Frommer's®

Tahiti & French Polynesia

1st Edition

by Bill Goodwin

Here's what the critics say about Frommer's:

"Amazingly easy to use. Very portable, very complete."
—*Booklist*

"Detailed, accurate, and easy-to-read information for all price ranges."
—*Glamour Magazine*

"Hotel information is close to encyclopedic."
—*Des Moines Sunday Register*

"Frommer's Guides have a way of giving you a real feel for a place."
—*Knight Ridder Newspapers*

1807
WILEY
2007
BICENTENNIAL

Wiley Publishing, Inc.

Published by:

Wiley Publishing, Inc.

111 River St.
Hoboken, NJ 07030-5774

ISBN-13: 978-0-470-00986-4
ISBN-10: 0-470-00986-1

Editor: Leslie A. Shen
Production Editor: Michael Brumitt
Cartographers: Liz Puhl/Tim Lohnes
Photo Editor: Richard Fox
Anniversary Logo Design: Richard Pacifico
Production by Wiley Indianapolis Composition Services

Front cover photo: Tahiti: huts on pillars, local people in canoe in foreground
Back cover photo: French Polynesia, Marquesas: horse on hilltop above ocean

For information on our other products and services or to obtain technical support, please contact our Customer Care Department within the U.S. at 800-762-2974, outside the U.S. at 317-572-3993 or fax 317-572-4002.

Wiley also publishes its books in a variety of electronic formats. Some content that appears in print may not be available in electronic formats.

Manufactured in the United States of America

5 4 3 2 1

Contents

List of Maps

About the Author

Bill Goodwin began his writing career as an award-winning newspaper reporter and then served as legal counsel and speechwriter for two influential U.S. senators—Sam Nunn of Georgia and the late Sam Ervin of North Carolina. In 1977 he and a friend said goodbye to office life and sailed a 41-foot yacht from Annapolis, Maryland, through the Panama Canal to the Marquesas Islands, the Tuamotu Archipelago, and Tahiti. He left the boat in Papeete and, with girlfriend and backpack, explored Tahiti, Moorea, and the Society Islands for as long as the local immigration authorities would allow. He has returned for extended visits many times since, most devoted to researching and writing *Frommer's South Pacific*. At home, he also is the author of *Frommer's Virginia*.

Dedication

To my father,
with love and grateful thanks for supporting my being a writer
rather than a lawyer.

Acknowledgments

I owe a debt of gratitude to many individuals and organizations for their assistance, information, and advice without which it would have been impossible to research and write this book. This is especially true of Dany Panero, Céline Teihotaata, Al Keahi, Jonathan Reap, and Leila Laille of Tahiti Tourisme, French Polynesia's terrific tourist information bureau.

My deep personal thanks go to Anne Simon, Curtis and Judy Moore, Suzanne McIntosh, Nancy Monseaux, and Max Parrish, who have tended the home front while I was away in the islands; to Bill and Donna Wilder, who introduced me to the intricacies of Tahiti and who once loaned me their home on Moorea; and to my sister, Jean Goodwin Santa Maria, who has consistently given much-needed moral support. I am truly blessed to have these wonderful folks in my life.

—Bill Goodwin

An Invitation to the Reader

In researching this book, we discovered many wonderful places—hotels, restaurants, shops, and more. We're sure you'll find others. Please tell us about them, so we can share the information with your fellow travelers in upcoming editions. If you were disappointed with a recommendation, we'd love to know that, too. Please write to:

Frommer's Tahiti & French Polynesia, 1st Edition
Wiley Publishing, Inc. • 111 River St. • Hoboken, NJ 07030-5774

An Additional Note

Please be advised that travel information is subject to change at any time—and this is especially true of prices. We therefore suggest that you write or call ahead for confirmation when making your travel plans. The authors, editors, and publisher cannot be held responsible for the experiences of readers while traveling. Your safety is important to us, however, so we encourage you to stay alert and be aware of your surroundings. Keep a close eye on cameras, purses, and wallets, all favorite targets of thieves and pickpockets.

Other Great Guides for Your Trip:

Frommer's South Pacific
Frommer's Australia
Frommer's New Zealand
Frommer's Southeast Asia

Frommer's Star Ratings, Icons & Abbreviations

Every hotel, restaurant, and attraction listing in this guide has been ranked for quality, value, service, amenities, and special features using a **star-rating system.** In country, state, and regional guides, we also rate towns and regions to help you narrow down your choices and budget your time accordingly. Hotels and restaurants are rated on a scale of zero (recommended) to three stars (exceptional). Attractions, shopping, nightlife, towns, and regions are rated according to the following scale: zero stars (recommended), one star (highly recommended), two stars (very highly recommended), and three stars (must-see).

In addition to the star-rating system, we also use **seven feature icons** that point you to the great deals, in-the-know advice, and unique experiences that separate travelers from tourists. Throughout the book, look for:

Finds	Special finds—those places only insiders know about
Fun Fact	Fun facts—details that make travelers more informed and their trips more fun
Kids	Best bets for kids and advice for the whole family
Moments	Special moments—those experiences that memories are made of
Overrated	Places or experiences not worth your time or money
Tips	Insider tips—great ways to save time and money
Value	Great values—where to get the best deals

The following **abbreviations** are used for credit cards:

AE	American Express	DISC	Discover	V	Visa
DC	Diners Club	MC	MasterCard		

Frommers.com

Now that you have this guidebook to help you plan a great trip, visit our website at **www.frommers.com** for additional travel information on more than 3,500 destinations. We update features regularly to give you instant access to the most current trip-planning information available. At Frommers.com, you'll find scoops on the best airfares, lodging rates, and car rental bargains. You can even book your travel online through our reliable travel booking partners. Other popular features include:

- Online updates of our most popular guidebooks
- Vacation sweepstakes and contest giveaways
- Newsletters highlighting the hottest travel trends
- Online travel message boards with featured travel discussions

The Best of Tahiti & French Polynesia

Tahiti and her sister islands in French Polynesia have conjured up romantic images of an earthly paradise since European sailors brought home tales of their tropical splendor and uninhibited people in the 1770s. When I washed ashore 2 centuries later, I quickly understood why these remote outposts still enjoy such a reputation. In fact, I was so smitten that I stayed here for 7 months, as long as the gendarmes would allow in those days.

You may wish you had planned a longer trip yourself, for here are some of the most beautiful islands in the world—if not *the* most beautiful. They are blessed with gorgeous beaches, and their lagoons offer fabulous diving and spectacular snorkeling.

And then there are the islanders who live here. Their fabled history has provided fodder for famous books and films, their storied Polynesian culture inspires hedonistic dreams, and their big smiles and genuine hospitality are prime attractions.

Even today, you are likely to encounter bare breasts on the beaches here, for these islands are indeed French as well as Polynesian. Unlike other South Pacific countries, where the preaching of 19th-century puritanical missionaries took deeper root, here you will discover a marvelous combination of both *joie de vivre* and *laissez-faire*. Add the awesome beauty of the islands and you'll quickly see why this is one of the world's top honeymoon destinations.

In this chapter, I point out the best of the best—not necessarily to pass qualitative judgment, but to help you choose among the surprisingly many options the islands have to offer. I list them here in the order in which they appear in the book. For a preview of what each of these little specks of land has to offer, see "The Islands in Brief," in chapter 2.

1 The Most Beautiful Islands

"In the South Seas," Rupert Brooke wrote in 1914, "the Creator seems to have laid himself out to show what He can do." How right the poet was, for here lie some of the world's most dramatically beautiful islands. In my opinion, the best of the lot have jagged mountain peaks plunging into aquamarine lagoons.

Here are some that you see on the travel posters and in the brochures:

- **Moorea:** To my mind, Moorea is the most beautiful island in the world. Nothing I have ever seen compares with its sawtooth ridges and the great dark-green hulk of Mount Rotui separating glorious Cook's and Opunohu bays. The view from Tahiti of Moorea's dinosaur-like skyline is unforgettable. See chapter 5.
- **Huahine:** Although Moorea and Bora Bora get most of the ink, Huahine is

almost as gorgeous, with mountain-surrounded bays that almost rival Moorea's. But since it is off the well-beaten tourist track, it still retains an air of old Polynesia. Relatively unhurried by both tourists and the pressures of modern life, its residents still greet you with a big smile and have time to sit and chat. See chapter 6.

- **Bora Bora:** The late James Michener thought Bora Bora was the most beautiful island in the world. Although tourism has turned this gem into a sort of expensive South Seas Disneyland since Michener's day, development hasn't altered the incredible beauty of Bora Bora's basaltic tombstone towering over a lagoon ranging in color from yellow to deep blue. See chapter 8.

- **Maupiti:** Another unspoiled jewel, Maupiti is nearby Bora Bora in miniature, but without any modern hotels or resorts. Like Bora Bora, its mountainous central island towers over a crystal-clear lagoon. See chapter 9.

- **Rangiroa, Tikehau, Manihi and Fakarava:** I lump these atolls together because they are equally beautiful. Each has a string of islets enclosing large lagoons, like giant lakes in the middle of the ocean. See chapter 10.

- **Hiva Oa and Nuku Hiva:** Two more islands that are equally gorgeous, the two main Marquesas Islands are high and mountainous, with cliffs and steep ridges outlining numerous valleys descending to the edge of the sea. See chapter 11.

2 The Best Beaches

Because all but a few of the islands are surrounded by coral reefs, there are few surf beaches here. Most of those on Tahiti have heat-absorbing black volcanic sand. Except in the Marquesas, which is almost devoid of coral, most islands (and all but a few resorts) have bathtublike lagoons that lap on white-coral sands draped by coconut palms. Here are a few that stand out from the many (the French word for "beach" being *plage*):

- **La Plage de Maui** (Tahiti): Bordering the southern shore of Tahiti Iti, the main island's peninsula, this strip of white sand is far and away the best beach on Tahiti. The lagoon is suitable for swimming, and there's an excellent snack bar beside the beach. See chapter 4.

- **Mareto Plage Publique** (Moorea): Although it isn't as picturesque as Moorea's Temae Plage Publique (see below), this beach between Cook's and Opunohu bays sits between a coconut grove and the lagoon. See chapter 5.

- **Temae Plage Publique** (Moorea): The northeastern coast of Moorea is fringed by a nearly uninterrupted stretch of white-sand beach that commands a glorious view: across a speckled lagoon to Tahiti, sitting on the horizon across the Sea of the Moon. See chapter 5.

- **Avea Beach** (Huahine): My favorite resort beach is at Relais Mahana, a small hotel on Auea Bay near Huahine's southern end. Trees grow along the white beach, which slopes into a lagoon deep enough for swimming at any tide. The resort's pier goes out to a giant coral head, a perfect and safe place to snorkel, and the lagoon here is protected from the trade winds, making it safe for sailing. See chapter 6.

- **Matira Beach** (Bora Bora): Beginning at the Hotel Bora Bora, this fine ribbon of sand stretches around skinny Matira Point, which forms the island's southern extremity, all the way to the Club Med. The eastern side has views of the sister islands of Raiatea and Tahaa. See chapter 8.

- **Plage Tereia** (Maupiti): Like Matira Beach on Bora Bora, this white-sand beach wraps around a peninsula on Maupiti's main island. Unlike Matira, however, you'll likely have this one all to yourself, since there are no resorts on Maupiti. See chapter 9.

- **Les Sables Rose/The Pink Sands** (Rangiroa): At a remote corner of Rangiroa's lagoon, the world's second largest, lies a gorgeous beach made up of pink sand. It's well worth the hour-long boat ride from Rangiroa's hotels. See chapter 10.

3 The Best Honeymoon Resorts

Whether you're on your honeymoon or not, French Polynesia is a marvelous place for romantic escapes. After all, romance and the islands have gone hand-in-hand since the young women of Tahiti gave rousing, bare-breasted welcomes to the 18th-century European explorers.

Back in those days, everyone here lived in a proverbial little grass shack by the beach. The modern resorts have elevated that concept into luxurious guest bungalows, many built on stilts out over the lagoons. I've never stayed anywhere as romantic as these thatch-roofed overwater units, most with glass panels in their floors for viewing fish swimming below. If their indoor luxuries aren't enough, you can climb down the steps leading from your front deck and go skinny-dipping in the warm waters below. The overwater bungalows help make French Polynesia—especially Bora Bora—one of the world's most famous honeymoon destinations. Naturally, they are the most expensive accommodations here.

One caveat is in order: Many overwater bungalows are relatively close together, meaning that your honeymooning next-door neighbors will be within earshot if not eyeshot. ("It can be like watching an X-rated video," a hotel manager once confessed, "but without the video.") Therefore, if you're seeking a high degree of privacy and seclusion, these won't necessarily be your best choice.

The top resorts are variations on the same theme: A beachside central complex with restaurant, bar, and other public facilities flanked by individual guest bungalows in a coconut grove. From the shoreline, piers reach out to the overwater units. I point out the top resorts island-by-island in the paragraphs below, but please read the reviews in the chapters that follow before making your choice.

- **Tahiti:** Most visitors now consider Tahiti to be a way station to the other islands, but the **Inter-Continental Resort Tahiti** (p. 100) has overwater bungalows that face the dramatic outline of Moorea across the Sea of the Moon. Some of those at **Le Meridien Tahiti** (p. 102) also have this view.

- **Moorea:** The units at the **Club Bali Hai** (p. 132) are among the oldest—and the least expensive—overwater bungalows in the islands, but they enjoy an unparalleled view of the jagged mountains surrounding Cook's Bay. Some overwater units at the **Sofitel Moorea Beach Resort** (p. 130) actually face Tahiti across the Sea of the Moon, and they're built over Moorea's most colorful lagoon. The **Moorea Pearl Resort** (p. 130) has a few bungalows perched on the edge of the clifflike reef, making for superb snorkeling right off your front deck. You'll have more luxurious options at the **Inter-Continental Resort & Spa Moorea** (p. 134).

- **Huahine:** After a few days on Bora Bora, many couples today are opting to end their honeymoons by decompressing on Huahine or Tahaa (see below). On Huahine, the American-owned **Te Tiare Beach Resort** (p. 151) is one of the smallest and most intimate retreats in French Polynesia. Its units have some of the largest decks of any overwater bungalows (one side is completely shaded by a thatch roof).

- **Tahaa:** The most charming of all overwater units are at the **Le Taha'a Private Island & Spa** (p. 167), a luxurious resort on a small islet off Tahaa. Some of these have views of Bora Bora on the horizon.

- **Bora Bora:** This most famous—and crowded—of French Polynesia's honeymoon islands has several hundred overwater bungalows, and many more will be here by the time you plan your trip. Meantime, the largest and most luxurious are at the **Bora Bora Nui Resort Luxury Collection** (p. 182), although they don't look out to tombstonelike Mount Otemanu, rising across the famous lagoon. Along with Cook's Bay on Moorea, this is one of the most photographed scenes in the entire South Pacific. For that, you have to stay at the **Sofitel Motu** (p. 185) or at the

Hotel Bora Bora (p. 183). Other bungalows at the Hotel Bora Bora sit right on the reef's edge, providing fantastic snorkeling. Ashore, the Hotel Bora Bora has large, luxurious bungalows that boast their own courtyards with swimming pools. Equally private, though less luxe, are the garden units at the **Bora Bora Pearl Beach Resort** (p. 183); you can cavort to your heart's content in their wall-enclosed patios, which have sun decks and splash pools. The smaller but well-appointed overwater units at the friendly **Hotel Maitai Polynesia** (p. 186) are the least expensive on Bora Bora.

- **Tuamotu Archipelago:** Out at the huge atoll of Rangiroa, the **Hotel Kia Ora** (p. 206) has bungalows over the world's second-largest lagoon. It also boasts beachside units with Jacuzzi pools set in their front porches. On the adjacent atoll, the **Tikehau Pearl Beach Resort** (p. 212) resides on its own small islet, affording more privacy than most other French Polynesian resorts. Some overwater bungalows actually sit over the rip tides in a pass that lets the sea into the lagoon. On Manihi atoll, units at the **Manihi Pearl Beach Resort** (p. 215) are cooled by the almost constantly blowing trade winds.

4 The Best Family Resorts

There are no Disney Worlds or other such attractions in the islands. As I point out in the "Family Travel" section in chapter 2 (p. 32), most tourism here is aimed at honeymooners and other couples. In fact, most resorts in French Polynesia are designed specifically for romance, not the product thereof. Accordingly, most resorts house their guests in individual bungalows best occupied by two people. That's not to say that children won't have a fine time here, for

more and more resorts are making provisions for families as well as honeymooners. Kids who like being around the water will enjoy themselves the most.

Here are a few family-friendly resorts:

- **Inter-Continental Resort Tahiti** (Tahiti): Tahiti's best all-around resort has a few overwater bungalows, but most units are hotel rooms that interconnect, thus giving families who can afford them two or more units in which to roam. See p. 100.

- **Radisson Plaza Resort Tahiti** (Tahiti): The lagoon off the black-sand beach at the Radisson Plaza is subject to dangerous rip tides, but kids can play in the walk-in swimming pool. If you don't mind bunking the youngsters on the living-room sofa, you parents can sleep upstairs in a two-story "duplex" suite. See p. 104.
- **Club Bali Hai** (Moorea): Along with an awesome view of Cook's Bay, the Club Bali Hai has numerous units with kitchens, a benefit of its being about half time-share. It lacks the organized activities of the Inter-Continental Resort & Spa Moorea (see below), but you will pay considerably less for a unit here. See p. 132.
- **Inter-Continental Resort & Spa Moorea** (Moorea): The most notable exception to French Polynesia's couples-mainly hotels is the Inter-Continental Resort & Spa Moorea, which has an attractive pool, a safe lagoon, the widest selection of watersports in French Polynesia, and a top-flight kids' program. See p. 134.
- **Bora Bora Lagoon Resort & Spa** (Bora Bora): This upscale resort on an islet off Bora Bora has a two-bedroom villa among its inventory, a plus for well-heeled families. See p. 182.
- **Bora Bora Nui Resort & Spa Luxury Collection** (Bora Bora): This large and swanky resort has a variety of accommodations, including hotel-style units that interconnect. Buffet breakfasts are included in the rates, another plus for families. See p. 182.
- **Bora Bora Pearl Beach Resort** (Bora Bora): Families can opt for one of Pearl's beachside one-bedroom villas. See p. 183.
- **Le Meridien Bora Bora** (Bora Bora): In addition to romantic overwater bungalows, this Meridien has units beside a shallow, man-made lagoon, a safe haven for children playing in the water. The youngsters can also both play and learn in the resort's award-wining sea turtle rescue and breeding program.

5 The Best Historical & Cultural Experiences

The Tahitians are justly proud of their ancient Polynesian culture as well as the unique modern history that sets them apart from all other Pacific Islanders. Below are the best ways to learn about the people, their lifestyle, and their history.

- **La Maison James Norman Hall/ James Norman Hall's Home** (Tahiti): The co-author of *Mutiny on the Bounty* and other books set in the South Pacific lived most of his adult life on Tahiti. His family maintains his former home as a fascinating museum. See p. 80.
- **Marché Municipal/Municipal Market** (Tahiti): Papeete's large, teeming market is a wonderful place to examine tropical foodstuffs as well as to buy handicrafts. It's especially busy before dawn on Sunday. See p. 80.
- **Musée de Tahiti et Ses Isles/ Museum of Tahiti and Her Islands** (Tahiti): This terrific lagoonside museum recounts the geology, history, culture, flora, and fauna of French Polynesia. It's worth a stop just for the outstanding view of Moorea from its coconut-grove setting. See p. 80.
- **Musée Gauguin/Gauguin Museum** (Tahiti): The great French painter Paul Gauguin lived and worked on Tahiti's south coast from 1891 until moving to Hiva Oa in the Marquesas Islands, where he died. This museum has a few of his original works, but is

best at tracing his adventures in French Polynesia. See p. 81.

- **Tiki Theatre Village** (Moorea): Built to resemble a pre-European Tahitian village, this cultural center has demonstrations of handicraft making and puts on a nightly dance show and feast. It's a bit commercial, and the staff isn't always fluent in English, but this is the only place in French Polynesia where one can sample the old ways. See p. 123.

- **Maeva *Marae*** (Huahine): The ancient Tahitians gathered to worship their gods and hold other ceremonies at stone temples known as *marae*. More than 40 of these structures have been restored near the village of Maeva and are a highlight of any visit to Huahine. See p. 147.

- **Taputapuatea *Marae*** (Raiatea): French Polynesia's largest and most important *marae* sits beside the lagoon on Raiatea. Archaeologists have uncovered bones apparently from human sacrifices from beneath its 45m-long (150-ft.) grand altar. See p. 160.

- **Tohua Papa Nui/Paul Gauguin Cultural Center** (Hiva Oa): This small museum recounts Paul Gauguin's last days on Hiva Oa, where he died in 1903. It's worth a visit to see the exact replicas of his original paintings executed by a team of French artists. See p. 237.

6 The Best of the Old South Seas

The islands are developing rapidly, with modern, fast-paced cities like Papeete replacing what were once sleepy backwater ports. But there are still remnants of the old South Seas days of coconut planters, beach bums, and missionaries.

- **Huahine:** Of the major French Polynesian islands, Huahine has been the least affected by tourism, and its residents are still likely to give you an unprompted Tahitian greeting, *"Ia orana!"* Agriculture is still king on Huahine, which makes it the "Island of Fruits." There are ancient *marae* (temples) to visit, and the only town, tiny **Fare,** is little more than a collection of Chinese shops fronting the island's wharf, which comes to life when ships pull in. See chapter 6.

- **Tahaa:** With no towns and barely a village, Tahaa is still predominately a vanilla-growing island—as sweet aromas will attest. One of French Polynesia's top resorts is on a small islet off Tahaa, but otherwise this rugged little island takes you back to the way Moorea used to be. See chapter 7.

- **Maupiti:** Not long ago, residents of Maupiti voted down a proposal to build an upscale resort on their gorgeous little island, thus leaving it as a day trip from Bora Bora or as an unspoiled retreat for those who can do without maximum luxuries—or the English language. Maupiti looks like Bora Bora; locals boast that it's like Bora Bora used to be. See chapter 9.

- **The Tuamotu Archipelago:** Whether you choose to visit Rangiroa, Tikehau, Manihi, or Fakarava, you will find modern Polynesian life relatively undisturbed by modern ways, except for the many black-pearl farms in their lagoons. See chapter 10.

- **The Marquesas Islands:** The infrequently visited Marquesas group harkens back to the early 19th century, when Herman Melville and others jumped off whaling ships and disappeared into their haunting valleys. See chapter 11.

7 The Best Dining Experiences

Wherever the French go, fine food and wine are sure to follow, and French Polynesia is no exception. You will get good food everywhere here, but these are a few of the best places to sample fine fare.

- **Auberge du Pacifique** (Tahiti): Award-winning chef Jean Galopin has been blending French and Polynesian cuisines at his lagoonside restaurant—with a removable roof to let in starlight—since 1974. He's even written a cookbook about Tahitian cooking. See p. 108.

- **Le Coco's** (Tahiti): Not far from Auberge du Pacific, you'll have a fine view of Moorea from the patio at Le Coco's, specializing in light *nouvelle* cuisine. See p. 109.

- **Le Lotus** (Tahiti): The most romantic setting of any French Polynesian restaurant is in this overwater dining room at the Inter-Continental Resort Tahiti. Even if the food weren't gourmet French and the service highly efficient and unobtrusive, the view of Moorea on a moonlit night makes an evening here special. See p. 109.

- **Linareva Floating Restaurant and Bar** (Moorea): With luck, you won't get queasy while dining at Chef Eric Lussiez's charming restaurant, which occupies the original ferry that plied the waters between Tahiti and Moorea. His menu highlights fresh seafood excellently prepared in the classic French fashion. See p. 141.

- **Le Mahogany** (Moorea): After 30 years at the former Hotel Bali Hai, Chef François Curtien now works his magic at Le Mahogany, one of the best food values on Moorea. See p. 138.

- **Le Mayflower** (Moorea): Mainly locals in the know frequent this roadside restaurant, Moorea's best. The sauces are delightfully light, as are the prices for such good food. See p. 142.

- **Restaurant Quai des Pecheurs** (Raiatea): Beach bums aren't likely to visit Raiatea, but those of you who charter yachts likely will find your way to this casual restaurant in Raiatea's Gare Maritime. Spicy tuna steak in a Creole sauce will make your mouth water. See p. 169.

- **Bloody Mary's Restaurant & Bar** (Bora Bora): A fun evening at French Polynesia's most famous restaurant is a must-do when on Bora Bora. That's because Bloody Mary's offers the most unique and charming dining experience in the islands. Come early for a drink at the friendly bar, and then pick your fresh seafood from atop a huge tray of ice. After eating heavy French fare elsewhere for a few days, the sauceless fish from the grill will seem downright refreshing. See p. 189.

- **Kaina Hut** (Bora Bora): Local ingredients are fused into Continental fare under the high thatch roof of the Kaina Hut. Italian gnocchi here is made not of potato but of breadfruit. See p. 189.

- **La Villa Mahana** (Bora Bora): Corsican chef Damien Rinaldi Devio also offers relief from traditional French sauces at his romantic little restaurant, where he uses "exotic" spices to enliven fresh fish and beef dishes. See p. 189.

- **TOPdive Restaurant** (Bora Bora): Romance reigns under the high thatch roof of this restaurant perched beside the lagoon. Seafood *nouvelle* style is the specialty. See p. 190.

8 The Best Island Nights

An editor once asked me why I didn't write more about nightlife in the islands other than Tahiti. "Let me put it this way," I replied. "Most of the visitors out here are honeymooners and other couples. On most islands you get up in the morning and spend all day sightseeing or playing in the lagoon. You come back to your hotel, shower, go to dinner, and watch a Tahitian dance show, which will be over by 9pm. If you can't figure out what to do between 9pm and midnight on your honeymoon, that's not my problem!"

In other words, don't come to the islands expecting opera and ballet, or Las Vegas–style floor shows either. Other than pub-crawling to bars and nightclubs in Papeete, evening entertainment here consists primarily of feasts of island foods followed by traditional dancing.

Of course, the Tahitian hip-swinging traditional dances are world famous. They are not as lewd and lascivious today as they were in the days before the missionaries arrived, but they still have plenty of suggestive movements to the primordial beat of drums; see "A Most Indecent Song & Dance" (p. 113).

Every hotel will have at least one dance show a week. The best are on Tahiti, especially the thrice-weekly performances at the Inter-Continental Resort Tahiti that feature one of the best troupes, the **Grande Danse de Tahiti** (p. 114). Also good are the Friday and Saturday evening shows at the **Captain Bligh Restaurant and Bar** (p. 114).

Moorea offers two excellent opportunities. The **Inter-Continental Resort & Spa Moorea** (p. 143) stages a spectacular beachside show on Saturday nights. The **Club Bali Hai** (p. 143) has a free performance at 6pm on Wednesday, followed by an a la carte barbecue, making it also a very good value.

If you want to see the very best Tahitian dancing, come here in July during the annual *Heiva Nui* festival, when the top troupes compete on the Papeete waterfront. Plan early, since tickets can be hard to come by if you wait until the last minute. See the "French Polynesia Calendar of Events" (p. 24) for details.

9 The Best Buys

Take some extra money along, for you'll likely spend it on black pearls, handicrafts, and tropical clothing.

See "Shopping," in chapter 4, for an overall discussion and the "Shopping" sections in the individual destination chapters for the best shops on the other islands.

- **Black Pearls:** Few people will escape French Polynesia without buying at least one black pearl. That's because the shallow, clear-water lagoons of the Tuamotu Archipelago are the world's largest producers of the beautiful dark orbs. The seemingly inexhaustible supply has resulted in fierce competition by vendors ranging from market stalls to high-end jewelry shops.

- **Handicrafts:** Although many of the items you will see in island souvenir shops are actually made in Asia, locally produced handicrafts are among the best buys. The most widespread are hats, mats, and baskets woven of *pandanus* or other fibers, usually by women who have maintained this ancient art to a high degree. Woodcarvings are also popular, especially those from the Marquesas Islands. Many carvings in some large stores, however, tend to be produced for the tourist trade and often lack the imagery of bygone days;

some may also be machine-produced these days.

- **Tropical Clothing:** Colorful hand-screened, hand-blocked, and hand-dyed fabrics are very popular in the islands for making dresses or the wrap-around skirt known as *pareu*. Many pareus are hand-painted, some almost works of art. Others are produced when heat-sensitive dyes are applied by hand to gauzelike cotton, which is then laid in the sun for several hours. Flowers, leaves, and other designs are placed on the fabric, and as the heat of the sun darkens and sets the dyes, the shadows from these objects leave their images behind on the finished product.

10 The Best Diving & Snorkeling

All the islands have excellent scuba diving and snorkeling, and all but a few of the resorts have their own dive operations or can easily make arrangements with a local company.

The lagoons in French Polynesia are known less for colorful soft corals than for the wide variety of sealife they contain. Both the number and variety of colorful tropical fish are astounding. Stingrays and manta rays are prevalent, and some in the Society Island lagoons are quite friendly to humans, the result of their having been hand fed (you'll see them hanging around the waterside restaurants after dark, hoping for handouts).

Rare is the diver who doesn't encounter sharks here, though most will be of the relatively harmless reef varieties—black tip, silver tip, white tip, and grey. The most visited islands now have shark-feeding encounters (see "The Best Offbeat Travel Experiences," at the end in this chapter). Hammerheads and other large sharks live outside the reef and in the passes leading into the lagoons.

Most dive sites are along or just outside the barrier reefs and within short boat rides of the resorts.

Serious divers can opt to explore the lagoons and reefs of Bora Bora, Raiatea, Tahaa, and Huahine in the live-aboard *Tahiti Aggressor* (see p. 51).

If you like to snorkel, you're in for a few treats, whether on a shark-feeding excursion with other tourists or just swimming off your hotel. In some cases, snorkelers can go out with scuba divers.

The best diving and snorkeling are at **Rangiroa, Tikehau, Manihi,** and **Fakarava** in the Tuamotu Archipelago, where the huge lagoons harbor an incredible variety of fish and sharks. Go to Rangiroa to see sharks; go to the others to see more fish than you imagined ever existed. See chapter 10.

The atolls are also home to heart-stopping "ride the rip" dives and snorkeling trips, on which you literally ride the tidal current through the passes into the lagoons. See "The Best Offbeat Travel Experiences," below.

11 The Best Sailing

Sailboats based on Tahiti and Moorea will take you out for a spin, or even to the late Marlon Brando's island of Tetiaroa, but the best sailing here is among the Leeward Islands of Raiatea, Tahaa, Bora Bora, and Huahine. Having arrived here originally via yacht from the East Coast of the United States, I can say without qualification that the sailing among the Leeward Islands is world class.

French Polynesia's center for charter-yacht sailing is **Raiatea,** where rentals are available from several companies (including the Moorings, the outstanding American company).

Raiatea shares a lagoon with **Tahaa,** its rugged sister island. Tahaa is indented with long bays sheltering numerous picturesque anchorages, and you can sail completely around it without leaving the lagoon.

If you are reasonably skilled at "blue water" offshore sailing, both Bora Bora and Huahine are just 32km (20 miles) away, albeit in opposite directions. Most of the charter-boat companies will let you leave the boat in either Huahine or Bora Bora, so you won't have to beat back to Raiatea after your week or so of knocking around the islands.

Details are in "Seeing the Islands by Cruise Ship & Yacht," in chapter 2.

12 The Best Offbeat Travel Experiences

Some cynics might say that a visit to French Polynesia itself is an offbeat experience, but there are three things to do here that are really unusual.

- **Getting Asked to Dance** (everywhere): I've seen so many traditional dance shows that I now stand by the rear door, ready to beat a quick escape before those lovely young women in grass skirts can grab my hand and force me to make a fool of myself trying to gyrate my hips up on the stage. It's part of the tourist experience at all resorts, and it's all in good fun.

- **Swimming with the Sharks** (Bora Bora): A key attraction in Bora Bora's magnificent lagoon is to snorkel with a guide, who actually feeds a school of sharks as they thrash around in a frenzy. I prefer to leave this one to the Discovery Channel. See p. 178.

- **Riding the Rip** (Rangiroa, Manihi, and Fakarava): Divers and snorkelers will never forget the flying sensation as they ride the strong currents ripping through passes into the lagoons at Rangiroa and Manihi. See "Rangiroa" and "Manihi," in chapter 10.

Planning Your Trip to Tahiti & French Polynesia

Thanks to many tons of euros pouring in from Paris, French Polynesians enjoy a relatively high standard of living. The flip side of that coin is that everyone pays high prices for almost everything, locals and visitors alike. As one resident of these gorgeous islands says, "You must pay for paradise."

Indeed, you can pay a king's ransom to vacation here, but French Polynesia doesn't have to cost you both arms and both legs. In this chapter, I will introduce the islands and advise you on how to plan your trip, hopefully so that you will pay a reasonable amount for this modern paradise.

In planning your trip, keep in mind why you are coming here and what your priorities are. You can scuba dive to exhaustion or just sit on the beach with a trashy novel. You can share a 300-room hotel with package tourists or get away from it all in an overwater bungalow. You can hide away with your lover or join your fellow guests at lively dinner parties. You can totally ignore the islanders around you or enrich your own life by learning about theirs. You can listen to the day's events on CNN International or see what the South Seas were like a century ago. Lacking the ability to read minds, I must leave those decisions to you.

1 The Islands in Brief

French Polynesia sprawls over an area of 5.2 million sq. km (2 million sq. miles) in the eastern South Pacific. That's about the size of Europe, excluding the former Soviet Union countries, or about two-thirds the size of the continental United States. The 130 main islands, however, consist of only 3,885 sq. km (1,500 sq. miles), an area smaller than the American state of Rhode Island. Only 245,500 or so souls inhabit these small specks.

The territory's five major island groups differ in terrain, climate, and, to a certain extent, people. With the exception of the Tuamotu Archipelago, an enormous chain of low coral atolls northeast of Tahiti, all but a few are "high" islands; that is, they are the mountainous tops of ancient volcanoes eroded into jagged peaks, deep bays, and fertile valleys. All have fringing, or barrier coral reefs, and blue lagoons worthy of postcards.

THE SOCIETY ISLANDS

The most strikingly beautiful and most frequently visited destinations in the South Pacific are the **Society Islands,** so named by Capt. James Cook, the great English explorer, in 1769 because they lay relatively close together (see "French Polynesia Yesterday: History 101," p. 243). These include Tahiti and its nearby companion Moorea, which are also known as the Windward Islands because they sit to the east, the direction of the prevailing trade wind.

French Polynesia & the South Pacific

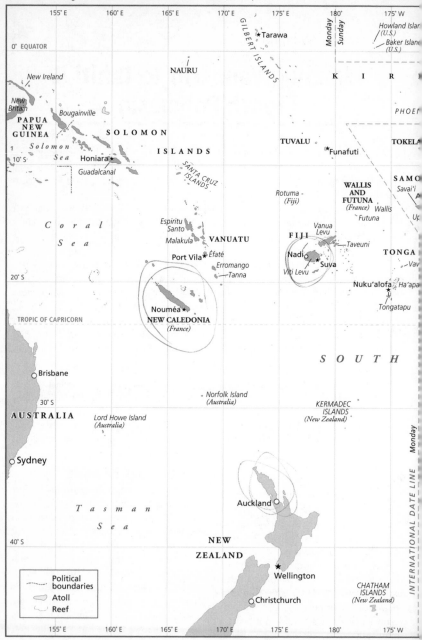

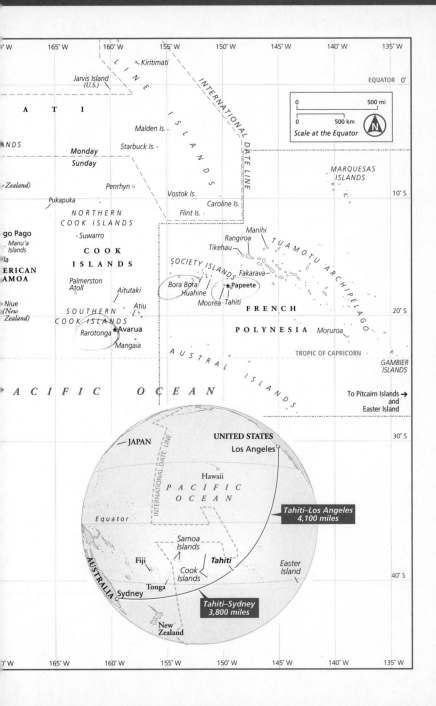

French Polynesia

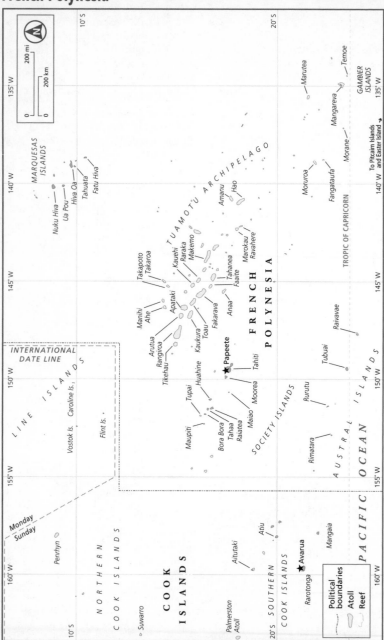

Tahiti is the most developed island in French Polynesia. Don't be surprised when you take the freeway from the airport into the noisy, bustling capital of Papeete. Chic bistros and high-rise shopping centers long ago replaced the city's stage-set wooden Chinese stores, and the glass and steel of luxury resorts out in the suburbs have supplanted its cheap waterfront hotels. If you're into cities, Papeete will be right up your alley. Even if you're not, Tahiti is well worth seeing, especially its fine museums devoted to the painter Paul Gauguin, to the writer James Norman Hall, and to the islanders themselves.

Most modern visitors bypass these jewels and quickly head to **Moorea,** just 20km (12 miles) west of Tahiti. The short journey is like being transported to another world. Moorea's mountain peaks and fingerlike bays are world-renowned for their awesome beauty. Even though parts of Moorea are beginning to seem like Papeete suburbs, the island still retains more of old Polynesia than does Tahiti. It also has numerous white-sand beaches, which are in short supply on Tahiti, where most sand is of the black volcanic variety.

To the northwest lie Bora Bora, Huahine, Raiatea, Tahaa, Maupiti, and several smaller islands. Because they are downwind of Tahiti, they are also called the Leeward Islands.

One of the world's top honeymoon destinations, **Bora Bora** is French Polynesia's tourism dynamo, with more resorts than any other island. **Huahine** is almost as beautiful as Moorea and Bora Bora, but with only a handful of hotels, it retains much of its old-Polynesian charm. The administrative center of the Leeward Islands, **Raiatea** lacks beaches, but the deep lagoon it shares with Tahaa makes it the sailing capital of French Polynesia. **Tahaa** has only recently opened to tourism, with one of French Polynesia's top resorts now sitting out on a small reef islet. Virtually unscathed by tourism but a favorite retreat of French residents of Tahiti, **Maupiti** has a few locally owned pensions. It can be visited on a day trip from Bora Bora.

THE TUAMOTU ARCHIPELAGO

Across the approaches to Tahiti from the east, the 69 low-lying atolls of the **Tuamotu Archipelago** run for 1,159km (720 miles) on a line from northwest to southeast. The early European sailors called them the "Dangerous Archipelago" because of their tricky currents and because they virtually cannot be seen until a ship is almost on top of them. Even today, they are a wrecking ground for yachts and inter-island trading boats. Two of them, Moruroa and Fangataufa, were used by France to test its nuclear weapons between 1966 and 1996. Others provide the bulk of Tahiti's well-known black pearls. **Rangiroa,** the world's second-largest atoll and the territory's best scuba-diving destination, is the most frequently visited. Neighboring **Tikehau,** with a much smaller and shallower lagoon, also has a modern resort hotel, as does **Manihi,** the territory's major producer of black pearls. To the south, the reef at **Fakarava** encircles the world's third-largest lagoon.

Out here you'll find marvelous snorkeling and diving in massive lagoons stocked with a vast array of sealife. As I mention in chapter 3, "Suggested Tahiti & French Polynesia Itineraries," the atolls may seem anticlimactic after you've seen the high islands, so I suggest visiting them before exploring the Society Islands.

THE MARQUESAS ISLANDS

Made famous in 2002 by the *Survivor* television series, the **Marquesas** are a group of 10 high islands some 1,208km (750

Impressions

It is no exaggeration to say, that to a European of any sensibility, who, for the first time, wanders back into these valleys—away from the haunts of the natives—the ineffable repose and beauty of the landscape is such, that every object strikes him like something seen in a dream; and for a time he almost refuses to believe that scenes like these should have a commonplace existence.

—Herman Melville, 1847

miles) northeast of Tahiti. They are younger than the Society Islands, and because a cool equatorial current washes their shores, protecting coral reefs have not enclosed them. As a result, the surf pounds on their shores, there are no encircling coastal plains, and the people live in a series of deep valleys that radiate out from central mountain peaks. The Marquesas have lost their once-large populations to 19th-century disease and the 20th-century economic lure of Papeete; today, their sparsely populated, cloud-enshrouded valleys have an almost haunting air about them. Most visitors get to the Marquesas via *Aranui 3* cruises (see "Seeing the Islands by Cruise Ship & Yacht," later in this chapter). Only two of them—**Nuku Hiva** and **Hiva Oa**—have international-standard hotels.

THE AUSTRAL & GAMBIER ISLANDS

With no hotels or resorts, the **Austral Islands,** south of Tahiti, are seldom visited. They are part of a chain of high islands that continues westward into the Cook Islands. The people of the more temperate Australs, which include Rurutu, Raivavae, and Tubuai, once produced some of the best art objects in the South Pacific, but these skills have passed into time. Far on the southern end of the Tuamotu Archipelago, the **Gambier Islands** are part of a semisubmerged, middle-aged high island similar to Bora Bora. The hilly remnants of the old volcano are scattered in a huge lagoon, which is partially enclosed by a barrier reef marking the original outline of the island before it began to sink. The largest of these remnant islands is Mangareva.

2 Visitor Information

The best source of up-to-date information in advance is **Tahiti Tourisme,** B.P. 65, 98713 Papeete, French Polynesia (© **50.57.00;** fax 43.66.19; www.tahiti-tourisme.pf).

You can also contact Tahiti Tourisme's overseas offices or representatives:

- **United States:** 300 N. Continental Blvd., Suite 160, El Segundo, CA 90245 (© **310/414-8484;** fax 310/414-8490; www.tahiti-tourisme.com); and 122 E. 42nd St., Suite 608, New York, NY 10168 (© **212/599-8484**).
- **Australia:** Paramour Productions, 362 Riley St., Surry Hills, NSW 2010

(© **1300 655 563** toll free in Australia, or 02/9281-6020; fax 02/9211-6589; www.tahiti-tourisme.com.au)
- **New Zealand:** 200 W. Victoria St., Suite 2A (P.O. Box 106192), Auckland (© **09/368-5262;** fax 09/368-5263; www.tahiti-tourisme.co.nz)
- **United Kingdom:** BGB & Associates, 7 Westminster Palace Gardens, Artillery Row, London SW1P 1RL (© **20/7233-2300;** fax 20/7233-2301; www.tahiti-tourisme.co.uk)
- **France:** 28 bd. Saint Germain, 75005 Paris (© **01/55426434;** fax 01/55426120; www.tahiti-tourisme.fr)

- **Germany:** Travel Marketing Romberg, Swartzbachstrasse, 32 40822, Mettman bei Dusseldorf (✆ **2104/286672;** fax 2104 912673; www.tahiti tourisme.de)
- **Italy:** Aigo, Piazza Castello, 3 20 124 Milano (✆ **02/66-980317;** fax 02/66-92648; www.tahiti-tourisme.it)
- **Chile:** Officina de turismo de Tahiti y sus islas, av. 11 de Septiembre 2214, Of. 116, Casila 16057, Santiago 9 (✆ **251-2826;** fax 233-1787; www.tahiti-tourisme.cl)
- **Japan:** Tahiti Tourist Promotion Board, Tokyo City Air Terminal 2F 42-1, Nihonbashi-Hakozakicho, Chuo-ku, Tokyo 103-0015 (✆ **3/3639-0468;** fax 3/3665-0581; www.tahiti-tourisme.jp)

Once you're in Papeete, you can get maps, brochures, and other information at the **Tahiti Manava** visitors bureau (✆ **50.57.12;** www.tahiti-manava.pf), located in the cruise-ship welcome center on the waterfront, on boulevard Pomare at the foot of rue Paul Gauguin. See "Fast Facts: Tahiti," in chapter 4.

Local tourism committees run information booths on Moorea, Huahine, Raiatea, and Bora Bora (see "Fast Facts" in chapters 5, 6, 7, and 8, respectively).

Be sure to pick up the *Tahiti Beach Press,* a free weekly English-language newspaper that lists special events and current activities. Copies are available in most hotel lobbies.

USEFUL WEBSITES

The U.S. Department of State maintains a **Travel Advisory** (✆ **202/647-5225**) to keep you abreast of political or other problems throughout the world. It posts travel warnings and other timely information on its website, www.travel.state.gov.

The Tahiti-based **Agence Tahitienne de Presse** (www.tahitipresse.pf) is the best source for breaking local news as well as events and weather. Click on the "English version" link.

The East-West Center at the University of Hawaii gathers news from French Polynesia and other islands on its **Pacific Islands Report** website, http://pidp.east westcenter.org/pireport. It includes links to newspapers, news services, and universities.

Other useful websites include:

- **www.airtahitimagazine.com**, with articles from Air Tahiti's in-flight magazine.
- **www.diving-tahiti.com**, for general information and links to dive operators in all of the islands.
- **www.frommers.com**, especially the message boards, where you can read what other travelers have to say about Tahiti and French Polynesia.
- **www.meteo.pf**, the official site of Météo France, the local weather service.
- **www.polynesianislands.com**, with coverage of all the South Pacific islands.
- **www.tahiti.com**, which has been around since 1994.
- **www.tahiti-explorer.com** and its affiliated **www.tahiti-guide.com**, with details about most resorts.
- **www.tahiti-nui.com**, where you can see what the weather is doing in Papeete and on Bora Bora through Tahiti Nui Travel's live webcams.
- **www.tahitisun.com**, with links to several other sites that offer a host of information about each island.

3 Entry Requirements & Customs

ENTRY REQUIREMENTS
PASSPORTS

For information on how to get a passport, go to "Passports" in the "Fast Facts" section of this chapter: The websites listed provide downloadable passport applications as well as the current processing fees. For an up-to-date, country-by-country

Tips **Getting Hitched in the Islands**

The islands are marvelous places for a honeymoon. Getting married in French Polynesia, however, is another matter, due to a required 30-day residency. That is, you have to stay here at least a month before you can get a marriage license. On the other hand, most resorts have romantic wedding packages including traditional ceremonies, often right on the beach, so many couples get legally hitched at home, and then go through it again here. Others come here to reaffirm their vows.

---

listing of passport requirements around the world, go to the "Foreign Entry Requirement" page of the U.S. State Department's website at **www. travel.state.gov**.

VISAS

All visitors except French nationals are required to have a **passport** that will be valid for 6 months beyond their intended stay, as well as a **return or ongoing ticket.** French citizens must bring their national identity cards.

Citizens and nationals of the United States, Canada, Argentina, Bermuda, Bolivia, Brunei, Chile, Costa Rica, Croatia, the Czech Republic, Ecuador, El Salvador, Estonia, Guatemala, Honduras, Hungary, Japan, Latvia, Lithuania, Malaysia, Mexico, New Zealand, Nicaragua, Panama, Paraguay, Poland, Singapore, Slovakia, Slovenia, South Korea, and Uruguay may visit for up to 1 month without a visa.

Nationals of Andorra, Australia, the European Union countries, Monaco, Switzerland, Iceland, Liechtenstein, Norway, St. Martin, and the Vatican, can stay up to 3 months without a visa.

Citizens from all other countries (including foreign nationals residing in the U.S.) must get a visa before leaving home. French embassies and consulates overseas can issue "short stay" visas valid for 1 to 3 months, and they will forward applications for longer visits to the local immigration department in Papeete. *Note:* Visas issued by French embassies and consulates do not entitle you to visit

Tahiti without being stamped *"valable pour la Polynésie Française"*—valid for French Polynesia.

In the United States, the **Embassy of France** is at 4102 Reservoir Road NW, Washington, DC 20007 (✆ **202/944-6000;** www.info-france-usa.org). There are French consulates in Boston, Chicago, Detroit, Houston, Los Angeles, Miami, New Orleans, New York, and San Francisco.

MEDICAL REQUIREMENTS

No vaccinations are required unless you are coming from a yellow fever, plague, or cholera area. For information on medical requirements and recommendations, see "Health & Safety," p. 27.

CUSTOMS
WHAT YOU CAN BRING INTO FRENCH POLYNESIA

Customs allowances are 200 cigarettes or 50 cigars, 2 liters of spirits or 2 liters of wine, 50 grams of perfume, ¼ gram of toilet water, 500 grams of coffee, 100 grams of tea, and 30,000CFP (US$300) worth of other goods. Narcotics, dangerous drugs, weapons, ammunition, and copyright infringements (that is, pirated video- and audiotapes) are prohibited. Pets and plants are subject to stringent regulations (don't even think of bringing your dog).

WHAT YOU CAN TAKE HOME FROM FRENCH POLYNESIA

Returning **United States** citizens who have been in French Polynesia for at least

48 hours are allowed to bring back, once every 30 days, 200 cigarettes (age 18 and older), 1 liter of alcoholic beverages (age 21 and older), and US$800 worth of merchandise duty-free. You'll be charged a flat rate of 4% duty on the next US$1,000 worth of purchases. Be sure to have your receipts handy, since you must list every item if you're over the duty-free limits. On mailed gifts, the duty-free limit is US$100. You cannot bring jewelry or other items made of black coral or whalebone into the United States. Nor can you bring fresh foodstuffs; tinned foods, however, are allowed.

For more information about what you can bring back and the corresponding fees, download the invaluable free pamphlet *Know Before You Go* at www.cbp.gov (click on "Travel" and then "Know Before You Go"). Or request the pamphlet from **U.S. Customs & Border Protection (CBP),** 1300 Pennsylvania Ave., NW, Washington, DC 20229 (© 877/ 287-8667).

Citizens of **Canada** can write for the booklet *I Declare,* issued by the **Canada Border Services Agency** (© 800/461-9999 in Canada, or 204/983-3500; www.cbsa-asfc.gc.ca).

Citizens of the **United Kingdom** can contact **HM Revenue & Customs** (© 0845/010-9000, or 020/8929-0152 from outside the U.K.; www.hmce.gov. uk) for information.

Citizens of **Australia** can request the helpful *Know Before You Go* brochure from consulates or customs offices. For more information, call the **Australian Customs Service** (© 1300/363-263) or log on to www.customs.gov.au.

Citizens of **New Zealand** can pick up a free pamphlet, *New Zealand Customs Guide for Travellers, Notice no. 4,* available at consulates and Customs offices. For more information, contact **New Zealand Customs Service,** The Customhouse, 17–21 Whitmore St., Box 2218, Wellington (© 04/473-6099 or 0800/428-786; www.customs.govt.nz).

4 Money

CURRENCY

Although the local government wants to shift French Polynesia to the European euro, the official currency will continue to be the **French Pacific franc (CFP)** through at least 2007.

The CFP comes in coins up to 100CFP and in colorful notes ranging from 500CFP into the millions.

The value of the CFP is pegged to the European euro at a rate of **1€** = 119CFP. That means the value of the CFP remains steady against the euro but fluctuates against the U.S. dollar and other currencies. I have seen US$1 worth as much as 170CFP and as little as 75CFP. Recently, it has hovered around 100CFP per buck, so I have used the rate of **US$1 = 100CFP** (or 1CFP = US1¢) to compute the equivalent U.S. dollar prices given in parentheses after the CFP prices in this book.

You can go to **www.xe.com/ucc** and find out the present exchange rates.

Tips Small Change

When you change money (or after you've withdrawn local currency from an ATM), ask for some small bills or loose change. Petty cash will come in handy for public transportation (local taxi drivers never seem to have change for large bills). Consider keeping the small money separate from your larger bills, so that it's readily accessible and you'll be less of a target for theft.

The CFP & the U.S. Dollar

As a rule of thumb, US$1 = approximately 100CFP is the rate of exchange used to calculate the U.S. dollar prices given in this book. This rate has fluctuated widely and may not be the same when you visit. Therefore, use the following table only as a guide.

CFP	US$	CFP	US$
100	$1.00	1,500	15.00
150	1.50	2,000	20.00
200	2.00	3,000	30.00
300	3.00	4,000	40.00
400	3.00	5,000	50.00
500	5.00	6,000	60.00
600	6.00	7,000	70.00
700	7.00	8,000	80.00
800	8.00	9,000	90.00
900	9.00	10,000	100.00
1,000	10.00	20,000	200.00

U.S. dollar and European euro notes (but not coins) are widely accepted as cash in the islands, although at less favorable exchange rates than at banks.

ATMs

The easiest and best way to get local currency is from an ATM (automated teller machine), sometimes referred to as a "cash machine" or "cashpoint." **Banque de Polynésie, Banque Socredo,** and **Banque de Tahiti** have offices with ATMs on the main islands. See the "Fast Facts" sections in the following chapters for bank and ATM locations (this is essential since some of the smaller islands do not have ATMs).

The ATMs operate in both French and English, but they are not always reliable at giving cash or cash advances. I have found Banque Socredo's ATMs to be more reliable than the other banks' machines. Be sure you know your **personal identification number (PIN)** for each credit and debit card—and find out your daily withdrawal limit before

you leave home. Visa cards are more likely to work than MasterCard. Bring some cash or traveler's checks with you just in case, and be prepared to put as many purchases as you can on your credit cards.

When I use my credit or debit cards, I get a better rate of exchange than if I had changed traveler's checks, and I avoid the local banks' fees for changing traveler's checks (see below). You will probably get a more favorable rate if you change your money in French Polynesia rather than before leaving home.

Visa and MasterCard tack on a 1% currency conversion fee, and many American banks add up to 5% as their own "foreign transaction fee." Visa and MasterCard have already converted the other currency into dollars by the time it hits your bank, so this additional fee is nothing but a rip-off. To my mind, it's also grounds for finding another bank.

How much you will pay depends entirely on your bank. I have a Capital One credit card that charges no foreign

> **Tips Getting Rid of Leftover Currency**
>
> If you're about to leave the South Pacific, use any leftover currency to pay part of your hotel bill. Put the rest on your credit card. This will save you the trouble of having to change it at the airport.

transaction fee (and it has no annual fee), but I have cards from other banks that do levy fees. Call your bank's customer service department for information on any applicable charges.

Also ask if your bank levies a fee even if you pay in dollars, or when you charge a U.S. dollar amount to an overseas company or website and the vendor sends the transaction through a foreign bank. You may be able to avoid fees by paying for your airfare and hotel in U.S. dollars before leaving home, such as through a travel agent.

CREDIT CARDS

MasterCard and Visa are widely accepted on the most-visited islands. American Express cards are taken only by major hotels and car-rental firms and by some restaurants. Don't count on using your Diners Club card except at the major hotels. Discover cards are not accepted in the islands. Always ask first, and when you're away from the main towns, don't count on putting anything on plastic.

TRAVELER'S CHECKS

Traveler's checks are something of an anachronism from the days before the ATM. I carry a few hundred dollars' worth in case the ATMs are broken, have run out of cash, or for some reason won't accept my credit or debit card, but I did not cash a single check during my recent 3-month trip. Banks in all the main towns will exchange—and most major hotels, resorts, restaurants, and car-rental firms will accept—traveler's checks issued by American Express, Bank of America, Citicorp, MasterCard, Thomas Cook, and Visa.

You won't necessarily be able to cash traveler's checks on many outer islands, which often have limited, if any, banking facilities, so read the applicable "Fast Facts" section in the following chapters before heading out. All French Polynesian banks charge at least 450CFP (US$4.50) per transaction to cash traveler's checks, regardless of the amount, so you should change large amounts each time to minimize this bite.

You can get traveler's checks at almost any bank or from an **American Express** office. You'll pay a service charge ranging from 1% to 4%. You can also get American Express traveler's checks over the phone by calling ⓒ **800/221-7282** (www.americanexpress.com); Amex gold and platinum cardholders who use this number are exempt from the 1% fee.

Visa offers traveler's checks at Citibank locations nationwide, as well as at several other banks. The service charge ranges between 1.5% and 2%. Call ⓒ **800/732-1322** (www.visa.com) for information. **MasterCard** also offers traveler's checks; call ⓒ **800/223-9920** (www.mastercard.com) for a location near you.

AAA members can obtain checks without a fee at most AAA offices.

5 When to Go

There is no bad time to go to French Polynesia, but some periods are better than others. The weather is at its best—comfortable and dry—in July and August, but this is the prime vacation and festival season. July is the busiest month because of the *Heiva Nui* festival (see "French Polynesia Calendar of Events," below).

Fun Fact **"Tahiti Time"**

There's an old story about a 19th-century planter who promised a South Pacific islander a weekly wage and a pension if he would come to work on his copra plantation. *Copra* is dried coconut meat, from which oil is pressed for use in soaps, cosmetics, and other products. Hours of backbreaking labor are required to chop open the coconuts and extract the meat by hand.

The islander was sitting by the lagoon, eating the fruit he had picked from nearby trees while hauling in one fish after another. "Let me make sure I understand correctly," said the islander. "You want me to break my back working for you for 30 years. Then you'll pay me a pension so I can come back here and spend the rest of my life sitting by the lagoon, eating the fruit from my trees and the fish I catch? I may not be sophisticated, but I am not stupid."

The islander's response reflects an attitude still prevalent in Tahiti and French Polynesia, where many people don't have to work in the Western sense. Here life moves at a slow pace. The locals call it "Tahiti time."

Consequently, do not count on the same level of service in hotels and restaurants as you might expect back home. The slowness is not slothful inattention; it's just the way things are done here. Your drink will come in due course. If you must have it immediately, order it at the bar. Otherwise, relax with your friendly hosts and enjoy their charming company.

Hotels on the outer islands are at their fullest during August, the traditional French vacation month, when many Papeete residents head for the outer islands to get away from it all. In other words, book your air tickets and hotel rooms for July and August as far in advance as possible.

May, June, September, and October offer the best combination of weather and availability of hotel rooms.

THE CLIMATE

Tahiti and the rest of the Society Islands enjoy a balmy tropical climate. Tropical showers can pass overhead at any time of the year. Humidity averages between 77% and 80% throughout the year.

The most pleasant time of year is the May-through-October austral winter, or **dry season,** when midday maximum temperatures average a delightful 82°F (28°C), with early morning lows of 68°F (20°C) often making a blanket necessary. Some winter days, especially on the south side of the islands, can seem quite chilly when a strong wind blows from Antarctica.

November through April is the austral summer, or **wet season,** when rainy periods can be expected between days of intense sunshine. The average maximum daily temperature is 86°F (30°C) during these months, while nighttime lows are about 72°F (22°C). An air-conditioned hotel room or bungalow will feel like heaven during this humid time of year.

The central and northern Tuamotus have somewhat warmer temperatures and less rainfall. Since there are no mountains to create cooling night breezes, these islands can experience desertlike hot periods between November and April.

The Marquesas are closer to the equator, and temperatures and humidity tend to be slightly higher than in Tahiti. Rainfall in the Marquesas is scattered throughout the year, but is most likely from June through August, exactly opposite that of the rest of French Polynesia. The trade winds reach that far north and temper the climate from April to October, but the Marquesas can see hot and sticky days the rest of the year.

The climate in the Austral and Gambier islands, which are much farther south, is more temperate year-round.

French Polynesia is on the far eastern edge of the South Pacific cyclone (hurricane) belt, and storms can occur between November and March.

Another factor to consider is the part of an island that you'll visit. Because the moist trade winds usually blow from the east, the eastern sides of the high, mountainous islands tend to be wetter all year than the western sides.

Also bear in mind that the higher the altitude, the lower the temperature. If you're going up in the mountains, be prepared for much cooler weather than you'd have on the coast.

Average Daytime Temperatures in Tahiti

	Jan	Feb	Mar	Apr	May	June	July	Aug	Sept	Oct	Nov	Dec
Temp °F	80.6	80.8	81.3	80.8	79.5	77.4	76.5	76.3	77	78.1	79.3	79.9
Temp °C	27	27.1	27.4	27.1	26.4	25.2	24.7	24.6	25	25.6	26.3	26.6

THE BUSY SEASON

July and August are the busiest tourist season in French Polynesia. That's when residents of Tahiti head to their own outer islands, in keeping with the traditional July-August holiday break in France. Many Europeans also visit the islands during this time. In addition, July brings the *Heiva Nui,* the territory's biggest annual festival (see "French Polynesia Calendar of Events," below), when locals flock to Tahiti to see or participate in dance contests.

Christmas through the middle of January is a good time to get a hotel reservation in the islands, but airline seats can be hard to come by, since thousands of islanders fly home from overseas.

HOLIDAYS

Like all Pacific Islanders, the Tahitians love public holidays and often extend them past the official day. For example, if Ascension Day falls on a Thursday, don't be surprised if some stores and even banks are closed through the weekend. Plan your shopping forays accordingly.

Public holidays are New Year's Day (government offices are also closed on Jan 2), Good Friday and Easter Monday, Ascension Day (40 days after Easter), Whitmonday (the seventh Mon after Easter), Missionary Day (Mar 5), Labor Day (May 1), Pentecost Monday (the first Mon in June), Bastille Day (July 14), Internal Autonomy Day (Sept 8), All Saints Day (Nov 1), Armistice Day (Nov 11), and Christmas Day.

Moments When the Moon Is Full

The islands are extraordinarily beautiful anytime, but the play of moonlight on the lagoons and ocean, along with the black silhouettes the mountains cast against the sky, make them magical when the moon is full. Keep that in mind when planning your trip—and especially if it's your honeymoon.

Tahiti Tourisme publishes an annual list of the territory's leading special events on its website (see "Visitor Information," earlier).

FRENCH POLYNESIA CALENDAR OF EVENTS

January

Chinese New Year. Parade, musical performances, demonstrations of martial arts, Chinese dances, and handicrafts. Between mid-January and mid-February.

International Oceania Film Documentary Festival (FIFO). More than 100 films produced by Pacific islanders are shown and judged in Papeete. Last weekend in January.

February

Tahiti Moorea Marathon. Prizes worth up to US$15,000 entice some of the world's best runners to trot 42km (26 miles) around Moorea. Second Saturday in February.

March

Coming of the Gospel. Gatherings on Tahiti commemorate the anniversary of the arrival of the London Missionary Society. March 5.

May

Billabong Pro. World-class surfers compete on the big waves off Teuhupoo on Tahiti Iti. First 2 weeks in May.

June

Tahiti Nui Cup Regatta. Cruising yachts sail among Raiatea, Tahaa, Huahine, and Bora Bora. First 10 days in June.

Miss Tahiti, Miss *Heiva*, Miss Moorea, and Miss Bora Bora Contests. Candidates from around the islands vie to win the titles. These are among the biggest annual events on the outer islands. Early to mid-June.

Tahiti International Golf Open. Local and international golfers compete at Atimaono Golf Course, Tahiti. Mid-June.

July

Heiva Nui ✦✦✦. This is the festival to end all festivals in French Polynesia. It was originally a celebration of Bastille Day on July 14, but the islanders have extended the shindig into a month-long blast (it is commonly called *Tiurai,* the Tahitian word for July). They pull out all the stops, with parades, outrigger canoe races, javelin-throwing contests, fire walking, games, carnivals, festivals, and reenactments of ancient Polynesian ceremonies at restored *maraes.* Highlight for visitors: An extraordinarily colorful contest to determine the best Tahitian dancing troupe for the year—never do the hips gyrate more vigorously. Airline and hotel reservations are difficult to come by during July, so book early and take your written confirmation with you. Last weekend in June through July.

August

Mini Fêtes. Winning dancers and singers from the *Heiva Nui* perform at hotels on the outer islands. All month.

September

Tourism Days. Islanders pay homage to overseas visitors, who get discounts. Last weekend in September.

October

Aitoman (Iron Man) Moorea Triathlon. Top-shape athletes swim, bike, and run on Moorea. If you're looking to sign up, go to www.tahititriathlon.pf. First Saturday in October.

Hawaiki Nui Va'a. Outrigger canoe racing, the national sport, takes center stage as international teams race from Huahine to Raiatea, Tahaa, and Bora Bora over 3 days. Find out more at www.hawaikinuivaa.pf. Early October.

Tahiti Carnival. Parades, floats, and much partying on the Papeete waterfront. Last week in October.

November

All Saints Day. Flowers are sold everywhere to families who put them on graves after whitewashing the tombstones. November 1.

December

Tiare Tahiti Flower Festival (The Tiare Days on Tahiti). Everyone on the streets of Papeete and in the hotels receives a *tiare Tahiti,* the fragrant gardenia that is indigenous to Tahiti. Dinner and dancing later. First week in December.

New Year's Eve. A big festival in downtown Papeete leads territory-wide celebrations. December 31.

6 Travel Insurance

The cost of travel insurance varies widely, depending on the cost and length of your trip, your age and health, and the type of trip you're taking, but expect to pay between 5% and 8% of the vacation itself. You can get estimates from various providers through **InsureMyTrip.com**. Enter your trip cost and dates, your age, and other information to obtain prices from more than a dozen companies.

Check your existing insurance policies and credit-card coverage before you buy travel insurance. You may already be covered for lost luggage, cancelled tickets, or medical expenses.

TRIP-CANCELLATION INSURANCE

Trip-cancellation insurance (TCI) helps you get your money back if you have to back out of a trip, if you have to go home early, or if your travel supplier goes bankrupt. Allowed reasons for cancellation can range from sickness to natural disasters (French Polynesia occasionally gets whacked by a hurricane). Trip-cancellation insurance is a good buy if you're getting tickets well in advance—who knows what the state of the world, or of your airline, will be in 9 months? Insurance policy details vary, so read the fine print—and especially make sure that your airline or cruise line is on the list of carriers covered in case of bankruptcy.

For more information, contact one of the following recommended insurers: **Access America** (© 866/807-3982; www.accessamerica.com), **Travelex Insurance Services** (© 888/457-4602; www.travelexinsurance.com), **Travel Guard International** (© 800/826-4919; www.travelguard.com), and **Travel Insured International** (© 800/243-3174; www.travelinsured.com).

MEDICAL INSURANCE

Hospitals and clinics are widespread in French Polynesia. The level of care is very good in Papeete, but elsewhere the quality varies. You can get a broken bone set

---

Tips Travel in the Age of Bankruptcy

Airlines can go bankrupt, so protect yourself by **buying your tickets with a credit card.** The Fair Credit Billing Act guarantees that you can get your money back from the credit card company if a travel supplier goes under (and if you request the refund within 60 days of the bankruptcy). **Travel insurance** can also help, but make sure it covers against "carrier default" for your specific travel provider. And be aware that if a U.S. airline goes bust midtrip, a 2001 federal law requires other carriers to take you to your destination (albeit on a space-available basis) for a fee of no more than $25, provided you rebook within 60 days of the cancellation.

and a coral scrape tended, but treating more serious ailments likely will be beyond the capability of the local hospital everywhere except in Tahiti. For this reason, I always buy a travel insurance policy that includes medical evacuation in case of life-threatening injury or illness. Otherwise, the cost of a flying ambulance would wipe out my life's savings.

Check with your insurer, particularly if you belong to an HMO, about the extent of its coverage while you're overseas. With the exception of certain HMOs and Medicare/Medicaid, your medical insurance should cover medical treatment—even hospital care—overseas (don't forget to bring your insurance ID card!). However, most out-of-country hospitals make you pay your bills up front, and then send you a refund after you've returned home and filed the necessary paperwork. If you do get medical treatment in the islands, save all of your receipts!

If you require additional medical insurance, try **MEDEX International** (✆ **800/527-0218** or 410/453-6300; www.medexassist.com) or **Travel Assistance International** (✆ **800/821-2828** or 202/331-1596; www.travelassistance. com; for general information on services, call the company's Worldwide Assistance Services, Inc., at ✆ **800/777-8710**).

LOST-LUGGAGE INSURANCE

On flights within the U.S., checked baggage is covered up to $2,500 per ticketed passenger. On international flights (including U.S. portions of international trips), baggage coverage is limited to approximately $9.07 per pound, up to approximately $635 per checked bag. If you plan to check items more valuable than what's covered by the standard liability, see if your homeowner's policy covers your valuables, get baggage insurance as part of your comprehensive travel-insurance package, or buy Travel Guard's "BagTrak" product.

If your luggage is lost, immediately file a lost-luggage claim at the airport, detailing the luggage contents. Most airlines require that you report delayed, damaged, or lost baggage within 4 hours of arrival. The airlines are required to deliver luggage, once found, directly to your house or destination free of charge.

CAR-RENTAL INSURANCE

If you hold a private auto insurance policy, you're probably covered in the United States, but not necessarily abroad, for loss or damage to the car and liability in case a passenger is injured. The credit card you used to rent the card also may provide some coverage. Check your own auto insurance policy, the rental company's policy, and your credit card policy for the extent of coverage.

Even if you have such coverage, rental-car companies in the islands are likely to require that you pay for any damages on the scene and sort it out with your insurer or credit card company when you get home. Given the hassles this can cause, I always buy the collision damage waiver and liability policies offered by the local companies. It adds to the cost, but it's a relatively small price to pay for peace of mind.

Tips **Healthy Travels to You**

The following government websites offer up-to-date health-related travel advice:

- **Australia:** www.smartraveller.gov.au
- **Canada:** www.hc-sc.gc.ca/index_e.html
- **U.K.:** www.dh.gov.uk/PolicyAndGuidance/HealthAdviceForTravellers/fs/en
- **U.S.:** www.cdc.gov/travel

7 Health & Safety

STAYING HEALTHY

Tahiti and French Polynesia pose no major health problem for most travelers, although it's a good idea to have your tetanus, hepatitis-A, and hepatitis-B vaccinations up to date.

There are plenty of mosquitoes (see "Insects & Other Critters," below), but they do not carry deadly endemic diseases such as malaria. From time to time the islands will experience an outbreak of **dengue fever,** a viral disease borne by the *Adës aegypti* mosquito, which lives indoors and bites only during daylight hours. Dengue is seldom fatal in adults, but you should take extra precautions to keep children from being bitten by mosquitoes if the disease is present. (For other special precautions that should be taken if you are traveling with kids, see "Specialized Travel Resources," below.)

Minor illnesses found on the islands include the common cold and the occasional outbreaks of influenza and conjunctivitis (pink eye).

Cuts, scratches, and all open sores should be treated promptly in the tropics. I always carry a tube of antibacterial ointment and a small package of adhesive bandages.

Throughout the islands, sexual relations before marriage—heterosexual, homosexual, and bisexual—are more or less accepted (abstinence campaigns fall on deaf ears). Both male and female prostitution is common in Papeete. HIV is present in the islands, so if you intend to engage in sex with strangers, you should exercise *at least* the same caution in choosing them, and in practicing safe sex, as you would at home.

Tap water is safe to drink only in the city of Papeete on Tahiti and on Bora Bora. You can buy bottled spring water in any grocery store. See "Fast Facts" in the chapters that follow for particulars.

If you have a chronic condition, you should consult your doctor before visiting the islands. For conditions like epilepsy, diabetes, or heart problems, wear a **Medic-Alert Identification Tag** (© 800/825-3785; www.medicalert.org), which will immediately alert doctors to your condition and give them access to your records through MedicAlert's 24-hour hot line.

By and large, medical care is very good in Papeete. Every island also has a government clinic, and some have doctors in private practice. I list **hospitals, doctors,** and **emergency numbers** in the "Fast Facts" section of each island chapter.

Overseas health-insurance plans are not accepted here, so you will likely have to pay all medical costs up front and be reimbursed later. See "Medical Insurance," under "Travel Insurance," above.

Remember to pack **prescription medications** in your carry-on luggage, and carry them in their original containers, with pharmacy labels affixed—otherwise, they won't make it through airport security. Also bring along copies of your prescriptions in case you lose your pills or run out. Carry the generic name of prescription medicines, since local pharmacies primarily carry medications manufactured

---

Tips Slather on the Sunscreen

The sun in these latitudes can burn your skin in a very short period of time—even on what seems like a cloudy day. Limit your exposure, especially during the first few days of your trip. Be particularly careful from 11am to 2pm. Use sunscreen with a high protection factor (SPF 30 or more) and apply it liberally. If you're going snorkeling, wear a T-shirt to avoid overexposure on your back.

Avoiding "Economy-Class Syndrome"

Deep vein thrombosis, or "economy-class syndrome," as it's known in the world of flying, is a blood clot that develops in a deep vein. It's a potentially deadly condition that can be caused by sitting in cramped conditions—such as an airplane cabin—for too long. During a flight (especially a long-haul flight), get up, walk around, and stretch your legs every 60 to 90 minutes to keep your blood flowing. Other preventative measures include frequent flexing of the legs while sitting, drinking lots of water, and avoiding alcohol and sleeping pills. If you have a history of deep vein thrombosis, heart disease, or another condition that puts you at high risk, some experts recommend wearing compression stockings or taking anticoagulants when you fly; always ask your physician about the best course for you. Symptoms of deep vein thrombosis include leg pain or swelling, or even shortness of breath.

in France, and the brand names might be different here than in the United States.

And don't forget **sunglasses** and an extra pair of **contact lenses** or **prescription glasses.**

STAYING SAFE

While international terrorism is a threat throughout the world, the islands are among the planet's safest destinations. Tight security procedures are in effect at Tahiti-Faaa International Airport, but once you're on the outer islands, you are unlikely to see a metal detector, nor is anyone likely to inspect your carry-on.

The islands have seen increasing property theft in recent years, however, including occasional break-ins at hotel rooms and resort bungalows. Although street crimes against tourists are still relatively rare, friends of mine who live here don't stroll off Papeete's busy boulevard Pomare after dark. For that matter, you should stay alert wherever you are after dusk.

Don't leave valuable items in your hotel room, in your rental car, or unattended anywhere. See the "Fast Facts" sections in the following chapters for specific precautions.

Women should not wander alone on deserted beaches at any time, since some Polynesian men may consider such behavior to be an invitation for instant amorous activity.

When heading outdoors, keep in mind that injuries often occur when people fail to follow instructions. Believe the experts who tell you to stay on the established trails. Hike only in designated areas, follow the marine charts if piloting your own boat, carry rain gear, and wear a life jacket when canoeing or rafting. Mountain weather can be fickle at any time. Watch out for sudden storms that can leave you drenched and send bolts of lightning your way.

The French gendarmes will come to rescue you if you get into trouble out in the wild, but believe me, they do not appreciate tourists blundering into trouble.

8 Specialized Travel Resources

TRAVELERS WITH DISABILITIES

Most disabilities shouldn't stop anyone from traveling, even in the islands, where ramps, handles, accessible toilets, automatic opening doors, telephones at convenient heights, and other helpful aids are just beginning to appear.

Some hotels provide rooms specially equipped for people with disabilities. These improvements are ongoing; inquire

Tips Insects & Other Critters

"You will find that we islanders are among the friendliest people in the South Pacific," a sign in an island resort advises its guests. "Amongst all the friendly people we also have the friendliest ants, roaches, geckos, crabs, and insects, who are all dying to make your acquaintance."

Indeed, the islands have multitudes of mosquitoes, roaches, ants, house-flies, and other insects. **Ants** are omnipresent here, so don't leave crumbs or dirty dishes lying around your room. Many beaches and swampy areas also have invisible **sand flies**—the dreaded "no-see-ums" or "no-nos"—which bite the ankles around daybreak and dusk.

Insect repellent is widely available in island shops. The most effective contain a high percentage of "deet" (N,N-diethyl-m-toluamide).

I light a **mosquito coil** in my non-air-conditioned room at dusk in order to keep the pests from flying in, and I start another one at bedtime. Grocery stores throughout the islands carry these inexpensive coils. I have found the Fish brand coils, made by the appropriately named Blood Protection Company, to work best.

Don't be frightened by those little **geckos** (lizards) crawling around the rafters of even the most expensive bungalows. They're harmless to us humans, but lethal to insects.

Also, don't be surprised to see a multitude of dogs, chickens, pigs, and squawking myna birds, even in the finest restaurants.

---

when making a reservation whether such rooms are available.

The major international airlines make special arrangements for persons with disabilities. Be sure to tell them of your needs when you reserve. Although most local airlines use small planes that are not equipped for passengers with disabilities, their staffs go out of their way to help everyone get in and out of the aircraft.

Many travel agencies offer customized tours and itineraries for travelers with disabilities. Among them are **Flying Wheels Travel** (© 507/451-5005; www.flying wheelstravel.com), **Access-Able Travel Source** (© 303/232-2979; www.access-able.com), and **Accessible Journeys** (© 800/846-4537 or 610/521-0339; www.disabilitytravel.com).

Avis Rent a Car has an "Avis Access" program that offers such services as a dedicated 24-hour toll-free number (© 888/879-4273) for customers with special travel needs; special car features such as swivel seats, spinner knobs, and hand controls; and accessible bus service.

Organizations that offer assistance to travelers with disabilities include **Moss-Rehab** (www.mossresourcenet.org), the **American Foundation for the Blind** (**AFB;** © 800/232-5463; www.afb.org), and **SATH (Society for Accessible Travel & Hospitality;** © 212/447-7284; www.sath.org). **AirAmbulance-Card.com** is now partnered with SATH and allows you to preselect top-notch hospitals and prepay for medically necessary airlift service in case of an emergency.

Also check out the quarterly magazine *Emerging Horizons* (www.emerginghorizons.com), and *Open World* magazine, published by SATH.

Tips   Be Careful in the Water

Most marine creatures in the lagoons here are harmless to humans, but some should be avoided. Always **seek local advice** before snorkeling or swimming in a lagoon away from the hotel beaches. Many dive operators conduct snorkeling tours. If you don't know what you're doing, go with them.

Because coral cannot grow in freshwater, the flow of rivers and streams into a lagoon creates narrow channels known as **passes** through the reef. Currents can be very strong in the passes, so stay in the protected, shallow water of the inner lagoons.

Coral cuts and scrapes should be washed and treated with a good antiseptic or antibacterial ointment as soon as possible.

Sharks are curious beasts that are attracted by bright objects such as watches and knives, so be careful what you wear in the water. Never swim alone if you have any suspicion that sharks might be present. If you do see a shark, don't splash in the water or urinate. Calmly retreat and get out of the water as quickly as you can, without creating a disturbance.

Those round things on the rocks and reefs that look like pin cushions are **sea urchins,** and their calcium spikes can be more painful than needles. A sea-urchin puncture can result in burning, aching, swelling, and discoloration (black or purple) around the area where the spines entered your skin. The best thing to do is pull out any protruding spines. The body will absorb the spines within 24 hours to 3 weeks, or the remainder of the spines will work themselves out. Again, contrary to poplar wisdom, do not urinate or pour vinegar on the embedded spines—this will not help.

Jellyfish stings can hurt like the devil, but are seldom life-threatening. Get any visible tentacles off your body right away, but not with your hands, unless you're wearing gloves. Use a stick or anything else that is handy. Then rinse the sting with salt- or freshwater, and apply ice to prevent swelling and to help control the pain. If you can find it at an island grocery store, Adolph's Meat Tenderizer is a great antidote.

The **stone fish** is so named because it looks like a piece of stone or coral as it lies buried in the sand on the lagoon bottom, with only its back and 13 venomous spikes sticking out. Its venom can cause paralysis and even death. You'll know by the intense pain if you're stuck. Serum is available, so get to a hospital at once.

Sea snakes, cone shells, crown-of-thorns starfish, moray eels, lionfish, and **demon stingers** can also be painful, if not deadly. The last thing any of these creatures wants is to tangle with a human, so keep your hands to yourself.

Lastly, *do not deface the reef.* You could land in the slammer for breaking off a gorgeous chunk of live coral to take home as a souvenir. The locals know what they can and cannot legally take from under the water, so buy your souvenir coral in a handicraft shop.

GAY & LESBIAN TRAVELERS

French Polynesia is a relatively friendly destination for gay men. Just remember that the AIDS virus is present here (see "Health & Safety," above).

In the islands, many families with a shortage of female offspring rear young boys as girls, or at least relegate them to female chores around the home and village. These males-raised-as-girls are known as *mahus*. Some of them grow up to be heterosexual; others become homosexual or bisexual and, often appearing publicly in women's attire, actively seek the company of tourists. Some dance the female parts in traditional island night shows. You'll see them throughout the islands. Many of them have traveled widely and speak English fluently, making them prime candidates for jobs in hotels and restaurants.

On the other hand, women were not considered equal in this respect in ancient times, so lesbians may not find the islands quite as friendly.

The **International Gay & Lesbian Travel Association** (IGLTA; © 800/448-8550 or 954/776-2626; www.iglta. org), the trade association for the gay and lesbian travel industry, offers an online directory of gay- and lesbian-friendly travel businesses; go to its website and click on "Members."

Many agencies offer tours and itineraries specifically for gay and lesbian travelers. Among them are **Above and Beyond Tours** (© 800/397-2681; www.abovebeyondtours.com), **Now, Voyager** (© 800/255-6951; www.nowvoyager.com), and **Olivia Cruises & Resorts** (© 800/631-6277; www.olivia.com).

Gay.com Travel (© 800/929-2268 or 415/644-8044; www.gay.com/travel or www.outandabout.com) is an excellent online successor to the popular *Out & About* print magazine. It provides regularly updated information about gay-owned, gay-oriented, and gay-friendly lodging, dining, sightseeing, nightlife, and shopping establishments in every important destination worldwide.

The following travel guides are available at many bookstores, or you can order them from any online bookseller: **Spartacus International Gay Guide** (Bruno Gmünder Verlag; www.spartacusworld.com/gayguide), **Odysseus: The International Gay Travel Planner** (Odysseus Enterprises Ltd.), and the **Damron** guides (www.damron.com), with separate, annual books for gay men and lesbians.

SENIOR TRAVELERS

Children are cared for communally in the islands' extended family systems, and so are senior citizens. Many islanders live with their families from birth to death. Consequently, the local governments don't provide as many programs and other benefits for persons of retirement age as in the United States and other Western countries. You won't find many senior discounts.

Nevertheless, mention the fact that you're a senior citizen when you first make your travel reservations. All major airlines and many chain hotels offer discounts for seniors.

Elderhostel, 75 Federal St., Boston, MA 02110-1941 (© 877/426-8056; www.elderhostel.org), arranges study programs for those 55 and over (and a spouse or companion of any age) in the U.S. and in more than 80 countries around the world. Most include airfare, accommodations in university dormitories or modest inns, meals, and tuition. One recent trip included a 2-week cruise to the Marquesas Islands in French Polynesia.

Members of **AARP,** 601 E St. NW, Washington, DC 20049 (© 888/687-2277 or 202/434-2277; www.aarp.org), get discounts on hotels, airfares, and car rentals. AARP offers a wide range of benefits, including *AARP: The Magazine* and a monthly newsletter. Anyone over 50 can join.

Recommended publications offering travel resources and discounts for seniors include the quarterly magazine *Travel 50 & Beyond* (www.travel50andbeyond. com); *Travel Unlimited: Uncommon Adventures for the Mature Traveler* (Avalon); *101 Tips for Mature Travelers,* available from Grand Circle Travel (© **800/221-2610** or 617/350-7500; www.gct.com); and *Unbelievably Good Deals and Great Adventures That You Absolutely Can't Get Unless You're Over 50,* by Joann Rattner Heilman (McGraw-Hill).

FAMILY TRAVEL

Some of the larger hotels are beginning to cater to families. Best is the **Inter-Continental Resort & Spa Moorea,** on Moorea (p. 134).

For the most part, however, tourism in French Polynesia is still aimed primarily at honeymooners and other couples. To be blunt, the islands are better known for sand, sea, and sex than for babysitters, nannies, and playgrounds.

That's not to say you and your offspring won't have a marvelous time here. The islanders invariably love children and are very good at babysitting. Just make sure you get one who speaks English. The hotels can take care of this for you.

On the other hand, childhood does not last as long here as it does in Western societies. As soon as they are capable, children are put to work, first caring for their younger siblings and cousins and helping out with household chores, later tending the village gardens. It's only as teenagers, and then only if they leave their villages for Papeete, that they know unemployment in the Western sense. Accordingly, few towns and villages have children's facilities, such as playgrounds, outside school property.

Some resorts do not accept children at all; I point these out in the establishment listings, but you should ask to make sure.

Even if they do, check whether the hotel can provide cribs, bottle warmers, and other needs, and if they have children's menus.

Disposable diapers, cotton swabs, and baby food are sold in many main-town stores, but you should take along a supply of such items as children's aspirin, a thermometer, adhesive bandages, and any special medications. Make sure your children's vaccinations are up to date before you leave home. If your kids are very small, perhaps you should discuss your travel plans with your family doctor.

Remember to protect youngsters with ample sunscreen. Some other tips: Certain tropical plants and animals may resemble rocks or vegetation, so teach your youngsters to avoid touching or brushing up against rocks, seaweed, and other objects. If your children are prone to swimmer's ear, use vinegar or preventive drops before swimming in freshwater streams or lakes. Have them shower soon after swimming or suffering cuts or abrasions.

Rascals in Paradise, 1 Daniel Burnham Court, Suite 105-C, San Francisco, CA 94107 (© **415/921-7000;** www.rascals inparadise.com), specializes in South Pacific tours for families with kids, including visits with local families and children.

Recommended family travel websites include **Family Travel Forum** (www. familytravelforum.com), **Family Travel Network** (www.familytravelnetwork.com), **Traveling Internationally with Your Kids** (www.travelwithyourkids.com), and **Family Travel Files** (www.thefamily travelfiles.com).

WOMEN TRAVELERS

The islands are relatively safe for women traveling alone, but don't let the charm of warm nights and smiling faces lull you into any less caution than you would exercise at home. *Do not* wander alone on deserted beaches. In the old days, this was an invitation for sex. If that's what you want today, then that's what you're likely to get. Otherwise, it could result in your being raped.

And don't hitchhike alone, either.

Check out the award-winning website **Journeywoman** (www.journeywoman. com), a "real life" women's travel-information network where you can sign up for a free e-mail newsletter and get advice on everything from etiquette and dress to safety. Also see the travel guide *Safety and Security for Women Who Travel,* by Sheila Swan and Peter Laufer (Travelers' Tales, Inc.), for common-sense tips on safe travel.

STUDENT TRAVELERS

The South Pacific islands have one of the most developed backpacker industries in the world, but you won't find any student discounts here.

If you're going on to New Zealand or Australia, you'd be wise to arm yourself with an **international student I.D. card,** which offers substantial savings on plane tickets. It also provides basic health and life insurance and a 24-hour help line. The card is available from **STA Travel** (✆ 800/781-4040; www.statravel.com), the biggest student travel agency in the world. If you're not in North America, there's probably a local number in your country.

If you're no longer a student but are still under 26, you can get an **International Youth Travel Card (IYTC)** for the same price from the same people and it entitles you to some discounts (but not on museum admissions).

Travel CUTS (✆ 800/667-2887 or 416/614-2887; www.travelcuts.com) offers similar services for residents of both Canada and the U.S. Irish students may prefer to turn to **USIT** (✆ 01/602-1904; www.usitnow.ie), an Ireland-based specialist in student, youth, and independent travel.

SINGLE TRAVELERS

Having traveled alone through the islands for more years than I care to admit, I can tell you it's a great place to be unattached. After all, this is the land of smiles and genuine warmth toward strangers. The attitude soon infects visitors: All I've ever had to do to meet my fellow travelers is wander into a hotel bar, order a beer, and ask the persons next to me where they are from and what they have done here.

The hottest destination for singles is the **Club Med,** on Bora Bora (p. 186).

Unfortunately, the solo traveler is often forced to pay a "single supplement" charged by many resorts, cruise lines, and tours for the privilege of sleeping alone.

Travel Buddies Singles Travel Club (✆ 800/998-9099; www.travelbuddies worldwide.com), based in Canada, runs small, intimate, single-friendly group trips and will match you with a roommate free of charge. **TravelChums** (✆ 212/787-2621; www.travelchums. com) is an Internet-only travel-companion matching service with elements of an online personals–type site, hosted by the respected New York–based Shaw Guides travel service. The **Single Gourmet Club** (www.singlegourmet.com/chapters.php) is an international social, dining, and travel club for singles of all ages, with club chapters in 21 cities in the U.S. and Canada.

Many reputable tour companies also offer singles-only trips. **Singles Travel International** (✆ 877/765-6874; www. singlestravelintl.com) offers trips to places like London, Fiji, and the Greek Isles. **Backroads** (✆ 800/462-2848; www.backroads.com) offers more than 160 active-travel trips to 30 destinations worldwide, including Bali, Morocco, and Costa Rica.

For more information, check out Eleanor Berman's latest edition of *Traveling Solo: Advice and Ideas for More Than 250 Great Vacations* (Globe

Pequot), a guide with advice on traveling alone, either solo or as part of a group tour.

TRAVELING WITH PETS

Don't even think about bringing your pet. Fido will spend his vacation in quarantine until you're ready to fly home.

9 Planning Your Trip Online

SURFING FOR AIRFARES

The most popular online travel agencies are **Travelocity** (www.travelocity.com or www.travelocity.co.uk), **Expedia** (www.expedia.com, www.expedia.co.uk, or www.expedia.ca), and **Orbitz** (www.orbitz.com).

Other helpful websites for booking airline tickets online include:

- www.biddingfortravel.com
- www.cheapflights.com
- www.hotwire.com
- www.kayak.com
- www.lastminutetravel.com
- www.opodo.co.uk
- www.priceline.com
- www.sidestep.com
- www.site59.com
- www.smartertravel.com

It's a good idea to get a **confirmation number** and make a **printout** of any online booking transaction.

By all means check the websites of **airlines** that fly to the islands, as well as those of the package-tour companies specializing in French Polynesia, some of which sell air tickets separately from hotel rooms (see "Getting to Tahiti & French Polynesia," p. 38).

Most airlines now offer Web-only specials that even their phone agents know nothing about, so you can often shave a few bucks from a fare by booking directly through the website.

SURFING FOR HOTELS

In addition to **Travelocity, Expedia, Orbitz, Priceline,** and **Hotwire** (see above), the following websites will help you with booking hotel rooms online:

- www.hotels.com
- www.quickbook.com

- www.travelaxe.net
- www.travelweb.com
- www.tripadvisor.com

The best independent site for South Pacific hotel discount shopping is **www.travelmaxia.com**, where scores of properties throughout the South Pacific post their current specials. You can search by country for resorts, hotels, bed-and-breakfasts, dive operators, and cruises.

Another tactic is to check with the local **inbound tour operators.** In addition to selling tours and day trips to visitors already in the islands (that is, at hotel activities desks), these companies put together the local elements of tour packages—such as hotel rooms and airport transfers—for overseas wholesalers. They have the advantage of being on the scene and thus familiar with the properties. Some sell direct to inbound visitors as well as other tour companies. For example, **Tahiti Nui Travel** (www.tahitinui travel.com) has a variety of local packages in French Polynesia.

As with booking air tickets online, it's a good idea to get a confirmation number and make a printout of any online booking transaction.

SURFING FOR RENTAL CARS

All of French Polynesia's major car-rental firms are franchises; that is, they're owned by local interests and not by the big companies such as Avis and Budget. They're also relatively small operations. Consequently, you're unlikely to find them included in big discounts and special deals featured on the major firms' websites. The best deals will appear on their own sites, which I give in the chapters that follow.

Frommers.com: The Complete Travel Resource

For an excellent travel-planning resource, we highly recommend **Frommers. com** (www.frommers.com), voted Best Travel Site by *PC Magazine*. We're a little biased, of course, but we guarantee that you'll find the travel tips, reviews, monthly vacation giveaways, bookstore, and online-booking capabilities to be thoroughly indispensable. Special features include our popular **Destinations** section, where you can access expert travel tips, hotel and dining recommendations, and advice on the sights to see in more than 3,500 destinations around the globe; the **Frommers.com Newsletter,** with the latest deals, travel trends, and money-saving secrets; and our **Travel Talk** area featuring **Message Boards,** where Frommer's readers post queries and share advice, and where our authors sometimes show up to answer questions. Once you finish your research, the **Book a Trip** area can lead you to Frommer's preferred online partners' websites, where you can book your vacation at affordable prices.

All the major online travel agencies offer rental-car reservations services, so it never hurts to look there. Priceline and Hotwire work well for rental cars, too; the only mystery is which major rental company you get, and for most travelers the difference between Hertz, Avis, and Budget is negligible.

10 The 21st-Century Traveler

INTERNET ACCESS AWAY FROM HOME

E-mail is as much a part of life in French Polynesia as it is anywhere else these days. Although ADSL connections are available here (ADSL is not as fast as DSL or cable access in the U.S. and other countries, but is much speedier than dial-up connections), most Internet connections are still dial-up, which will seem glacially slow if you're used to DSL or cable.

Access is also relatively expensive. **MANA** (© **50.88.88;** www.mana.pf) is the only local Internet service provider (ISP), and it charges by the minute rather than by the month—and many hotels slap a whopping fee on top of that. (My Internet and phone bills for checking my e-mail and banking sites from Tahiti hotel rooms have topped US$50!) Consequently, don't expect people here to reply to your e-mail immediately. Patience definitely is a virtue when dealing with folks in French Polynesia.

The easiest way to check your e-mail on the Web is at your hotel, resort, or hostel, although you will pay a premium for the service. It's less expensive to go a **cybercafe.** I point these out under "Internet Access" in the "Fast Facts" sections in the following island chapters.

To retrieve your e-mail, ask your ISP if it has a Web-based interface tied to your existing e-mail account. If not, you can use the free **mail2web** service (www. mail2web.com) to view and reply to your home e-mail. For more flexibility, you may want to open a free, Web-based e-mail account with a service such as **Yahoo! Mail** (http://mail.yahoo.com). Your home ISP may be able to forward your e-mail to the Web-based account automatically.

Configuring Your Laptop

If you brought your laptop, you can log on directly from your hotel room via MANA's so called "Anonymous" dial-up service. MANA charges 85CFP (US85¢) per minute for access time; the cost of the local call will also be billed to your room. Your hotel may well add yet another charge, so it can become very expensive very quickly.

If you elect to go this route, here's how to set up your computer in Windows XP, 2000, and 98 (sorry, Mac users—MANA doesn't provide instructions for other platforms):

- Double-click on **Control Panel** in Windows XP (My Computer in Windows 98).
- Double-click **Network Connections** in XP (Dial-Up Networking in 98).
- Double-click **Create a New Connection** in XP (Make New Connection in 98).
- Name the new connection anything you want. I call mine "Tahiti."
- Click **Configure** and set the maximum speed of your modem to not more than 57,600kbps. Click **OK**.
- Leave the Area Code box blank; in the "Telephone Number" box, type (with no spaces) **0,368888** as the local access number (0 is the number dialed to reach an outside line from all French Polynesian hotels). Don't change the Country box. Click **OK**.
- After you have created your new connection, double-click **Network Connections** in XP (My Computer, Dial-Up Networking in 98) and the icon for your new connection. Click **Connect**. When the connection is made, enter **anonymous** as *both* your name and your password. (If your first try fails, retype both in all capital letters.)
- From then on, you can double-click **My Computer, Dial-Up Networking,** your local connection icon, and **Connect**. After the connection is made, load your browser, and you're online.

Since no major international ISP such as AOL or Earthlink has a local access number in the islands, you can't just plug in your laptop, program in the local access number, and go online as you would at home. On the other hand, you can use your own computer from any hotel room by dialing up via MANA's "Anonymous" service (see "Configuring Your Laptop," below). If you bring your laptop, be sure to include a **connection kit** with French power and phone adapters as well as spare phone and Ethernet cables.

Wi-Fi (wireless fidelity) "hotspots" are soon to be developed in Papeete, but for the time being don't count on finding one.

CELLPHONE USE

Known as "mobiles" over here, cellphones are prevalent throughout the islands. No international wireless company operates in French Polynesia, however, and many American phones won't work since French Polynesia uses the Global System for Mobiles (GSM) technology. Although this quasi-universal system is gaining in popularity, only T-Mobile and Cingular/AT&T Wireless use it in the U.S., while

Online Traveler's Toolbox

Veteran travelers usually carry some essential items to make their trips easier. Following is a selection of handy online tools to bookmark and use.

- **Airplane Food** (www.airlinemeals.net)
- **Airplane Seating** (www.seatguru.com or www.airlinequality.com)
- **Foreign Languages for Travelers** (www.travlang.com)
- **Maps** (www.mapquest.com)
- **Time and Date** (www.timeanddate.com)
- **Travel Warnings** (www.travel.state.gov, www.fco.gov.uk/travel, www.voyage.gc.ca, or www.dfat.gov.au/consular/advice)
- **Universal Currency Converter** (www.xe.com/ucc)
- **Visa ATM Locator** (www.visa.com), **MasterCard ATM Locator** (www.mastercard.com)
- **Weather** (www.intellicast.com or www.weather.com)

some Rogers customers in Canada are GSM. All Europeans and most Australians use GSM. Call your wireless company to see if your phone is GSM.

If you do have a GSM phone, you may be able to use it in the islands if your home provider has a roaming agreement with **Vini** (© **48.13.13;** www.vini.pf), the local cellphone company. Call your wireless operator and ask for "international roaming" to be activated for French Polynesia. I know Cingular does, for my American phone works quite well here.

There's one big problem if you want to both make and receive calls from within French Polynesia. I can make local calls within French Polynesia on my Cingular phone, but calling me requires expensive international calls for French Polynesians. In other words, their calls to my cellphone were routed to the United States and then back to French Polynesia!

You can get around this if (1) your GSM phone transmits and receives on the 900mHz band; (2) it has been "unlocked" from its SIM card, the removable computer chip that stores your and your provider's information; and (3) you buy a local SIM card from Vini.

Pre-paid SIM cards are available at stores displaying the VINI sign. The least expensive costs about 5,500CFP (US$55) and includes 30 minutes of outgoing calls. Incoming calls are free, but outgoing calls using a prepaid 5,500CFP card cost 183CFP (US$1.83) a minute, and that's assuming you use all of your 30 minutes.

The Travel Insider (www.thetravel insider.info) has an excellent explanation of all this, as well as a phone-unlocking service. Click on "Road Warrior Resources" and "International Cellphone Service."

In a worst-case scenario, you can always rent a phone from Vini.

Should you want to rent a phone or SIM card before leaving the U.S., good wireless rental companies offering phones for use in French Polynesia are **InTouch USA** (© **800/872-7626;** www.intouch global.com) and **RoadPost** (© **888/290-1606** or 905/272-5665; www.roadpost. com). InTouch will also, for free, advise you on whether your existing phone will work overseas; simply call © **703/222-7161** between 9am and 4pm EST, or go to http://intouchglobal.com/travel.htm.

11 Getting to Tahiti & French Polynesia

BY PLANE

A few cruise ships stop in the islands on their way across the Pacific Ocean (see "By Cruise Ship," later), yet today all but a handful of visitors arrive by air.

All international flights arrive at **Tahiti-Faaa International Airport (PPT),** on Tahiti's northwest corner, about 11km (7 miles) west of downtown Papeete. See "Arriving & Departing" in chapter 4 for details on getting from the airport to Papeete and other points on Tahiti.

THE AIRLINES

AIR TAHITI NUI (© 877/824-4846; www.airtahitinui.com) French Polynesia's award-winning national airline has more flights—all on relatively new Airbus planes—to and from Tahiti than any other airline.

Unlike flights on the other carriers, which leave Los Angeles shortly before midnight and arrive in Tahiti during the wee hours, some of Air Tahiti Nui's flights depart in the early afternoon California time and arrive in Papeete before dark, thus enabling you to connect to Moorea that evening. Most of its return flights are overnight, but you arrive in Los Angeles early enough in the morning to make convenient connections to other cities.

Air Tahiti Nui also has nonstop flights between New York's John F. Kennedy International Airport and Papeete, a 12-hour flight, but you don't have to land and change airlines in Los Angeles. The plane also keeps going to Sydney, which means you can fly between New York and Australia with only one stop, in Papeete.

Air Tahiti Nui also links Paris, Tokyo, and Auckland to Papeete, and it has a code-share arrangement with Virgin Atlantic permitting direct ticketing from London to Sydney (via Hong Kong) on Virgin Atlantic, thence to Papeete via Air Tahiti Nui. It also code-shares with American Airlines and Northwest Airlines, meaning frequent fliers of those carriers can use their miles to reach Tahiti.

AIR NEW ZEALAND (© 800/262-1234 or 310/615-1111; www.airnewzealand.com) As part of its far-flung island network, Air New Zealand has several flights a week linking Los Angeles and San Francisco to Tahiti, continuing on to the Cook Islands and Auckland. Its weekly "Coral Route" service links Fiji to Rarotonga in the Cook Islands, from where you can connect to and from Tahiti, Los Angeles, and Auckland.

Air New Zealand flies to several Australian cities, so Aussies can reach most of the South Pacific islands through Auckland. It links Tokyo, Hong Kong, Singapore, Seoul, Taipei, and Beijing to Auckland, with connections on to the islands. Air New Zealand is a member of the Star Alliance, which includes United Airlines and several other carriers, which means you can get to the islands from many cities in the United States, Canada, and Europe on an Air New Zealand flight even if your ticket is issued by one of these other airlines.

AIR FRANCE (© 800/321-4538; www.airfrance.com) The French national carrier flies to Tahiti from Paris, Los Angeles, and Tokyo.

HAWAIIAN AIRLINES (© 800/367-5320 in the continental U.S., Alaska, and Canada, or 808/838-1555 in Honolulu; www.hawaiianair.com) This Hawaiian-based airline has the only direct link between Honolulu and Tahiti, usually once a week except during Christmas, when Tahitians like to go shopping in Hawaii. You can fly from Los Angeles, San Francisco, Portland, or Seattle to Honolulu, and then change plans for

> ## Tips Getting through the Airport
>
> - In the U.S., travelers should arrive at the airport 1 hour before a domestic flight and 2 hours before an international flight; if you show up late, tell an airline employee and he or she will probably whisk you to the front of the line.
> - Beat the ticket-counter lines by using an airport electronic kiosk or even online check-in from your home computer, which allows you to print out boarding passes in advance. Curbside check-in is also a good way to avoid lines.
> - Bring a current, government-issued photo ID such as a driver's license or passport. Children under 18 do not need government-issued photo IDs for flights within the U.S., but they do for international flights to most countries.
> - Speed up security by removing your jacket and shoes before you're screened. In addition, remove metal objects such as big belt buckles. If you've got metallic body parts, a note from your doctor can prevent a long chat with the security screeners.
> - Use a TSA-approved lock for your checked luggage. Look for Travel Sentry certified locks at luggage or travel shops and Brookstone stores (or online at www.brookstone.com).

Tahiti. *Beware:* The plane change can result in delays and even an unexpected Hawaiian holiday.

JAPAN AIRLINES (© 800/525-3663; www.jal.co.jp)   The major Japanese carrier flies between Tokyo and Tahiti.

LANCHILE AIRLINES (© 800/735-5526; www.lanchile.com)   The Chilean national airline flies at least weekly between Santiago, Chile, and Tahiti by way of Easter Island.

QANTAS AIRWAYS (© 800/227-4500; www.qantas.com)   The Australian carrier has flights between Sydney and Tahiti.

FLYING FOR LESS: TIPS FOR GETTING THE BEST AIRFARE

The Pacific Ocean hasn't shrunk since it took 10 days and more than 83 hours in the air for Australian aviator Charles Kingsford Smith to become the first person to fly across it in 1928. Even though you can now board a jetliner in Los Angeles in the morning and be strolling under the palm trees of Tahiti by dark, the distances still run into the thousands of miles. Consequently, transportation costs may be the largest single expense of your trip to French Polynesia.

Be sure to shop all the airlines mentioned above to see which has the best deals. Keep calling and checking the websites if no attractive fare is available at first, since wholesalers and groups often reserve blocks of low-cost seats in advance but release some of them near the date of departure. Occasionally a carrier will hold a last-minute sale to get rid of unused seats, so always ask for the *lowest* fare.

SEASONAL & PROMOTIONAL FARES   Depending on the carrier, the South Pacific region has four airfare seasons: High, or peak, season is from December through February. One shoulder season includes March and April; a second runs from September through November. Least expensive, the basic season runs from May through August (when the weather is at its finest in the islands). Fares can vary by as much as 25%, depending on the season.

The major airlines serving Tahiti often have special fares, especially during the slower seasons. Check the airline websites or ask their reservations agents what special deals are offered when you want to fly. *Note:* The lowest-priced fares are often nonrefundable, require advance purchase of 1 to 3 weeks and a certain length of stay, and carry penalties for changing dates of travel.

DISCOUNTERS & CONSOLIDATORS Discounters are travel agents who buy airline seats and hotel rooms at wholesale prices and pass on some of their savings to you. Until recently they were the only way to get the big discounts, but today some wholesalers who specialize in the South Pacific engage in the same practice and are more likely to offer the best deals (see "Packages for the Independent Traveler," below).

There are still numerous discounters, many of them in the United States and abroad. Start by looking in Sunday newspaper travel sections; U.S. travelers should focus on the *New York Times, Los Angeles Times, Miami Herald,* and *Washington Post.* For less-developed destinations, small travel agents who cater to immigrant communities in large cities often have the best deals.

Many discounters—as well as some full-service travel agents—sell tickets provided by **consolidators,** which are sometimes called bucket shops. Consolidators buy and resell seats on the major international carriers that otherwise would go unfilled, especially during slow seasons. Consolidator deals can be riskier than direct buys from a carrier, but they can result in substantial savings on tickets that have fewer restrictions than you

would get with an advance-purchase ticket bought directly from an airline.

Beware, however, that bucket-shop tickets are usually nonrefundable or rigged with stiff cancellation penalties, often as high as 50% to 75% of the ticket price, and some put you on charter airlines with questionable safety records.

Generally, it's best to ask a travel agent to comparison shop for you. Always compare the deals he or she comes up with to those offered directly by the airlines and wholesalers, inquire about any and all restrictions there may be, and pay by credit card.

One reliable consolidator is **STA Travel** (© 800/781-4040; www.statravel.com), now the world's leader in student travel, thanks to its purchase of Council Travel (see "Student Travelers," earlier in this chapter). It also offers good fares for travelers of all ages. **Flights.com** (© 800/TRAV-800; www.flights.com) started in Europe and has excellent fares worldwide, but particularly to that continent. It also has local websites in 12 countries. **Air Tickets Direct** (© 800/778-3447; www.airticketsdirect.com) is based in Montreal and leverages the currently weak Canadian dollar for low fares.

BAGGAGE ALLOWANCES
How many bags you can carry on board and check (and how much they can weigh) varies somewhat by airline, so always check with your chosen carrier beforehand.

Only one rule is set in stone: Passengers on flights to or from the continental United States may check two bags each weighing up to 30kg (66 lb.), with total dimensions (height, width, and length) of both not exceeding 158cm (62 in.). The allowance on flights to and from Hawaii and the South Pacific may be limited to 30kg (66 lb.) per passenger in economy class, 32kg (70 lb.) in first and business class.

Although domestic U.S. allowances may be lower, you can check this much baggage if you're connecting to an international flight.

In general, first-class passengers on other international flights are entitled to 40kg (88 lb.) of checked luggage, business-class passengers to 30kg (66 lb.), and economy-class passengers to 20kg (44 lb.). Some airlines, including Air New Zealand and Air Pacific, strictly enforce these limits and make you pay extra for each kilogram over the maximum.

In addition to a small handbag or purse, all international passengers are permitted one carry-on bag with total measurements not exceeding 115cm (45 in.). Carry-on hoarders can stuff all sorts of things into a laptop bag; as long as it has a laptop in it, it's still considered a personal item (remember, however, you must remove your laptop and pass it through security separately).

Pack carefully and bring evidence of your international ticket with you, as the baggage limit on both of French Polynesia's domestic airlines is 20kg (44 lb.) per person if you're connecting with an international flight within 7 days, but it's 10kg (22 lb.) per person if you're not. You will face a substantial extra charge for excess weight. You can leave your extra belongings in the storage room at your hotel or at Tahiti-Faaa International Airport (see "Arriving & Departing" in chapter 4).

LONG-HAUL FLIGHTS: HOW TO STAY COMFORTABLE

There is no place for a plane to land between Los Angeles and Papeete, so the 7½-hour flights are all nonstop. The trip takes about 12 hours from New York, 7½ hours from Sydney, and 5½ hours from Auckland. In other words, many of you will be in for long-haul flights to get here.

Here are some tips on how to stay comfortable during your flight:

- Your choice of airline and airplane will definitely affect your legroom.

Find more details about U.S. airlines at **www.seatguru.com**. For international airlines, the research firm Skytrax has posted a list of average seat pitches at **www.airlinequality.com**.

- Emergency exit seats and bulkhead seats typically have the most legroom. Emergency exit seats are usually left unassigned until the day of a flight (to ensure that able-bodied persons fill the seats); it's worth getting to the ticket counter early to snag one of these spots for a long flight. Many passengers find that bulkhead seating (the row facing the wall at the front of the cabin) offers more legroom, but keep in mind that bulkheads are where airlines often put baby bassinets, so you may be sitting next to an infant.

- To have two seats for yourself in a three-seat row, try for an aisle seat in a center section toward the back of coach. If you're traveling with a companion, book an aisle and a window seat. Middle seats are usually booked last, so chances are good you'll end up with three seats to yourselves.

- Ask about entertainment options. Many airlines offer seatback video systems that let you choose your movies or play video games—but only on some of their planes. (Boeing 777s are your best bet.)

- To sleep, avoid the last row of any section or the row in front of an emergency exit, as these seats are the least likely to recline. Avoid seats near highly trafficked toilet areas and in the back of many jets—these can be narrower than those in the rest of coach. You also may want to reserve a window seat so you can rest your head and avoid being bumped in the aisle.

- Get up, walk around, and stretch every 60 to 90 minutes to keep your blood flowing. See "Avoiding 'Economy-Class Syndrome,'" p. 28.

Flying with Film & Video

Never pack **film**—exposed or unexposed—in checked bags, because the new, more powerful airport scanners can fog film. The film you carry with you can be damaged by scanners as well. X-ray damage is cumulative; the faster the film, and the more times you put it through a scanner, the more likely the damage. Film under 800 ASA is usually safe for up to five scans. If you're taking your film through additional scans, U.S. regulations permit you to demand hand inspections. In international airports, you're at the mercy of officials. Store your film in clear baggies so you can remove it easily before you go through scanners. Keep in mind that airports are not the only places where your camera may be scanned: Highly trafficked attractions are X-raying visitors' bags with increasing frequency.

Most photo-supply stores sell pouches designed to block X-rays. The pouches fit both film and loaded cameras. They should protect your film in checked baggage, but they may also raise alarms and result in a hand inspection.

You'll have little to worry about if you are traveling with a **digital camera.** Unlike film, which is sensitive to light, the digital camera and its storage cards are not affected by airport X-rays, according to Nikon.

Carry-on scanners will not damage **videotape** in video cameras, but the magnetic fields emitted by the walk-through security gateways and handheld inspection wands will. Always place your loaded camcorder on the screening conveyor belt or have it hand-inspected. Be sure your batteries are charged, as you may be required to turn the device on to ensure that it's what it appears to be.

- Drink water before, during, and after your flight to combat the lack of humidity in airplane cabins. Avoid alcohol, which will dehydrate you.
- If you're flying with kids, don't forget to carry on toys, books, pacifiers, and chewing gum to help them relieve ear pressure buildup during ascent and descent.

BY CRUISE SHIP

Although the days of great liners plying the Pacific are long gone, occasionally it may be possible to reach the islands on a cruise ship making an around-the-world voyage or being repositioned, say, from Alaska to Australia. In addition to Princess Cruises (see below), other companies likely to have ships in the South Pacific include **Cunard Line** (© **800/528-6273;** www.cunardline.com), whose vessels include the *Queen Elizabeth II,* and **Orient Lines** (© **800/333-7300;** www.orientlines.com).

Most sell tickets through travel agents, although some offer them directly to the public on their websites.

At press time, the only company whose ships regularly visit more than one country covered in this book is **Princess Cruises** (© **800/774-6237;** www.princesscruises.com). Some of its *Tahitian Princess* itineraries are extended from French Polynesia to the Cook Islands and Samoa.

Tips Coping with Jet Lag

Except for Air Tahiti Nui's afternoon departures from Los Angeles bound for the islands (see "The Airlines," above), flights from North America leave after dark, which means you will fly overnight and cross at least two time zones. This invariably translates into jet lag. Here are some tips for combating this malady:

- Reset your watch to your destination time before you board the plane.
- Drink lots of water before, during, and after your flight. Avoid alcohol.
- Exercise and sleep well for a few days before your trip.
- Daylight is the key to resetting your body clock. At the website for **Outside In** (www.bodyclock.com), you can get a customized plan of when to seek and avoid light.
- If you need help getting to sleep earlier than you usually would, some doctors recommend taking either the hormone melatonin or the sleeping pill Ambien—but not together. Take 2 to 5 milligrams of melatonin about 2 hours before your planned bedtime.

Lindblad Expeditions (© 800/EXPEDITION; www.expeditions.com) occasionally has exploratory voyages from Easter Island to Tahiti, from there to Fiji, and from Fiji to Papua New Guinea.

You can also go to **www.cruisecritic.com**, where you can check out cruises throughout the world; **www.cruise411.com**, which has itineraries, deck plans, and other information; and **www.cruisepage.com**, with reviews of more than 300 ships.

Your best bet for steaming through the islands, however, is to fly to Tahiti and take one of the ships based here (see "Seeing the Islands by Cruise Ship & Yacht," later in this chapter).

12 Packages for the Independent Traveler

Package tours are simply a way to buy the airfare, accommodations, and other elements of your trip (such as car rentals, airport transfers, and sometimes even activities) at the same time and often at discounted prices. They usually provide the best bargains available, especially to expensive French Polynesia.

Note that package tours are not the same thing as escorted tours, which are structured tours with a group leader. Scant few escorted tours go to Tahiti, except as add-ons to tours primarily of Australia and New Zealand.

Before you invest in a package deal, always ask about the **cancellation policy.** Can you get your money back? Is there a deposit required? Also ask about the **accommodations** choices, prices, and what types of rooms are offered; then look up the hotels' reviews in a Frommer's guide and check their rates online for your specific dates of travel. Finally, look for **hidden expenses.** Ask whether airport departure fees and taxes, for example, are included in the total cost—they rarely are.

Packages are often listed in the travel section of many Sunday newspapers. Or check ads in magazines such as *Arthur Frommer's Budget Travel Magazine, Travel + Leisure, National Geographic Traveler,* and *Condé Nast Traveler.*

Airlines also offer air-and-hotel packages, so be sure to check the websites of **Air Tahiti Nui, Air New Zealand,** and the other South Pacific carriers (see "The Airlines," earlier).

Below, in alphabetical order, are some reputable American-based companies that sell package tours to French Polynesia. Some will discount air tickets and hotel rooms separately—that is, not as part of a package. Be sure to shop among them to see who has the best deals.

- **Blue Pacific Vacations** (© 800/798-0590; www.bluepacificvacations.com), a division of France Vacations, is headed by John Biggerstaff and Ken Jordan, two veterans of Tahiti tourism. They will customize tours to most French Polynesian islands.
- **Brendan Worldwide Vacations** (© 800/421-8446 or 818/785-9696; www.brendanvacations.com) provides packages to French Polynesia.
- **Go-Today** (© 800/227-3235; www.go-today.com), based in Washington State, offers packages to French Polynesia at discount prices.
- **Islands in the Sun** (© 800/828-6877 or 310/536-0051; www.islandsinthesun.com), the largest and oldest Tahiti travel specialist, was started in the 1960s by the late Ted Cook, a pioneer in modern Tahiti tourism.
- **Jetabout Island Vacations** (© 800/348-8145; www.jetabouttahitivacations.com), of El Segundo, Calif., offers a wide variety of packages to Tahiti.
- **Journey Pacific** (© 800/704-7094; www.journeypacific.com) is a Las Vegas–based agency offering packages to Tahiti.
- **Pacific Destination Center** (© 800/227-5317; www.pacific-destinations.com) is owned and operated by Australian-born Janette Ryan, who offers some good deals to the islands.
- **Pleasant Holidays** (© 800/742-9244; www.pleasantholidays.com), a huge company best known for its Pleasant Hawaiian and Pleasant Mexico operations, offers packages to French Polynesia.
- **Tahiti Discount Travel** (© 877/426-7262; www.tahiti-discounttravel.com) is owned by former employees of the defunct Discover Wholesale Travel, once the leader in budget packages. They feature some of the lowest-priced packages to French Polynesia.
- **Tahiti Legends** (© 800/200-1213; www.tahiti-legends.com) is run by former officials of Islands in the Sun. It sells tours to French Polynesia, the Cook Islands, and Fiji under the name **Pacific Legends** (www.pacificlegends.com).
- **Tahiti Vacations** (© 800/553-3477; www.tahitivacation.com) is a subsidiary of Air Tahiti, French Polynesia's domestic airline. It frequently offers the least expensive packages available to Tahiti and Moorea.

13 The Active Traveler

The islands are a dream if you're an active traveler, and especially if you're into diving, snorkeling, swimming, boating, and other watersports. You can also play golf and tennis, or hike into the jungle-clad mountainous interiors of the islands. Kayaking on the lagoons is popular everywhere. There's good biking along the many roads skirting colorful lagoons. You can engage in these activities virtually everywhere, although some islands are better than others. I point out the best in the chapters that follow, but here's a brief rundown of my favorites.

BIKING

Relatively flat roads circle most of the islands covered in this book, making for easy and scenic bike riding. In fact, bicycles are one of my favorite means of getting around. It's simple and inexpensive to rent bikes on all the islands in French

Polynesia. Many hotels and resorts provide bikes for their guests to use.

DIVING & SNORKELING

Most of the islands have very good to great diving and snorkeling. Virtually every lagoon-side resort has a dive operator, and many will let snorkelers go along. The live-aboard dive boat *Tahiti Aggressor* operates in French Polynesia (see "Seeing the Islands by Cruise Ship & Yacht," below).

French Polynesia is famous for its bountiful sealife, from harmless tropical fish to hammerhead sharks. You'll see plenty of creatures at Moorea, Bora Bora, Huahine, Raiatea, and Tahaa, but the best diving and snorkeling are in the huge lagoons of Rangiroa, Tikehau, Manihi, and Fakarava in the Tuamotu Islands. See chapters 5, 6, 7, 8, and 10.

Most resorts offer dive packages to their guests, and the American-based **PADI Travel Network** (© 800/729-7234; www.padi.com) puts together packages for divers of all experience levels.

DEEP-SEA FISHING

Charter boats on many islands will take you in search of marlin, swordfish, tuna, mahimahi, and other game fish.

French Polynesia has two ways to cast your line while living aboard in luxury. Based in Bora Bora, the *Taravana* is a 50-foot sail-powered game-fishing boat (see chapter 8). In the Tuamotus, **Haumana Cruises** (www.tahiti-haumana-cruises.com) uses a 17-cabin yacht (see "Seeing the Islands by Cruise Ship & Yacht," below).

GOLF & TENNIS

Frankly, this is generally not the place for a vacation consisting primarily of golf and tennis.

At press time, French Polynesia's lone course, on the south coast of Tahiti, was about to be joined by a new set of links on Moorea. See chapter 5.

HIKING

These aren't the Rocky Mountains, nor are there blazed trails out here, but hiking in the islands is a lot of fun.

Tahiti and Moorea have several trails into the highlands, some of which run along spectacular ridges. You'll need a guide for the best hikes, but you can easily hire them on both islands. See chapters 4 and 5.

HORSEBACK RIDING

Although I prefer sipping a cold drink, a great way to experience a glorious South Pacific sunset is from the back of a horse while riding along a white-sand beach. You can do just that on Moorea and Huahine (see chapters 5 and 6). Ranches on Moorea and Huahine also have daytime rides into the mountains.

SAILING

All but a few beachfront resorts have canoes, kayaks, small sailboats, sailboards, and other toys for their guests' amusement. Since most of these properties sit beside protected lagoons, using these craft is not only fun, but also relatively safe. It's most fun where you can paddle or sail across a lagoon to uninhabited islets out on the reef, such as on Moorea's northwest coast. See chapter 5.

You can rent bareboat yachts (that is, without captains) in the Leeward Islands, where **The Moorings** (© 800/535-7289; www.moorings.com) and **Sunsail Yacht Charters** (© 800/327-2276; www.sunsail.com) have operations based on Raiatea. For details, go to "Seeing the Islands by Cruise Ship & Yacht," below.

14 Getting Around Tahiti & French Polynesia

BY PLANE

Air Moorea (© 86.41.41; fax 86.42.99; www.airmoorea.com) provides shuttle service between Tahiti-Faaa International Airport and Temae Airport on Moorea. Its small planes (and I do mean small)

Tips Air Tahiti Fares & a Money-Saving Pass

Air Tahiti's most recent one-way adult fares on the usual visitor's circuit are as follows (double the fare for round-trips between any two islands; halve the cost for children):

Papeete to Moorea	4,200CFP (US$42)
Moorea to Huahine	14,400CFP (US$144)
Moorea to Bora Bora	20,700CFP (US$207)
Huahine to Raiatea	6,100CFP (US$61)
Raiatea to Bora Bora	7,000CFP (US$70)
Bora Bora to Papeete	17,600CFP (US$176)
Bora Bora to Rangiroa	26,600CFP (US$266)
Rangiroa to Papeete	17,700CFP (US$177)
Papeete to Hiva Oa	35,200CFP (US$352)

You can save by buying an **Air Tahiti Pass** over these popular routes. For example, the "Bora Bora Pass" permits travel over the popular Papeete–Moorea–Huahine–Bora Bora–Papeete route for about 34,700CFP (US$347), which is 10,300CFP (US$103) less than the full adult fares. The "Bora Bora-Tuamotu Pass" adds Rangiroa, Tikehau, Manihi, and Fakarava. There's also a Marquesas extension to these plans as well as a "Marquesas Pass" if you're only going to Nuku Hiva and Hiva Oa. Whether you save anything will depend on how many islands you plan to visit, so add up the regular fares and compare to the price of the passes. All travel must be completed within 28 days of the first flight, and other restrictions apply. See **www.airtahiti.pf** for details.

leave Faaa on the hour and half-hour daily from 6 to 9am, then on the hour from 10am to 3pm, and on the hour and half-hour again from 4 to 6pm. Each plane turns around on Moorea and flies back to Tahiti. The fare is about 3,100CFP (US$31) each way. Air Moorea's little terminal is on the east end of Tahiti-Faaa International Airport (that's to the left as you come out of Customs). Air Moorea will take you from the airport to your Moorea hotel for 500CFP (US$5) each way, but *you must buy your transfer ticket in Papeete.* It is not available after you arrive on Moorea.

Air Moorea is owned by **Air Tahiti** (© **86.42.42;** fax 86.40.99; www.air tahiti.pf), which provides daily flights between Papeete and all the main islands.

Since Air Tahiti is the only scheduled carrier to the islands other than Moorea, it's wise to reserve your seats as early as possible.

Air Tahiti's central downtown Papeete walk-in reservations office is at the corner of rue du 22 Septembre and rue du Maréchal Foche (© **47.44.00**). It also has an office in the Tahiti-Faaa International Airport terminal (© **86.41.84**).

The **baggage limit** on both of these airlines is 20kg (44 lb.) per person if you're connecting with an international flight within 7 days, but 10kg (22 lb.) per person if you're not. You will face a substantial extra charge for excess weight. You can leave your extra belongings in the storage room at your hotel or at

---

Tips **Always Reconfirm**

Once here, *always* reconfirm your return flight as soon as you arrive on an outer island, primarily so that Air Tahiti will know where to reach you in case of a schedule change. Avoid booking a return flight from an outer island on the same day your international flight is due to leave for home; give yourself plenty of leeway in case the weather, mechanical problems, or scheduling conflicts prevent the plane from getting to and from the outer island on time.

Tahiti-Faaa International Airport (see "Arriving & Departing" in chapter 4).

Check-in times vary from 1 to 2 hours in advance, so ask Air Tahiti when you should arrive at the airport.

An alternative to taking Air Tahiti's scheduled flights is chartering a plane and pilot from **Air Moorea, Air Tahiti, Air Archepels** (✆ **81.30.30;** www.air archipels.com), or **Wan Air** (✆ **50.44. 18;** www.wanair.pf). **Polynesia Hélicoptères** (✆ **86.60.29;** www.polynesia-helicopter.com) charters helicopters. When the total cost is split among a large enough group, the price per person could be less than airfare on a scheduled airline.

BY FERRY TO MOOREA

Two companies, **Aremiti** (✆ **50.57.57;** www.aremiti.pf) and **Moorea Ferry** (✆ **86.87.47** on Tahiti, or 56.34.34 on Moorea; www.mooreaferry.pf), run ferries between the Papeete waterfront and Vaiare, a small bay on Moorea's east coast. It can seem like madness when the boats arrive and depart at the wharves, so take your time and be sure to get on one of the fast catamarans, which take 30 minutes to cover the 19km (12 miles) between the islands. The *Aremiti V,* the *Aremiti Ferry,* and the *Moorea Express* are all fast catamarans. Don't get on the *Moorea Ferry,* which can take an hour. The one-way fare on any ferry, whether fast or slow, is about 900CFP (US$9).

In general, one or another of them departs Papeete at about 6am, 7:30am, 9am, noon, 1:30pm, 3pm, and 5pm, with extra voyages on Friday and Monday (Moorea is a popular weekend retreat for Papeete residents). Pick up a copy of the schedules at the ferry dock and carry them with you throughout your visit.

Buses meet all ferries (except the midday departures from Papeete) to take you to your hotel or other destination on Moorea; the fare is 300CFP (US$3) per person. From Vaiare, they take about 1 hour to reach the northwest corner of Moorea.

BY SHIP TO THE OUTER ISLANDS

You can go by ship from Papeete to Huahine, Raiatea, Tahaa, and Bora Bora, but it's by no means the quickest or most comfortable way to travel, nor the most reliable.

Once used as a Tahiti–Moorea ferry, the catamaran *Aremiti 4* (✆ **50.57.57;** www.aremiti.pf) is the fastest of the lot. It usually departs Papeete at 8am on Wednesday and Sunday for Huahine and Raiatea. It arrives in Huahine at noon, at Raiatea at 1:30pm. It then returns over the same route, arriving back at Papeete about 6pm on the same day. The *Aremiti 4* has airline-style seats and a bar, but no cabins. One-way fares from Papeete are about 4,770CFP (US$48) to Huahine, 5,500CFP (US$55) to Raiatea.

Two cargo ferries, the *Vaeanu* (✆ **41. 25.35;** fax 41.24.34; torehiatetu@mail. pf) and the *Hawaiki* **Nui** (✆ **45.23.24;** fax 45.24.44; sarlstim@mail.pf), make three voyages a week. Both have passenger

---

Moments **Breaking into Tahitian Song**

I was on the last ferry from Moorea to Tahiti when a Tahitian passenger, obviously on his way home from work, started playing a guitar. Within seconds, everyone onboard spontaneously began singing Tahitian songs. If you're lucky, you'll witness something like this and be in for a very special moment.

---

cabins. Usually they depart Papeete about 4pm, arrive at Huahine during the night, and go on to the other Leeward Islands the next day. They return from Bora Bora over the reverse route. Contact the ship owners for fares and schedules, which are at the mercy of the weather and mechanical condition of the ships.

Once in the Leeward Islands, you can make the gorgeous voyage between Bora Bora and Raiatea on the *Maupiti Express* (© **67.66.69** on Bora Bora, 66.37.81 on Raiatea; maupitiexpress@mail.pf). This small, fast ferry usually departs Bora Bora for Tahaa and Raiatea at 7am on Monday, Wednesday, and Friday, returning to Bora Bora in the late afternoon. It stops at Tahaa in both directions. On Tuesday, Thursday, and Saturday, it sails from Bora Bora to Maupiti, departing at 8:30am and returning in the late afternoon. In other words, it's possible to make day trips from Bora Bora to Raiatea or Maupiti. Fares on either route are 2,500CFP (US$25) one-way, 3,500CFP (US$35) round-trip.

Except for the excellent *Aranui 3*, which is as much cruise vessel as cargo ship (see "Seeing the Islands by Cruise Ship & Yacht," below), ships to the Tuamotu, Marquesas, Gambier, and Austral groups keep somewhat irregular schedules in terms of weeks or even months, not days. I once met a young Australian who took a boat to Rapa in the Austral Islands, expecting to return in a few weeks to Papeete. The ship broke down and went into the repair yard on Tahiti, stranding him for 3 months on Rapa, where he survived on coconuts and

the generosity of local residents. Consequently, I cannot recommend them. If you're interested, contact Tahiti Tourisme for a list of inter-island schooners, their fares, and approximate schedules from Tahiti Tourisme. You had best have a 3-month visa to stay in French Polynesia.

BY RENTAL CAR

Avis and **Europcar** have rental-car agencies (*locations de voiture* in French) on Tahiti, Moorea, Huahine, Raiatea, and Bora Bora. **Hertz** is present on Tahiti, Raiatea, and Bora Bora. See the "Getting Around" sections in the following chapters for details.

A valid **driver's license** from your home country will be honored in French Polynesia.

Service stations are fairly common on Tahiti, but only in the main villages on the other islands. Expect to pay about twice as much per gallon of gas as in the United States.

Driving is on the **right-hand side** of the road, as in North America and continental Europe.

All persons in a vehicle must wear **seat belts.** If you drive or ride on a scooter or motorbike, **helmets** (*casques,* pronounced "casks") are mandatory.

Speed limits are 40kmph (24 mph) in the towns and villages, and 80kmph (48 mph) on the open road. The limit is 60kmph (36 mph) for 8km (5 miles) on either side of Papeete. The general rule on the Route 5 freeway between Papeete and Punaauia, on Tahiti's west coast, is 90kmph (54 mph), although there is one

> **Tips Drive Defensively!**
>
> Except for the four-lane expressways leading into Papeete, the roads here are narrow and winding. Add a penchant for speeding on the part of some locals, and you have the recipe for danger. If you rent a vehicle, keep your eyes on the road and drive defensively at all time.

short stretch going down a hill where it's officially 110kmph (66 mph).

Drivers on the main rural roads have the right of way. In Papeete, priority is given to vehicles entering from the right side, unless an intersection is marked with a traffic light or a stop or yield sign. This rule differs from those of most other countries, so be especially careful at all intersections, especially those marked with a *priorité à droite* (priority to the right) sign, and give way accordingly.

Drivers are required to **stop for pedestrians** at marked crosswalks, but on busy streets, don't assume that drivers will politely stop for you when you try to cross.

Traffic lights in Papeete may be difficult to see, since some of them are on the far left-hand side of the street instead of on the driver's side of the intersection.

15 Seeing the Islands by Cruise Ship & Yacht

The Society Islands are ideal grounds for cruise ships, since it's barely an hour's steam from Tahiti to Moorea, half a day's voyage on to Huahine, and less than 2 hours each among Huahine, Raiatea, Tahaa, and Bora Bora. That means the ships spend most days and nights at anchor in lovely lagoons, allowing passengers plenty of time to explore the islands and play in the water. Bear in mind, however, that you will see a lot more of the ship than you will of the islands.

Cruises could also be an affordable way to see the islands in style, since the prices usually include all meals, wine with lunch and dinner, soft drinks, and most onboard activities. You might even find a deal that includes airfare to and from Tahiti.

Likewise, these are wonderful islands for chartering a yacht and setting sail on your own.

TAKING A CRUISE

In addition to the ships below, keep an eye out for the *Star Flyer,* a 170-passenger, sail-driven vessel that is to begin cruises out of Papeete in 2007. It's operated by **Star Clippers** (✆ **800/442-0552** or 305/442-0550; www.starclippers.com).

ADVENTURES ON THE
ARANUI ✵✵✵

The working cargo ship *Aranui 3* (✆ **800/972-7268** in the U.S., or 42.62.40 in Papeete; fax 43.48.89; www.aranui.com) is the most interesting way to visit the out-of-the-way Marquesas Islands. Outfitted for up to 200 passengers, this 386-foot freighter makes regular 15-day round-trips from Papeete to 6 of the 10 Marquesas Islands, with stops on the way at Fakarava and Rangiroa in the Tuamotus. While the crew loads and unloads the ship's cargo, passengers spend their days ashore experiencing the islands and islanders. Among the activities: picnicking on beaches, snorkeling, visiting villages, and exploring archaeological sites. Experts on Polynesian history and culture accompany most voyages.

Accommodations are in 10 suites, 12 deluxe cabins, 63 standard cabins, and dormitories. The suites and cabins all have private bathrooms. Suites and deluxe cabins have windows and doors opening to outside decks, and their bathrooms are equipped with bathtubs as well as showers. Standard cabins lack outside doors and have portholes instead of windows. The ship has a restaurant, bar, boutique, library, video lounge, and pool.

The ship's primary job is to haul cargo, so it does not have stabilizers and other features of a luxury liner. In other words, do not expect the same level of comfort, cuisine, and service as on the other ships cruising these waters. If you only want to sit by the pool, eat prodigious quantities of fine food, and smoke cigars, the *Aranui* may not be your cup of tea. But for those who want to go places relatively few people visit, and learn a lot in the process, then it is an excellent choice.

Fares for the complete voyage range from about US$1,980 for a dormitory bunk to US$4,950 per person for suites. All meals are included, but you have to pay your own bar bill and your airfare to and from Tahiti.

LUXURY ON THE *PAUL GAUGUIN* ★★

The 157m (513-ft.), 318-passenger *Paul Gauguin* (© 877/505-5370 or 904/776-6123 in the U.S., or 54.51.00 in Papeete; www.rssc.com) is the most luxurious of Tahiti's cruise ships. It spends most of its year making 7-day cruises through the Society Islands, but occasionally extends to Rarotonga in the Cook Islands and to the Tuamotu and Marquesas islands. All of the ship's seven suites and about half of its 152 staterooms have private verandas or balconies (the least expensive lower-deck units have windows or portholes). All are luxuriously appointed with minibars, TVs and VCRs, direct-dial phones, and marble bathrooms with full-size tubs. Most have queen-size beds, although some have two twins. Per-person double-occupancy fares for the 1-week Society Islands cruises start at about US$1,800 per person.

A LOT OF COMPANY ON THE *TAHITIAN PRINCESS*

Operated by **Princess Cruises** (© 800/774-6237 or 904/527-6660; www.princesscruises.com), the 700-passenger *Tahitian Princess* makes 10-night voyages through French Polynesia and to Rarotonga in the Cook Islands. Formerly a Renaissance Cruises ship, this is the largest vessel operating in French Polynesia, so you won't have the same intimacy as on the other vessels. It's also the least expensive, with special fares sometimes offered during the slow seasons. Passengers can make use of a sun deck, pool, fitness center, casino, cabaret lounge, two bars, and four restaurants. Shore excursions are offered, but unlike the *Paul Gauguin* and the *Wind Star,* the *Tahitian Princess* doesn't have a stern platform to support onboard watersports activities. Almost 70% of the 280 staterooms and 62 suites open to private terraces. Prices start at US$1,850 per person for an interior stateroom.

An identical vessel, the *Pacific Princess,* cruises part of the year in French Polynesia,

---

Fun Fact **Phoning Like a Local**

The custom in the Tuamotu and Marquesas islands is to group telephone numbers in two, such as 960 569, but in most of French Polynesia, the local phone numbers are presented as three two-digit numbers—for example, 42.29.17. If you ask someone for a number, he or she will say it like this: *"quarante-deux, vingt-neuf, dix-sept"* in French or "forty-two, twenty-nine, seventeen" in English.

and then repositions to other ports, including Sydney, Australia, from where it sails through the western Pacific.

DINING IN THE LAGOON WITH *BORA BORA CRUISES*

Bora Bora Cruises, B.P. 40186, Papeete (© **45.10.66;** fax 45.10.65; www.bora boracruises.com), uses the sleek, luxurious yachts *Tu Moana* and *Tia Moana* for 1-week cruises from Bora Bora to Huahine, Raiatea, and Tahaa. The identical ships measure in at 69m (226-ft.) and can carry up to 60 passengers in 30 staterooms spread over three decks. They are small enough to anchor closer to shore than the other ships. Consequently, passengers are treated to such extras as breakfast served in the lagoon (that's right, you actually sit at tables in the water) and movies shown on a beach. Fares are about US$4,600 per person.

DIVING FROM THE *TAHITI AGGRESSOR*

Serious intermediate and advanced divers can experience the lagoons of Bora Bora, Huahine, Raiatea, and Tahaa on the liveaboard *Tahiti Aggressor* (© **800/348-2628;** fax 985/384-0817; www.aggressor.com). Owned and operated by the Louisiana-based Aggressor Fleet, this nine-cabin, 36m (106-ft.) catamaran makes 1-week cruises starting at Bora Bora. The cost is about US$3,000 per person.

FLY-FISHING FROM THE *HAUMANA*

Fly-fishing plays second fiddle to just ordinary cruising, but if you like to fish, there is no better place to cast your line than from the *Haumana* (© **50.06.74;** fax 50.06.72; www.tahiti-haumana-cruises.com). This 33.5m (110-ft.), 42-passenger catamaran specializes in 3-, 4-, and 7-night cruises on the calm, shallow lagoons of Rangiroa and Tikehau in the Tuamotus, both well stocked with bone- and other game fish. Although the *Haumana*

is smaller than other ships, its 21 air-conditioned cabins all have large windows or portholes, queen beds, sofas or settees, minibars, TVs, VCRs, phones, and shower-only bathrooms with hair dryers. Rates range from US$2,130 to US$5,070 per person, double occupancy, including all meals, drinks, fishing, and kayak excursions.

CHARTERING A YACHT

If you're an experienced sailor, you can charter a yacht—with or without skipper and crew—and knock around some of the French Polynesian islands as the wind and your own desires dictate. The best place to start is Raiatea, which shares a lagoon with Tahaa, the only French Polynesian island you can circumnavigate entirely within a protective reef. Depending on the wind, Bora Bora and Huahine are relatively easy blue-water trips away.

The Moorings ✦✦✦, a respected charter company based in Florida (© **800/535-7289** or 727/535-1446; www.moorings.com), operates a fleet of sailboats based at **Apooti Marina,** on Raiatea's northern coast (© **66.35.93;** fax 66.20.94; moorings@mail.pf). That's a few minutes' sail to Tahaa. Depending on the size of the boat—they range from 11 to 15m (36–50 ft.) in length—and the season, bareboat rates (that is, without skipper or crew) range from about US$415 to US$1,480 per vessel per day. Provisions are extra. The agency will check you out to make sure you and your party can handle a sailboat of this size; otherwise, you must pay extra for a skipper.

Sunsail Yacht Charters (© **800/327-2276** in the U.S., or 60.04.85 on Raiatea; www.sunsail.com) has a fleet of 11-to-15m (36–49 ft.) yachts based at Faaroa Bay on Raiatea. Its bareboat rates range from about US$360 to US$1,200 a day per boat, depending on size and season, plus provisions, skipper, and cook if you need them.

The French-owned **Tahiti Yacht Charter** (© 45.04.00; fax 45.76.00; www.tahitiyachtcharter.com) has 11m to 14m (36–49 ft.) yachts based at Papeete and Raiatea. It designs cruises throughout the territory, including lengthy voyages to the Tuamotus and Marquesas. Similar services are offered by **Archipel Croisiers,** on Moorea (© **56.36.39;** fax 56.35.87; www.archipels.com).

16 Tips on Accommodations

French Polynesia has a wide range of accommodations, from deluxe resort hotels to mom-and-pop guesthouses and dormitories with bunk beds.

TYPES OF ROOMS

My favorite type of hotel accommodates its guests in individual bungalows set in a coconut grove beside a sandy beach and quiet lagoon; if that's not the quintessential definition of the South Seas, then I don't know what is! Some of these are super-romantic bungalows that actually stand on stilts out over the reef (although I should point out that some of these overwater units tend to be close together and thus less private than bungalows ashore elsewhere). Others are as basic as tents. In between, they vary in size, furnishings, and comfort. In all, you get to enjoy your own place, one usually built or accented with thatch and other native materials but containing most of the modern conveniences. An increasing number of these accommodations are air-conditioned, which is a definite plus during the humid summer months from November through March. All but a few bungalows have ceiling fans, which will usually keep you comfortable during the rest of the year. Hotels of this style are widespread in the South Pacific.

SAVING ON YOUR HOTEL ROOM

The rate ranges quoted in this book are known in the hotel industry as **rack rates,** or published rates—that is, the maximum a property charges for a room. These prices are becoming less meaningful as more and more hotels engage in "yield management," under which they change their rates almost daily depending on how many people are booked in for a particular night. In other words, you may not know what the price of a room is until you call the hotel or book online for a particular date. Nevertheless, rack rates remain the best way of comparing prices.

You may be able to save on hotel rooms by booking them through the airlines, discounters, or wholesalers. One example is **Air New Zealand's "Go As You Please"** program, which offers reduced rates at a number of establishments everywhere that the airline flies. You book and pay for the rooms ahead through Air New Zealand's offices and agents (see "The Airlines," earlier in this chapter). You won't find this program online, so ask the airline for a brochure that lists the hotels and rates.

Just as consolidators pare the price of airline tickets by selling unused seats, so do hotel brokers get rid of rooms hoteliers don't think they can sell at full price. The brokers may not offer the best deals you can find, but they're worth calling. You're probably better off dealing directly with a hotel, but if you don't like bargaining, this is certainly a viable option. Most of them offer online reservations services as well. One reputable provider offering South Pacific rooms is **Hotel Discounts Reservations Network** (© **800/715-7666;** www.hoteldiscounts.com).

See "Planning Your Trip Online," earlier in this chapter, for tips on finding discounts on the Web.

LANDING THE BEST ROOM

Somebody has to get the best room in the house. It might as well be you.

Guesthouses & Family Accommodations

In general, you'll find a significant difference in quality between French Polynesia's moderate and inexpensive accommodations. Few establishments here are comparable in price or quality to the inexpensive motels found in abundance in the U.S., Canada, Australia, and New Zealand.

The local government is encouraging the development of guesthouses and family pensions, of which there are a growing number. Many owners have used government-backed loans to acquire one-room guest bungalows with attached bathrooms. Although the bungalows are identical, the owners have added decorative touches (in some cases quite tasteful, in others barely so).

Tahiti Tourisme inspects these establishments and distributes lists of those it recommends (see "Visitor Information" earlier); some are also recommended in this book. Many promote themselves through an organization known as **Haere-Mai** (www.haere-mai.pf). Local families operate most of them, so if you decide to go this route, an ability to speak some French may be essential.

You can start by joining the hotel's frequent-guest program, which may make you eligible for upgrades. A hotel-branded credit card usually gives its owner "silver" or "gold" status in frequent-guest programs for free.

Always ask about corner rooms. They're often larger and quieter, with more windows and light, and they often cost the same as standard rooms. When you make your reservation, ask if the hotel is renovating; if it is, request a room away from the construction. Ask about nonsmoking rooms, rooms with views, and rooms with twin, queen-, or king-size beds. If you're a light sleeper, request a room away from vending machines, elevators, bars, and discos. Ask for a room that has been most recently renovated or redecorated.

If you aren't happy with your room when you arrive, ask for a different one. Most lodgings will be willing to accommodate you if another room is available.

Here are some other questions to ask before you book a room:

- What's the view like? If you're a cost-conscious traveler, you might be willing to pay less for a bungalow in the garden, especially if you don't plan to spend much time in the room.
- Does the room have air-conditioning or just ceiling fans? It's an important consideration between November and March.
- Is there good ventilation in the room? Some older hotels don't have windows on both sides of the building, which prevents the cooling trade winds from circulating.
- What is the noise level outside the room? If nighttime entertainment takes place alfresco, you might want to find out when show time is over.
- What's included in the price? Your room may be moderately priced, but if you're charged for beach chairs, towels, sports equipment, and other amenities, you could end up spending more than you bargained for.
- Is there a hotel pool, and is it fresh- or saltwater?
- How far is the room from the beach?
- Are airport transfers included in the price?
- If it's off season, will any facilities be shut down while you're there?
- If you're single, ask if there's a singles program. If it's off season, inquire

---

Tips   It Could Pay to Ask

All hotels pay travel agents and wholesalers 30% or more of their rates for sending clients their way, and they may sell blocks of rooms at even more of a discount during slow periods. Some hotels may give you the benefit of at least part of this commission if you book directly instead of going through an airline or travel agent.

Many also have "local" rates for islanders, which they may extend to visitors if business is slack. It never hurts to ask politely for a discounted or local rate.

---

about the occupancy rate. If you're with a partner and looking for quiet, an empty resort might be fine; but if you're single and looking for fun, you might want to find a place that's a little more bustling.

- Are there children's programs?

- What is the dining plan—European Plan (EP; no meals), American Plan (AP; three meals), or Modified American Plan (MAP; breakfast and dinner)? You don't want to pay for three meals if you plan to eat out a lot.
- What is the cancellation policy?

17 Tips on Dining

Unlike other South Pacific countries, French Polynesia has a plethora of excellent restaurants. I'm not fabricating when I say I've seldom had a really bad meal here. And you're in for a special treat when ordering tomatoes and other locally grown vegetables, for more than likely they will be as fresh as if they had come from your own garden.

Many visitors are shocked at the high prices on the menus of their resorts' dining rooms, and in the grocery stores as well. Most foodstuffs are imported, and—except for sugar, flour, and a few other necessities—are subject to stiff duties. On the other hand, you won't have sales tax added to your bill, nor will you necessarily tip the waitstaff, as in the United States. In other words, Americans will not have to add up to 25% to the cost of restaurant meals. When all is said and done, restaurant prices outside the resort dining rooms are comparable to those in large Western cities. (See "Money-Saving Tips," below for how I save money on food here.)

LOCAL FARE: *MA'A TAHITI*

The Tahitians have adopted many Western and Chinese dishes, but they still consume copious quantities of *ma'a Tahiti* (Tahitian food), especially on Sunday. Like their ancestors, who had no crockery, Tahitians still cook meals underground in an earth oven, or *himaa*. Pork, chicken, fish, shellfish, leafy green vegetables (such as taro leaves), and root crops (such as taro and yams) are wrapped in banana and other leaves, placed on a bed of heated stones, covered with more leaves and earth, and left to steam for several hours. The results are quite tasty, since the steam spreads the aroma of one ingredient to the others, and liberal use of coconut cream adds a sweet richness.

Many restaurants serving primarily French, Italian, or Chinese cuisine also offer Tahitian dishes. One you will see virtually everywhere is *poisson cru,* French for "raw fish." It's the Tahitian-style salad of fresh tuna or mahimahi marinated in lime juice, cucumbers, onions, and tomatoes, all served in coconut cream. Chili is added to spice up a variation known as Chinese *poisson cru.*

Most of Tahiti's big resort hotels have at least one **tama'ara'a** (Tahitian feast) a week, followed by a traditional, hip-swinging dance show (see "A Most Indecent Song & Dance," p. 113).

SNACK BARS & LES ROULOTTES

Tahiti has three McDonald's, but locals still prefer their plethora of snack bars, which they call simply "snacks." You can get a hamburger and usually *poisson cru,* but the most popular item is the *casse-croûte,* a sandwich made from a crusty French baguette and ham, tuna, *roti* (roast pork), or *hachis* (hamburger), plus lettuce, tomatoes, and cucumbers—or even spaghetti. A *casse-croûte* usually costs about 300CFP (US$3) or less.

Also in this category are *les roulottes*—or portable meal wagons. A good friend of mine says he hates the idea of dining in a parking lot, but *les roulottes* are one of the best values here, with meals seldom topping 1,500CFP (US$15). They roll out after dark on most islands. The carnival-like ambience they create on the Papeete waterfront makes them a highlight of any visit to the city (see "Don't Miss *Les Roulottes,*" p. 112).

MONEY-SAVING TIPS

Despite the high prices, you don't have to go broke dining here. In addition to finding the nearest "snack," here are some ways to eat well on the least amount of money:

- Do not to eat at resort dining rooms, which charge a premium for food and drink. For example, a graze of the breakfast buffet can easily cost 3,000CFP (US$30) or more per person. You can have a perfectly good breakfast for less than half that at a snack bar or patisserie.
- Likewise, do not buy a hotel meal package except on remote islands,

where your resort's restaurant is your only choice. Dining out is as much a part of the French Polynesian experience as snorkeling.

- Order breakfast from room service if you don't want to go out and your hotel restaurant serves only an expensive buffet. Room service menus usually are *a la carte,* meaning you can order individual items whose total may be much less than the full buffet price.
- Dine at *restaurants conventionné,* which get breaks on the government's high duty on imported alcoholic beverages. Wine and mixed drinks in these establishments cost significantly less than elsewhere. You can also order *vin ordinaire* (table wine) served in a carafe to save money. The chef buys good-quality wine in bulk and passes the savings on to you.
- Take advantage of *plats du jour* (daily specials), especially at lunch, and *prix-fixe* (fixed-priced) menus, often called "tourist menus." These three- or four-course offerings are usually made from fresh produce direct from the market.
- Consider sharing a starter course. Unlike some American menus, which list the main course as an "entree," here an entree is the first course, and it is likely to be a more substantial serving than an American "appetizer." If you have a light appetite, an entree could suffice as your only course, or you can share one with your mate or a friend. Discreetly glance at other tables to check portion sizes before ordering.
- Make your own snacks or perhaps a picnic lunch to enjoy at the beach. Every village has at least one grocery store. Fresh French bread costs about 55CFP (US55¢) everywhere, and most stores carry cheeses, deli meats, vegetables, and other sandwich

makings, many imported from France. Locally brewed Hinano beers sell for about 200CFP (US$2) or less in grocery stores, versus 500CFP (US$5) or more at the hotel bars, and bottles of decent French wine cost a fraction of restaurant prices.

18 Recommended Reading

Rather than list the hundreds of books about Tahiti and French Polynesia, I have picked some of my favorites that are likely to be available in the United States and Canada, either in bookstores or at your local library. A few out-of-print island classics have been reissued in paperback by **Mutual Publishing, LLC,** 125 Center St., Suite 210, Honolulu, HI 96816 (© **808/732-1709;** fax 808/734-4094; www.mutualpublishing.com).

GENERAL

If you have time for only one South Pacific book, read *The Lure of Tahiti* (1986). Editor A. Grove Day, himself an islands expert, includes 18 short stories, excerpts from other books, and essays. There is a little here from many of the writers mentioned below, plus selections from captains Cook, Bougainville, and Bligh.

The National Geographic Society's book *The Isles of the South Pacific* (1971), by Maurice Shadbolt and Olaf Ruhen,

and Ian Todd's *Island Realm* (1974) are somewhat out-of-date coffee-table books, but they have lovely color photographs. *Living Corals* (1979), by Douglas Faulkner and Richard Chesher, shows what you will see underwater.

HISTORY & POLITICS

Several early English and French explorers published accounts of their exploits, but *The Journals of Captain James Cook* stand out as the most exhaustive and evenhanded. Edited by J. C. Beaglehole, they were published in three volumes (one for each voyage) in 1955, 1961, and 1967. A. Grenfell Price edited many of Cook's key passages and provides short transitional explanations in *The Explorations of Captain James Cook in the Pacific* (1971).

The explorers' visits and their consequences in Tahiti, Australia, and Antarctica are the subject of Alan Moorehead's excellent study *The Fatal Impact: The Invasion of the South Pacific, 1767–1840*

⌒ Fun Fact Mutiny on the *Bounty*

The most famous movies about the South Pacific are two *Mutiny on the Bounty* films based on the novel by Charles Nordhoff and James Norman Hall. The 1935 version starred Clark Gable as Fletcher Christian and Charles Laughton as a tyrannical Captain Bligh. (It was actually the second film based on the *Bounty* story; the first was an Australian production, starring Errol Flynn in his first movie role.) Although the 1935 version contained background shots of 40 Tahitian villages, most of the movie was filmed on Santa Catalina, off the California coast; neither Gable nor Laughton visited Tahiti. The 1962 remake with Marlon Brando and Trevor Howard in the Gable and Laughton roles, however, was actually filmed on Tahiti. It was the beginning of Brando's tragic real-life relationship with Tahiti. A 1984 version, *The Bounty,* not based on Nordhoff and Hall, was filmed in Opunohu Bay on Moorea and featured Mel Gibson as Christian and Anthony Hopkins as a more sympathetic (and historically accurate) Bligh.

Impressions

I have often been mildly amused when I think that the great American novel was not written about New England or Chicago. It was written about a white whale in the South Pacific.

—James A. Michener, *Return to Paradise*, 1951

(1966), a colorful tome loaded with sketches and paintings of the time.

Three other very readable books trace Tahiti's postdiscovery history. Robert Langdon's *Tahiti: Island of Love* (1979) takes the island's story up to 1977. David Howarth's *Tahiti: A Paradise Lost* (1985) covers more thoroughly the same early ground covered by Langdon, but stops with France's taking possession in 1842. *The Rape of Tahiti* (1983), by Edward Dodd, covers the island from prehistory to 1900.

Mad About Islands (1987), by A. Grove Day, follows the island exploits of literary figures Herman Melville, Robert Louis Stevenson, Jack London, and W. Somerset Maugham. Also included are Charles Nordhoff and James Norman Hall, coauthors of the so-called "Bounty Trilogy" and other works about the islands (see "Fiction," below). *A Dream of Islands* (1980), by Gavan Dawes, tells of the missionary John Williams as well as of Melville, Stevenson, and the painter Paul Gauguin, who spent the final years of his life in French Polynesia.

PEOPLES & CULTURES

Bengt Danielsson, a Swedish anthropologist who arrived in Tahiti on Thor Heyerdahl's *Kon Tiki* raft in 1947 and spent the rest of his life there, painted a broad picture of Polynesian sexuality in *Love in the South Seas* (1986). Heyerdahl tells his tale and explains his theory of Polynesian migration (since debunked) in *Kon Tiki* (1950). In 1936, Heyerdahl and his wife lived for a year in the Marquesas; his book *Fatu-Hiva: Back to Nature* (1975) provides an in-depth look at Marquesan life at the time. Robert Lee Eskridge

spent a year on Mangareva; his charming book is titled, appropriately, *Manga Reva* (1931; reprinted by Mutual in 1986).

FICTION

Starting with Herman Melville's *Typee* (1846) and *Omoo* (1847)—semifictional accounts of his adventures in the Marquesas and Tahiti, respectively—the islands have spawned a wealth of fiction. (Though set in the South Pacific Ocean, Melville's 1851 classic, *Moby Dick,* does not tell of the islands.)

After Melville came Julien Viaud, a French naval officer who fell in love with a Tahitian woman during a sojourn in Tahiti. Under the pen name Pierre Loti, he wrote *The Marriage of Loti* (1880; reprinted by KPI in 1986), a classic tale of lost love.

W. Somerset Maugham's *The Moon and Sixpence* (1919) is a fictional account of the life of Paul Gauguin. Maugham changed the name to Charles Strickland and made the painter English instead of French. (Gauguin's own novel, *Noa Noa,* was published in English in 1928, long after his death.) Maugham also produced a volume of South Pacific short stories, *The Trembling of a Leaf* (1921; reprinted by Mutual in 1985). My favorite Maugham story is "The Fall of Edward Bernard," about a Chicagoan who forsakes love and fortune at home for "beauty, truth, and goodness" in Tahiti.

Next on the scene were Charles Nordhoff and James Norman Hall (more about them in chapter 4). Together they wrote the most famous of all South Pacific novels, *Mutiny on the Bounty* (1932). They followed that enormous success with two other novels: *Men*

Against the Sea (1934), based on Captain Bligh's epic longboat voyage after the mutiny, and *Pitcairn's Island* (1935), about Lt. Fletcher Christian's demise on the mutineers' remote hideaway.

(For a nonfiction retelling of the great tale, see Caroline Alexander's *The Bounty: The True Story of the Mutiny on the Bounty* [2003].)

Nordhoff and Hall later wrote *The Hurricane* (1936), a novel set in American Samoa that has been made into two movies filmed in French Polynesia. Hall also wrote short stories and essays, collected in *The Forgotten One* (1986).

The second most famous South Pacific novel appeared just after World War II—

Tales of the South Pacific (1947), by James A. Michener. A U.S. Navy historian, Michener spent much of the war on Espiritu Santo, in the New Hebrides (now Vanuatu). Richard Rodgers and Oscar Hammerstein turned the novel into the musical *South Pacific*, a huge Broadway hit; it was later made into the blockbuster movie.

Michener toured the islands a few years later and wrote *Return to Paradise* (1951), a collection of essays and short stories. The essays describe the islands as they were after World War II but before tourists began to arrive via jet aircraft—in other words, near the end of the region's backwater, beachcomber days.

FAST FACTS: Tahiti & French Polynesia

The following facts apply to French Polynesia in general. For more specific information, see the "Fast Facts" sections in chapters 4 through 11.

American Express The territory's one full-service representative is in Papeete. See "Fast Facts" in chapter 4.

Bookstores Only Tahiti and Moorea have well-stocked bookstores (see "Fast Facts" in chapters 4 and 5). Many hotel boutiques sell colorful picture books of the islands.

Business Hours Although many shops in downtown Papeete stay open during the long lunch break, general shopping and business hours are from 7:30 to 11:30am and 2 to 5pm Monday through Friday, 8am to noon on Saturday. In addition to regular hours, most grocery stores are also open Saturday from 2 to 6pm and Sunday from 6 to 8am (that's right: They're open for 2 hours on Sunday).

Car Rentals See "Getting Around Tahiti & French Polynesia," p. 45.

Currency See "Money," p. 19.

Driving Rules See "Getting Around Tahiti & French Polynesia," p. 45.

Drug Laws Plenty of pot may be grown up in the hills, but possession and use of dangerous drugs and narcotics are subject to long jail terms.

Drugstores Drugstores are known as *pharmacies* in French. See "Fast Facts" in the chapters that follow for locations of local pharmacies.

Electricity Electrical power is 220 volts, 50 cycles, and the plugs are the French kind with two round, skinny prongs. Most hotels have 110-volt outlets for shavers only, so you will need a converter and adapter plugs for your other appliances. Some hotels, especially those on the outer islands, have their own generators, so ask at the reception desk what voltage is supplied.

Embassies & Consulates The **United States** has a consular agent here (© **50.80.95;** fax 50.80.96; usconsular@mail.pf), whose main function is to facilitate local residents in applying for visas from the U.S. embassy in Suva, Fiji. Australia, Austria, Belgium, Chile, Denmark, Finland, Germany, Italy, Monaco, the Netherlands, New Zealand, Norway, South Korea, Sweden, and the United Kingdom have honorary consulates in Papeete. Tahiti Tourisme can provide their phone numbers (see "Visitor Information," earlier in this chapter).

Emergencies/Police If you are in a hotel, contact the staff. Otherwise, the **emergency police** phone number is © **17** throughout the territory.

Etiquette & Customs Even though many women go topless and wear the skimpiest of bikini bottoms at the beach (although I saw more exposed bums than boobs during my recent visit), the Tahitians have a sense of propriety similar to what you find in any Western nation. Don't offend them by engaging in behavior that would not be permissible at home. Evening attire for men is usually a shirt and slacks; women typically wear a long, brightly colored dress (slacks or long skirts help to keep biting sand flies away from your ankles). Shorts are acceptable during the day almost everywhere. Outside Papeete, the standard attire for women is the colorful wraparound sarong known in Tahitian as a *pareu,* which can be tied in a multitude of ways into a dress, blouse, or skirt.

Holidays See "French Polynesia Calendar of Events," p. 24.

Gambling You can play "Lotto," the French national lottery.

Hospitals Highly qualified specialists practice on Tahiti, where some clinics possess state-of-the-art diagnostic and treatment equipment; nevertheless, public hospitals tend to be crowded with local residents, who get free care. Most visitors use private doctors or clinics. Larger hotels have English-speaking physicians on call. Each of the smaller islands has at least one infirmary (see "Fast Facts" in chapters 4 through 11). Overseas health insurance plans are not recognized, so remember to get receipts at the time of treatment.

Insects There are no dangerous insects in French Polynesia. The only real nuisances are mosquitoes and tiny, nearly invisible sand flies known locally as "nonos," elsewhere as "no-see-ums." They appear at dusk on most beaches here. Wear trousers or long skirts and plenty of insect repellent (especially on the feet and ankles) to ward off the no-nos. If you forget to bring insect repellent, look for the Off or Dolmix Pic brands at the pharmacy.

Internet Access See "The 21st-Century Traveler," p. 35, and "Fast Facts" in chapters 4 through 11.

Language French is the official language, although most local Polynesians also speak Tahitian. English is understood in the hotels and other tourist-oriented business. See "Languages" in Appendix A (p. 255).

Laundry Tahiti and Raiatea have laundromats. See "Fast Facts: Tahiti," p. 76, and "Fast Facts: Raiatea & Tahaa," p. 158.

Legal Aid Check with your hotel staff if you get into legal trouble. Lawyers are known as *avocats* in French.

Liquor Laws Regulations about where and when you can drink are liberal. Anyone over 18 can purchase alcoholic beverages, and some bars in Papeete stay open until the wee hours on weekends. Official *conventionné* restaurants and hotels pay reduced duty on imported alcoholic beverages, so they will cost less there than at local bars and clubs. Most grocery stores sell beer, wine, and spirits.

Lost & Found Be sure to tell all of your credit card companies the minute you discover your wallet has been lost or stolen and file a report at the nearest police precinct. Your credit card company or insurer may require a police report number or record of the loss. Most credit card companies have an emergency toll-free number to call if your card is lost or stolen; they may be able to wire you a cash advance immediately or deliver an emergency credit card in a day or two. American Express, MasterCard, and Visa do not have local numbers to call to report a lost or stolen credit card, but all three will accept collect calls from overseas.

Mail Letters usually take about a week to 10 days to reach overseas destinations in either direction. Mailing addresses in French Polynesia consist of post office boxes (*boîtes postales* in French, or B.P. for short) but no street numbers or names. Local addresses have postal codes, which are written before the city or town name. (If you send a letter to French Polynesia from the U.S., do *not* put the postal code after the name of the town; otherwise, the U.S. Postal Service may dispatch it to a zip code within the United States.) See "Fast Facts" in chapters 4 through 11 for locations of local post offices.

Maps Tahiti Tourisme distributes free maps of each island. Each weekly edition of the free *Tahiti Beach Press* carries artistic island and Papeete maps. Librairie Vaima, a large bookstore in Papeete's Vaima Centre, sells several *cartes touristiques*. The most detailed map is *Tahiti: Archipel de la Société*, published by the Institut Géographique National. Although it dates to 1994 and doesn't include every new road on Tahiti, it shows all the Society Islands in detail, including topographic features. The full-color *Guide Touristique de Tahiti et ses Isles* shows the precise locations of all hotels and pensions.

Newspapers & Magazines The *Tahiti Beach Press,* an English-language weekly devoted to news of Tahiti's tourist industry, runs features of interest to visitors as well as ads for hotels, restaurants, real-estate agents, car-rental firms, and other businesses that cater to tourists. Establishments that buy ads in it give away copies for free. The daily newspapers, *La Dépêche de Tahiti* and *Les Nouvelles,* are in French. Le Kiosk in front of the Vaima Centre, on boulevard Pomare in Papeete, sells some international newspapers and magazines.

Passports Allow plenty of time before your trip to apply for a passport; processing normally takes 3 weeks, but can take longer during busy periods (especially spring). And keep in mind that if you need a passport in a hurry, you'll pay a higher processing fee.

   For Residents of Australia: You can pick up an application from your local post office or any branch of Passports Australia, but you must schedule an interview at the passport office to present your application materials. Call the **Australian Passport Information Service** at ⓒ **131-232,** or go to www.passports. gov.au.

   For Residents of Canada: Passport applications are available at travel agencies throughout Canada or from the central **Passport Office,** Department of

Foreign Affairs and International Trade, Ottawa, ON K1A 0G3 (© **800/567-6868**; www.ppt.gc.ca).

For Residents of Ireland: You can apply for a 10-year passport at the **Passport Office,** Setanta Centre, Molesworth Street, Dublin 2 (© **01/671-1633**; www.irl gov.ie/iveagh). Those under 18 and over 65 must apply for a €12 3-year passport. You can also apply at 1A South Mall, Cork (© **021/272-525**) and at most main post offices.

For Residents of New Zealand: You can pick up a passport application at any New Zealand Passports Office or download it from the website. Call the **Passports Office** at © **0800/225-050** (in New Zealand) or 04/474-8100, or log on to www.passports.govt.nz.

For Residents of the United Kingdom: To pick up an application for a standard 10-year passport (5-yr. passport for children under 16), visit your nearest passport office, major post office, or travel agency or contact the **United Kingdom Passport Service** (© **0870/521-0410**; www.ukpa.gov.uk).

For Residents of the United States: Whether you're applying in person or by mail, you can download passport applications from the U.S. State Department website at **www.travel.state.gov**. To find your regional passport office, either check the U.S. State Department website or call the **National Passport Information Center** (© **877/487-2778**).

Radio & TV French Polynesia has government-operated AM radio stations with programming in French and Tahitian. Several private AM and FM stations in Papeete play mostly American and British musical numbers in English; the announcers, however, speak French. Two government-owned television stations broadcast in French. Most hotels pick up a local satellite service, which carries CNN International in English. The government-owned radio and TV stations can be received throughout the territory via satellite. Moorea has an American-style cable system with CNN, ESPN, and HBO, all in English.

Safety See "Health & Safety," earlier in this chapter.

Smoking Although antismoking campaigns and hefty tobacco taxes have reduced the practice to a large extent, cigarette smoking is still more common in French Polynesia than in Western countries (this is a *French* place, after all, and the French are more interested in living well than in living long). Most office buildings and the airlines are smoke-free, but nonsmoking sections in restaurants are relatively rare. Not all hotels have nonsmoking rooms, so don't assume you'll get a nonsmoking room without asking for one.

Taxes Local residents do not pay income taxes; instead, the government imposes stiff duties on most imported goods. It also levies a value-added tax (VAT, or *TVA* in French) on most goods and services, including restaurant and hotel bills. Only the TVA on set pearls is refundable in the European fashion (see "Shopping" in chapter 4). These taxes will not be added to your bills in the American fashion, but you will see the 10% tax tacked onto your hotel bills and another 50CFP to 200CFP (50¢–$1.50) per night for the Tahiti, Moorea, and Bora Bora communes.

Telephones Direct international dialing is available to all telephone and fax numbers in French Polynesia. The international country code is **689**.

There are no domestic area codes; just dial the six-digit local number.

Public pay phones are located at all post offices and are fairly numerous elsewhere on Tahiti, less so on the other islands. You must have a *télécarte* to call from public pay phones (coin phones are history here). Digital read-outs on the phones tell you how many *unites* you have left on a card. The cards are sold at all post offices, most hotel front desks, and many shops in 1,500CFP, 2,000CFP, and 5,000CFP (US$15, US$20, and US$50) sizes.

For directory assistance: Dial © **19** for local numbers, © **12** for international assistance. The operators speak English. You can also look up numbers online at **www.annuaireopt.pf** (it's in French).

To make international calls: Dial **00,** and then the country code (**1** for the U.S. and Canada), followed by the area code and phone number.

The direct-dial charge from French Polynesia to the U.S., Europe, Australia, and New Zealand is 103CFP (US$1.03) per minute. You can make calls through your hotel, though with a surcharge, which can more than double the fee.

You'll need a GSM cellphone for it to work in French Polynesia (see "The 21st-Century Traveler," earlier in this chapter).

Time Zone Local time in the most visited islands is 11 hours behind Greenwich Mean Time. I find it easier to think of it as 5 hours behind U.S. Eastern Standard Time or 2 hours behind Pacific Standard Time. Translated: When it's noon in California, it's 10am in Tahiti. When it's noon on the U.S. East Coast, it's 7am in Tahiti. Add 1 hour to the Tahiti time during daylight saving time.

The Marquesas Islands are 30 minutes ahead of the rest of the territory.

French Polynesia is on the east side of the International Date Line; therefore, Tahiti has the same date as the United States, the Cook Islands, and the Samoas, and is a day behind Australia, New Zealand, Fiji, and Tonga.

Tipping Despite inroads (credit card forms now have a "tip" line here), tipping is considered contrary to the Polynesian custom of hospitality. In other words, tipping is not expected unless the service has been truly beyond the call of duty. Some hotels accept contributions to the staff Christmas fund.

Useful Phone Numbers Here are some useful phone numbers:

Air Moorea, Papeete: © **86.41.41**

Air Tahiti, Papeete: © **86.42.42**

Tahiti Manava Visitors Bureau, Papeete: © **50.57.12**

Tahiti Tourisme, Los Angeles, Calif.: © **310/418-8484**

U.S. Centers for Disease Control International Traveler's Hotline: © **404/332-4559**

U.S. Department of State Travel Advisory © **202/647-5225** (24 hrs.)

U.S. Passport Agency © **202/647-0518**

Water Tap water is consistently safe to drink only in Papeete and on Bora Bora. Well water in the Tuamotu Islands tends to be brackish; rainwater is used there for drinking. You can buy bottled water at every grocery. The local brands Vaimato and Eau Royal are much less expensive than imported French waters.

Weights & Measures French Polynesia is on the metric system.

Suggested Tahiti & French Polynesia Itineraries

People often ask me where they should go in Tahiti and French Polynesia. Lacking the ability to read minds, I do not have an easy answer. In other words, it all depends on what you want to see and do on your own vacation. What I like is not necessarily what will interest you—but what I can do is give you the benefit of my expertise and advice so that you don't waste your valuable vacation time.

If you live in the United States, Canada, or Europe, the long flights here and back mean you can easily burn a day getting to the islands and a day returning home. A week's worth of vacation suddenly becomes 5 days. If possible, therefore, you should spend more than 1 week out here.

However you construct your own itinerary, first find out the airlines' schedules and book both your international and Air Tahiti domestic interisland flights well in advance. This is especially true of the domestic flights; do not wait until you arrive in the islands to take care of this important chore.

And remember the old travel agent's rule: Do not stay at the most luxurious property first. Anything after that will seem inferior, and you may go home disappointed. For example, most resorts on Moorea are neither as luxurious nor as picturesque as those on Bora Bora, so if you can afford to island-hop, start but don't end your visit on Moorea. And even after the luxuries of Bora Bora, you won't regret ending your trip with a bit of pampered chill time at Te Tiare Beach Resort on Huahine (p. 151) or the exquisite Le Taha'a Private Island & Spa (p. 167) on Tahaa.

1 The Grand Tour in 2 Weeks

This itinerary takes you to all the hot spots: Tahiti, Moorea, Huahine, and Bora Bora—plus a few days in Rangiroa, the largest atoll in the Tuamotu Archipelago. I suggest going to Rangiroa first because after seeing the awesome mountainous beauty of the Society Islands, it may seem anticlimactic to end your trip at a flat atoll. Tikehau, Manihi, or Fakarava, Rangiroa's Tuamotuan sisters, are also worthy alternatives to Rangiroa (see chapter 10).

An exceptional alternative—or a terrific add-on if you have a month to spend here—would be a cruise from Papeete to the Marquesas Islands on the *Aranui 3* (p. 49).

For the typical 10-day highlight-hitting tour (or honeymoon, as the case may be), leave off Rangiroa and forget Tahiti except while waiting for your flight home. Begin your visit on Moorea, then go to Bora Bora, and finish on Huahine (or Tahaa if you can afford to stay at Le Taha'a Private Island & Spa; p. 167).

The Grand Tour in 2 Weeks

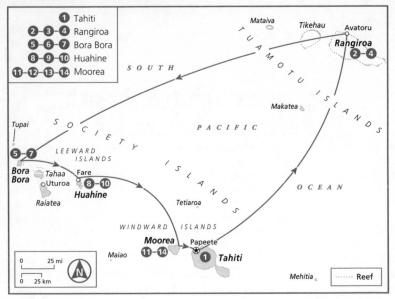

1 Tahiti
2 – 3 – 4 Rangiroa
5 – 6 – 7 Bora Bora
8 – 9 – 10 Huahine
11 – 12 – 13 – 14 Moorea

Mataiva Tikehau Avatoru
Rangiroa 2 – 4

TUAMOTU ISLANDS

SOUTH

Makatea

Tupai

SOCIETY

LEEWARD ISLANDS

PACIFIC

5 – 7
Bora Bora Tahaa Fare
Uturoa 8 – 10
Huahine

Raiatea Tetiaroa

OCEAN

ISLANDS

WINDWARD ISLANDS

Maiao **Moorea** Papeete
11 – 14 1 **Tahiti**

0   25 mi
0   25 km

N

Mehitia ----- Reef

Day 1: Circling Tahiti

Unless you arrive in the afternoon or early evening on one of Air Tahiti Nui's flights, you'll probably get here in the wee hours, so spend your first morning on a guided half-day **circle island tour** of Tahiti (p. 85). You won't have to drive or find your way around, so it's a good method of recovering while seeing the island. After a long French lunch, take a **walking tour** of downtown Papeete (p. 82). Even if you aren't staying in a hotel on Tahiti's west coast, head over there to watch the sunset over Moorea, one of the region's most awe-inspiring sights.

Days 2–4: Riding the Rip on Rangiroa

The world's second-largest lagoon demands a full day's excursion by boat to one of its two key sites: **Les Sables Rose (The Pink Sands)** or the **Blue Lagoon** (p. 205). Devote a full day to one of these trips. My choice would be the Blue Lagoon, actually a small lagoon within

the large lagoon, though it's hard to pass up the Pink Sands, one of the great beaches here. On another day, don your snorkel or diving gear and **ride the rip tide** through the main pass into the lagoon. Be sure to watch the dolphins playing in Tiputa Pass at sunset

Days 5–7: Feeding the Sharks on Bora Bora

A nonstop flight from Rangiroa will bring you to beautiful **Bora Bora,** which many consider the world's most beautiful island. Spend part of your first day here exploring the interior by four-wheel-drive "safari expedition" (p. 178). Devote a full day to a lagoon tour by boat, the top thing to do on Bora Bora. You'll get a fish-eye view of the island's dramatic peak, snorkel while watching your guide feed a school of reef sharks, and enjoy a fresh-fish lunch on a small islet on the fringing reef (p. 178). Have dinner one night at **Bloody Mary's Restaurant and Bar** (p. 189), another night at **Villa Mahana** (p. 189).

Days ⑧–⑩: Touring Old Polynesia on Huahine 👁👁

After the mile-a-minute activities on Bora Bora, **Huahine** will seem like a reserved Polynesian paradise. Spend your first morning on a tour of the historic *maraes* (ancient temples) at Maeva village with Paul Atallah of **Island Eco Tours** (p. 147). The next day, tour the lagoon, swim, snorkel, or go horseback riding. I always have a sunset drink while watching the boats coming and going at **Fare,** the island's charming main town.

Days ⑪–⑭: Sightseeing on Moorea 👁👁👁

While the lagoons are the highlights at Rangiroa and Bora Bora, the ruggedly gorgeous interior draws my eyes on **Moorea.** Whether it's via a regular guided tour, a four-wheel-drive safari excursion, or on your own, go up to the **Belvédère** overlooking **Cook's** and **Opunohu** bays. Moorea's lagoon does have its good features, especially dolphin-watching excursions led by **Dr. Michael Poole** (p. 125). And don't miss a nighttime show at **Tiki Theatre Village,** one of the region's best cultural centers (p. 125). Moorea is only 7 minutes by plane from Tahiti, which makes it a snap to connect to Papeete and your flight home.

2 Tahiti & Moorea in 1 Week

This itinerary outlines how you can spend your time on a low-end, 1-week package tour, most of which offer discounted prices for airfare and a week on Tahiti and nearby Moorea. Even if you don't buy a package, this is still the least expensive way to sample the islands, since you won't be forking out a few hundred quid for interisland airfares and paying the relatively high prices on Bora Bora. You'll get to visit fabled Tahiti and spend a few days frolicking on Moorea. You can pick and choose from this itinerary if you are laying over for a day or two on Tahiti while crossing the Pacific.

Day ❶: Exploring Papeete

Get over your flight by taking it easy on the beach or around the pool this morning. Head into downtown **Papeete** in time for a long French lunch; then take a walking tour of this busy but fascinating city (p. 82). Head back to your hotel for some relaxation before watching the sun setting over Moorea.

Day ❷: Circling Tahiti 👁👁

You can either rent a vehicle or take a guided tour around Tahiti's coastal road (p. 92). Either way, stop at **James Norman's Home** (p. 80), the **Gauguin Museum** (p. 81), and the **Museum of Tahiti and Her Islands** (p. 80), all of which will inform you about Tahiti's interesting history. If you drive yourself, take along a swimsuit and beach towel for a visit to **Maui Beach,** Tahiti's top sands (p. 89.) At night, watch one of the dance shows at the hotels (p. 114).

Day ❸: Taking a Safari Expedition into Tahiti's Interior 👁👁👁

You may think you have seen all of Tahiti after your round-island tour, but not so. A **safari expedition** by four-wheel-drive vehicle (p. 93) will take you into the mountainous interior, which is a very different world from the coastal road. If the weather permits, these trips follow the **Papenoo Valley** into Tahiti's extinct volcanic crater. Have dinner at *les roulottes,* the carnival-like meal wagons on the Papeete waterfront.

Tahiti & Moorea in 1 Week

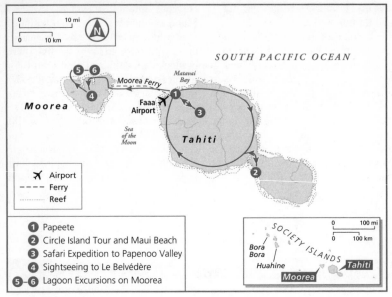

SOUTH PACIFIC OCEAN

Matavai Bay

Moorea Ferry

Faaa Airport

Moorea

Sea of the Moon

Tahiti

✈ Airport
---- Ferry
.... Reef

1 Papeete
2 Circle Island Tour and Maui Beach
3 Safari Expedition to Papenoo Valley
4 Sightseeing to Le Belvédère
5 – 6 Lagoon Excursions on Moorea

SOCIETY ISLANDS

Bora Bora
Huahine
Moorea
Tahiti

Day 4: Sightseeing on Moorea ★★★

An early morning ferry or plane ride will get to Moorea in time to take a tour of this gorgeous island's north shore, home of the picturesque **Cook's** and **Opunohu bays** and the awesome view over them from **Le Belvédère** lookout. My favorite trip is a four-wheel-drive safari excursion (p. 124), which will take you to the sights plus a ride into the interior and a dip under a waterfall. After dark, take in the extraordinary dance show at **Tiki Theatre Village** (p. 125).

Day 5: Getting Wet in the Moorea Lagoon ★★★

Spending a day out on the water is a must on Moorea, and every hotel offers a half- or full-day **lagoon excursion** (p. 125). The usual route takes you across the water to a *motu* (small islet) out on the

reef for some swimming, snorkeling, and a barbecue lunch, perhaps of fish your crew caught on the way out.

Day 6: Dolphin Watching on Moorea ★★★

You may have spotted dolphins playing on your Moorea lagoon excursion, but you'll learn a lot more about these friendly mammals on a trip with American marine biologist **Dr. Michael Poole** (p. 125), who has identified some 150 of them as Moorea residents.

Day 7: Finishing Up

You will need to return to Tahiti this afternoon to await your flight home, since most planes leave after dark or in the early morning hours. Have your last supper taking in the glorious view down over Papeete from **Le Belvédère** (p. 110).

3 The Leeward Islands in 10 Days

The Leeward Islands of Huahine, Raiatea, Tahaa, and Bora Bora are very different from Tahiti, or even Moorea, for that matter. With the exception of Bora Bora, which

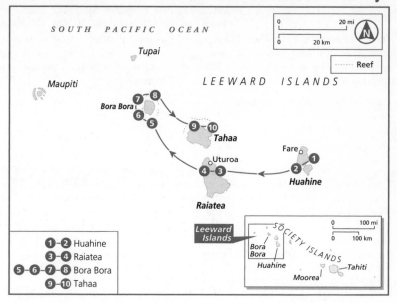

is French Polynesia's tourism magnet, all are relatively undeveloped. Except when cruise ships are in port, they will let you see what Polynesia is like without hordes of fellow visitors.

Days ①–②: Touring Old Polynesia on Huahine 🐢🐢

Lovely Huahine will give you a chance to relax and chill after your international flight. On your first morning, take an informative tour of the historic *maraes* (ancient temples) at Maeva village with Paul Atallah of **Island Eco Tours** (p. 147). Have lunch at **Restaurant Mauarii** on gorgeous **Avea Beach** (p. 154), one of French Polynesia's finest. On your second day, get out on the water with a lagoon excursion, or perhaps go horseback riding. I always have a sunset drink at **Restaurant Temarara** while watching the boats coming and going at **Fare,** the island's charming main town.

Days ③–④: A History Lesson on Raiatea 🐢🐢🐢

If you can spare a day away from the beach, for it has none, Raiatea will let you

see Polynesia *sans* tourists—except when cruise ships dock at **Uturoa,** the island's only town and the administrative center of the Leeward Islands. You will get a good lesson in Polynesian history by spending this morning on a tour with Bill Kolans of **Almost Paradise Tours** (p. 162). Bill will take you to **Taputapuatea Marae,** the largest and most impressive ancient *marae* in French Polynesia (p. 160). You can spend your second day out on the lagoon, which Raiatea shares with Tahaa.

Days ⑤–⑧: Enjoying the Lagoon on Bora Bora 🐢🐢🐢

Two days is barely enough to experience the beauty of Bora Bora and its lagoon, but you can make the most of them by spending half of your first day on a four-wheel-drive safari expedition (p. 178). Devote all of the next day to a lagoon excursion, which invariably will include a shark-feeding stop, a picnic on a small islet, and time for snorkeling (p. 178). Be sure to have dinner at **Bloody Mary's Restaurant and Bar** (p. 189) one night, and at **Villa Mahana** (p. 189) the other night.

Days ❾–❿: Chilling in Luxury on Tahaa ✷✷✷

The best way to come down after all the activities of this week is at **Le Taha'a**

Private Island & Spa, on a small reef islet off Tahaa (p. 167). While you're here, take a safari excursion into the interior of Tahaa. (If Le Taha'a Private Island & Spa is too rich for your blood, finish your trip on Moorea.)

4 The Tuamotu & Marquesas Islands in 2 Weeks

Your French Polynesian experience will be much richer if you really do get off the well-worn Tahiti–Moorea–Bora Bora tourist track and visit islands even less developed than Huahine, Raiatea, and Tahaa. (Although four islands in the Tuamotu Archipelago have first-class resorts, the far-flung atolls still meet this criterion.) The Marquesas Islands are even farther off the beaten path. Indeed, they are like a world removed from the rest of French Polynesia, since their Polynesian residents have a different culture and even speak a different language than the Tahitians.

Since Air Tahiti has at least one flight a week between Rangiroa in the Tuamotus to Hiva Oa in the Marquesas, it's possible to combine the two groups in this itinerary. Air Tahiti doesn't fly between the Tuamotus every day, either, so your precise itinerary will hinge on its current schedule. Depending on the flights, you can start on Manihi or Tikehau instead of Fakarava (see chapter 10). The easy alternative to all this is taking a 2-week cruise through the Tuamotus and Marquesas on the *Aranui 3* (p. 49).

Days ❶–❸: Exploring a Large Lagoon & an Old Village on Fakarava

An early morning flight from Papeete should put you in Fakarava in time to play in French Polynesia's second-largest lagoon. Spend your full second day here on a lagoon excursion, especially one that will take you to **Tetamanu** village (p. 216), where you'll see the ruins of an 1834 vintage Catholic church before swimming in the lagoon, riding the rip tide in the adjacent pass, and enjoying a beachside picnic.

Days ❹–❻: Swimming with the Sharks at Rangiroa ✷✷✷

As I noted in the Grand Tour earlier, the world's second-largest lagoon demands full-day excursions by boat to its two key sites: **Les Sables Rose (The Pink Sands)**

and the **Blue Lagoon** (p. 205). On your third day, don your snorkeling or diving gear and **ride the rip tide** through Tiputa Pass into the lagoon. Be sure to watch the dolphins playing in Tiputa Pass at sunset, and don't miss sampling the local vintages at **Cave de Rangiroa** (p. 204). Have dinner one night at **Relais de Josephine,** another night at **Restaurant Le Kai Kai** (p. 209).

Days ❼–❿: Following Paul Gauguin to Hiva Oa ✷✷✷

The Air Tahiti flight from Rangiroa to Hiva Oa, administrative center of the Marquesas Islands, will eat up half a day, so spend your first afternoon exploring the village of **Atuona.** The French painter Paul Gauguin died in Atuona in 1903, so visit his grave and the **Tohua Papa**

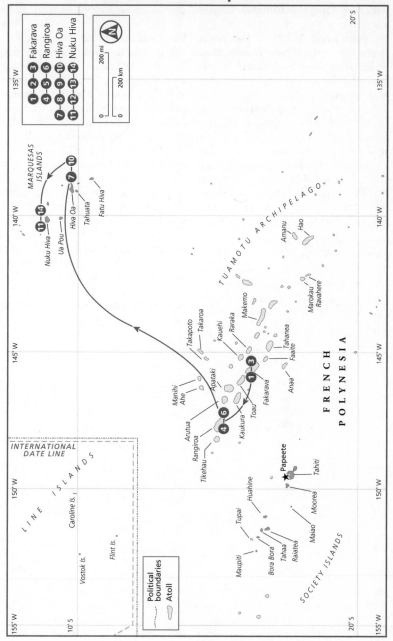

Nui/Paul Gauguin Cultural Center, where you will see meticulous copies of his great works (p. 237). The center shares space with **Espace Jacques Brel,** dedicated to the French singer Jacques Brel, who also expired here and is buried near Gauguin. Spend the next day on an expedition to lovely **Puamau** village (p. 238), beside a gorgeous settlement next to a half-moon beach. The snakelike road along on the northeast coast is virtually chiseled into the cliffs above the sea, so the ride out and back will occupy a full day. On another day, you can go fishing, hiking, or exploring the Atuona area on mountain bike or horseback (p. 239).

Days ⑪–⑭: "Surviving" on Nuku Hiva ★★

The *Survivor* TV series brought Nuku Hiva to the world's attention when it was taped here in 2002, but you'll have a better chance of seeing **Taipivai Valley,** where Herman Melville hid after jumping ship in the early 1900s (p. 229). Unless the local helicopter is operating, it's at least a 2-hour ride by four-wheel-drive vehicle across three mountain ranges from the airport to **Taiohae,** Nuku Hiva's only town. Spend half a day exploring the town and the **Herman Melville Memorial** beside its picturesque bay, including a visit to **Taetae Tupuna He'e Tai,** where American Rose Corser shows a fine collection of Marquesan art and sells exquisite handicrafts (p. 232). Later on, you can veg on the town's black-sand beach. Devote the next day to an excursion to the Taipivai Valley and **Hatiheu,** an enormously beautiful bay on the north coast and home to ancient *marae* with tikis resembling the mysterious statues on Easter Island (p. 229). On your next-to-last day, you can go hiking or horseback riding (p. 231). You will need all of Day 14 for the ride back to the airport and the 3-hour Air Tahiti flight to Papeete.

Tahiti

Large and abundant, Tahiti is the modern traveler's gateway to French Polynesia, just as it was for Capt. James Cook and the other late-18th-century discoverers who used it as a base to explore the South Pacific. In later years, the capital city, **Papeete,** became a major shipping crossroads. Located on Tahiti's northwest corner, the city curves around what is still French Polynesia's busiest harbor.

There wasn't even a village here until the 1820s, when Queen Pomare set up headquarters along the shore, and merchant ships and whalers began using the harbor in preference to the less protected Matavai Bay to the east. A simple town of stores, bars, and billiard parlors sprung up quickly, and between 1825 and 1829 it was a veritable den of iniquity. It grew even more after the French made it their headquarters upon taking over Tahiti in 1842. A fire nearly destroyed the town in 1884, and waves churned up by a cyclone did severe damage in 1906. In 1914, two German warships shelled the harbor and sank the French navy's *Zélée*.

Papeete is a very different place today. Vehicles of every sort now crowd boulevard Pomare, the broad avenue along Papeete's waterfront, and the four-lane expressway linking the city to the trendy suburban districts of Punaauia and Paea on the west coast. Indeed, suburbs are creeping up the mountains overlooking

the city and sprawling for miles along the coast in both directions. The island is so developed and so traffic-clogged that many Tahitians commute up to 2 hours in each direction on weekdays. Many are moving to Moorea, a mere 30-minute ferry ride away.

But there is a bright side to Tahiti's development: Using money from a post-nuclear-testing economic restructuring fund, Papeete has done a remarkable job in refurbishing its waterfront, including a cruise-ship terminal and a classy park where families gather and the city celebrates its festivals. It's a real treat now to walk along the promenade fronting this storied South Seas port.

Papeete's chic shops, busy Municipal Market, and lively mix of French, Polynesian, and Chinese cultures are sure to invigorate any urbanite. If you're looking for old-time Polynesia, on the other hand, you will find it on Tahiti's rural east and south coasts and especially on its peninsula, Tahiti Iti. Its three fine museums are reason enough for me to spend a day or two here.

Even if you plan to leave immediately for Moorea, Bora Bora, and the other less developed islands, most of you will have to spend at least a few hours here, since all international flights land at Faaa on the northwest coast of this legendary and still very beautiful island.

1 Arriving & Departing

ARRIVING

All international flights arrive at **Tahiti-Faaa International Airport,** 7km (4 miles) west of downtown Papeete. With its runway built on a landfill over the reef, it is French Polynesia's only international airport.

Tahitian musicians are usually on hand to welcome international flights, and they will keep you entertained while you wait in line to have your passport stamped at Immigration. Once you've cleared Customs, you will see a **visitor information booth** straight ahead. Start there for maps and other information. If you're on a tour or have made other prior arrangements, representatives of the local tour operators will be holding signs announcing their presence.

Pick up some pocket money at **Banque de Polynésie,** to the left as you exit Customs, or at **Banque Socredo,** to the right. Both have ATMs, and Banque Socredo has a machine that will change U.S. dollars and other major notes into French Pacific francs.

I have spent many an hour waiting for flights at the open-air, 24-hour **snack bar** to the right. There's a **McDonald's** next to Air Tahiti's domestic departure lounge, also to the right.

GETTING TO YOUR HOTEL

Unless you're on a package tour or your hotel has arranged a transfer, your only choice of transportation to your hotel between 10pm and 6am will be a **taxi.** Official fares from 8pm to 6am are 1,500CFP (US$15) to the hotels on the west coast, 2,500CFP (US$25) to downtown. Add 100CFP (US$1) for each bag.

If you arrive when the local buses are running and are in reasonably good physical condition, you can haul your baggage across the parking lot in front of the terminal, climb the stairs to the main road, and flag one down. See "Getting Around Tahiti," below, for details.

If you're driving a rental car, take **Route 1 West** to the Inter-Continental Resort Tahiti, the Sofitel Tahiti Resort, or Le Meridien Tahiti. **Route 1 East** passes the Sheraton Hotel Tahiti on its way to downtown Papeete. If you're going to downtown, watch for the **Route 5** signs directing you to the expressway connecting Papeete to the west coast. See "Getting Around Tahiti," below, for more information.

BAGGAGE STORAGE

Most hotels will store your baggage for free. The airport's **baggage storage room** is in the parking lot in front of the international departures gate. It's the small building behind the pavilion where Tahitian women often sell leis and flower crowns. It isn't cheap: Charges range from 640CFP (US$6.40) per day for regular-size bags to 1,100CFP (US$11) for surfboards, bicycles, and other large items. The room opens 2 hours before every international flight departs. Regular hours are Monday from 4am to 7pm, Tuesday through Thursday from 5am to 11pm, Saturday from 5am to 12:30am, and Sunday and holidays from 1pm to 12:30am. MasterCard and Visa are accepted.

DEPARTING

Check-in time for departing international flights is 3 hours before flight time; for domestic flights, be there 2 hours in advance. All of your bags must be screened for

Tahiti

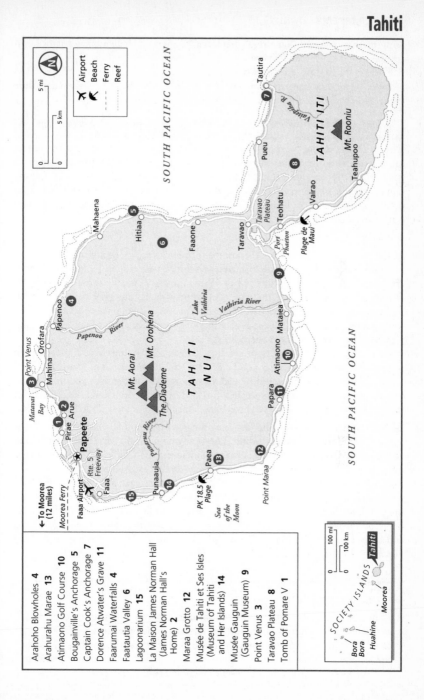

SOUTH PACIFIC OCEAN

SOUTH PACIFIC OCEAN

TAHITI ITI

TAHITI NUI

Mt. Rooniu

Tautira

Pueu

Teahupoo

Vairao

Teohatu

Taravao Plateau

Port Phaeton

Plage de Maui

Taravao

Faaone

Vaihiria River

Lake Vaihiria

Mataiea

Atimaono

Papara

Point Maraa

Paea

PK 18.5 Plage

Sea of the Moon

Punaauia

Faaa

Faaa Airport

Rte. 5 Freeway

Papeete

Arue

Pirae

Mahina

Orofara

Point Venus

Matavai Bay

Papenoo

Papenoo River

Punaruu River

Mt. Aorai

Mt. Orohena

The Diademe

Hitiaa

Mahaena

Vaitepiha R.

Teohatu

← To Moorea
(12 miles)

Moorea Ferry

Airport ✈
Beach ✦
Ferry – – –
Reef · · · ·

N

5 mi
5 km

Arahoho Blowholes **4**
Arahurahu Marae **13**
Atimaono Golf Course **10**
Bougainville's Anchorage **5**
Captain Cook's Anchorage **7**
Dorence Atwater's Grave **11**
Faarumai Waterfalls **4**
Faatautia Valley **6**
Lagoonarium **15**
La Maison James Norman Hall
  (James Norman Hall's
  Home) **2**
Maraa Grotto **12**
Musée de Tahiti et Ses Isles
  (Museum of Tahiti
  and Her Islands) **14**
Musée Gauguin
  (Gauguin Museum) **9**
Point Venus **3**
Taravao Plateau **8**
Tomb of Pomare V **1**

SOCIETY ISLANDS

Bora Bora
Huahine
Moorea
Tahiti

100 mi
100 km

both international and domestic flights leaving Papeete. (There are few security procedures at the outer-island airstrips.)

There is no airport departure tax for either international or domestic flights.

Note: There is no bank or currency exchange bureau in the international departure lounge, so change your money before clearing Immigration.

2 Getting Around Tahiti

Except for the Route 5 expressway between Papeete and Punaauia, and the north-south cross-island road, the island's highway system consists primarily of Route 1, a paved road running for 116km (72 miles) around Tahiti Nui, plus roads halfway down each side of Tahiti Iti. From the isthmus, a road partially lined with trees wanders up to the high, cool Plateau of Taravao, with pastures and pines more like provincial France than the South Pacific.

BY BUS

Although it might appear from the number of vehicles scurrying around Papeete that everyone owns a car or scooter, the average Tahitian gets around by local bus. Modern buses have replaced all but a few of Tahiti's famous *le trucks,* those colorful vehicles called "trucks" because the passenger compartments are gaily painted wooden cabins mounted on the rear of flatbed trucks. The last of them operate between downtown Papeete and Centre Moana Nui, a shopping complex south of the Sofitel Tahiti Resort. Elsewhere, look for modern buses.

Once upon a time, *le trucks* would stop for you almost anywhere, but today you must catch them and the buses at official stops (called *arrêt le bus* in French).

The villages or districts served by each bus are written on the sides and front of the vehicle. **Fares** within Papeete are 130CFP (US$1.30) until 6pm and 200CFP (US$2) thereafter. A trip to the end of the line in either direction costs about 750CFP (US$7.50).

BUSES GOING WEST The few remaining *le trucks* and all short-distance buses going west are painted red and white. They line up on rue du Maréchal-Foch behind the Municipal Market and travel along rue du Général-de-Gaulle, which becomes rue du Commandant-Destremeau and later route de-l'Ouest, the road that circles the island. Buses run along this route as far as the Centre Moana Nui (south of the Sofitel Tahiti Resort) Monday through Friday at least every 30 minutes from 6am to 6pm, once an hour between 6pm and midnight. Except for *le trucks* serving tourists at the hotels on the west coast, there is irregular service on Saturday, none on Sunday. Trucks and buses labeled Faaa, Maeva Beach, and Outuamaru will pass the airport and the Sheraton Hotel Tahiti and Inter-Continental Resort Tahiti.

Tips Around Tahiti by Bus?

Although you had to walk across the Taravao isthmus, it was once possible to circumnavigate Tahiti by *le truck* in a single day. Today the long-distance buses run only from 6am to noon on weekdays, so it is virtually impossible to go all the way around the island in any reasonable amount of time. I recommend renting a vehicle or taking a guided circle island tour instead.

Impressions

Edward called for him in a rickety trap drawn by an old mare, and they drove along a road that ran by the sea. On each side of it were plantations, coconut and vanilla; now and then they saw a great mango, its fruit yellow and red and purple among the massy green of the leaves, now and then they had a glimpse of the lagoon, smooth and blue, with here and there a tiny islet graceful with tall palms.

—W. Somerset Maugham, "The Fall of Edward Bernard," 1921

BUSES GOING EAST Short-distance buses going east are painted green and white. They line up in the block west of the Banque de Polynésie on boulevard Pomare, opposite the cruise-ship terminal and near the Municipal Market and rue Paul Gauguin. They proceed out of town via avenue du Prince-Hinoi, passing the cut-off for Hotel Le Royal Tahitien and the Radisson Plaza Resort Tahiti on their way to Pirae, Arue, and Mahina. They run frequently from 6am to 5pm as far as the Mahina. No buses run at night, so you must rent a car or take a taxi to and from the Radisson and Le Royal Tahitien after dark and on weekends.

LONG-DISTANCE BUSES Buses going in either direction to Tahiti's south coast and Tahiti Iti are painted orange and white. They line up next to the Tahiti Manava visitors bureau on boulevard Pomare at rue Paul Gauguin. They run on the hour from 6am to noon Monday through Friday, but there is only one afternoon trip at 4:30pm back to the villages. They do not run nights or weekends.

BY TAXI

Papeete has a large number of taxis, although they can be hard to find during the morning and evening rush hours, especially if it's raining. You can flag one down on the street or find them gathered at one of several stations. The largest gathering points are on boulevard Pomare near the market (© **42.02.92**) and at the Centre Vaima (© **42.60.77**). Most taxi drivers understand some English.

Taxi fares are set by the government and are posted on a board at the Centre Vaima taxi stand on boulevard Pomare. Few cabs have meters, so be sure that you and the driver have agreed on a fare before you get in. Note that *all fares are increased by at least 20% from 8pm to 6am.* A trip anywhere within downtown Papeete during the day starts at 1,000CFP (US$10) and goes up 120CFP (US$1.20) for every kilometer after the first one during the day, 240CFP (US$2.40) at night. As a rule of thumb, the fare from the Papeete hotels to the airport or vice versa is about 1,700CFP (US$17) during the day; from the west-coast hotels to the airport, it is about 1,000CFP (US$10). A trip to the Gauguin Museum on the south coast costs 10,000CFP (US$100) one-way. The fare for a 4-hour journey all the way around Tahiti is about 16,000CFP (US$160). Drivers may charge an extra 50CFP to 100CFP (US50¢–US$1) per piece of luggage.

BY RENTAL CAR

Avis (© **800/331-1212** or 41.93.93; www.avis.com), **Hertz** (© **800/654-3131** or 42.04.72; www.hertz.com), and **Europcar** (© **800/227-7368** or 45.24.24; www.europcar.com) all have agencies on Tahiti. Europcar is slightly less expensive than the others, with rates starting at 1,850CFP (US$18.50) a day plus 41CFP (US41¢) per kilometer, or 8,600CFP (US$86) a day with unlimited kilometers. You get a better

---

Tips **Get Unlimited Kilometers If Driving around Tahiti**

If you rent a car, consider the unlimited kilometer rate if you intend to drive around Tahiti, since the round-island road is 114km (72 miles) long, not counting Tahiti Iti.

---

deal on the unlimited rate if you rent for more than 1 day. Collision damage waiver insurance costs an additional 1,500CFP (US$15) a day on the per-kilometer plans, but is included in the unlimited kilometer rate.

The best local rental company is **Daniel Location de Voitures,** in the Faaa airport terminal (*©* **81.96.32;** fax 85.62.64; daniel.location@mail.pf). Its unlimited kilometer rates start at 8,020CFP (US$80) per day.

DRIVING HINTS   In Papeete, priority is given to vehicles entering an intersection from the right side. This rule does not apply on the four-lane boulevard Pomare along the waterfront, but be careful everywhere else, as drivers on your right will expect you to yield the right of way at intersections where there are no stop signs or traffic signals. Be prepared to deal with numerous **traffic circles** in and near town. You must give way to traffic already in the circles.

Outside of Papeete, priority is given to vehicles that are already on the round-island road. The main round-island road is a divided highway east and west of Papeete, which means that to make a left turn, you will have to turn around at the next traffic circle and drive back to your destination.

PARKING   Parking spaces can be as scarce as chicken teeth in downtown Papeete during the day. You must pay to park in most on-street spaces from 8am to 5pm Monday through Saturday; the cost is 100CFP (US$1) per hour, payable by tickets sold at numerous shops and newsstands displaying **Parc Chec** signs. Put the *parc chec* ticket on the dashboard inside the vehicle (not outside under the windshield wiper, where it will be stolen). There are several municipal parking garages, including one under the Hôtel de Ville (Town Hall); enter off rue Collette between rue Paul Gauguin and rue d'Ecole des Frères. Some large buildings, such as the Centre Vaima, have garages in their basements. Frankly, if I'm not staying downtown, I usually leave my car at the hotel and take a bus into the city during workdays.

FAST FACTS: Tahiti

The following facts apply specifically to Tahiti. For more information, see "Fast Facts: Tahiti & French Polynesia," in chapter 2.

American Express The American Express representative is **Tahiti Tours,** on rue Jeanne-d'Arc (*©* **54.02.50;** fax 42.25.15), across from the Centre Vaima in downtown Papeete. The mailing address is B.P. 627, 98713 Papeete, Tahiti, French Polynesia.

Bookstores **Librairie Vaima,** on the second level of the Centre Vaima (*©* **45.57. 57**), has some English-language novels and a wide selection of books on French Polynesia, many of them in English and some of them rare editions. It also has maps of the islands. **Le Kiosk** in front of the Centre Vaima sells the *International*

Herald Tribune, Time, and *Newsweek,* as does **La Maison de la Presse,** on boulevard Pomare at Quartier du Commerce (© **50.93.93**).

Business Hours Although some shops stay open over the long lunch break, most businesses are open Monday through Friday from 8 to 11:30am and 2 to 5pm, give or take 30 minutes, since "flex hours" help alleviate Tahiti's traffic problem. Saturday hours are 8 to 11:30am, although some shops in the Centre Vaima stay open Saturday afternoon as well. The Papeete Municipal Market is a roaring beehive from 5 to 7am on Sunday, and many of the nearby general stores are open during those hours. Except for some small groceries, most other stores are closed on Sunday.

Camera/Film Film and 1-hour color-print processing are available at several stores in downtown Papeete. One of the best is **Tahiti Photo,** in the Centre Vaima (© **42.97.34**), where you can get help in English.

Currency Exchange **Banque de Polynésie, Banque de Tahiti,** and **Banque Socredo** each has at least one branch with ATMs on boulevard Pomare, along with many suburban locations. See "Money," in chapter 2.

Drugstores **Pharmacie du Vaima,** on rue du Général-de-Gaulle at rue Georges La Garde behind the Centre Vaima (© **42.97.73**), is owned and operated by English-speaking Nguyen Ngoc-Tran, whose husband runs Pharmacie Tran on Moorea. Pharmacies rotate night duty, so ask your hotel staff to find out which one is open after dark.

Emergencies/Police If you are in a hotel, contact the staff. Otherwise, the **emergency police** phone number is © **17** (but don't expect the person on the other end of the line to speak English). The **central gendarmerie** is at the inland terminus of avenue Pouvanaa Oopa (© **42.02.02**).

Eyeglasses Papeete has several opticians, including **Optique Vaima,** in the Centre Vaima (© **42.77.54**).

Hairdressers/Barbers The staff of the beauty salons in the Inter-Continental Resort Tahiti speaks English.

Healthcare Both **Clinque Cardella,** on rue Anne-Marie-Javouhey (© **42.80.10**), and **Clinic Paofai,** on boulevard Pomare (© **43.77.00**), have highly trained specialists and some state-of-the-art equipment. They are open 24 hours.

Internet Access Every hotel here has Internet access for its guests, but you will have more fun at American expatriate Nina Piermatti's **Tiki Soft Café,** on rue Paul Gauguin at the Rond Pont de L'Est traffic circle (© **88.93.98**). At Nina's computer terminals, you can check your e-mail while sipping a cup of French roast java or a glass of freshly squeezed fruit juice (or munching on a healthy salad or sandwich). Dial-up access costs 250CFP (US$2.50) for 15 minutes, 1,000CFP (US$10) for an hour; high-speed or wireless laptop connections are 350CFP (US$3.50) for 15 minutes, 1,000CFP (US$10) per hour. Open Monday through Wednesday from 8am to 8:30pm, Thursday and Friday from 8:30am to 10:30pm. Nina has wine tastings here Wednesday from 5 to 8pm. Friday night is gay friendly.

Cybernesia Tahiti, on the second level of the Vaima Centre (© **85.43.67**), has both dial-up and wireless access for 20CFP (US20¢) for the first 10 minutes,

15CFP (US15¢) per minute thereafter. It has English keyboards and the Skype telephone program on some of its computers, and it will also burn your digital photos to CD. Open Monday through Friday from 8am to 6pm, Saturday from 9am to 4pm. **La Maison de la Presse,** on boulevard Pomare at Quartier du Commerce (© **50.93.93**), also has English keyboards. It charges 250CFP (US$2.50) for each 15 minutes spent online.

If you need to check your email after dark, the **business center** at Faaa airport (© **83.63.88**) is open until midnight Monday through Saturday (from 8am Mon, Wed, and Fri; from 6am Tues, Thurs, and Sat). It charges 300CFP (US$3) for 15 minutes and can also put your photos on CDs.

Laundry **Laverie Gauguin,** 64 rue Paul Gauguin, at Pont de l'Est (© **43.71.59**), has wash-dry-fold service for 2,200CFP (US$22) a load. Open Monday through Friday from 7am to 5:30pm.

Libraries The **Office Territorial D'Action Culturelle (Territorial Cultural Center),** on boulevard Pomare, west of downtown Papeete (© **42.88.50**), has a small library of mostly French books on the South Pacific and other topics. Hours are 8am to 5pm Monday through Friday, except on Wednesday when it closes at 4pm.

Post Office The main post office is on boulevard Pomare, a block west of the Centre Vaima; open from 7am to 6pm Monday through Friday, 8 to 11am Saturday. The branch post office at the Tahiti-Faaa International Airport terminal is open from 6 to 10:30am and noon to 2pm Monday through Friday, and from 6 to 9am on Saturday, Sunday, and holidays.

Restrooms Both **Tahua Vaite** (the park by the cruise-ship terminal at rue Paul Gauguin) and **Place Toata** (on the western end of downtown) have free and clean public toilets.

Safety Papeete has seen increasing street crime in recent years. The busy parks on boulevard Pomare along the waterfront are generally safe, but be very careful if you wander onto the side streets after dark.

Telephones The main post office, the cruise-ship terminal, and Place Toata all have pay phones, where you can use a *télécarte* to make local and international calls. See "Fast Facts: Tahiti & French Polynesia," in chapter 2, for more information about pay phones and international calls.

Visitor Information The **Tahiti Manava visitors bureau** (© **50.57.12**; www.tahiti-manava.pf), in the cruise-ship welcoming center on the waterfront on boulevard Pomare at the foot of rue Paul Gauguin, is open 7:30am to 5pm Monday through Friday, 1 to 4pm Saturday, and 8am to noon on holidays. It's also open on Sunday if cruise ships are in port.

Water You can drink the tap water in Papeete and its nearby suburbs, which includes all the hotels, but not out in the rural parts of Tahiti. Bottled water is available in all grocery stores.

3 Tahiti's Top Attractions

Tahiti is shaped like a figure eight lying on its side. The "eyes" of the eight are two extinct, eroded volcanoes joined by the flat Isthmus of Taravao. The larger, western part of the island is known as *Tahiti Nui* ("Big Tahiti" in Tahitian), while the smaller eastern peninsula beyond the isthmus is named *Tahiti Iti* ("Little Tahiti"). Together they comprise about 670 sq. km (258 sq. miles), about two-thirds the size of the island of Oahu in Hawaii.

Tahiti Nui's volcano has been eroded over the eons so that now long ridges, separating deep valleys, march down from the crater's ancient rim to the coast far below. The rim itself is still intact, except on the north side, where the Papenoo River has cut its way to the sea. The highest peaks, **Mount Orohena,** 2,206m (7,353 ft.), and **Mount Aora,** 2,045m (6,817 ft.), tower above Papeete. Another peak, the toothlike Mount Te Tara O Maiao, or the **Diadème,** at 1,308m (4,360 ft.), can be seen from the eastern suburb of Pirae but not from downtown.

With the exception of the east coast of Tahiti Iti, where great cliffs fall into the lagoon, and a few places where the ridges end abruptly at the water's edge, the island is skirted by a flat coastal plain. Tahiti's residents live on this plain, in the valleys, or on the hills adjacent to the plain.

Arahurahu Marae ✮✮ Arahurahu is the only *marae*—an ancient temple or meeting place—in all of Polynesia that has been fully restored, and it is maintained like a museum. Although not nearly as impressive as the great lagoonside *marae* on Huahine and Raiatea (see chapters 6 and 7, respectively), this is Tahiti's best example of ancient Polynesian temples and meeting places, and its exhibit boards do a good job of explaining the significance of each part. For example, the stone pens near the entrance were used to keep the pigs to be sacrificed to the gods. Arahurahu is used for the reenactment of old Polynesian ceremonies during the July *Heiva Nui* celebrations.

Paea, 23km (14 miles) west of Papeete. No phone. Free admission. Daily 24 hr.

Lagoonarium de Tahiti If you won't be diving or snorkeling in the lagoons, then you will enjoy a visit to this underwater viewing room surrounded by pens containing reef sharks, sea turtles, and many colorful species of tropical fish. It's part of the Captain Bligh Restaurant and Bar (p. 108). The view of Moorea from here is terrific.

Punaauia, 12km (7 miles) west of Papeete. ✆ **43.62.90.** Admission 500CFP (US$5) adults, 300CFP (US$3) children under 12. Daily 9am–5:30pm.

Tips **Bone Up on History**

A knowledge of French Polynesia's background will prove very useful as you see the sights, many of which have historical significance. I strongly recommend reading Appendix A before setting out and referring back to it as you go. Also consider buying a copy of the late Bengt Danielsson's *Tahiti: Circle Island Tour Guide.* French and English editions are available in the local bookstores. As noted in "Recommended Reading" (p. 56), Danielsson arrived in French Polynesia on Thor Hyerdahl's *Kon Tiki* raft in the late 1940s. He lived here the rest of his life and understood Polynesian culture as well as any European.

Fun Fact **Shipwrecked**

While researching the novel *Pitcairn's Island,* which he co-authored with Charles Nordhoff, James Norman Hall disappeared for several months in 1933 after being shipwrecked near Mangareva, between Tahiti and Pitcairn.

La Maison de James Norman Hall (James Norman Hall's Home) ✸✸✸   This marvelous museum is a required stop for all of us who have ever dreamed of writing successful novels in a lovely lagoonside house. James Norman Hall was a U.S. army pilot in France during World War I, when he was shot down behind German lines and held prisoner. He met Charles Nordhoff in Paris shortly after the war, and together they wrote *The Lafayette Flying Corp,* the story of the American unit that fought for France before the U.S. entered the war. In 1920, they moved to Tahiti, where they sailed around on copra schooners and wrote *Faery Lands of the South Seas.* In 1932, they published *Mutiny on the Bounty,* the first of their three novels about the incident and its aftermath (*Men Against the Sea* and *Pitcairn's Island* are the others). It was turned into the 1935 movie starring Clark Gable and Charles Laughton, and the 1962 remake with Marlon Brando. Hall and Nordhoff penned several more books about the islands, including *Hurricane,* which was also turned into two movies.

Hall and his wife, Sarah Teraireia Winchester Hall, lived their entire married lives here in Arue. Their family manages the house, which is an exact reproduction of their home, and has stocked it with Hall's typewriter, original manuscripts, and tons of heirlooms and memorabilia. (One of the three Oscars won by his son, the late Hollywood cinematographer Conrad L. Hall, is here.) The office is adorned with photographs of him with Zane Grey, Robert Dean Frisbee, and other men-of-the-pen when they dropped by for visits. One of Hall's grandsons still lives on the property, so you will need permission to visit his grave on the hill above the house. Staff members lead 30-minute tours and sell coffee and soft drinks. The free parking lot is across the highway beside the lagoon; if coming from Papeete, you'll have to turn around at the next traffic circle and come back to reach it.

Arue, 5.5km (3¼ miles) east of Papeete. ✆ **50.01.60.** www.jamesnormanhallhome.pf. Admission 600CFP (US$6). Tues–Sat 9am–4pm. Closed public holidays.

Marché Municipale (Municipal Market) ✸✸✸   An amazing array of fruits, vegetables, fish, meat, handicrafts, and other items are sold under the big tin pavilion of Papeete's bustling public market. Unwritten rules dictate that Tahitians sell fruits and traditional vegetables (such as taro and breadfruit), Chinese sell European and Chinese vegetables, and Chinese and Europeans serve as butchers and bakers. If your stomach can handle it, look for hogs' heads hanging in the butcher stalls. The market is busiest early in the mornings, but it's like a carnival here from 5 to 7am every Sunday, when people from the outlying areas of Tahiti, and even from the other islands, arrive to sell their produce. (*Note:* The pickings are slim by 8am.) A Tahitian string band plays during lunch at the upstairs snack bar, which purveys inexpensive island chow.

Papeete, between rue du 22 Septembre and rue François Cardella, 1 block inland from bd. Pomare. No phone. Free admission. Mon–Fri 5am–6pm, Sat 5am–1pm, Sun 4–8am.

Musée de Tahiti et Ses Isles (Museum of Tahiti and Her Islands) ★★★ Set in a lagoonside coconut grove with a gorgeous view of Moorea, this ranks as one of the best museums in the South Pacific. On display are the geological history of the islands, including a terrific topographic map; their sea life, flora, and fauna; and the history and culture of their peoples. Exhibits are devoted to traditional weaving, tapa-cloth making, early tools, body ornaments, tattooing, fishing and horticultural techniques, religion and *maraes*, games and sports, warfare and arms, deaths and funerals, and writers and missionaries (note the 1938 *Tahitian Bible*). Most, but not all, of the display legends are translated into English. Start in the air-conditioned exhibit hall to the left as you enter and proceed outside. Give yourself at least 30 minutes here, preferably an hour.

Punaauia, 15km (9 miles) west of Papeete. ☎ **58.34.76.** Admission 600CFP (US$6) adults, free for children. Tues–Sun 9:30am–5:30pm. Turn toward the lagoon at the Total station and follow the signs.

Musée Gauguin (Gauguin Museum) ★★★ This museum/memorial to Paul Gauguin, the French artist who lived in the Mataiea district from 1891 until 1893, owns a few of his sculptures, wood carvings, engravings, and a ceramic vase. It has an active program to borrow his major works, however, and one might be on display during your visit. Otherwise, the exhibits are dedicated to his life in French Polynesia. It's best to see them counterclockwise, starting at the gift shop (which sells excellent prints and reproductions of his works). The originals are in the first gallery. An interesting display in the last gallery shows who owns his works today. The museum has a lagoonside restaurant, although most visitors have lunch at the nearby Restaurant du Musée Gauguin, at PK 50.5 (p. 94).

The museum is adjacent to the lush **Harrison W. Smith Jardin Botanique (Botanical Gardens),** which was started in 1919 by Harrison Smith, an American who left a career teaching physics at the Massachusetts Institute of Technology and moved to Tahiti. He died here in 1947. His gardens, which now belong to the public, are home to a plethora of tropical plants from around the world. This is the wettest part of Tahiti, so bring an umbrella.

Mataiea, 51km (32 miles) west of Papeete. ☎ **57.10.58.** Museum admission 600CFP (US$6) adults, 300CFP (US$3) children 12–18. Gardens 600CFP (US$6), free for children under 12. Daily 9am–5pm.

Point Venus ★★★ Capt. James Cook observed the transit of the planet Venus in 1769 at Point Venus, Tahiti's northernmost extremity. The low, sandy peninsula covered with ironwood (casuarina) trees is about 2km (1¼ miles) from the main road. Captains Wallis, Cook, and Bligh landed here after anchoring their ships offshore, behind the reef in Matavai Bay. Cook made his observations of the transit of Venus across the sun in 1769 from a point between the black-sand beach and the meandering river that cuts the peninsula in two. The beach and the parklike setting around the tall white lighthouse, which was completed in 1868 (notwithstanding the 1867 date over the door), are popular for picnics. There is a snack bar, a souvenir and handicraft shop, and toilets.

Mahina, 10km (6 miles) east of Papeete. No phone. Free admission. Daily 4am–7pm, snack bar and souvenir shop daily 8am–5pm.

> **Tips** **Get a New Map**
>
> The independence-leaning government of President Oscar Temaru announced as we were going to press that it plans to change the names of several Papeete avenues and *rues* from French to Polynesian. For example, avenue Bruat is now avenue Pouvanaa Oopa, to honor the father of French Polynesia's independence movement. Be sure to pick up a new map at the Tahiti Manava visitors bureau on the waterfront.

WALKING TOUR   PAPEETE

Start:	Tahiti Manava visitors bureau.
Finish:	Papeete Town Hall.
Time:	2 hours.
Best Time:	Early morning or late afternoon.
Worst Time:	Midday or Sunday when most establishments are closed.

Begin at the Tahiti Manava visitors bureau in Tahua Vaiete, the park by the cruise-ship dock, at the foot of rue Paul Gauguin. Stroll westward along Boulevard Pomare. Opposite the tuna-boat dock, you'll see:

❶ Centre Vaima

The chic shops in Papeete's first shopping mall are a mecca for the city's French and European residents (the Municipal Market still attracts mostly Tahitians). The infamous Quinn's Bar stood in the block east of the Centre Vaima, where the Noa Noa boutique is now. The Centre Vaima takes its name from the Vaima Restaurant, everyone's favorite eatery in those days, which it replaced.

Across the four-lane boulevard from the Vaima is the wooden boardwalk along:

❷ The Quay

Cruising yachts from around the world congregate here from April to September, and resident boats are docked here all year. Beyond them, on the other side of the harbor, is **Motu Uta,** once a small natural island belonging to Queen Pomare but now home of the wharves and warehouses of Papeete's shipping port. The reef on the other side has been filled to make a breakwater and to connect Motu Uta by road to

Fare Ute, the industrial area and French naval base to the right. The inter-island boats dock alongside the filled-in reef, and their cargoes of *copra* (dried coconut meat) are taken to a mill at Fare Ute, where coconut oil is extracted and later shipped overseas to be used in cosmetics.

Walk west along the waterfront, past the main post office, next to which is:

❸ Parc Bougainville

This shady park next to the post office is named for Antoine de Bougainville, the French explorer who landed on Tahiti in 1768, less than a year after British Capt. Samuel Wallis got here, thus a little too late to get credit for its discovery. There is no statue of Wallis on Tahiti, but Bougainville's likeness stands here in the park. Two naval cannons flank it. The one nearest the post office was on the *Seeadler,* Count von Luckner's infamous World War I German raider, which ran aground in the Cook Islands after terrifying the British and French territories of the South Pacific. The other was on the French navy's *Zélée.* Bougainville's statue stands between the guns.

Walk westward to the traffic circle at the foot of avenue Pouvanaa Oopa, where you'll find:

Walking Tour: Papeete

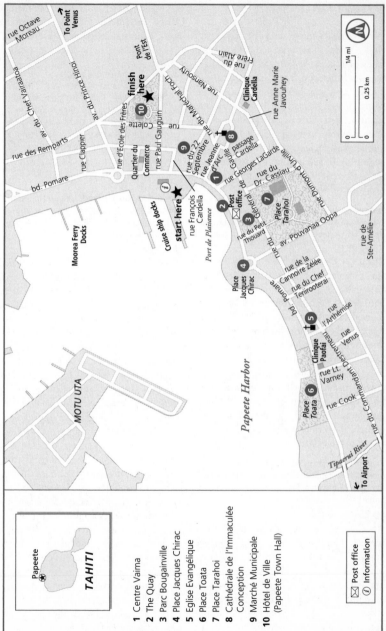

TAHITI

Papeete ✴

1 Centre Vaima
2 The Quay
3 Parc Bougainville
4 Place Jacques Chirac
5 Eglise Evangélique
6 Place Toata
7 Place Tarahoi
8 Cathédrale de l'Immaculée Conception
9 Marché Municipale
10 Hôtel de Ville (Papeete Town Hall)

⊠ Post office
ⓘ Information

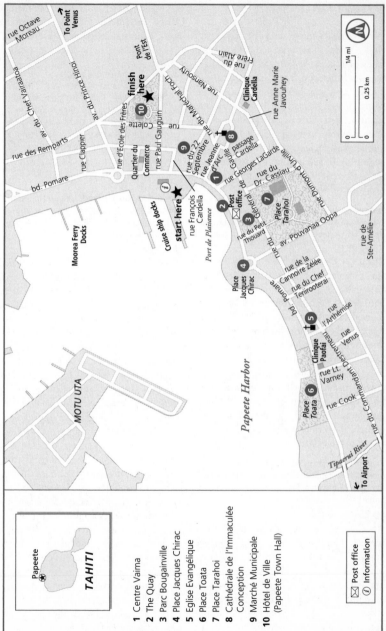

start here
finish here

Cruise ship docks
Moorea Ferry Docks
MOTU UTA
Papeete Harbor
Port de Plaisance
Tipaerui River

To Point Venus
To Airport

rue Octave Moreau
rue du Chef Vairaatoa
av. du Prince Hinoi
rue des Remparts
rue Clappier
bd. Pomare
rue d'Ecole des Frères
Quartier du Commerce
rue Paul Gauguin
rue Colette
rue du Maréchal Foch
Pont de l'Est
rue Nansouty
rue du Frère Alain
Clinique Cardella
rue Anne Marie Javouhey
rue du 22 Septembre
rue Jeanne d'Arc
rue Gal passage Cardella
rue Georges LaGarde
rue du Dr. Cassiau
rue Dumont d'Urville
av. de l'Uranie
rue François Cardella
Post office
rue du Général
rue du Petit Thouard
Place Tarahoi
av. Pouvanaa Oopa
rue de Ste-Amélie
Place Jacques Chirac
rue de la Cannoire Zélée
rue du Chef Teriirooterai
rue l'Arthémise
rue Venus
Clinique Paofai
rue Lt. Destremeau Varney
Place Toata
rue Cook
rue du Commandant Destremeau
bd. Pomare

N

1/4 mi
0.25 km

83

❹ Place Jacques Chirac

Few projects exemplify Papeete's vast road improvements more than the big traffic circle, under which pass the four busy lanes of boulevard Pomare. On the harbor side, the semicircular-shaped park is known as Place Jacques Chirac, whose name created quite a stir because French tradition says not to name a public place after a living president. Underneath is a public parking garage. The park is the beginning of recent landfills, which have replaced a black-sand beach that used to run west of here.

Keep going west along the waterfront, to rue l'Arthémise, where you can't miss the big beige church on the mountain side of the boulevard, known as:

❺ Eglise Evangélique

An impressive steeple sits atop Eglise Evangélique, the largest Protestant church in French Polynesia. The local evangelical sect grew out of the early work by the London Missionary Society. Today the pastors are Tahitian. Outrigger canoe racing is Tahiti's national sport, and the *va'a*—those long, sleek vessels seen cutting the harbor during lunchtime and after work—used to be kept on a black-sand beach across the boulevard from the church. A section of the landfill across is now reserved for them.

Continue west along boulevard Pomare for 6 more blocks. You'll see a few remaining stately old colonial homes across the boulevard. On the harbor side, you will come to:

❻ Place Toata

Another economic restructuring fund project, Place Toata is also built on the landfill. The park is a favorite gathering place for office workers during the day and families at night. They come to stroll, take in the view, and dine at inexpensive snack bars. Place Toata's outdoor amphitheater hosts concerts all year (Joe Cocker played here recently) and the national dance competition during the huge *Heiva Nui* festival in July. Next door, on

the banks of Tipaerui River, stands the **Office Territorial d'Action Culturelle,** Tahiti's cultural center and library.

> **TAKE A BREAK**
> Comparable to *les roulottes* (see "Don't Miss *Les Roulottes,*" p. 112) but permanently here, Place Toata's open-air snack bars are great for cold drinks, ice-cream cones, or even a complete lunch. There are also clean public restrooms here.

Turn around and backtrack east on boulevard Pomare to Parc Bougainville (see no. 3, above), cut through the park, and proceed to the spacious grounds of:

❼ Place Tarahoi

Place Tarahoi, Papeete's governmental center, was royal property in the old days. Queen Pomare, who ruled Tahiti when the French annexed it in 1842, had her mansion here. After taking over, the French used the impressive home as their headquarters. It is long gone, but today is replicated by the Papeete Town Hall (see no. 10, below). As you face the grounds, the buildings on the right house the French government and include the home of the president of French Polynesia. The modern building on the left is the Territorial Assembly. You can walk around the hallways of the Assembly building during business hours. In front stands a monument to Pouvanaa a Oopa (1895–1977), a Polynesian from Huahine who became a hero fighting for France in World War I and then spent the rest of his life battling for independence for his home islands. During the 1960s and '70s, he spent 15 years in prison in France, but he returned home in time to see more local autonomy granted to the territory. In fact, his fellow Tahitians promptly sent him back to Paris as a member of the French Senate.

Continue 2 more blocks along rue du Général-de-Gaulle, past the rear of Centre Vaima, to:

Impressions

To those who insist that all picturesque towns look like Siena or Stratford-on-Avon, Papeete will be disappointing, but to others who love the world in all its variety, the town is fascinating. My own judgment: any town that wakes each morning to see Moorea is rich in beauty.

—James A. Michener, *Return to Paradise*, 1951

⑧ Cathédrale de l'Immaculée Conception

Tahiti's oldest Catholic church, Cathédrale de l'Immaculée Conception houses a series of paintings of the Crucifixion. It's a cool, quiet, and comforting place to worship or just to contemplate.

Rue du Général-de-Gaulle becomes rue du Maréchal-Foch past the church. Follow it for a block. Bear left at rue Colette and continue until you come to the:

⑨ Marché Municipale

Take a stroll under the large tin pavilion of Papeete's Municipal Market and examine the multitude of fruits and vegetables offered for sale (see "Tahiti's Top Attractions," earlier).

After sampling the market and the marvelous handicrafts stalls along its sidewalk and upstairs, walk along rue Colette 2 more blocks, until you come to the:

⑩ Hôtel de Ville (Papeete Town Hall)

This is a magnificent replica of Queen Pomare's mansion, which once stood at Place Tarahoi. The impressive structure, with its wraparound veranda, captures the spirit of the colonial South Pacific. This *Hôtel de Ville* or *Fare Oire* (French and Tahitian, respectively, for "town hall") was dedicated in 1990 by French President François Mitterand during an elaborate celebration. Walk up the grand entrance steps to catch a cool breeze from the broad balconies.

From here you can find your way back to Vaima Centre and some much-needed refreshment at its open-air cafes (see "Where to Dine," later in this chapter).

4 The Circle Island Tour ★★

A **Circle Island Tour,** or a drive around Tahiti, is the best way to spend a day seeing the island's outlying sights and a bit of old Polynesia away from Papeete's bustle. It can be done even if you're staying on Moorea (see "Touring Tahiti from Moorea . . . & Vice Versa," p. 97).

The road around Tahiti Nui is 114km (72 miles) long. It's 54km (32 miles) from Papeete to Taravao along the east coast and 60km (40 miles) returning along the west coast. If your car has a trip meter, reset it to zero; if it doesn't, make note of the total kilometers on the odometer at the outset.

On the land side of the road are red-topped concrete **kilometer markers** (*pointes kilomètres* in French, or *PK* for short). They tell the distance every kilometer between Papeete and the Isthmus of Taravao, that is, the distance from Papeete to Taravao in each direction, not the total number of kilometers around the island. The large numbers facing the ocean are the number of kilometers from Papeete; the numbers facing you as you drive along are the number of kilometers you have to go to Papeete or Taravao, depending on your direction. Distances between the PKs are referred to in tenths of kilometers; for example, PK 35.6 would be 35.6km from Papeete.

⌐ *Tips* **Avoid Rush Hour & Check on Road Work**

If you drive yourself around Tahiti, avoid getting snarled in morning and evening weekday rush hours. Landslides between PK 44 and PK 45 on the east coast can close the round-island road, so ask the car-rental agent or the staff at the Tahiti Manava visitors bureau if it is open all the way around.

THE NORTH & EAST COASTS OF TAHITI NUI

Proceeding clockwise from Papeete, you'll leave town by turning inland off boulevard Pomare and following the broad **avenue du Prince-Hinoi,** the start of the round-island road.

FAUTAUA VALLEY, LOTI'S POOL & THE DIADEME

It's not worth the side trip, but at PK 2.5, a road goes right into the steep-walled **Fautaua Valley** and the **Bain Loti,** or Loti's Pool. Julien Viaud, the French merchant mariner who wrote under the pen name Pierre Loti, used this pool as a setting for his novel *The Marriage of Loti,* which recounted the love of a Frenchman for a Tahitian woman. Now part of Papeete's water-supply system, the pool is covered in concrete. Don't take any chances in this traffic, but try for a look up the valley to the **Diadème,** a rocky outcrop protruding like a crown from the interior ridge. (I think it looks like a single, worn molar sticking up from a gum.) The road goes into the lower part of the valley and terminates at the beginning of a hiking trail up to the **Fautaua Waterfall,** which plunges over a cliff into a large pool 300m (985 ft.) below. The all-day hike to the head of the valley is best done with a guide (see "Golf, Hiking & Watersports," later in this chapter).

TOMB OF POMARE V 👁👁

At PK 4.7, turn left at the sign and drive a short distance to a Protestant churchyard commanding an excellent view of Matavai Bay to the right. The **tomb** with a Grecian urn on top was built in 1879 for Queen Pomare. Her remains were removed a few years later by her son, King Pomare V, who abdicated in return for a French pension and later died of too much drink. Now he is buried here, and tour guides like to say the urn is not an urn at all but a liquor bottle, which makes it a monument not to Pomare V but to the cause of his death.

LA MAISON DE JAMES NORMAN HALL (JAMES NORMAN HALL'S HOME) 👁👁👁

At PK 5.4, on the mountain side of the road just east of the small bridge, stands the home of **James Norman Hall,** coauthor with Charles Nordhoff of *Mutiny on the Bounty.* See "Tahiti's Top Attractions," earlier.

ONE TREE HILL 👁👁

At PK 8, past the new Radisson Plaza resort, you'll come to the top of **One Tree Hill,** so named by Capt. James Cook because a single tree stood on this steep headland in the late 1700s. For many years it was the site of a luxury hotel, now closed. Pull into the roundabout at the entrance and stop for one of Tahiti's most magnificent vistas. You'll look down on the north coast all the way from Matavai Bay to Papeete, with Moorea looming on the far horizon.

POINT VENUS ⭑⭑⭑

At PK 10, turn left at Super Marché Venus Star and drive to **Point Venus,** Tahiti's northernmost point, where Capt. James Cook observed the transit of the planet Venus in 1769 (see "Tahiti's Top Attractions," earlier).

PAPENOO VALLEY

At PK 17.1, Tahiti's longest bridge crosses its longest river at the end of its largest valley at one of its largest rural villages—all named **Papenoo.** The river flows down to the sea through the only wall in Tahiti Nui's old volcanic crater. Opened since I was last here, a new cross-island road goes up the valley, literally through the mountains (via a tunnel), and down to Tahiti's south shore. Four-wheel-drive vehicles go into the valley on rugged excursions (see "Safari Expeditions," later).

ARAHOHO BLOWHOLES

At PK 22, the surf pounding against the headland at **Arahoho** has formed overhanging shelves with holes in them. As waves crash under the shelves, water and air are forced through the holes, resulting in a geyserlike phenomenon. One shoots up at the base of a cliff on the mountain side of the road, but be careful because oncoming traffic cannot see you standing there. Pull into the overlook (with free parking and toilets) west of the sharp curve. There's a local snack bar across the road, and a black-sand beach is within sight.

CASCADES DE TEFAARUMAI (FAARUMAI WATERFALLS) ⭑⭑

At PK 22.1, a sign on the right just past the blowhole marks a somewhat paved road that leads 1.5km (1 mile) up a small valley to the **Cascades de Faarumai,** Tahiti's most accessible waterfalls. The drive itself gives a glimpse of how ordinary rural Tahitians live in simple wood houses surrounded by bananas and breadfruit. Park near the stand of bamboo trees and take a few minutes to read the signs, which explain a romantic legend. Vaimahuta falls are an easy walk; Haamaremare Iti and Haamaremarerahi falls are a 45-minute climb up a more difficult trail. Vaimahuta falls plunge straight down several hundred feet from a hanging valley into a large pool. Bring insect repellent.

MAHAENA BATTLEFIELD

At PK 32.5, the Tahitian rebellion came to a head on April 17, 1844, when 441 French troops charged several times and many poorly armed Tahitians dug in near the village of **Mahaena.** The Tahitians lost 102 men and the French, 15. It was the last set battle of the rebellion.

BOUGAINVILLE'S ANCHORAGE ⭑

At PK 37.6, a plaque mounted on a rock on the northern end of the bridge at Hitiaa commemorates the landing of the French explorer **Bougainville,** who anchored just

---

Impressions

The air was full of that exquisite fragrance of orange blossom and gardenia which is distilled by night under the thick foliage; there was a great silence, accentuated by the bustle of insects in the grass, and that sonorous quality, peculiar to night in Tahiti, which predisposes the listener to feel the enchanting power of music.

—Pierre Loti (Julien Viaud), The Marriage of Loti, 1880

offshore when he arrived in Tahiti in 1768. The two small islands on the reef, Oputotara and Variararu, provided slim protection against the prevailing trade winds, and Bougainville lost six anchors in 10 days trying to keep his ships off the reef. Tahitians recovered one and gave it to the high chief of Bora Bora, who in turn gave it to Captain Cook in 1777.

FAATAUTIA VALLEY

At PK 41.8 begins a view of **Faatautia Valley,** which looks so much like those in the Marquesas that in 1957 director John Huston chose it as a location for a movie version of *Typee,* Herman Melville's novelized account of his ship-jumping adventures among the Marquesans on Nuku Hiva in the 1840s. The project was scrapped after another of Huston's Melville movies, *Moby Dick,* bombed at the box office. The uninhabited valley surely looks much today as it did 1,000 years ago.

TARAVAO

At PK 53, after passing the small-boat marina, the road climbs up onto the **Isthmus of Taravao,** separating Tahiti Nui from Tahiti Iti. At the top are the stone walls of **Fort Taravao,** which the French built in 1844 to bottle up what was left of the rebellious islanders on the Tahiti Iti peninsula during the French-Tahitian War of 1844–48. Germans stuck on Tahiti during World War II were interned here. It is now used as a French army training center. The village of **Taravao,** with its shops, suburban streets, and churches, has grown up around the military post. Its snack bars are good places for refueling stops.

THE TAHITI ITI PENINSULA

Tahiti Iti is much less sparsely populated and developed than its bigger twin, Tahiti Nui. Paved roads dead-end about halfway down its north and south sides. A series of cliffs plunges into the sea on Tahiti Iti's rugged east end. While the north shore holds historical interest, the south coast has Tahiti's best beach and its top surfing spot.

TARAVAO PLATEAU

If you have to choose one of three roads on Tahiti Iti, take the one by the school and stadium. It dead-ends high up into the rolling pastures of the **Taravao Plateau.** It begins at the traffic signal on the north-coast road to Tautira and runs up through cool pastures reminiscent of rural France, with huge trees lining the narrow paved road. At more than 360m (1,200 ft.) high, the plateau is blessed with a refreshing, perpetually spring-like climate. Near the end of the road, you'll come to the **Taravao Plateau Overlook,** where you'll have a spectacular view of the entire isthmus and down both sides of Tahiti Nui.

THE NORTH COAST TO TAUTIRA

The road on the north coast of Tahiti Iti goes for 18km (11 miles) to the sizable village of **Tautira,** which sits on its own little peninsula. Captain Cook anchored in the bay off Tautira on his second visit to Tahiti in 1773. His ships ran aground on the reef while the crews were partying one night. He managed to get them off, but lost several anchors in the process. One of them was found in 1978 and is now on display at the Museum of Tahiti and Her Islands, which you will come to on the west side of the island.

A year after Cook landed at Tautira, a Spanish ship from Peru named the *Aguila* landed here, and its captain claimed the island for Spain. It was the third time Tahiti had been claimed for a European power. He also put ashore two Franciscan priests. The *Aguila* returned a year later, but the priests had had enough of Tahiti and sailed back to Peru.

When you enter the village, bear left and drive along the scenic coast road as far as the general store, where you can buy a cold soft drink and snack. If you can hold out longer, I usually take my break at La Plage de Maui snack bar on Tahiti Iti's south coast (see below).

THE SOUTH COAST TO TEAHUPOO
The picturesque road along the south coast of Tahiti Iti skirts the lagoon, passing through small settlements. Novelist Zane Grey had a deep-sea-fishing camp at PK 7.3, near the village of **Toahotu,** from 1928 to 1930. He caught a silver marlin that was about 4m (14 ft.) long and weighed more than 454kg (1,000 lbs.)—even after the sharks had had a meal on it while Grey was trying to get it aboard his boat. He wrote about his adventures in *Tales of Tahitian Waters.*

According to Tahitian legends, the demigod Maui once made a rope from his sister Hina's hair and used it to slow down the sun long enough for Tahitians to finish cooking their food in their earth ovens (a lengthy process). He accomplished this feat while standing on the reef at a point 8.5km (5 miles) along the south-coast road. Beyond Maui's alleged footprints, now under the road, the **Bay of Tapueraha** provides the widest pass and deepest natural harbor on Tahiti. It was used as a base by a large contingent of the French navy during the aboveground nuclear tests at Moruroa atoll in the 1960s and 1970s. Some of the old mooring pilings still stand just offshore.

Reminiscent of the great Matira Beach on Bora Bora, **La Plage de Maui (Maui Beach)** ✹✹✹ borders the bay and is the best strip of white sand on Tahiti. Get out of the car and take a break at the lagoonside snack bar here. A cave, known as the **Caverne de Maui,** is a short walk inland.

Near Vairao village, you'll pass the modern **IFREMER: Le Centre Océanologique du Pacifique (Pacific Oceanographic Center),** which conducts research into black-pearl oysters, shrimp farming, and other means of extracting money from seawater. The buildings were formerly used for France's nuclear testing program.

The south-coast road ends at **Teahupoo,** the famous *"village de surf,"* whose beachside park overlooks the big waves curling around Havaa Pass. World-class boarders compete in the Billabong Pro tournament here every May. A footbridge crosses the

Impressions
It came upon me little by little. I came to like the life here, with its ease and its leisure, and the people, with their good-nature and their happy smiling faces.
—W. Somerset Maugham, "The Fall of Edward Bernard," 1921

Impressions

Tahiti has unique sex freedom. A bitter critic of the island has sneered that its charm is explainable solely in terms of the "erotic mist" that hangs over the island . . . . I remember as a boy poring over the accounts of early navigators and coming repeatedly upon that cryptic phrase "so we put into Tahiti to refresh the men."

—James A. Michener, 1951

Tirahi River, where a trail begins along Tahiti Iti's rugged eastern shoreline. It's a strenuous and sometimes dangerous hike done only with a guide (see "Golf, Hiking & Watersports," later in this chapter).

THE SOUTH COAST OF TAHITI NUI

As you leave Taravao, heading back to Papeete along Tahiti's south coast, note that the PK markers begin to decrease the nearer you get to Papeete. The road rims casuarina-ringed **Port Phaeton,** which cuts nearly halfway across the isthmus. Port Phaeton and the **Bay of Tapueraha** to the south are Tahiti's finest harbors, yet European settlement and most development have taken place on the opposite side of the island, around Papeete. The shrimp you'll order for dinner come from the aqua farms in the bay's shallow waters.

PAPAEARI

At PK 52 stands Tahiti's oldest village. Apparently the island's initial residents recognized the advantages of the south coast and its deep lagoons and harbors, for word-of-mouth history says they came through the Hotumatuu Pass in the reef and settled at **Papeari** sometime between A.D. 400 and 500. Robert Keable, author of *Simon Called Peter,* a best-selling novel about a disillusioned clergyman, lived here from 1924 until he died in 1928 at the age of 40. His home, now a private residence, stands at PK 55. Today Papeari is a thriving village whose residents often sell fruits and vegetables at stands along the road.

MUSEE GAUGUIN (GAUGUIN MUSEUM) ✸✸✸

At PK 51.2 is the entrance to the museum/memorial to Paul Gauguin, who lived near here from 1891 until 1893 (see "Tahiti's Top Attractions," earlier). The museum sits in the lush **Harrison W. Smith Botanical Gardens,** started in 1919 by American Harrison Smith. The museum and gardens are open daily from 9am to 5pm. There's a snack bar here, but your best bet is to continue west.

VAIHIRIA RIVER AND VAIPAHI GARDENS

At PK 48, in the village of Mataiea, the main road crosses the Vaihiria River. The new cross-island road from Papenoo on the north coast terminates here. An 11km (7.3-mile) track leads to **Lake Vaihiria,** at 465m (1,550 ft.) above sea level. It is Tahiti's only lake and is noted for its freshwater eels. Cliffs up to 900m (3,000 ft.) tall drop to the lake on its north side. Also in Mataiea is the lush **Jardin Vaipehi (Vaipehi Gardens),** a cool and refreshing spot with an oft-photographed waterfall and a bubbling natural spring. The garden is lush with elephant ears, tree ferns, ground orchids, jade vines, and other tropical vegetation. A planned renovation project is to emphasize its historical importance, since ancient Tahitian nobles followed the path to the springs in order to be spiritually purified.

ATIMAONO

At PK 41 begins the largest parcel of flat land on Tahiti, site of **Atimaono Golf Course,** French Polynesia's only links. Irishman William Stewart started a cotton plantation here during the American Civil War. Nothing remains of the plantation, but it was Stewart who brought the first Chinese indentured servants to Tahiti. See "Golf, Hiking & Watersports," below.

DORENCE ATWATER'S GRAVE

At PK 36, on the lagoon side of the road in Papara village, stands a Protestant church, under whose paved yard is buried **Dorence Atwater,** American consul to Tahiti after the Civil War. Captured while serving in the Union Army, Atwater was assigned to the hospital at the infamous Confederate prisoner-of-war camp at Andersonville, Ga., where he surreptitiously recorded the names of Union soldiers who died in captivity. He later escaped and brought his lists to the federal government, thus proving that the Confederacy was keeping inaccurate records. His action made him a hero in the eyes of the Union Army. He eventually moved to the south coast of Tahiti, married a daughter of a chief of the Papara district, and at one time invested in William Stewart's cotton venture.

MARAA GROTTO

At PK 28.5, on Tahiti's southwest corner, the road turns sharply around the base of a series of headlands, which drop precipitously to the lagoon. Deep into one of these cliffs goes the **Maraa Grotto,** also called the Paroa Cave. It's actually two caves, both with water inside, and they go much deeper into the hill than appears at first glance. Park in the lot, not along the road, and enter at the gazebo to reach the larger of the two caves. A short trail leads from there to the smaller cave and a miniwaterfall.

THE WEST COAST OF TAHITI NUI

North of Maraa, the road runs through the Paea and Punaauia suburbs of Papeete. The west coast is the driest part of Tahiti, and it's very popular with Europeans, Americans, and others who have built homes along the lagoon and in the hills overlooking it and Moorea.

ARAHURAHU MARAE ⟪⟪

At PK 22.5, a small road on the right of Magasin Laut leads to a narrow valley, on the floor of which sits the restored **Arahurahu Marae** (see "Tahiti's Top Attractions," earlier).

MUSÉE DE TAHITI ET SES ISLES ⟪⟪⟪

At PK 15.1, turn left at the gas station and follow the signs through a residential area to the lagoon and the **Musée de Tahiti et Ses Isles (Museum of Tahiti and Her Islands),** one of the South Pacific's best museums (see "Tahiti's Top Attractions," earlier).

⟨Fun Fact⟩ R. L. S. Was Here

Robert Louis Stevenson spent 2 months at Tautira in 1888, working on *The Master of Ballantrae,* a novel set not in Tahiti but in Scotland. Stevenson's mother was with him in Tautira. After she returned to London, she sent the local Protestant church a silver Communion service, which is still being used today.

Finds   **Take a Break**

Sitting beside the sands of Maui Beach, **La Plage de Maui** snack bar (© **74.71. 74**) is a great place to stop for refreshment while taking in the gorgeous scenery, or perhaps a dip in the shallow lagoon. Owners Rose Wilkinson and Alain Corre, both veterans of the Sofitel Moorea Beach Resort on Moorea, offer reasonably priced burgers, steaks, *poisson cru* (marinated fish), ice cream, and other temptations. Open daily 10am to 6pm. No credit cards.

PUNARUU VALLEY

On a cloudless day, you will have a view up the **Punaruu Valley** to the Diadème as you drive from the museum back to the main road. Power lines mar the view, but it's worth stopping to take a look. Tahitian rebels occupied the valley during the 1844–48 war, and the French built a fort to keep them there (the site is now occupied by a television antenna). Later the valley was used to grow oranges, most of which were shipped to California. Villagers sell the now-wild fruit at roadside stands during July and August.

The Route 5 expressway goes as far south as the Punaruu River, just north of the Tahiti Museum. Instead of taking the overpass onto the expressway, stay in the right lane to the traffic circle under the overpass. The first exit off the circle will take you up into the Punaruu Valley. The second exit leads to the Route 5 expressway. The third is Route 1, the old two-lane coast road, which will take you to the Lagoonarium.

THE LAGOONARIUM

At PK 11.4, the **Captain Bligh Restaurant and Bar** has a terrific view of Moorea and is home to the **Lagoonarium de Tahiti,** an underwater viewing room (see "Tahiti's Top Attractions," earlier).

After the Lagoonarium, Route 1 soon joins the four-lane Route 5 expressway, which passes shopping centers and marinas in Punaauia. It splits just before the Sofitel Tahiti Resort. The left lanes feed into the Route 5 expressway, which roars back to Papeete. The right lanes take you along Route 1, the old road that goes past the west-coast hotels and the Tahiti-Faaa International Airport before returning to town.

ORGANIZED TOURS AROUND THE COASTAL ROAD

Several companies offer tours along the coastal road around Tahiti Nui. They're a good way to see the island without hassling with traffic, and they're an especially fine way to spend your first day here, since you can see the island while recovering from jet lag.

If one is scheduled while you're here, I recommend Tahiti Tourisme's **Le Tere Faati** tour, which takes you around the island via open-air *le truck,* with Tahitian musicians entertaining you all the way. It stops at waterfalls, a beach, Tautira, the Vapahi Garden, and in Paea. It may not, however, include the James Norman Hall, Gauguin, and Tahiti museums. These all-day excursions leave the Office Territorial d'Action Culturelle (Cultural Center), on boulevard Pomare at Place Toata, at 8am and return at 5:30pm. They cost just 2,000CFP (US$20) for adults, 500CFP (US$5) for children under 15. Check with your hotel activities desk or call Tahiti Tourisme (© **50.57.00**) to find out the schedule and to make reservations.

Also good is English-speaking William Leteeg's **Adventure Eagle Tours** (℃ 77.20. 03). William takes you around in an air-conditioned van and lends his experiences growing up on the island to his commentaries. Other options include **Tahiti Tours** (℃ 54.02.50; www.tahiti-tours.com), **Tahiti Nui Travel** (℃ 42.40.10; www.tahiti-nui.com), and **Marama Tours** (℃ 50.74.74; www.maramatours.com). They have reservations desks in several hotels. Expect to pay about 5,000CFP (US$50) for a half-day tour and 9,500CFP (US$95) for an all-day tour, plus entrance fees to the museums, other attractions, and lunch, usually at the Restaurant du Musée Gauguin.

For a spectacular bird's-eye view of Tahiti or Moorea, take a sightseeing ride with **Polynesia Hélicoptères** (℃ 86.60.29; www.polynesia-helicopter.com). The flights are anything but inexpensive, but if you can afford it, they are well worth the price of about 16,000CFP (US$160) for a flight over Tahiti Nui, 29,000CFP (US$290) for a flight over Tahiti Iti, 26,000CFP (US$260) for a spectacular view of Moorea, or 29,000CFP (US$290) to fly out to Tetiaroa, the late Marlon Brando's atoll. Those fares are per person, with a minimum of four passengers required. The flights last between 20 and 45 minutes, depending on where you go. Reserve as far in advance as possible.

5 Safari Expeditions ★★★

So-called safari expeditions into Tahiti's interior offer a very different view of the island—and some spectacular views at that. Riding in the back of open, four-wheel-drive vehicles, you follow narrow, unpaved roads through Tahiti's central crater, usually

The Moon & Six Million

In 1891, a marginally successful Parisian painter named Paul Gauguin left behind his wife and six children and sailed to Tahiti. He wanted to devote himself to his art, free of the chains of civilization.

Instead of paradise, Gauguin found a world that suffered from some of the same maladies as did the one from which he fled. Poverty, sickness, and frequent disputes with church and colonial officials marked his decade in the islands. He had syphilis, a bad heart, and an addiction to opium.

Gauguin disliked Papeete and spent his first 2 years in the rural Mataiea district, on Tahiti's south coast, where a village woman asked what he was doing there. Looking for a girl, he replied. The woman immediately offered her 13-year-old daughter Tehaamana, the first of Gauguin's early teenage Tahitian mistresses. One of them bore him a son in 1899.

Tehaamana and the others figured prominently in Gauguin's impressionistic masterpieces, which brought fame to Tahiti but did little for his own pocketbook. After 649 paintings and a colorful career, immortalized by W. Somerset Maugham in *The Moon and Sixpence,* Gauguin died penniless in 1903.

At the time of his death, on Hiva Oa in the Marquesas Islands, a painting by Gauguin sold for 150 French francs. Today, on the rare occasion when one comes on the market, it fetches far in excess of US$6 million.

Finds **Take a Break**

The circle island tour buses deposit their passengers for lunch at the lagoonside **Restaurant du Musée Gauguin,** at PK 50.5 (© **57.13.80**), which is worth a stop just for its phenomenal view of Tahiti Iti. The lunch buffet costs about 2,650CFP (US$27) per person Monday through Saturday, 3,500CFP (US$35) on Sunday; sandwiches are also available. Open daily from noon to 3pm. A less expensive option is **Beach Burger,** at PK 39 (© **57.41.03**), west of the golf course at Atimaono. In addition to burgers, it offers salads, steaks, Chinese fare, and pizzas. Open Sunday through Thursday from 6am to 8pm, Friday and Saturday from 6am to 9:30pm.

via the breathtaking Papenoo Valley. Weather permitting, you'll reach altitudes of 1,440m (4,800 ft.) on the sides of the island's steep interior ridge. The cool temperatures at the higher elevations are refreshing, as is a swim in a cold mountain stream.

Tahiti Safari Expedition (© **42.14.15;** www.tahiti-safari.com) has been the best outfitter since owner Patrice Bordes pioneered the concept in 1990. He charges about 5,500CFP (US$55) per person for a half-day trip, 9,500CFP (US$95) for a full day. Patrice usually stops at a restaurant in the Papenoo Valley, where you can buy lunch, or you can bring your own picnic. Don't forget a bathing suit, towel, hat, sunscreen, insect repellent, and camera. These are popular trips with limited space, so reserve as early as possible at any hotel activities desk.

6 Golf, Hiking & Watersports

GOLF

The 18-hole, 6,255m (6,839-yd.) **Atimaono Golf Course,** PK 40.2 (© **57.43.41**), sprawls over the site of William Stewart's cotton plantation. A clubhouse, pro shop, restaurant, bar, locker rooms, showers, swimming pool, spa pool, and driving range are on the premises. The club is open daily from 8am to dark. Greens fees are about 5,500CFP (US$55). The hotel activities desks can book all-day golf outings for about 24,000CFP (US$240) for one golfer, 35,000 (US$350) for two, including greens fees, equipment, lunch, and transportation to and from the course.

HIKING

Tahiti has a number of hiking trails, such as the cross-island Papenoo Valley–Lake Vaihiria route. Another ascends to the top of Mount Aorai, and another skirts the remote and wild eastern coast of Tahiti Iti. This is not the Shenandoah or some other American or New Zealand national park with well-marked trails, and the French gendarmes do not take kindly to rescuing tourists who become lost trying to scale one of Tahiti's peaks. Downpours can occur in the higher altitudes, swelling the streams that most trails follow, and the nights can become bitterly cold and damp. Which side of the island is the rainy side can shift from one day to the next, depending on which way the wind blows. In addition, the quick-growing tropical foliage can quickly obscure a path that was easily followed a few days before. Permits are required to use some trails that cross government land.

Accordingly, always go with a guide or on organized hikes such as those offered by **Tahiti Evasion** (© **56.48.77;** www.tahitievasion.com). This Moorea-based company has all-day treks into the Fautaua valley, home of Loti's Pool; the Orofero Valley on Tahiti's south coast; and to the top of Mount Aorai, the island's third-highest peak. The treks start at 5,200CFP (US$52) per person. Hikes along the wild, uninhabited east coast of Tahiti Iti take 3 days of walking and 2 nights of camping (call for prices). All except the Mount Aorai climb are rated as easy walks. Tahiti Evasion will also organize hiking-and-watersports trips of up to 3 weeks throughout the islands.

You can also check with the **Tahiti Manava visitors bureau** in Papeete (© **50.57.12;** www.tahiti-manava.pf) for the names of guides and hiking clubs.

WATERSPORTS

Based at the Inter-Continental Resort Tahiti, **Aquatica Dive Centre and Nautical Activities** (© **53.34.96**) offers the most comprehensive list of watersports activities, and you don't have to be a hotel guest to partake. Some sample prices: snorkeling gear rental, 2,000CFP (US$20); snorkeling trips, 4,000CFP (US$40); water-skiing, 4,500CFP (US$45); and kayak rental, 1,800CFP (US$18) per hour. A two-tank dive including equipment and a guide costs 11,000CFP (US$110); an introductory dive, 6,000CFP (US$60).

SCUBA DIVING   Tahiti is not in the same diving league as the other French Polynesian islands. You can see plenty of smaller fish here, but don't expect daily encounters with sharks, rays, and other large creatures, which are plentiful around the other islands. The popular dive sites are on the west coast of Tahiti Nui, from Papeete down to Punaauia, and off the southern coast of Tahiti Nui. **The Aquarium,** near the end of the Faaa airport runway, and in clear view of Moorea, attracts both divers and snorkelers to see fish swimming around coral heads and several wrecks, including a small aircraft (it didn't crash; it was moved here in the 1990s). Nearby is another aircraft and the hulks of two cargo vessels.

With the exception of **Aquatica Dive Centre and Nautical Activities,** at the Inter-Continental Resort Tahiti (see above), and **Top Dive Tahiti,** based at the Sheraton Hotel Tahiti (© **83.51.26;** www.topdive.com), Tahiti's dive operators cater primarily to local residents, which means you should bring your own equipment. It also helps if you can speak French. Go to Eleuthera Plongee Tahiti's website, **www.dive-tahiti. com**, for more information.

SNORKELING & SWIMMING   Most beaches on Tahiti have black volcanic sand, not the white variety most of us expect in the South Pacific. The most convenient of these is the public beach in front of **Hotel Le Royal Tahitien** (© **50.40.40**), in Pirae 4km (2½ miles) east of downtown (see "Where to Stay," below). There is some white

---

Moments Watching the Sun Paint Moorea

I was born to see sights, and no matter how many times I visit French Polynesia, I never tire of its incredible natural beauty. I always spend sunset of my first day at the Inter-Continental Resort Tahiti, on the west coast, depleting up my camera battery as the sun paints another glorious red-and-orange sky over Moorea's purple ridges.

Marlon's *Mana*

The late Marlon Brando did more than star in the remake of *Mutiny on the Bounty* when he came to Tahiti in 1960. He fell in love with his beautiful Tahitian co-star, Tarita Terepaia, the 19-year-old daughter of a Bora Bora fisherman. At first Tarita reportedly wasn't attracted to the then-dashing actor, but his good looks and charm must have won out, for she later became his wife and the mother of two of his children.

Brando also fell for Tetiaroa, an atoll 42km (25 miles) north of Tahiti and Moorea. In the old days, this cluster of 12 flat islets surrounding an aqua-marine lagoon was the playground of Tahiti's high chiefs, who frequently were joined by the *Ariori,* traveling bands of sexually explicit entertainers and practitioners of infanticide (see "The Islanders," in Appendix A). High-ranking women would spend months doing a bit of make-over on Tetiaroa, resting in the shade to lighten their skin and gorging on starchy foods to broaden their girth. Chiefly men and women were said to possess the mys-tical power ancient Polynesians called *mana,* and the bigger the body, the more the mana.

For a time, a British dentist who married into the royal family owned Tetiaroa, but it was abandoned when Brando bought it in 1966. He turned one of his islets into a refuge for Tetiaroa's thousands of seabirds. He built a retreat for himself on a second islet and a small, rather rustic resort on a third.

Guests at the resort would seldom see the actor, on whose waistline Tetiaroa apparently worked its expansive magic. During the day he would stay at home in the shade, playing with his radios and computers. At night he would go fishing and lobstering.

A series of hurricanes almost blew his resort away in 1983, and Brando's relationship with Tahiti turned to human disaster a decade later when his son Christian—by his first wife, actress Anna Kashfi—shot and killed the boyfriend of his half-sister, Cheyenne, in Brando's Hollywood home. A year later Cheyenne, then 25, hung herself at Tarita's home on Tahiti. Brando did not attend her funeral; in fact, he never again returned to Tahiti.

Ex-wife Tarita operated the resort, mostly as a day-trip and weekend des-tination from Tahiti, until shortly before Brando's death in 2004. Richard Bailey, a long-time family friend and developer of the Inter-Continental Resort Tahiti and other hotels here, has announced plans to build an upmar-ket, environmentally friendly resort on Tetiaroa.

sand among the pebbles at the **PK 18.5 Plage de Publique (Public Beach),** on the west coast at the Punaauia-Paea border. It has a restaurant and snack bar. The best beach of all is **Plage de Maui** on Tahiti Iti (see "The Tahiti Iti Peninsula: The South Coast to Teahupoo" under "The Circle Island Tour," earlier). It's a long haul, but its white sands, clear lagoon, and snack bar make it worth the trip.

SURFING   Tahiti is famous for world-class surfing, especially Teuhupoo on Tahiti Iti, home of the annual Billabong Pro championships in May. The best big waves crash on jagged reefs offshore, however, so you could be turned into hamburger meat if you've never surfed before. On the other hand, **Ecole de Surf Tura'i Mataare (Tahiti Surf School; ℂ 41.91.37**; www.tahitisurfschool.info) teaches half-day surfing and body-boarding courses for 4,800CFP (US$48), or you can take private lessons for 12,000CFP (US$120). It's a good way to find out if you have what it takes to "hang ten."

7 Shopping

There's no shortage of things to buy on Tahiti, especially in Papeete. Black pearls and handicrafts are sure to tempt you. The selection is widest here, but prices on some items may be better on Moorea.

If you just can't live without visiting a modern shopping mall, head for the **Centre Moana Nui,** on the main road in Punaauia about .5km (¼ mile) south of the Sofitel Tahiti Resort. Here you'll find a huge Carrefour supermarket, several boutiques, a snack bar with excellent hamburgers, a hairdresser, a bar, banks with ATMs, and a post office (open Mon–Fri 8am–5pm, Sat 8am–noon). The local **Centre Artisinant** stands across the parking lot under a teepee-shaped roof (see "Handicrafts," below).

Duty-free shopping is very limited, with French perfumes the best deal. **Duty Free Tahiti (ℂ 42.61.61**), on the street-level waterside of the Centre Vaima, is the largest duty-free shop. Its specialties are Seiko, Lorus, and Cartier watches and Givenchy, Yves St. Laurent, Chanel, and Guerlain perfumes. The **airport departure lounge** has two duty-free shops.

BLACK PEARLS

Papeete has scores of *bijouteries* (jewelry shops) that carry black pearls in a variety of settings. Some stalls in Papeete's Municipal Market sell pearls, but give them a miss

---

Tips Touring Tahiti from Moorea . . . & Vice Versa

You can take a circle island tour or safari expedition of Tahiti even if you're staying on Moorea. Catch an early flight or ferry to Papeete, go on the tour or safari expedition, and return to Moorea in the late afternoon. Let the tour companies know you're coming from Moorea when you make your reservation so they can meet you at the airport or ferry dock. If you do it yourself, the rental-car companies can have a vehicle waiting on Tahiti. **Avis (ℂ 56.32.68** on Moorea) has special packages including air or ferry fares and a car on Tahiti, starting at 9,600CFP (US$96) via ferry and a 1-day rental.

By the same token, I would spend a day on Moorea even if I had a short lay-over on Tahiti. You can easily arrange it yourself by ferry or plane, but you will need a rental vehicle on Moorea (Avis or Europcar will have one waiting for you at the Moorea airport or ferry dock). An alternative is to take a Moorea day tour, such as those offered by **Tahiti Nui Travel (ℂ 54.02.00**; www.tahitinui travel.com). It charges between 10,300CFP and 14,100CFP (US$103–US$141), depending on whether you fly or take the ferry. Call or book at any hotel activi-ties desk.

Tips Pick a Clear Day

The safari expeditions do not go into the mountains when the weather is bad, and even if it's not raining, clouds atop the mountains can obscure what would otherwise be some fantastic views. It's best, therefore, to pick as clear a day as possible for this thrilling outing. Your best chance for that will be during the drier austral winter, June through early September.

---

and buy yours from an experienced, reputable dealer. Most of these stores are in or around the Centre Vaima, along boulevard Pomare, and in the Quartier du Commerce, the narrow streets off boulevard Pomare between rue Paul Gauguin and rue d'Ecole des Frères north of the Municipal Market.

Your beginning point should be the **Musée de la Perle Robert Wan,** on the rue Jeanne d'Arc side of the Centre Vaima (© **45.21.22**). Named for Robert Wan, the man who pioneered the local industry back in the 1960s, this museum explains the history of pearls from antiquity, the method by which they are cultured, and the things to look for when making your selection. The museum is open Monday through Saturday from 9:30am to noon and 1 to 4:15pm. Admission is 600CFP (US$6) per person.

Adjoining the museum, **Tahiti Perles** (© **45.05.05**) carries only excellent-quality pearls and uses only 18-karat gold for its settings, so the prices tend to be high. Tahiti Perles has outlets on all the main islands.

On the second level of the Centre Vaima, **Sibani Perles Joallier** (© **41.36.34**) carries the jewelry line of Didier Sibani, another pioneer of the local industry. European-style elegance is the theme here and at the other Sibani outlets throughout the islands.

HANDICRAFTS

Although most of the inexpensive souvenir items sold here are made in Asia, many local residents, especially on the outer islands, produce a wide range of seashell jewelry, rag dolls, needlework, and straw hats, mats, baskets, and handbags. I love the *tivaivai,* colorful appliqué quilts stitched together by Tahitian women as their great-grandmothers were shown by the early missionaries. You can also buy exquisite shell chandeliers like those adorning many hotel lobbies.

The most popular item by far is the cotton *pareu,* or wraparound sarong, which everyone wears at one time or another. They are screened, blocked, or printed by hand in the colors of the rainbow. The same material is made into other tropical clothing and various items such as bedspreads and pillowcases. Pareus are sold virtually everywhere a visitor might wander.

The **Papeete Municipal Market** ✶✶✶ is the place to shop (see "Tahiti's Top Attractions," earlier). It has stalls both upstairs and on the surrounding sidewalk, where local women's associations offer a wide selection of handicrafts at reasonable prices. The market is one of the few places where you can regularly find pareus for 1,000CFP (US$10), bedspreads made of the colorful tie-dyed and silk-screened pareu material, and tivaivai quilts. By and large, cloth goods are sold at the sidewalk stalls; those upstairs have a broader range of shell jewelry and other items.

Several villages have *centres artisanats,* where local women display their wares. The one in Punaauia, in the Centre Moana Nui parking lot south of the Sofitel Tahiti

Resort, is the best place to look for tivaivai quilts, which sell for about 35,000CFP (US$350).

For finer-quality handicrafts, such as wood carvings from the Marquesas Islands, shell chandeliers, tapa lamp shades, or mother-of-pearl shells, try **Tamara Curios,** on rue du Général-de-Gaulle in Fare Tony (© **42.54.42**).

Buying Your Black Pearl ✿✿✿

French Polynesia is the world's largest producer of cultured black pearls. They are cultured by implanting a small nucleus into the shell of a live *Pinctada margaritifera,* the oyster used here, which then coats it with nacre, the same lustrous substance that lines the mother-of-pearl shell. The nacre produces dark pearls known as "black" but whose actual color ranges from slightly grayer than white to black with shades of rose or green. Most range in size from 10mm to 17mm (slightly less than a ½ in. to slightly less than ¾ in.).

Size, color, luster, lack of imperfections, and shape determine a pearl's value. No two are exactly alike, but the most valuable are the larger ones that are most symmetrical and have few dark blemishes, and whose color is dark with the shades of a peacock showing through a bright luster. A top-quality pearl 13mm (½ in.) or larger will sell for US$10,000 or more, but there are thousands to choose from in the $300-to-$1,000 range. Some small, imperfect-but-still-lovely pearls cost much less.

So many pearls were being produced a few years ago that many small pearl farms closed. Competition is still fierce among the islands' shops (or their agents—commissioned tour guides and bus and taxi drivers), some of which will bombard you with sales pitches almost from the moment you arrive. Even at the highest-end shops, discounting is *de rigeur.* Despite the general rule to avoid haggling in French Polynesia, you shouldn't pay the price marked on a pearl or a piece of jewelry until you have politely asked for a discount.

With most tourists now spending minimum time on Tahiti in favor of the other islands, you might find pearl prices in Papeete to be lower than on Moorea and Bora Bora. That's not always the case, so you should look in shops like **Ron Hall's Island Fashion Black Pearls** (on Moorea) and **Matira Pearls** (on Bora Bora) before making a purchase in Papeete (see "Shopping" in chapters 5 and 8, respectively). Your salesperson over there is more likely to speak English fluently.

You can get a refund of the 16% **value added tax** (TVA) included in the price of set pearls (but not on loose pearls). The TVA is not added after the purchase like an American sales tax, so you won't see it. Don't believe them if they say you can't get a refund because they've already taken the TVA off a reduced price. Truth is, they'll have to send the government 16% of whatever price you paid. Ask your dealer how to get your money back by sending them an official form after you have left the country (you can mail it after clearing Immigration at Faaa).

Impressions

It's a comfort to get into a pareu when one gets back from town . . . I should strongly recommend you to adopt it. It's one of the most sensible costumes I have ever come across. It's cool, convenient, and inexpensive.
                    —W. Somerset Maugham, "The Fall of Edward Bernard," 1921

TROPICAL CLOTHING

You've arrived in Tahiti and you notice that everyone under the sun is wearing print sundresses or flowered aloha shirts. Where do you go to get yours?

Each hotel has at least one boutique carrying tropical clothing, including pareus. The prices there reflect the heavy tourist traffic, but they aren't much worse than at the stores in Papeete. Clothing, to put it bluntly, is dear in French Polynesia.

On boulevard Pomare, stop in **Marie Ah You** (© **42.03.31**) and **Aloha Boutique** (© **42.87.52**), both in the block west of the Vaima Centre. Their selections for women are trendy and a bit expensive.

Tahiti Art, in Fare Tony on boulevard Pomare just west of the Vaima Centre, (© **42. 97.43**), specializes in block-printed traditional designs (as opposed to the swirls and swooshes with leaves and flowers popular on most pareus). Its designs are the most unique in town.

8 Where to Stay

With a few exceptions, you will find Tahiti's accommodations in three areas: on the west coast, where most properties enjoy at least a partial view of Moorea; in the suburbs east of Papeete, where the beaches are of black volcanic sand; and in the city of Papeete, where you can sample urban life *a la Tahitien.* Consider staying at one of the west-coast or Papeete city hotels near the airport if you're stopping here for just a night on your way to or from the other islands or a cruise ship. This is especially true if your connecting flight departs during the horrendous traffic of a weekday morning or evening rush hour.

THE WEST COAST
EXPENSIVE

Inter-Continental Resort Tahiti ✶✶✶   This is the best all-around resort on Tahiti. Built in the 1960s as the Tahiti Beachcomber Travelodge, it was more recently named the Inter-Continental Tahiti Beachcomber Resort. Most folks here still call it "the Beachcomber," and many would like a return to its old, familiar name. It sits at Tataa Point on the island's northwest corner, from whence souls supposedly leaped to the ancient Polynesian homeland. Today planes leap into the air from the nearby airport at Faaa, although the jet noise seldom penetrates the rooms here. It has a range of accommodations, including smaller rooms dating from its original Travelodge incarnation, newer and more spacious "Panoramic" rooms, and overwater bungalows with unimpeded views of Moorea. Whatever the vintage, all units are now luxuriously appointed with the likes of canopy beds and marble bathrooms, and all have private patios or balconies with views of Moorea. The original overwater units are smaller than the newer models on the resort's south end, which have separate sitting areas and steps leading from their decks into the lagoon.

Tahiti Accommodations & Dining

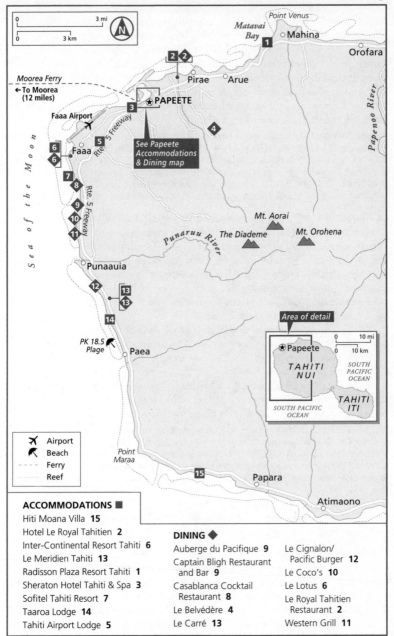

ACCOMMODATIONS ■

Hiti Moana Villa **15**
Hotel Le Royal Tahitien **2**
Inter-Continental Resort Tahiti **6**
Le Meridien Tahiti **13**
Radisson Plaza Resort Tahiti **1**
Sheraton Hotel Tahiti & Spa **3**
Sofitel Tahiti Resort **7**
Taaroa Lodge **14**
Tahiti Airport Lodge **5**

DINING ◆

Auberge du Pacifique **9**
Captain Bligh Restaurant and Bar **9**
Casablanca Cocktail Restaurant **8**
Le Belvédère **4**
Le Carré **13**

Le Cignalon/ Pacific Burger **12**
Le Coco's **10**
Le Lotus **6**
Le Royal Tahitien Restaurant **2**
Western Grill **11**

The resort doesn't have a natural beach, but bulkheads separate the sea from white imported sand. Or you can frolic in two pools—one in a large complex sitting lagoon-side before the main building or the other smaller pool with water cascading over its horizon (and apparently into the lagoon). The latter is adjacent to the romantic **Le Lotus** (p. 109), one of the Tahiti's best restaurants. Features here include an all-night lobby bar and the best watersports center on Tahiti. I love to stay here between jaunts to the outer islands because I can clean my dirty clothes in the free washers and dry-ers, a real money-saver given the exorbitant cost of laundry services (buy your soap powder before the boutique closes at 7pm).

B.P. 6014, 98702 Faaa (8km/5 miles west of Papeete). (C) **800/327-0200** or 86.51.10. Fax 86.51.30. www.tahiti. interconti.com. 214 units. 34,800CFP–59,400CFP (US$384–US$594) double; 76,100CFP–84,000CFP (US$761–US$840) suite; 51,600CFP–74,400CFP (US$516–US$744) overwater bungalow. AE, DC, MC, V. **Amenities:** 2 restaurants; 2 bars; 2 outdoor pools; tennis courts; health club; Jacuzzi; watersports equipment/rentals; concierge; activities desk; car-rental desk; 24-hr. business center with high-speed Internet access; salon; 24-hr. room service; massage; babysitting; laundry service; washers and dryers. *In room:* A/C, TV, dataport, minibar, coffeemaker, hair dryer, iron, safe.

Le Meridien Tahiti ★★   Two blocks from the Museum of Tahiti and Her Islands, this luxury resort sits alongside one of Tahiti's few white-sand beaches. It's an excellent choice—provided you don't have to get to Tahiti-Faaa International Airport to catch a flight during the weekday morning traffic jam, when the usual 15-minute ride can take considerably longer. The Melanesian-inspired architecture is stunning, with swayback shingle roofs evoking the "spirit houses" of Papua New Guinea. Imported sand surrounding the wade-in pool compensates for the pebbly beach and shallow lagoon here. The best accommodations are 12 overwater bungalows, but note that unlike most others, they have neither glass panels in their floors for fish-watching nor steps into the lagoon from their porches. The luxuriously appointed guest quarters have balconies, but try to get a north-facing unit for a Moorea view. Le Meridien pro-vides complimentary *le truck* shuttles into Papeete twice a day and on two evenings a week. **Le Carré** (p. 109) is one of the best resort dining rooms in French Polynesia. A shopping center next door has a grocery store, hairdresser, pharmacy, post office, restaurants, and a patisserie for inexpensive breakfasts.

B.P. 380595, 98718 Punaauia (15km/9 miles south of Papeete, 8km/5 miles south of the airport). (C) **800/225-5843** or 47.07.07. Fax 47.07.08. www.starwoodtahiti.com. 150 units. 35,000CFP (US$350) double; 45,000CFP–85,000CFP (US$450–US$850) suite; 50,000CFP (US$500) overwater bungalow. AE, DC, MC, V. **Amenities:** 2 restaurants; 2 bars; outdoor pool; tennis court; health club; watersports equipment/rentals; concierge; activities desk; car-rental desk; 24-hr. room service; babysitting; laundry service; Wi-Fi. *In room:* A/C, TV, dataport, minibar, coffeemaker, hair dryer, iron, safe.

Tips It Pays to Shop for Room Rates

Like many big hotels these days, those in French Polynesia adjust their room rates according to such factors as the season and how many guests they expect to have on a given day, and many offer Internet specials on their websites. Accordingly, their published "rack rates"—which I am compelled to give in this book—are nearly meaningless. For example, Le Meridien Tahiti recently offered an Internet special of 17,000CFP (US$170) a night for a standard room, less than half the rack rate of 35,000CFP (US$350). In other words, it can pay bountifully to shop around. See also "Tips on Accommodations" (p. 52).

Sofitel Tahiti Resort   Recently given a thorough facelift, this midrise hotel was built in the 1960s to resemble a modern version of a terraced Mayan pyramid. Formerly the Sofitel Maeva Beach Tahiti, it sits beside Maeva Bay and a gray-sand beach of the same name. The murky lagoon off the beach isn't as good for swimming and snorkeling as for anchoring numerous yachts, whose masts slice the beach's view of Moorea. The smallish rooms are equipped with modern European amenities (the bright, lime-green bathrooms nearly blinded me) and open to balconies. Those on the upper floors on the north (or "beach") side have partial views of Moorea, while those on the garden side look south along Tahiti's west coast. The Maeva Beach is often featured in some of the least expensive package tours. While adequate if cost is a major consideration, don't expect the same amount of space, luxuries, or amenities as at the Inter-Continental Resort Tahiti or Le Meridien.

B.P. 6008, 98702 Faaa (7.5km/4 miles west of Papeete). ✆ **800/763-4835** or 86.66.00. Fax 41.05.05. www. sofitel.com. 230 units. 29,500CFP–37,500CFP (US$295–US$375) double; 55,500CFP (US$555) suite. AE, DC, MC, V. **Amenities:** 2 restaurants; 2 bars; outdoor pool; tennis courts; watersports equipment/rentals; concierge; activities desk; car-rental desk; limited room service; babysitting; laundry service. *In room:* A/C, TV, minibar, coffeemaker, hair dryer, iron, safe.

MODERATE
Hiti Moana Villa ✦   Beside the lagoon in Papara, on the southwest coast, this is one of Tahiti's better family-operated pensions. Owner Steve Brotherson keeps everything running smoothly, while his mother, Henriette, tends the lush gardens and goldfish pond. Half the units here are standard government-issue bungalows; that is, each consists of one room for living and sleeping, an attached bathroom, and a front porch. They can also grab noise from the round-island road, so consider paying more for a one-bedroom lagoonside unit, each of which has an ocean view from its front porch. There is no beach on the premises, but you can swim in the pool or rent a canoe, kayak, or motorboat to play in the lagoon. English-speaking Steve will take you on a guided tour of the island. Restaurants, snack bars, and grocery stores are nearby.

B.P. 20055, 98718 Papara (PK 32 in Papara). ✆ **57.93.93.** Fax 57.94.44. www.papeete.com/moanavilla. 8 units. 10,000CFP–14,500CFP (US$100–US$145). AE, MC, V. 2-night minimum stay required. **Amenities:** Outdoor pool; watersports equipment/rentals; coin-op washer and dryer. *In room:* TV, kitchen, no phone.

INEXPENSIVE
Taaroa Lodge   Avid surfer Ralph Sanford bought the two bungalows at his humble lagoonside establishment in ritzy Paea as prefabricated kits in New Zealand; hence, they are larger and have more character than the cookie-cutter *fares* found at most small family-run establishments here. And their porches present million-dollar views of Moorea, especially the one sitting beside the bulkhead along the lagoon. Each has a kitchen, TV, and ceiling fan. Behind them, an A-frame chalet houses a room with double bed downstairs and a six-bed dormitory in the loft. The communal kitchen stays busy, as do Ralph's free kayaks (bring your own snorkeling gear). Grocery stores and snack bars are short walks away. In my opinion, this is the top backpacker accommodation on Tahiti, even if you do have to stay at least 2 nights.

B.P. 498, 98713 Papeete (PK 18.2 in Punaauia). ✆ and fax **58.39.21.** www.taaroalodge.com. 1 room, 2 bungalows, 6 dorm beds (shared bathroom). 6,000CFP (US$60) double, 10,000CFP (US$100) bungalow, 2,500CFP (US$25) dorm bed. Rates include breakfast. MC, V. 2-night minimum stay. **Amenities:** Communal kitchen; free kayaks. *In room (bungalows only):* TV, kitchen, coffeemaker, no phone.

EAST OF PAPEETE

EXPENSIVE

Radisson Plaza Resort Tahiti *ℰ*   This modern resort opened in 2004 beside a beach of deep black sand on Matavai Bay, where the 18th-century explorers dropped anchor. A huge, turtle-shaped thatch roof covers most of the central complex, which holds a restaurant, bar, arts-and-crafts center, full-service spa, and cozy library devoted to author James Norman Hall. Outside is a horizon-edge pool beside the beach. Currents create an undertow here, so heed the "Dangerous Sea" signs when swimming in the lagoon. Seven hotel buildings hold the accommodations, which include standard rooms, two-story townhouse-style "duplexes" (their upstairs bedrooms have their own balconies), suites, and—my favorites—rooms with hot tubs romantically placed behind louvers on the balconies. Furnishings and decor are tropical with a European flair. Try to get a unit in buildings numbered 1 through 3, which have views of Moorea on the horizon (those in buildings 4 through 7 look out to an empty horizon). The Radisson sends a shuttle to downtown Papeete each morning and afternoon, but public buses do not run out here after 5pm, meaning you will need to rent a car or take a taxi to get to and from downtown after dark. All units have high-speed Internet ports, making this a very good bet for business travelers with expense accounts for rental cars. As at Le Meridien Tahiti, rush-hour traffic can make for a long trek to the airport from here.

B.P. 14170, 98701 Arue (on Matavai Bay, 7km/4.2 miles east of downtown). ℰ **800/333-3333** or 48.88.88. Fax 48.88.89. www.radisson.com/aruefrp. 165 units. 32,000CFP–38,000CFP (US$320–US$380) double; 41,300CFP–42,600CFP (US$413–US$426) suite. AE, DC, MC. V. **Amenities:** Restaurant; 2 bars; outdoor pool; health club; spa; Jacuzzi; watersports equipment/rentals; activities desk; car-rental desk; business center; salon; 24-hr. room service; massage; babysitting; laundry service; concierge-level rooms. *In room:* A/C, TV, high-speed dataport, minibar, coffeemaker, hairdryer, iron, safe.

MODERATE

Hotel Le Royal Tahitien *ℰℰ* (Value)   One of the top values in French Polynesia, this American-owned hotel is the only moderately priced place on the island with its own beach, a stretch of deep black sand from which its suburban neighbors fish and swim. And long-time Australian-born manager Lionel Kennedy (a die-hard baseball fan) and his English-speaking staff are Tahiti's best when it comes to friendly, personalized service. Sitting in an expansive lawn and lush garden traversed by a small stream, the swimming pool sports a Jacuzzi and a waterfall cascading over rocks. The spacious guest rooms are in contemporary two-story wood-and-stone buildings that look like an American condominium complex. Colorful bedspreads and seat cushions add an island ambience to the rooms, however, and the tropics definitely pervade **Le Royal Tahitien Restaurant** (p. 110), a fine, moderately priced establishment with a 1937 vintage thatch ceiling. Both the beachside restaurant and adjacent bar are popular with local businesspeople. A local band plays on Friday and Saturday evenings. Your fellow guests are likely to be businesspersons living on the other islands and travelers who have made their own arrangements (that is, few groups stay here). It's very popular, so reserve as soon as possible. As with the Radisson Plaza (see above), you will need to rent a car or take a taxi if going downtown after dark, since the last local bus passes here about 5pm.

B.P. 5001, 98716 Pirae (4km/2½ miles east of downtown). ℰ **818/843-6068** or 50.40.40. Fax 50.40.41. www.hotel royaltahitien.com. 40 units. 18,000CFP (US$180) double. AE, DC, MC, V. Take a Mahina bus or follow av. Prince Hinoi to the Total and Mobil stations opposite each other; turn around at next traffic circle and return; turn right to hotel. **Amenities:** Restaurant; bar; outdoor pool; Jacuzzi; laundry service. *In room:* A/C, TV, fridge, coffeemaker.

IN PAPEETE
EXPENSIVE

Sheraton Hotel Tahiti & Spa 😴😴   A 15-minute walk to downtown and a quick drive to the airport, this state-of-the-art hotel stands on the site of the old Hotel Tahiti, whose massive thatch-roofed public areas hosted many a local soiree. With Tahiti's largest meeting space, the Sheraton still serves as one of the city's prime gathering places. Curving steps under a huge shell chandelier lead down to Quinn's Bar, an overwater dining room, and an expansive courtyard with restaurant and lagoonside swimming pool, which helps compensate for the lack of beach here. A hot tub perched atop a pile of rocks beside the pool offers a terrific view of Moorea. Except for 10 suites, which have one or two bedrooms, the spacious units are virtually identical except for the vistas off their private balconies. "Superior" units directly face Moorea, but you actually pay less for them since they are slightly smaller than the "deluxe lagoon" units facing the open ocean or harbor (someone who's never been to Tahiti must have devised that policy). This is a very good choice for a short layover when you don't need a beach. Top Dive, one of French Polynesia's best operators, has a base here.

B.P. 416, 98713 Papeete (1km/½ mile west of downtown, 6km/3½ miles east of the airport). © 800/325-3535 or 86.48.48. Fax 86.48.40. www.sheratontahiti.com. 200 units. 30,000CFP–37,000CFP (US$300–US$370) double; 55,000CFP–85,000CFP (US$550–US$850) suite. AE, DC, MC, V. **Amenities:** 2 restaurants; bar; outdoor pool; health club; spa; concierge; activities desk; car-rental desk; salon; limited room service; massage; babysitting; laundry service; Wi-Fi. *In room:* A/C, TV, dataport, minibar, coffeemaker, hair dryer, iron, safe.

MODERATE

Hotel Le Mandarin   Attractive primarily to business travelers and cost-conscious tourists heading to the cruise ships, this Chinese-accented hotel is a bit shopworn but is in a somewhat quieter downtown location—on rue Collette opposite the Town Hall—than is the Hotel Tiare Tahiti Noa Noa (see below). My friend Dick Beaulieu likes to stay at Le Mandarin when he comes over from Fiji because its central-city location puts him close to most offices and many restaurants, thus avoiding a bundle in taxi fares. Most rooms are rather smallish, but many have narrow balconies with mountain views. There's a coffee shop in the hotel, and **Le Mandarin** dining room next door is one of the city's better Chinese restaurants.

B.P. 302, 98713 Papeete. © 50.33.50. Fax 42.16.32. 37 units. 15,000CFP–17,000CFP (US$150–US$170) double. AE, MC, V. **Amenities:** 2 restaurants; 2 bars; laundry service. *In room:* A/C, TV, dataport, fridge.

Hotel Tiare Tahiti Noa Noa   This upstairs, five-story facility, on boulevard Pomare a block west of the Centre Vaima, is simple but clean. Amenities are scarce, but the friendly front-desk staffers speak English and are adept at helping you arrange tours and other activities. Many overseas guests here are on low-budget package tours or are heading to one of the cruise ships. The rooms are minimally furnished and can be noisy, since most face directly onto the busy boulevard. Be sure to request a unit on the upper floors, which are quieter and have better views from their slim, unfurnished balconies. Continental breakfast is available in an open-air room on the second floor.

B.P. 2359, 98713 Papeete. © 50.01.00. Fax 43.68.47. hoteltiaretahiti@mail.pf. 38 units. 16,300CFP–17,000CFP (US$163–US$170) double. AE, MC, V. **Amenities:** Restaurant (breakfast only); laundry service. *In room:* A/C, TV.

INEXPENSIVE

Ahitea Lodge *Finds*   Tucked away on an alley between Prince Hinoi and Chef Vairaatoa avenues, about 5 blocks inland from the Moorea ferry docks, this modern, two-story house provides an oasis in the midst of a closely packed Tahitian neighborhood. A high fence surrounds the house and lush yard with an outdoor pool and a pond stocked with tropical fish. The least expensive units are in an attached building, but these all share toilets and showers, and they have small fresh-air vents instead of windows. Preferable are bedrooms in the main house, especially those upstairs that open to a balcony overlooking the pool and pond. Best of these is a corner unit with TV, fridge, private bathroom, and air-conditioning (it is the only air-conditioned unit here); it is so popular that you should reserve it several months in advance. The hosts provide a tropical breakfast in the communal kitchen each morning. As with Pension Puea (see below), staying here will expose you to modern urban life as lived by middle- and working-class Tahitians.

Av. Chef Vairaatoa, 98713 Papeete. ✆ **53.13.53.** Fax 42.09.35. www.ahitea-lodge.com. 13 units (9 with bathroom). 8,500CFP–15,500CFP (US$85–US$155). Rates include tropical breakfast. AE, MC, V. **Amenities:** Outdoor pool, communal kitchen. *In room:* A/C (1 unit), TV (2 units), fridge (1 unit), no phone.

Pension Puea *(Finds* About a block from Ahitea Lodge (see above), this simple but friendly pension appeals to backpackers and other cost-conscious travelers who want to stay without frills in Papeete. Guests swap yarns in the TV lounge under a lean-to roof, which covers the open-air communal kitchen and lounge with plastic tables and chairs (breakfast is served here daily). The bright, well-ventilated rooms are all upstairs. Largest and best are the three air-conditioned family units with either two double beds or a double and a single. One of these also has a private bathroom (the other units share two toilets and two showers). To my mind, this is the best place to unload your backpack in Papeete, but it lags behind the west coast's Taaroa Lodge (see above).

B.P. 5597, 98716 Pirae (87 rue Pasteur Octave Moreau, Papeete). ✆ **85.43.43.** Fax 42.09.35. pension.puea@mail.pf. 6 units (5 with shared bathroom). 6,500CFP–8,500CFP (US$65–US$85). MC, V. Rates include tropical breakfast. **Amenities:** Communal kitchen. *In room:* A/C (3 units), no phone.

Tahiti Airport Lodge Perched on the side of a hill in the Cité de l'Air housing development above the airport, Charlie and Margarite Bredin's simple but clean and friendly bed-and-breakfast commands a spectacular view of Moorea from its lovely, open-air guest lounge. Unfortunately, you won't get this view from any of the rather dark rooms, which range from ample motel-size units with king-size beds and private bathrooms down to tiny shared-bathroom units barely big enough to accommodate a double bed. All rooms have fans and electric mosquito deterrents, and all showers dispense hot water. The house is a steep, 5-minute climb from the round-island road, but Charlie will pick you up from the airport or the bus stop. Charlie and Margarite speak English as well as French.

B.P. 2580, 98713 Papeete (PK 5.5, opposite Tahiti-Faaa International Airport). ✆ **82.23.68.** Fax 82.25.00. 10 units (4 with bathroom). 6,000CFP–8,000CFP (US$60–US$80) double. Rates include breakfast and airport transfers. No credit cards. *In room:* No phone.

9 Where to Dine

Tahiti has a plethora of excellent French, Italian, and Chinese restaurants. The ones recommended below are but a few of many; don't hesitate to strike out on your own.

Food is relatively expensive in French Polynesia, whether on the shelves of grocery stores or placed before you at a restaurant or snack bar, so be sure to see my money-saving tips under "Tips on Dining" (p. 54).

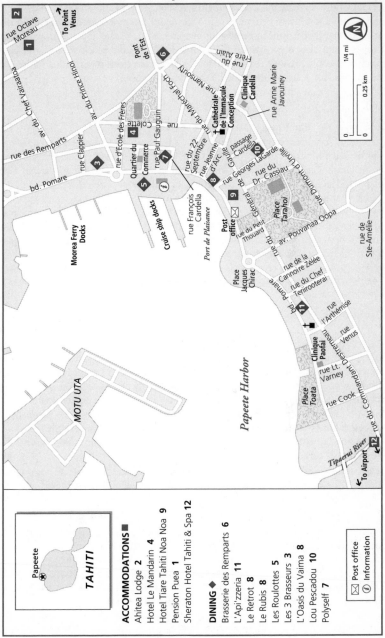

Papeete Accommodations & Dining

TAHITI

Papeete

ACCOMMODATIONS ■
Ahitea Lodge **2**
Hotel Le Mandarin **4**
Hotel Tiare Tahiti Noa Noa **9**
Pension Puea **1**
Sheraton Hotel Tahiti & Spa **12**

DINING ◆
Brasserie des Remparts **6**
L'Api'zzeria **11**
Le Retrot **8**
Le Rubis **8**
Les Roulottes **5**
Les 3 Brasseurs **3**
L'Oasis du Vaima **8**
Lou Pescadou **10**
Polyself **7**

⊠ Post office
ⓘ Information

107

Downtown Papeete has a **McDonald's** at the corner of rue du Général-de-Gaulle and rue du Dr. Cassiau behind Centre Vaima, and there's a second on the main road in Punaauia. If you want to make your own meals or a picnic, the downtown **Champion** supermarket is on rue du Général-de-Gaulle in the block west of the Eglise Evangélique. On the west coast, head for the huge **Carrefour** supermarket in the Centre Moana Nui, south of the Sofitel Tahiti Resort.

THE WEST COAST
EXPENSIVE

Auberge du Pacifique ✹✹✹ TAHITIAN/TRADITIONAL FRENCH   This lagoonside restaurant has been among Tahiti's finest since 1974. Owner Jean Galopin was named a Maître Cuisinier (Master Chef) de France in 1987, in large part because of his unique blending of French and Tahitian styles of cooking. He has shared many of his techniques in a popular cookbook, *La Cuisine de Tahiti et des Iles*. His *fafa* (chicken and taro leaves steamed in coconut milk) is in marked contrast with what comes out of a local himaa on a Sunday afternoon. The roof over the main dining room opens to reveal the twinkling stars above. Guests are welcome to visit the air-conditioned wine cellar and choose from among excellent French vintages. A special tourist menu features *poisson cru* and main courses such as a light mahimahi soufflé.

PK 11.2, Punaauia. ✆ **43.98.30.** Reservations recommended, especially on weekends. Main courses 2,600CFP–4,000CFP (US$26–US$40). Tourist menu 5,000CFP (US$50). AE, MC, V. Mon–Sat 11:30am–2:30pm and 6:30–10pm.

Captain Bligh Restaurant and Bar   TRADITIONAL FRENCH   One of Tahiti's last large, thatch-roofed buildings covers this restaurant beside the lagoon (you can toss bread crumbs to the fish swimming just over the railing). The food is not the best on the island, but you can't beat the old Tahitian charm. Specialties of the house are grilled steaks and lobster. Get here early to graze the all-you-can-eat lunchtime salad bar, which is so popular with locals that it quickly disappears. One of the island's top Tahitian dance troupes performs here Friday and Saturday nights after a seafood buffet—the 5,000CFP (US$50) per-person price is an excellent value compared to the resort hotels' buffets and dance shows. You can sample local food at the *ma'a Tahiti* buffet Sunday at noon. A pier goes out to the Lagoonarium here (see "Tahiti's Top Attractions," earlier).

At the Lagoonarium, PK 11.4, Punaauia. ✆ **43.62.90.** Reservations recommended on weekends. Burgers 1,300CFP (US$13); lunch salad bar 1,700CFP (US$17); main courses 1,800CFP–3,400CFP (US$18–US$34). AE, MC, V. Tues–Sun 11am–2:30pm and 6:30–10pm; bar 9am–10pm.

Casablanca Cocktail Restaurant ✹✹ FRENCH/MEDITERRANEAN   Perched beside the yachts moored in Marina Taina, this casual restaurant is very popular with local residents, especially on weekends, when live music is featured (make Fri and Sat reservations at least 2 days in advance). Couscous on Wednesday night also draws a crowd. The main menu features French treatments of local seafood with some island twists. The menu is in French, but the friendly staff will help you decipher *le carte*. Try to get a table in one of the romantic gazebos out in the yard.

PK 9, Punaauia, at Marina Taina. ✆ **43.91.35.** Reservations recommended. Main courses 2,600CFP–4,200CFP (US$26–US$42); fixed-price dinner 4,900CFP (US$49). AE, MC, V. Daily noon–2pm and 7–10pm. Heading south, turn right into marina after first traffic circle.

Le Carré 🦋🦋 FRENCH Although not on a par with Le Lotus at the Inter-Continental Resort Tahiti (see below), Le Meridien Tahiti's fine-dining outlet has tables under a round thatch roof and romantically posited out on the deck with a view of both the beach and the resort's wade-in swimming pool—but not of Moorea. Although basically French, the cuisine has numerous island influences, such as sautéed scallops served in a "beggar's purse" of taro leaves with sauce of curry and coconut milk. The fixed-price dinners offer two or three courses.

At Le Meridien Tahiti, PK 15, Punaauia. 📞 **47.07.07.** Reservations recommended. Main courses 2,900CFP–3,800CFP (US$29–US$38). Fixed-price dinners 5,200CFP–7,600CFP (US$52–US$76). AE, DC, MC, V. Daily noon–2pm and 7–10pm.

Le Coco's 🦋🦋 FRENCH Along with Le Lotus (see below), this lagoonside restaurant shares top rank as Tahiti's most romantic place to dine, especially the tables out on the lawn, where you will have a gorgeous look at Moorea. Other tables shaded by a thatch cabana also share the view. The cuisine is light in the French nouvelle cuisine tradition, with island influences such as shrimp marinated in lime juice and coconut milk. If your credit card can withstand 12,400CFP (US$124) per person, you will be surprised during the five-course, fixed-price "at the humor of the chef" menu. There's also a scaled-down tourist menu. Arrive early enough for a drink or glass of fine champagne while the sun sets over Moorea.

PK 13.5, Punaauia. 📞 **58.21.08.** Reservations recommended. Main courses 2,650CFP–3,800CFP (US$27–US$38). Tourist menu 5,850CFP (US$59). AE, MC, V. Daily 11:30am–1:30pm and 7–9:30pm.

Le Lotus 🦋🦋🦋 CONTINENTAL/FRENCH With two round, thatch-roofed dining rooms extending over the lagoon and enjoying an uninterrupted view of Moorea, the Inter-Continental Resort Tahiti's Le Lotus has the best setting of any restaurant in French Polynesia. The widely spaced tables are all at the water's edge (a spotlight between the two dining rooms shines into the lagoon, attracting fish in search of a handout). The gourmet French fare and attentive but unobtrusive service more than live up to this romantic scene. Your choices will depend on which of Europe's top master chefs has accepted the resort's invitation to take a working vacation here. No matter who's in residence, you're in for a gastronomic delight.

At Inter-Continental Resort Tahiti, PK 7, Faaa. 📞 **86.51.10,** ext. 5512. Reservations highly recommended. Main courses 4,200CFP–5,000CFP (US$42–US$50). AE, DC, MC, V. Daily noon–2:30pm and 6:30–9:30pm.

MODERATE
Western Grill 🆔 AMERICAN After a few weeks of French fare, my American stomach begins to yearn for some good ol' Yankee food. Granted, the Western Grill is a theme restaurant—the wagon wheels, swinging saloon doors, country music, and waitstaff in cowboy hats evoke the American West—but it's also the best place on Tahiti to get a grilled steak *sans* buttery sauce. Rump steak Texas, filet Nebraska, brochette de coyote, lamb chops Geronimo: You get the picture. The "menu Pat Garrett" includes a plat du jour with an appetizer, dessert, and a glass of home-brew from Papeete's Les 3 Brasseurs (see below), which shares owners. Burgers and a TV room make this a good place to bring any young Yanks you may have in tow.

PK 12.6, Punaauia. 📞 **41.30.56.** Reservations recommended on weekends. Burgers 1,500CFP–1,700CFP (US$15–US$17); main courses 1,600CFP–2,400CFP (US$16–US$24). MC, V. Mon–Fri 11:45am–2:30pm and 7–9:30pm; Sat 7–9:30pm.

Value   **Dining with a Belle View**

I like to spend my last evening on Tahiti up at **Le Belvédère** (© **42.73.44**), for this innlike establishment has a spectacular view of the city and Moorea from its perch 600m (2,000 ft.) up in the Fare Ape Valley above Papeete. The restaurant provides round-trip transportation from your hotel up the narrow, one-lane, winding, switchback road that leads to it (I don't encourage anyone to attempt this drive in a rental car). Take the 5pm pickup so you'll reach the restaurant in time for a sunset cocktail. They'll drop you back at the airport if you're leaving that night. The specialty of the house is fondue Bourguignonne served with six sauces. The 5,900CFP (US$59) fixed-price meal includes three courses, wine, and transportation, so it is a reasonably good value. The quality of the cuisine doesn't match the view, however, so treat the evening as a sightseeing excursion, not as a fine-dining experience. Reservations are required; American Express, MasterCard, and Visa are accepted. Closed Wednesdays.

INEXPENSIVE

Le Cignalon/Pacific Burger _Value_ PIZZA/SNACK BAR   Cost-conscious guests at Le Meridien Tahiti walk next door to Pacific Burger, the open-air snack-bar side of this otherwise Italian restaurant, for good, reasonably priced salads, _poisson cru,_ sashimi, pizzas from a wood-fired oven, burgers (beef, chicken, or fish), grilled rib-eye steaks, and fish with or without sauce. A big tarp covers plastic patio tables and chairs in front of the fast-food–style counter. The menu is in French and English. The Tahiti Museum is a few blocks away, so this is a good place to stop for refreshment on your round-island tour.

PK 15, Punaauia, next to Le Meridien Tahiti. © **42.40.84.** Reservations not accepted. Burgers 450CFP–850CFP (US$4.50–US$8.50); pizza 1,000CFP–1,500CFP (US$10–US$15); main courses 1,300CFP–2,300CFP (US$13–US$23). MC, V. Tues–Thurs 10am–3pm and 5:30–9pm, Fri–Sun 10am–3pm and 5:30–9:30pm (burgers and hot dogs only 3–5pm Sun).

EAST OF PAPEETE

Le Royal Tahitien Restaurant ★★ _Value_ INTERNATIONAL   Occupying an open-air building constructed in 1937 beside the black-sand beach in Pirae, the Hotel Le Royal Tahitien's dining room provides both charm and views of the lagoon and Moorea to accompany its very good international fare. Like the hotel, it also offers excellent value for the quality of its food. The cuisine is primarily French, such as fresh mahimahi in meunière sauce, but you will find island influences here, such as very good _poisson cru_ and chicken in a pineapple sauce. Locals flock here for the big lunchtime salads, as well as for live music in the adjacent bar on Friday and Saturday evenings. Be sure to talk baseball with Australian-born Lionel Kennedy, the hotel's general manager.

At Hotel Le Royal Tahitien, PK 4, Pirae. Reservations recommended at dinner. Main courses 1,950CFP–3,250CFP (US$20–US$33). Tourist menu 3,700CFP (US$37). AE, DC, MC, V. Daily 6:30–10am, 11:30am–2:30pm, and 7–10pm.

IN PAPEETE

It was closed for vacation during my recent visit, but my foodie friend Dick Beaulieu dined at **L'O a la Bouche,** on Passage Carella behind the Vaima Centre (© **45.29.76**). He had only one word to describe the Provençal lamb and _magret_ of duck: "Superbe!"

Open for lunch Monday through Friday, dinner Monday through Saturday. Let me know what you think.

EXPENSIVE

Le Rubis ★★ REGIONAL/TRADITIONAL FRENCH   Faux grape vines (*rubis* in French) hang from the ceilings of this casual but elegant restaurant, and the mat-lined walls are adorned with numerous paintings of wine bottles and vineyards. The decor will get you in the mood to select from one of Tahiti's most extensive lists of French vintages, many of them offered by the glass. The menu suggests a match for each item. Shrimp in a sweet, slightly curried coconut-cream sauce is the star here, or you can opt for the same sauce over fresh tuna. Salmon in puff pastry and traditional French versions of steak, veal, lamb, and duck are all tasty.

16 rue Jeanne d'Arc, in Vaima Centre. ℭ **43.25.55.** Reservations recommended. Main courses 2,000CFP–3,600CFP (US$20–US$36). AE, MC, V. Tues–Thurs 11am–2pm and 6–10pm, Fri 11am–2pm and 6pm–1am, Sat 6pm–2am, Sun 6–10pm.

MODERATE

Brasserie des Remparts ★ FRENCH   The blues cascade from speakers at this American-style, brass-and-dark-wood pub, whose food is much better than at the otherwise comparable Les 3 Brasseurs (see below). Despite the 5¢-PAY-TOILET sign and other American memorabilia hanging on the walls, the chow is definitely French, with the likes of andouille sausage in mustard sauce, mahimahi meunière, an Alsatian-style casserole, Moroccan couscous, and rib-eye steaks with Roquefort, pepper, or béarnaise sauces. The French country–style *paysan* and other plate-size salads make healthy meals unto themselves. Try for a sidewalk table.

Av. Georges Clemenceau, at Rond Pont de L'Est traffic circle. ℭ **42.80.00.** Reservations recommended Fri–Sat. Main courses 1,600CFP–2,250CFP (US$16–US$23). AE, MC, V. Mon–Fri 6am–1am, Sat 8am–3pm.

L'Api'zzeria ★ (Value ITALIAN   On par with Lou Pescadou (see below) but with a garden setting, this restaurant in a grove of trees across from the waterfront has been serving very good pizza and pasta since 1968. I prefer a table outside under the trees rather than inside, which resembles an Elizabethan waterfront tavern accented with nautical relics. The food, on the other hand, is definitely Italian. Both pizzas and tender steaks are cooked in a wood-fired oven. The menu also features spaghetti, fettuccine, lasagna, steak Milanese, veal in white or Marsala wine sauce, and grilled homemade Italian sausage.

Bd. Pomare, between rue du Chef Teriirooterai and rue l'Arthémise. ℭ **42.98.30.** Reservations not accepted. Pizzas and pastas 420CFP–1,750CFP (US$4.20–US$18); meat courses 1,500CFP–2,600CFP (US$15–US$26). MC, V. Mon–Sat 11:30am–10pm.

Les 3 Brasseurs FRENCH   The quality of its food and service tends to be up and down, but this microbrewery with sidewalk tables is a fine spot for a cold one while waiting for the Moorea ferry at the docks across the boulevard. The tabloid menu is all in French, but the waitstaff speaks enough English to explain the offerings. Choose from sandwiches, salads, roast chicken served hot or cold, or grilled steaks, mahimahi, and tuna plain or with optional French sauces. *Jarret de porc,* smoked ham hocks served with sautéed potatoes and sauerkraut, reminds me of the Southern soul food of my youth. The best deal here is the *croque brasseurs,* a ham sandwich served under melted Gruyère cheese and accompanied by a beer and a green salad with excellent vinaigrette dressing, all for 900CFP (US$9).

Bd. Pomare, between rue Prince Hinoi and rue Clappier, opposite Moorea ferry docks. *C* **50.60.25.** Reservations not accepted. Sandwiches and salads 900CFP–1,700CFP (US$9–US$17); main courses 1,300CFP–2,400CFP (US$13–US$24). MC, V. Daily 9am–1am.

Lou Pescadou *C* *Value* ITALIAN   A lively young professional clientele usually packs this quintessential Italian trattoria (red-and-white-checked tablecloths, dripping candles on each table, Ruffino bottles hanging from every nook and cranny). They come for good, fresh, and tasty Italian fare at reasonable prices (be prepared to wait for a table). The individual-size pizzas are cooked in a wood-fired oven; the excellent pasta dishes include lasagna, spaghetti, and fettuccine under tomato, carbonara, and Roquefort sauces.

Rue Anne-Marie Javouhey at passage Cardella. *C* **43.74.26.** Reservations not accepted. Pizzas and pastas 600CFP–1,050CFP (US$6–US$11); meat courses 1,650CFP–2,650CFP (US$17–US$27). MC, V. Mon–Sat 11:30am–2pm and 6:30–11pm. Take the narrow passage Cardella, a 1-block street that looks like an alley, directly behind Centre Vaima.

Value **Don't Miss *Les Roulottes***

_____

Although prices in some hotel dining rooms and restaurants here can be shocking, you don't need to spend a fortune to eat reasonably well in French Polynesia. In fact, the best food bargains in Papeete literally roll out after dark on the cruise-ship docks: portable meal wagons known as *les roulottes.*

Some owners set up charcoal grills behind their trucks and small electric generators in front to provide plenty of light for the diners, who sit on stools along either side of the vehicles. A few operate during the daytime, but most begin arriving about 6pm. The entire waterfront soon takes on a carnival atmosphere, especially on Friday and Saturday nights. So many cruise-ship passengers and other tourists eat here that most truck owners speak some English.

The traditional menu includes charbroiled steaks or chicken with french fries (known, respectively, as *steak frites* and *poulet frites*), familiar Cantonese dishes, *poisson cru,* and *salade russe* (Russian-style potato salad, tinted red by beet-root juice) for 950CFP to 1,500CFP (US$9.50–US$15) per plate. Glassed-in display cases along the sides of some trucks hold actual examples of what's offered at each (not exactly the most appetizing exhibits, but you can just point to what you want rather than fumbling in French). You'll find just as many trucks specializing in crepes, pizzas, couscous, and waffles *(gaufres).* Even if you don't order an entire meal at *les roulottes,* stop for a crepe or waffle and enjoy the scene.

Although they now have permanent homes, the open-air restaurants at **Place Toata,** on the western end of the waterfront, were born as roulottes, and they still offer the same fare and prices as their mobile siblings. They're open for lunch Monday through Saturday, for dinner Friday and Saturday.

Fun Fact   A Most Indecent Song & Dance

The young girls whenever they can collect 8 or 10 together dance a very indecent dance which they call Timorodee singing most indecent songs and useing most indecent actions in the practice of which they are brought up from their earlyest Childhood.

—Capt. James Cook, after seeing his first Tahitian dance show in 1769

The Tahitian dances described by the great explorer in 1769 left little doubt as to the temptations that inspired the mutiny on the *Bounty* a few years later. At the time Cook arrived, the Tahitians would stage a *heiva* (festival) for almost any reason, from blessing the harvest to celebrating a birth. After eating meals cooked in earth ovens, they would get out the drums and nose flutes and dance the night away. Some of the dances involved elaborate costumes, and others were quite lasciviously and explicitly danced in the nude or seminude, which added to Tahiti's reputation as an island of love.

The puritanical Protestant missionaries would have none of that and put an end to dancing in the early 1820s. Of course, strict prohibition never works, and Tahitians—including a young Queen Pomare—would sneak into the hills to dance. Only after the French took over in 1842 was dancing permitted again, and then only with severe limitations on what the dancers could do and wear. A result of these varied restrictions was that most of the traditional dances performed by the Tahitians before 1800 were nearly forgotten within 100 years.

You'd never guess that Tahitians ever stopped dancing, for after tourists started coming in 1961 they went back to the old ways. Today traditional dancing is a huge part of their lives—and of every visitor's itinerary. No one goes away without vivid memories of the elaborate and colorful costumes, the thundering drums, and the swinging hips of a Tahitian *tamure* in which young men and women provocatively dance around one another.

The *tamure* is one of several dances performed during a typical dance show. Others are the *o'tea*, in which men and women in spectacular costumes dance certain themes, such as spear throwing, fighting, or love; the *aparima*, the hand dance, which emphasizes everyday themes, such as bathing and combing one's hair; the *hivinau*, in which men and women dance in circles and exclaim *"hiri haa haa"* when they meet each other; and the *pata'uta'u*, in which the dancers beat the ground or their thighs with their open hands. It's difficult to follow the themes without understanding Tahitian, but the color and rhythms (which have been influenced by faster, double-time beats from the Cook Islands) make the dances thoroughly enjoyable.

INEXPENSIVE

In addition to checking your e-mail, you can get a healthy salad or sandwich at American expatriate Nina Piermatti's **Tiki Soft Café,** on rue Paul Gauguin at the Rond Point de L'Est traffic circle (© **88.93.98**). See "Fast Facts: Tahiti," earlier in this chapter.

Le Retrot FRENCH/ITALIAN/SNACKS You'll find better food elsewhere, but this Parisian-style sidewalk cafe is Papeete's best place to rendezvous or to grab a quick bite, a drink, or an ice cream while watching the world pass along the quay. A diverse selection of salads, sandwiches, pizzas, and pasta gets attention from the cafe crowd.

Bd. Pomare, front of Centre Vaima, on waterfront. (✆ **42.86.83**. Reservations not necessary. Salads, sandwiches, and burgers 450CFP–1,200CFP (US$4.50–US$12); pizza and pastas 800CFP–1,900CFP (US$8–US$19); main courses 1,800CFP–2,100CFP (US$18–US$21). AE, MC, V. Daily 6am–midnight.

L'Oasis du Vaima SNACK BAR You'll find me having a breakfast of a small quiche or a tasty pastry with strong French coffee at this kiosklike building on the southwest corner of Centre Vaima. In addition to dishing out ice cream and milkshakes to passersby at a sidewalk counter, it serves up a variety of goodies, from crispy *casse-croûtes* to two substantial *plats-du-jour* selections each day, on a covered dining terrace and in an air-conditioned dining room upstairs.

Rue du Général-de-Gaulle at rue Jeanne d'Arc (at the corner of Centre Vaima, opposite Cathédrale de l'Immaculée Conception). (✆ **45.45.01**. Reservations not necessary. Sandwiches, burgers, quiches, and small pizzas 350CFP–900CFP (US$3.50–US$9); meals 1,500CFP–2,000CFP (US$15–US$20). No credit cards. Mon–Sat 5am–5pm.

Polyself CAFETERIA I have stopped by this cafeteria for a quick breakfast or lunch for years. The stainless-steel counter in this air-conditioned, no-smoking establishment presents a selection of sandwiches, salads, Chinese dishes, and French fare such as chicken in cream sauce. No English is necessary; just point to what you want. Dim-sum dumplings augment such traditional French breakfast fare as croissants and coffee, or you can order eggs cooked any way you like them. The food isn't among the best in town, but you get a lot of it for the money.

Rue Paul Gauguin, between bd. Pomare and rue Colette. (✆ **43.25.32**. Reservations not accepted. Sandwiches and salads 100CFP–250CFP (US$1–US$2.50); main courses 600CFP–950CFP (US$6–US$9.50). No credit cards. Mon–Fri 5am–12:30pm.

10 Island Nights on Tahiti

A 19th-century European merchant wrote of the Tahitians, "Their existence was in never-ending merrymaking." In many respects this is still true, for after the sun goes down, Tahitians like to make merry as much today as they did in the 1820s, and Papeete has lots of good choices for visitors who want to join in the fun.

TAHITIAN DANCE SHOWS 🌴🌴🌴

Traditional Tahitian dancing isn't as indecent as it was in Captain Cook's day (see "A Most Indecent Song & Dance," above), but seeing at least one show should be on your agenda. You'll have plenty of chances, since nightlife on the outer islands consists almost exclusively of dance shows at the resorts, usually in conjunction with a feast of Tahitian food.

Each of Tahiti's big resort hotels has shows at least 1 night a week. Not to be missed is the **Grande Danse de Tahiti** 🌴🌴🌴 troupe, which usually performs at the Inter-Continental Resort Tahiti (✆ **86.51.10**) on Wednesday, Friday, and Saturday evenings (the Sat show is a reenactment of the dance that seduced the crew of HMS *Bounty*). Call the resort to confirm the schedule. Another good place to catch a show is the **Captain Bligh Restaurant and Bar** (✆ **43.62.90**), which usually has them on Friday and Saturday at 8:30pm. Expect to pay from 5,000CFP (US$50) for the show and dinner at the Captain Bligh to 8,500CFP (US$85) at the big resorts.

Impressions

They have several negative comments on the beachcombing life in Tahiti: Not much cultural life. No intellectual stimulus. No decent library. Restaurant food is disgraceful . . . But I noticed that Saturday after Saturday they turned up at Quinn's with the most dazzling beauties on the island. When I reminded them of this they said, "Well that does compensate for the poor library."
—James A. Michener, *Return to Paradise*, 1951

PUB CRAWLING

Papeete has a nightclub or watering hole to fit anyone's taste, from upscale private *(privé)* discotheques to down-and-dirty bars and dance halls where Tahitians strum on guitars while sipping on large bottles of Hinano beer (and sometimes engage in a fisticuffs after midnight). If you look like a tourist, you'll be allowed into the private clubs. Generally, everything gets to full throttle after 9pm (except on Sun, when most pubs are closed). None of the clubs are inexpensive. Expect to pay a cover of at least 1,000CFP (US$10), which will include your first drink. After that, beers cost at least 500CFP (US$5), with most mixed drinks in the 1,000CFP-to-1,500CFP (US$10–US$15) range.

The narrow rue des Ecoles is the heart of Papeete's *mahu* district, where male transvestites hang out. The **Piano Bar** (© **42.88.24**) is the most popular of the "sexy clubs" along this street, especially for its late-night strip shows featuring female impersonators. It's open daily from 3pm to 3am. The multistory **Mana Rock Cafe,** at boulevard Pomare and rue des Ecoles (© **48.36.36**), draws a more mixed crowd to its bars and discotheque (you can check your e-mail between sips here).

You're unlikely to be groped or get into a fight at **Hotel Le Royal Tahitien,** in Pirae (© **50.40.40**), which has a live band for dancing on Friday nights. The moderate-price seaside restaurant here has very good food for the money, so you can make Friday a dining-and-dancing evening. See p. 110 for details.

You don't have to pay to be entertained on Friday, which is "cruise-ship day" on the Papeete waterfront. Arts and crafts are on display, and Tahitians make music from 8am to 5pm at the Tahiti Manava visitors bureau at the foot of rue Paul Gauguin. Tahitian bands perform afterwards out on Place Vaiate by the cruise-ship docks.

5

Moorea

Like most visitors to French Polynesia, I soon grab the ferry to Moorea, just 20km (12 miles) west of Tahiti. James Michener may have thought Bora Bora to be the world's most beautiful island, but Moorea is my choice. In fact, it's so stunningly gorgeous that I have trouble keeping my eyes on the road here. Hollywood often uses stock shots of Moorea's jagged mountains, deep bays, and emerald lagoons to create a South Seas setting for movies that don't even take place in French Polynesia.

Geologists attribute Moorea's rugged, otherworldly beauty to a great volcano, the northern half of which either fell into the sea or was blown away in a cataclysmic explosion, leaving the heart-shaped island we see today. In other words, Moorea is only half of its old self. The remaining rim of the crater has eroded into the jagged peaks and spires that give the island its haunting, dinosaur-like profile. Cathedral-like Mount Mouaroa—Moorea's trademark "Shark's Tooth" or "Bali Hai Mountain"—shows up on innumerable postcards and on the 100CFP coin.

Mount Rotui stands alone in the center of the ancient crater, its black cliffs and stovepipe buttresses dropping dramatically into Cook's Bay and Opunohu Bay, two dark-blue fingers that cut deep into Moorea's interior. These mountainshrouded bays are certainly among the world's most photographed bodies of water.

Perched high up on the crater's wall, the Belvédère overlooks both bays, Mount Rotui, and the jagged old crater rim curving off to left and right. Do not miss the Belvédère, for it is one of the South Pacific's most awesome panoramas.

With traffic choking Tahiti, and Moorea only a 30-minute ferry ride away from Papeete, the island is already a bedroom community for its big sister. Still, it has maintained its Polynesian charm to a large extent. Its hotels and resorts are spread out enough that you don't feel like you're in a tourist trap, and the locals don't feel inundated by us. They still have time to stop and talk with visitors.

Most of the Moorea's 15,000 or so residents live on its fringing coastal plain, many of them in small settlements where lush valleys meet a lagoon enclosed by an offshore coral reef. This calm blue lagoon makes Moorea ideal for swimming, boating, snorkeling, and diving. Unlike the black sands of Tahiti, white beaches stretch for miles on Moorea.

Impressions

From Tahiti, Moorea seems to have about 40 separate summits: fat thumbs of basalt, spires tipped at impossible angles, brooding domes compelling to the eye. But the peaks which can never be forgotten are the jagged saw-edges that look like the spines of some forgotten dinosaur.
— James A. Michener, *Return to Paradise*, 1951

1 Getting Around Moorea

Where you stay and most of what you will want to see and do lie on Moorea's north coast, between the ferry wharf at **Vaiare** and the area known as **Haapiti** on the island's northwestern corner. A large Club Med dominated Haapiti until it closed in 2002, and locals still say "Club Med" when referring to this area.

All ferries from Papeete land at Vaiare on Moorea's east coast 5km (3 miles) south of **Temae Airport** (see "Getting Around Tahiti & French Polynesia," in chapter 2).

BY BUS

The only scheduled buses on Moorea are those that carry passengers from and to the morning and afternoon ferries at Vaiare. Tell the drivers where you're going; they will show you which vehicle is going to your hotel. The trip from Vaiare to the end of the line at the old Club Med site takes about 1 hour. The buses also return from the Petite Village shopping center in Haapiti to Vaiare, leaving the shopping center about 1 hour prior to each ferry departure. They go by the hotels, so ask the front-desk staff when you can expect the next bus to pass. Or you can flag them down along the road elsewhere. The one-way fare is 300CFP (US$3), regardless of direction or length of ride.

BY TAXI

Unless you catch a ferry bus or rent a vehicle, you're at the expensive mercy of Moorea's taxi owners, who don't run around looking for customers. The only **taxi stand** is at the airport (✆ **56.10.18**). It's staffed daily from 6am to 6pm. Your hotel desk can call one for you, or else phone **Pero Taxis** (✆ **56.14.93**), **Albert Tours** (✆ **56. 13.53**), or **Justine Taxi** (✆ **77.48.26**). Make advance reservations for service between 6pm and 6am.

Taxi fares are 800CFP (US$8) during the day, 1,700CFP (US$17) at night, plus 110CFP (US$1.10) per kilometer. They double from 8pm to 6am. Expect to pay about 2,000CFP (US$20) one-way from the ferry or airport to the Cook's Bay area, about 4,000CFP (US$40) one-way from the airport or Cook's Bay to the Haapiti area, and less for stops along the way. Be sure that you understand what the fare will be before you get in.

BY RENTAL CAR & SCOOTER

Avis (✆ **800/331-1212** or 56.32.68; www.avis.com) and **Europcar** (✆ **800/227-7368** or 56.34.00; www.europcar.com) both have booths at the Vaiare ferry wharf and at several hotels. Although I usually rent from Avis, Europcar is the more widespread and slightly less expensive of the two, with unlimited-kilometer rates starting at 8,600CFP (US$86) a day. The local firm **Albert Rent-a-Car** (✆ **56.13.53**) is the least expensive, with unlimited-kilometer rates starting at 8,000CFP (US$80) for a day. Insurance is included in all rates, but gasoline is not.

In addition to automobiles, Avis also rents little "Fun Cars" (noisy contraptions with two seats and no top) and somewhat larger (and safer) open-air Be-Up vehicles. Both are fun to drive on sunny days. So are scooters, which Europcar and Albert rent starting at 4,800CFP (US$48) for 4 hours and 6,000CFP (US$60) for 24 hours, including gas, full insurance, and unlimited kilometers.

Making reservations for cars and scooters is a very good idea, especially on weekends, when many Tahiti residents come to Moorea.

BY BICYCLE

The 60km (36-mile) road around Moorea is relatively flat. The two major hills are on the west side of Cook's Bay and just behind the Sofitel Moorea Beach Resort (the latter is worth the climb, as it has a stupendous view of Tahiti). Some resorts have bikes for their guests to use, and **Europcar** (see above) rents mountain bikes for about 1,600CFP (US$16) for 8 hours, 2,000CFP (US$20) for all day.

FAST FACTS: Moorea

The following facts apply specifically to Moorea. For more information, see "Fast Facts: Tahiti & French Polynesia," in chapter 2.

Bookstores **Kina Maharepa,** in the Maharepa shopping center (© **56.22.44**), has English-language novels and magazines. **Supersonics,** in Le Petit Village shopping center opposite Club Med (© **56.14.96**), carries some English-language magazines and newspapers.

Camera/Film The hotel boutiques, along with the aforementioned **Kina Maharepa** and **Supersonics** (see above), all sell film.

Currency Exchange **Banque Socredo, Banque de Tahiti,** and **Banque de Polynésie** have offices and ATMs in or near the Maharepa shopping center. Banque de Polynésie has an ATM and a currency-exchange machine (but not an office) in Le Petit Village shopping center in Haapiti. Bring cash or traveler's checks if you're staying on the northwest corner, or be prepared to put most of your expenditures on a credit card. Banks are open Monday through Friday from 8am to noon and 1:30 to 4:30pm.

Drugstores **Pharmacie Tran,** in Maharepa (© **56.10.51**), is open Monday through Friday from 7:30am to noon and 2 to 6pm, Saturday from 8am to noon and 3:30 to 6pm, and Sunday and holidays from 8 to 11am. The owner, Tran Thai Thanh, is a Vietnamese refugee who speaks English.

Emergencies/Police The **emergency police** phone number is © **17.** The phone number for the **gendarmerie** in Cook's Bay is © **56.13.44.** Local police have offices at Pao Pao (© **56.13.63**) and at Haapiti (© **56.10.84**), near Club Med.

Eyeglasses Try **Optique Moorea** in the Maharepa shopping center (© **56.55.44**).

Healthcare The island's **infirmary,** which has an ambulance, is at Afareaitu on the southwest coast (© **56.24.24**). Several doctors are in private practice; ask your hotel staff for a recommendation.

Internet Access Every hotel has Internet access for its guests. In Cook's Bay, the restaurant **Maria Tapas** (© **55.01.70;** www.mariatapas.com) has fast Internet access for 250CFP (US$2.50) for 15 minutes (see p. 140 for more information). Computers are available Monday through Thursday from 9am to 11pm, Friday from 9am to 1am. In Haapiti, **Polynesian Arts,** in Le Petit Village (© **56.22.00**), also has fast access at 20CFP (US20¢) a minute. Open Monday through Saturday from 8:30am to 6pm. You can burn your digital photos onto CDs at either place.

Post Office Moorea's main post office is in the Maharepa shopping center. It's open Monday through Thursday from 7:30am to noon and 1:30 to 4pm, Friday from 7:30am to noon and 1:30 to 3pm, and Saturday from 7:30 to 9:30am. A

THE TRAVELOCITY GUARANTEE

...THAT SAYS EVERYTHING YOU BOOK WILL BE RIGHT, OR WE'LL WORK WITH OUR TRAVEL PARTNERS TO MAKE IT RIGHT, RIGHT AWAY.

To drive home the point,
we're going to use the word "right" in every single sentence.

Let's get right to it. Right to the meat! Only Travelocity guarantees everything about your booking will be right, or we'll work with our travel partners to make it right, right away. Right on!

Here's a picture taken smack dab right in the middle of Antigua, where the Guarantee also covers you.

The Guarantee covers all but one of the items pictured to the right.

Now, you may be thinking, "Yeah, right, I'm so sure." That's OK; you have the right to remain skeptical. That is until we mention help is always right around the corner. Call us right off the bat, knowing our customer service reps are there for you 24/7. Righting wrongs. Left and right.

For example, what if the ocean view you booked actually looks out at a downright ugly parking lot? You'd be right to call – we're there for you. And no one in their right mind would be pleased to learn the rental car place has closed and left them stranded. Call Travelocity and we'll help get you back on the right track.

Now if you're guessing there are some things we can't control, like the weather, well you're right. But we can help you with most things – to get all the details in righting,* visit travelocity.com/guarantee.

*Sorry, spelling things right is one of the few things not covered under the Guarantee.

I'd give my right arm for a guarantee like this, although I'm glad I don't have to.

travelocity
You'll never roam alone.

post office in Papetoai village is open Monday through Thursday from 7:30am to noon and 1:30 to 4pm, Friday from 7:30am to noon and 1:30 to 3pm, and Saturday from 8 to 10am.

Taxes Moorea's municipal government adds 100CFP to 150CFP (US$1–US$1.50) per night to your hotel bill. Don't complain: The money helps keep the island litter-free.

Visitor Information The **Moorea Visitors Bureau,** B.P. 1121, 98279 Papetoai (© **56.29.09;** www.gomoorea.com), has an office at Le Petit Village shopping center in Haapiti. Open Monday through Thursday from 8am to 4pm (more or less; they sometimes change). The bureau also has an unstaffed booth at the Temae Airport where you can pick up maps and brochures any time.

Water Tap water on Moorea is not safe to drink, so buy bottled water at any grocery store. Some hotels filter their water; ask if it's safe before drinking from the tap.

2 Exploring Moorea: The Circle Island Tour ⭐⭐⭐

The sights of Moorea may lack great historical significance, but the physical beauty of the island makes a tour—at least of Cook's and Opunohu bays and up to the Belvédère lookout—a highlight of any visit here. There are few places on earth this gorgeous.

As on Tahiti, Moorea's round-island road—about 60km (36 miles) long—is marked every kilometer with a PK post. Distances are measured between the intersection of the airport road with the main round-island coastal road and the village of Haapiti on Moorea's opposite side. In other words, the distances indicated on the PKs increase from the airport in each direction, reaching 30km near Haapiti. They then decrease as you head back to the airport.

The hotel activities desks offer tours around Moorea and up to the Belvédère lookout in the interior. **Albert Tours** (© **56.13.53**) and **Moorea Explorer** (© **56.12.86**) have half-day circle island tours, including the Belvédère, for about 3,300CFP (US$33) per person. The tour buses all stop at one black-pearl shop or another (guess who gets a commission when you buy the pearl of your dreams?). See "Buying Your Black Pearl" (p. 99) and "Shopping," later in this chapter, before making a purchase.

TEMAE & MAHAREPA

Begin at the airstrip on Moorea's northeast corner. The airstrip is on the island's only sizable area of flat land. At one time it was a *motu,* or small island, sitting on the reef by itself. Humans and nature have since filled the lagoon except for Lake Temae,

---

Impressions

Nothing on Tahiti is so majestic as what faces it across the bay, for there lies the island of Moorea. To describe it is impossible. It is a monument to the prodigal beauty of nature.

—James A. Michener, *Return to Paradise,* 1951

Fun Fact **Pai's Spear**

Tahitian lore says the legendary hero Pai made the hole in the top of Mount Tohiea when the god of thieves attempted to steal Mount Rotui in the middle of the night. Pai threw his spear from Tahiti and pierced Mount Tohiea. The noise woke up Moorea's roosters, whose commotion alerted the citizenry to put a stop to the dastardly plan.

---

which you can see from the air if you fly to Moorea. A resort with Moorea's first golf course is being built here.

Head west from the junction of the round-island road and airport road. **Temae,** 1km (½ mile) from the junction, supplied the dancers for the Pomare dynasty's court in the 19th century and is still known for the quality of its performers. Herman Melville spent some time here in 1842 and saw the famous, erotic *upaupa,* which he called the "lory-lory," performed clandestinely, out of sight of the missionaries.

The relatively dry north shore between the airport and the entrance to Cook's Bay is **Maharepa,** the island's commercial center. The road skirts the lagoon and passes the Moorea Pearl Resort & Spa and soon reaches the island's main shopping center.

COOK'S BAY 🟔🟔🟔

As the road curves to the left, you enter **Cook's Bay,** the fingerlike body of water virtually surrounded on three sides by the jagged peaks lining the semicircular "wall" of Moorea. The tall thumb with a small hole in its top is **Mount Tohiea.** Coming into view as you drive farther along the bay is **Mount Mauaroa,** Moorea's trademark cathedral-like "Shark's Tooth" mountain buttressed on its right by a serrated ridge.

Huddled along the curving beach at the head of the bay, the village of **Pao Pao** is the site of Moorea's public schools. The **Marché Municipale (Municipal Market)** is open Monday through Saturday from 5am to 5pm and Sunday from 5 to 8am. Unlike Papeete's market, this one has slim pickings; locals come here primarily to buy fresh fish. The paved road that seems to run through the school next to the bridge cuts through the valley between Cook's Bay and Opunohu Bay. It intersects with the main road between Opunohu Bay and the Belvédère lookout.

The small **St. Joseph's Catholic Church** sits on the shore on the west side of Cook's Bay, at PK 10 from the airport. Inside is a large mural that artist Peter Heyman painted in 1946 and an altar decorated with mother-of-pearl. From the church, the road climbs up the side of the hill, offering some fine views, and then descends back to the lagoon's edge.

Watch on the left for the road leading inland to **Jus de Fruits de Moorea (Moorea Fruit Juices;** ✆ **56.22.33**), a factory and distillery that turns the island's produce into the Rotui juices and the potently alcoholic Tahiti Drink you will see in every grocery store. I like to refresh here by tasting the yummy fruit liqueurs. Every souvenir imaginable is for sale, too. Hours are Monday through Thursday from 8:30am to 4:30pm, Friday and Saturday from 8:30am to 3:30pm.

OPUNOHU BAY 🟔🟔🟔

Towering over you is jagged **Mount Rotui,** the huge green-and-black rock separating Moorea's two great bays. Unlike Cook's Bay, Opunohu is virtually devoid of development,

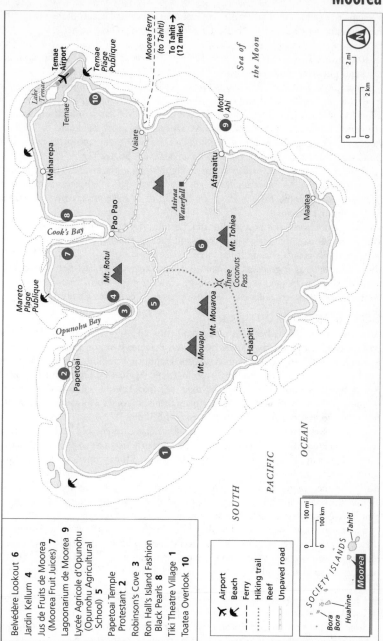

Moorea

Moorea Ferry
(to Tahiti)
To Tahiti →
(12 miles)

Sea of
the Moon

2 mi
2 km

Temae
Airport

Temae
Plage
Publique

Lake
Temae

Temae

Maharepa

Vaiare

Motu
Ahi

Afareaitu

Atiraa
Waterfall ■

Pao Pao

Cook's Bay

Mt. Rotui

Mt. Tohiea

Three
Coconuts
Pass

Maatea

Mt. Mouaroa

Mt. Mouapu

Haapiti

Mareto
Plage
Publique

Opunohu Bay

Papetoai

SOUTH
PACIFIC
OCEAN

Belvédère Lookout **6**
Jardin Kellum **4**
Jus de Fruits de Moorea
(Moorea Fruit Juices) **7**
Lagoonarium de Moorea **9**
Lycée Agricole d'Opunohu
(Opunohu Agricultural
School) **5**
Papetoai Temple
Protestant **2**
Robinson's Cove **3**
Ron Hall's Island Fashion
Black Pearls **8**
Tiki Theatre Village **1**
Toatea Overlook **10**

✈ Airport
↙ Beach
– – – Ferry
········ Hiking trail
Reef
Unpaved road

100 mi
100 km

SOCIETY ISLANDS

Moorea

Tahiti

Bora
Bora

Huahine

a testament to efforts by local residents to maintain the natural beauty of their island (they have ardently resisted efforts to build a luxury resort and golf course here).

As soon as the road levels out, you can look through the trees to yachts anchored in **Robinson's Cove,** one of the world's most photographed yacht anchorages. Stop here and put your camera to work.

Near the cove, at PK 17.5, stands **Jardin Kellum,** the bayside home and botanical garden of the late Medford and Gladys Kellum, an American couple who once owned all of Opunohu Valley. The Kellums arrived here in 1925, aboard Medford's parents' converted lumber schooner, and they lived for 65 years in a clapboard colonial-style house. Their daughter, Marimari Kellum, resides here today and gives tours of the home and garden to groups who book in advance (© **56.18.52**).

From the garden, the road soon curves right along a black-sand beach backed by shade trees and the Opunohu Valley at the head of the bay. The beach was turned into Matavai Bay on Tahiti for the 1983 production of *The Bounty,* starring Mel Gibson and Anthony Hopkins.

The major cruise ships now anchor in Opunohu Bay rather than in Cook's Bay, and you soon will pass the dock where they land their passengers. Although the location is gorgeous, it is also remote from shops, restaurants, and other facilities. Locals say the relocation was engineered by Moorea's most aggressive black-pearl merchant so that the ships' passengers would go ashore closer to his shop in Haapiti rather than competing dealers in Cook's Bay (see "Shopping," later in this chapter).

BELVÉDÈRE LOOKOUT ✸✸✸

After the bridge by the beach, a paved road runs up Moorea's central valley through pasture land, across which Warren Beatty and Annette Benning strolled in their flop movie *Love Affair* (the scenes with Katharine Hepburn were filmed in the white house on the hill to your right). You can stop at **Lycée Agricole d'Opunohu (Opunohu Agricultural School),** on the main road (© **56.11.34;** www.formation-agricole-opunohu.org), to see vanilla and other plantations. It's open Monday through Friday from 8am to 4:30pm, Saturday from 9am to 12:30pm.

At the head of the valley, the road climbs steeply up the old crater wall to the restored **Titiroa Marae,** which was part of a concentration of *maraes* and other structures. Higher up, you'll pass an archery platform used for competition (archery was a sport reserved for high-ranking chiefs and was never used in warfare in Polynesia). A display in the main *marae* parking lot explains the history of this area. You can walk among the remains of the temples, now shaded by towering Tahitian chestnut trees that have grown up through the cobblestone-like courtyards.

The narrow road then ascends to **Belvédère Lookout,** whose awesome panorama of the valley and the bays on either side of Mount Rotui is unmatched in the South Pacific. You won't want to be without film or camera batteries here. There's a snack bar in the parking lot, so grab a cold drink or ice cream while you take in this remarkable vista.

Impressions

Seen for the first time by European Eyes, this coast is like nothing else on our workaday planet; a landscape, rather, of some fantastic dream.
—Charles Nordhoff and James Norman Hall, *Mutiny on the Bounty,* 1933

Moments **The View from Belvédère Lookout**

If the view from Le Belvédère restaurant on Tahiti doesn't thrill me enough, the scene from the Moorea lookout of the same name certainly does. I never tire of standing at the base of that cliff and watching dramatic Mount Rotui separate the deep-blue fingers of Cook's and Opunohu bays.

PAPETOAI

Back on the coastal road, the sizable village of **Papetoai** was the retreat of the Pomare dynasty in the 1800s and the base from which Pomare I launched his successful drive to take over all of Tahiti and Moorea. It was also headquarters for the London Missionary Society's work throughout the South Pacific. The road to the right, past the new post office, leads to the octagonal **Papetoai Temple Protestant,** built on the site of a *marae* dedicated to Oro, son of the supreme Taaroa and the god of war. The original church was constructed in the 1820s, and although advertised as the oldest European building still in use in the South Pacific, the present structure dates from the late 1880s.

HAAPITI

From Papetoai, the road runs through the Haapiti hotel district at Pointe Hauru, Moorea's northwestern corner. A long stretch of white-sand beach wraps around the point and conspires with two islets out on the reef's edge and great sunset views to make the Haapiti area popular with tourists. Beginning in the 1970s, a 300-bungalow Club Med generated much business here, including Le Petit Village shopping center across the road. Although it closed in 2002, many locals still refer to the Club Med when giving directions. The area has been a bit depressed since the club closed. Still, this is your last chance to stop for refreshment before the sparsely populated southern half of Moorea. There are several choices here (see "Where to Dine," later in this chapter).

About 4km (2½ miles) beyond Le Petit Village, look for the **Tiki Theatre Village** *⭐⭐⭐*, a cultural center that consists of thatch huts on the coastal side of the road. It's the only place to see what a Tahitian village looked like when Captain Cook arrived, so pull in. See "Tiki Theatre Village," below, for details.

When the first Europeans arrived, the lovely, mountain-backed village of **Haapiti** was home to the powerful Marama family, which was allied with the Pomares. It became a center of Catholic missionary work after the French took over the territory, and it is one of the few villages whose Catholic church is as large as its Protestant counterpart. Stop here and look up behind the village for a view of Mount Mouaroa from a unique perspective.

THE SOUTH COAST

South of Haapiti, just as the road curves sharply around a headland, is a nice view of a small bay with the mountains towering overhead (there's no place to park on the headland, so stop and walk up for the view). In contrast to the more touristy north shore, the southeast and southwest coasts have retained an atmosphere of old Polynesia.

The village of **Afareaitu,** on the southeast coast, is the administrative center of Moorea, and the building that looks like a charming hotel across from the village church actually is the island's *mairie,* or town hall.

About half a kilometer (¼ mile) beyond the town hall, opposite an A-frame house on the shore, an unpaved road runs straight between several houses and then continues uphill to the **Atiraa Waterfall** 𝒜𝒜. Often called Afareaitu Waterfall, its water plunges more than 32m (100 ft.) down a cliff, into a small pool. You can drive partway to the falls and then walk 20 minutes up a steep, slippery, and muddy trail. Wear shoes or sandals that have good traction if you make this trek, for in places the slippery trail is hacked into a steep hill; if you slip, it's a long way down to the rocks below. Villagers will be waiting at the beginning of the footpath to extract a small fee.

Beyond Afareaitu, the small bay of **Vaiare** is a beehive of activity when the ferries pull in from Papeete. On workdays, commuters park their vehicles at least 1km (½ mile) in either direction from the wharf.

TOATEA OVERLOOK & TEMAE PLAGE PUBLIQUE 𝒜𝒜𝒜

Atop the hill north of the Sofitel Moorea Beach Resort is the **Toatea Overlook** 𝒜𝒜𝒜. Here you'll have a magnificent view of the hotel, the green lagoon flecked with brown coral heads, the white line of the surf breaking on the reef, the deep blue of the Sea of the Moon, and all of Tahiti rising magnificently from the horizon. There's a parking area at the overlook.

The unpaved road to the right at the bottom of the hill leads to the **Temae Plage Publique,** Moorea's finest stretch of public beach. Follow the left fork through the coconut grove to the lagoon. This is a continuation of the Sofitel Moorea Beach Resort's beach, except that here you don't have a staff to rake the leaves and coral gravel from the sand. Locals often sell snacks and souvenirs, especially on weekends. Bring insect repellent if you do your beaching here.

---

3 Safari Expeditions, Lagoon Excursions & Dolphin-Watching

SAFARI EXPEDITIONS 𝒜𝒜

You can see the sights and learn a lot about the island on a four-wheel-drive excursion through Moorea's mountainous interior. Every hotel activities desk can book you on one of these adventures. **Albert Tours** (⊘ 56.13.53) and **Moorea Explorer** (⊘ 56.12.86) both have them. I've been with Alex and Gheslaine Haamatearii's **Inner Island Safari Tours** (⊘ 56.20.09), which will take you through the valleys, up to Belvédère Lookout, and then down to a vanilla plantation in Opunohu Valley. They explain the island's flora and fauna along the way. The best trips end with a drive around Moorea's south coast and a hike up to Atiraa Waterfall for a refreshing swim (see "The South Coast" under "Exploring Moorea: The Circle Island Tour," above). Expect to visit a black-pearl shop and Jus de Fruits de Moorea (see "Cook's Bay," under "Exploring Moorea: The Circle Island Tour," above). These half-day trips cost between 4,000CFP and 5,000CFP (US$40–US$50) per person.

In a variation on this theme, **Mahana ATV Tours** (⊘ 56.20.44) takes you on all-terrain vehicles into the Opunohu Valley.

Moments **Tahiti in All Its Glory**

My neck strains every time I cross the hill behind Moorea's Sofitel Moorea Beach Resort, for there, across the Sea of the Moon, sits Tahiti in all its green glory. What amazement the early explorers must have felt when those mountains appeared over the horizon!

Tiki Theatre Village 🐾🐾🐾

The best cultural experience in French Polynesia is at **Tiki Theatre Village,** at PK 31, or 2km (1¼ miles) south of old Club Med (© **55.02.50;** www.tiki village.pf). Built in the fashion of ancient Tahitian villages, this cultural center has old-style *fares* (houses) in which the staff demonstrates traditional tattooing, tapa-cloth making and painting, wood and stone carving, weaving, cooking, and making costumes, musical instruments, and flower crowns. There's even a "royal" house floating out on the lagoon, where you can learn about the modern art of growing black pearls.

Tiki Theatre Village will even arrange a traditional beachside wedding. The bride is prepared with flowery *monoi* oil like a Tahitian princess, while the groom is tattooed (with a wash-off pen). Both wear traditional costumes.

The village is open Tuesday through Saturday from 11am to 3pm. Admission and a guided tour costs 1,200CFP (US$12).

Not to be missed is the authentic Tahitian feast and dance show here on Tuesday, Wednesday, Friday, and Saturday nights. The staff will pick you up from your hotel and deposit you on the beach for a rum punch and sunset. After they uncover the earth oven, they'll take you on a tour of the village. A buffet of both Tahitian and Western foods is followed by an energetic 1½-hour dance show with some of the most elaborate yet traditional costumes to be seen in French Polynesia. The dinner and show cost 7,900CFP (US$79) per person, or you can come for the 9pm show for 3,900CFP (US$39). Kids 3 to 12 pay half price. Add 1,150CFP (US$12) for round-trip transportation.

LAGOON EXCURSIONS 🐾🐾🐾

The lagoon around Moorea is not as beautiful or diverse as Bora Bora's, but it's worth a day's outing. Most hotel activities desks will book you on a lagoon excursion, the best way to experience the magnificent setting. The full-day version of these excursions invariably includes a "motu picnic"—a lunch of grilled fresh fish, *poisson cru,* and salads served on a little islet (*motu*) out on the reef. Quite often, the fresh fish is caught on the way. You'll have an opportunity to snorkel in the lagoon and learn how to husk a coconut. Some tours also include shark- and ray-feeding, one of the most interesting and exciting things to do in the water here. Wear shoes you don't mind getting wet. The cost is about 7,000CFP (US$70) per person.

Some lagoon excursions may take you to **Lagoonarium de Moorea,** on Motu Ahi off Afareaitu (© **78.31.15**). Like its counterpart on Bora Bora (see chapter 8), it allows you to snorkel in a fenced area with dolphins, small sharks, and other sealife. The islet also has a snack bar and scuba diving. You can also get here yourself, since the transfer boat leaves from PK 8 in Afareaitu. Fares are 2,300CFP (US$23) for adults and 1,500CFP (US$15) for children, including the use of kayaks and snorkeling gear. It's open daily.

DOLPHIN-WATCHING 🐾🐾🐾

One of the best things to do on Moorea is a dolphin- and whale-watching excursion led by American marine biologist **Dr. Michael Poole** (© **56.23.22** or 77.50.07;

www.drmichaelpoole.com). An expert on sea mammals and a leader in the effort to have French Polynesian waters declared a whale sanctuary, Dr. Poole will take you out beyond the reef to meet some of the 150 acrobatic spinner dolphins he has identified as regular Moorea residents. In calm conditions, and if the animals are agreeable, you can don snorkel gear and swim with them. You'll also be on the lookout for pilot whales that swim past year-round and giant humpback whales that frequent these waters from July to October. The half-day excursions cost about 7,000CFP (US$70) for adults, half price for kids, including pickup at most hotel docks. Make reservations in advance, and be prepared not to go if the sea isn't calm.

Among the many activities at the Inter-Continental Resort & Spa Moorea (see "Watersports," below) and by far the most popular for families is the **Moorea Dolphin Center** 𝒜𝒜 (✆ **55.19.48;** www.mooreadolphincenter.com). These intelligent sea mammals are sure to excite young and old alike. They live in a fenced area, although the center professes to be dedicated to their care and conservation. Kids 16 and older can join adults in snorkeling with the mammals in deeper water (all must be good swimmers) for 21,000CFP (US$210) per person. A 1-hour "dolphin discovery" excursion in shallow water costs 17,400CFP (US$174) per person. There's a 1-hour children's program (ages 5 to 11) that costs 10,800CFP (US$108) per kid, and there are family programs, too. Honeymooners can even go on their own private encounter.

4 Fishing, Hiking, Watersports & Other Outdoor Activities

By the time you arrive, Moorea may have a golf course, part of a resort being built near the airport at Temae. In the meantime, stay on Tahiti if you must play golf. Moorea has no public tennis courts, so pick a hotel that has them if tennis is important to you.

Most hotels have active watersports programs for their guests, such as glass-bottomed-boat cruises and snorkeling in, or sailing on, Moorea's beautiful lagoon.

FISHING

Chris Lilley, an American who has won several sportfishing contests, takes guests onto the open ocean in search of big game on his *Tea Nui* (✆ **55.19.19,** ext. 1903, or 56.15.08 at home; teanuiservices@mail.pf). You can go out for half a day for about 6,500CFP (US$65) per person, with a minimum of four required, or charter the boat for a whole day for about 66,000CFP (US$660). In keeping with South Pacific custom, you can keep the little fish you catch; Chris sells the big ones. Chris is based at the Inter-Continental Resort and Spa Moorea.

HIKING

You won't need a guide to hike from the coast road up the Opunohu Valley to Belvédère Lookout. Up and down will take most of a day. It's a level but hot walk along the valley floor and gets steep approaching the lookout. Bring lots of water.

Several unmarked hiking trails lead into the mountains, including one beginning in Cook's Bay and ending on the east coast near the Vaiare ferry dock, another from the southwest coast near Haapiti village across Three Coconuts Pass and into Opunohu Valley. Go with a guide on longer hikes up in the mountains. Moorea-based **Tahiti Evasion** (✆ **56.48.77;** www.tahitievasion.com) has half-day treks to the archeological sites in the Opunohu Valley, across Three Coconuts Pass between the Belvédère and the south coast, and to the Afareaitu waterfall and the pierced Mount Tohiea. Prices range from 4,000CFP to 6,000CFP (US$40–US$60) per person.

HORSEBACK RIDING

Landlubbers can go horseback riding along the beach and into the interior with **Ranch Opunohu Valley** (© **56.28.55**). Rates are about 6,000CFP (US$60) for a 1½-hour ride. Advance reservations are essential.

WATERSPORTS

The most extensive array of sporting activities is at the **Inter-Continental Resort and Spa Moorea** (© **55.19.19**), whose facilities can be used by both guests and visitors who are willing to pay. Options include scuba diving, parasailing (magnificent views of the bays, mountains, and reefs), water-skiing, wake boarding, scooting about the lagoon and Opunohu Bay on jet skis, viewing coral and fish from Aquascope boats, walking on the lagoon bottom while wearing diving helmets, line fishing, and speedboat rentals. Nonguests can also pay to use the pool, snorkeling gear, and tennis courts, and to be taken over to a small islet. Call the hotel for prices, schedules, and reservations, which are required.

SCUBA DIVING   Although Moorea's lagoon is not in the same league with those at Rangiroa, Fakarava, or even Bora Bora, its outer reef has some decent sites for viewing sea life, and especially the white- and black-tip reef sharks. Since the northern side of Moorea fell away from the rest of the island eons ago, the reef slopes away gently here, as opposed to the precipitous drop-offs found on Tahiti and most other South Pacific islands. The shallow lagoon has mostly dead coral, so you must dive to deeper depths in order to see the colors of the living reef.

Most sites are within short boat rides of the northwest-coast resorts and require dives of 10 to 20m (33–70 ft.). **The Tiki,** off the island's northwestern point, is popular thanks to the shark-feeding (as on Bora Bora, many dives feature shark-feeding, although not all of Moorea's operators engage in this practice). Even novice divers can pet the friendly rays at **Stingray World,** just off the Inter-Continental Resort and Spa Moorea. **Opunohu Canyons,** off the mouth of the bay, is another shark-feeding favorite. You can drift dive through **Taotoi Pass,** to the west of Opunohu Bay. Experienced divers can see a huge expanse of flat montipora coral at **The Roses,** at a depth of 30 to 40m (100–130 ft.) halfway between Opunohu and Cook's bays. Inside the lagoon, **The Wreck** is an old ship that was sunk to provide an artificial reef home to a multitude of fish.

The island's best dive operator is **TOPdive** (© **56.17.32**; www.topdive.com), with bases in Cook's Bay and at the Sheraton Moorea Lagoon Resort & Spa. Also excellent is Gilles Pétré's **Moorea Blue Nui Dive Center** (© **55.17.50**; www.bluenui.com) at the Moorea Pearl Resort & Spa. On the northwest coast, the Inter-Continental Resort & Spa Moorea is home to **Bathy's Club Moorea** (© **55.19.19**, ext. 1139), and **Scubapiti Moorea** (© **56.30.38**) resides at Hotel Les Tipaniers. All charge about 7,500CFP (US$75) for one dive, including equipment (gauges are metric).

SNORKELING & SWIMMING   Sharing the lagoon with the Sofitel Moorea Beach Resort, the **Temae Plage Publique (Tamae Public Beach)** has some of the island's best snorkeling, and it's relatively safe. Also good is the lagoon around the islets off Haapiti, but watch out for strong currents coming in and out of the nearby reef passes.

Another favorite with locals for sunning and swimming is **Mareto Plage Publique (Mareto Public Beach),** in a coconut grove west of the Sheraton Moorea between the two bays. Go around the barbed-wire fence on the eastern end.

The lagoon off Moorea's northwest corner is blessed with offshore motu, small islets where you can sunbathe, swim, and snorkel (but beware of strong currents), plus have lunch on **Motu Moea** (p. 141). You can rent a boat to get over there from **Moorea Locaboat** (© **78.13.39**), based next to Hotel Les Tipaniers, or take a transfer from **Tip Nautic** next door (© **73.76.73**) for 700CFP (US$7) round-trip. Tip Nautic also rents snorkel gear for 500CFP (US$5) for half a day and kayaks starting at 500CFP (US$5) per hour, and it has water-skiing and dolphin-watching trips as well.

5 Shopping

THE SHOPPING SCENE

The island's primary commercial center is at **Maharepa,** where you'll find black-pearl shops, banks, grocery stores, hairdressers, the main post office, and other services. The neocolonial buildings of **Le Petit Village** shopping center anchor the northwestern corner, where numerous stores sell *pareus,* T-shirts, and souvenirs. **Supersonics** (© **56. 29.73**) carries film, camera batteries, stamps, magazines, and other items. There's also a grocery store.

Boutiques and art galleries are numerous on Moorea, but they come and go as frequently as their owners arrive from France and then decide to go home. The shops I mention below have been around for a while. One of the most reliable places to look for pareus, tropical dresses, aloha shirts, bathing suits, T-shirts, shell jewelry, and handicrafts is **La Maison Blanche (The White House),** in Maharepa near the Moorea Pearl Resort & Spa (© **56.13.26**). It's housed in a whitewashed vanilla planter's house with railing enclosing a magnificent veranda, which alone makes it worth a stop. Open daily from 8:30am to 5pm.

ART

Galerie van der Heyde 🐸🐸   Dutch artist Aad van der Heyde has lived and worked on Moorea since 1964. One of his bold impressionist paintings of a Tahitian woman was selected for French Polynesia's 100CFP postage stamp in 1975, and his landscape of Bora Bora appeared on a 2004 stamp. Aad will sell you an autographed lithograph of the paintings. Some of his works are displayed on the gallery's garden wall. He has also produced excellent videos of the islands and will gladly sell you a copy on DVD. In addition, you'll see a small collection of pearls, wood carvings, tapa cloth, shell and coral jewelry, and primitive art from Papua New Guinea. Open Monday through Saturday from 8am to 5pm. East side of Cook's Bay. © **56.14.22.**

Sculpture Par Woody 🐸   Woody Howard was studying horticulture at the University of Hawaii when he came to Moorea in 1982 to work on Hotel Bali Hai's plantation. Like so many others, he stayed. You can visit his lagoonside workshop and, if he's not off searching for driftwood, watch him carving award-winning images of dolphins, fish, Polynesian wildlife, and women. He also has a reasonably priced selection of black pearls. Open Monday through Saturday from 8am to 5pm. Papetoai, between village and Inter-Continental Resort and Spa Moorea. © **56.37.00** or 56.17.73.

BLACK PEARLS

Moorea has more pearl shops than you can visit in a normal vacation. In fact, many of the stores will come looking for you, with offers of free transportation to and from your hotel or the cruise-ship landing in Opunohu Bay, and tour operators are likely to deposit you at the shop offering the highest commission at the end of your excursion. Always shop around—and read "Buying Your Black Pearl" (p. 99) before making your purchase.

Among several stores near the old Club Med site in Haapiti is **Tahia Collins** (© **55.05.00;** www.tahiacollins.com), formerly the Black Pearl Gem Company. Owner and chief designer Tahia Collins was a Miss Moorea and is a scion of the Albert Haring family (you will see the Albert name all over the island). Her husband, Marc Collins, was born in Hawaii of an American father and Tahitian mother. Theirs is the most aggressive pearl dealership on Moorea, and since they have the concession on some of the cruise ships, Tahia Collins will be the first dealer many of you will encounter here. Others worth visiting in this area are **Herman Perles** (© **56.42.79**) and **Pai Moana Pearls** (© **56.25.25**).

My favorites are the lower-key shops the other side of the island, to wit:

Ann Simon Boutique   The French owner of this shop, Ann Simon, specializes in darker pearls—those with rich blue and green hues—set in 18-karat gold. That combination makes them anything but inexpensive, but this is a good place to see what high-quality black pearls look like. Some of Ann's designs are unique. Open Monday through Saturday from 9am to 6pm. Maharepa, west of the post office. © 56.44.55.

Authentic Black Pearls/Yann Olivier Collection   Two doors removed from Ann Simon Boutique, this is another fine shop for top-quality pearls, which designer Yann Olivier uses in his unique jewelry designs. Open Monday through Friday from 9am to noon and 1 to 5:30pm. Maharepa, west of the post office. © 56.29.96.

Eva Perles ✸   Eva Frachon, the friendly French owner of this little shop, graduated from the University of Wisconsin at Oshkosh with a bachelor's degree in photography and art metals; thus, she does her own creative settings, and she speaks American-style English. It's worth stopping to look at her selection of wood carvings from the Marquesas. Open Monday through Saturday from 9:30am to 5:30pm. Maharepa, opposite the post office. © 56.10.10.

Ron Hall's Island Fashion Black Pearls ✸✸✸ ✔Value   Ron Hall sailed from Hawaii to Tahiti with the actor Peter Fonda in 1974. Peter went home; Ron didn't. Now Ron and his son, Heimata, run this air-conditioned Moorea retail outlet. It's worth a stop to see the antiques and old photos, including one of the infamous Quinn's Bar and a William Leeteg painting of a Tahitian *vahine* (Ron's wife and Heimata's mother, Josée, was herself a championship Tahitian dancer). In 15 minutes of "pearl school," you will learn the basics of picking a pearl. They will have your selection set in a mounting of your choice, their prices are fair, and they donate 10% of every pearl purchase to Dr. Michael Poole's dolphin and whale research (see "Dolphin-Watching," p. 125). They also carry one of Moorea's best selections of bathing suits, aloha shirts, and T-shirts. Open Monday through Saturday from 9am to 6pm. East side of Cook's Bay. © 56.11.06.

6 Where to Stay

Most of Moorea's hotels and restaurants are grouped in or near Cook's Bay, between Cook's and Opunohu bays, or in the Haapiti district on the northwest corner of the island around the old Club Med site. With the exception of the Sofitel Moorea Beach Resort, those in or near Cook's Bay do not have the best beaches on the island, but the snorkeling is excellent and the views of the mountains are unsurpassed in the South Pacific. The establishments between the two bays have beaches, but they are a bit inconvenient to the facilities at both Cook's Bay and Haapiti. Those on the northwest corner have generally fine beaches, lagoons like giant swimming pools, and unobstructed views of the sunset, but not of Moorea's famous mountains. The areas are relatively far apart, so you might spend most of your time near your hotel unless you rent a vehicle or otherwise make a point to see the sights. An alternative is to split your stay between the areas.

THE COOK'S BAY AREA
EXPENSIVE

Moorea Pearl Resort & Spa ★★★   Forget a great view here, since this multi-faceted resort faces the open ocean, and its 28 overwater bungalows block most of the sea view. Snorkeling is excellent, however, especially from the decks of the 20 deluxe overwater bungalows perched out on the edge of the clifflike reef. They and 18 beach bungalows with private pools in their courtyards are the pick of a mixed litter of accommodations. Some of the garden bungalows are stand-alone, while others are in less private duplex units. All bungalows are identical inside, with tasteful native-wood accents, ceiling fans, king-size beds, and ample shower-only bathrooms. The least expensive units are 30 spacious hotel rooms in two-story blocks away from the lagoon. They all have king-size beds and balconies or patios, and eight family rooms add two single beds. Big thatch roofs cover a large dining room and pool-level bar, which hosts Tahitian dance shows twice a week. The smallish beach and big infinity swimming pool serve as centers for numerous outdoor activities.

B.P. 3410, 98728 Maharepa, Moorea. © 800/657-3275 or 55.17.50. Fax 55.17.51. www.pearlresorts.com. 95 units. 25,000CFP–30,000CFP (US$250–US$300) double; 39,000CFP–62,000CFP (US$390–US$620) bungalow. AE, DC, MC, V. **Amenities:** 2 restaurants; bar; outdoor pool; spa; Jacuzzi; watersports equipment/rentals; bike rentals; activities desk; car-rental desk; limited room service; massage; babysitting; laundry service. *In room:* A/C, TV, dataport, kitchen, minibar (bungalows only), fridge, coffeemaker, hair dryer, iron, safe.

Sofitel Moorea Beach Resort   On the island's northeast coast, this sprawling resort (formerly the Sofitel Ia Ora Moorea) was built in the 1960s and shuttered temporarily in 2005 for its first massive renovation since then. All of its original bungalows were replaced, and 19 new overwater units were added—which set off demonstrations by local environmentalists opposed to damaging the reef. It still sits beside one of the South Pacific's best lagoons and a long, lovely beach over which grape-leaf and casuarina trees hang. It's the only hotel with a view of Tahiti, whose green, cloud-topped mountains seem to climb out of the horizon beyond the reef.

B.P. 28, 98728 Maharepa, Moorea (Temae, on the northeast coast, facing Tahiti). © 800/763-4835, 55.03.55, or 41.04.04 in Papeete. Fax 41.05.05. www.accorhotels.com. 129 units. Check the website for post-renovation rates. AE, DC, MC, V. **Amenities:** 2 restaurants; bar; outdoor pool; 2 tennis courts; watersports equipment/rentals; bike rentals; activities desk; car-rental desk; massage; babysitting; laundry service. *In room:* A/C, TV, minibar, coffeemaker, hair dryer, iron, safe.

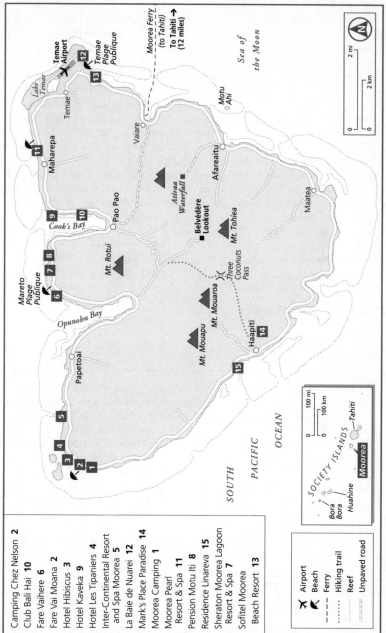

Camping Chez Nelson **2**
Club Bali Hai **10**
Fare Vaihere **6**
Fare Vai Moana **2**
Hotel Hibiscus **3**
Hotel Kaveka **9**
Hotel Les Tipaniers **4**
Inter-Continental Resort
and Spa Moorea **5**
La Baie de Nuarei **12**
Mark's Place Paradise **14**
Moorea Camping **1**
Moorea Pearl
Resort & Spa **11**
Pension Motu Iti **8**
Residence Linareva **15**
Sheraton Moorea Lagoon
Resort & Spa **7**
Sofitel Moorea
Beach Resort **13**

Airport
Beach
Ferry — · — · —
Hiking trail ·······
Reef
Unpaved road

MODERATE

Club Bali Hai *Value*   The last property operated by Moorea's two surviving Bali Hai Boys (see "The Bali Hai Boys," below), this basic hotel has an incredible view of Moorea's ragged mountains across Cook's Bay, a scene that epitomizes French Polynesia. Under a bayside thatch roof, **Snack l'Ananas Bleu (The Blue Pineapple)** restaurant serves breakfast and lunch (p. 140). It's also the scene for Muk McCallum's bring-your-own happy hours from 5:30 to 7pm Thursday through Tuesday, when he "talks story" about the good old days on Moorea. It's worth stopping by the club's Wednesday-night Tahitian dance shows, too. A swimming pool with a rock waterfall augments the manmade beach here. Half of the guest units are part of a time-share operation, but that means they come equipped with cooking facilities, which is a plus for budget-minded travelers. The overwater bungalows are the least expensive in French Polynesia, while the beachfront bungalows have huge bathrooms with gardens growing in them, another trademark of the Bali Hai Boys. Most other units are in one- or two-story motel-style buildings. All are simply but comfortably furnished. *Note:* Some units have air-conditioners in their bedrooms but not in their living areas, and the least expensive "budget units" do not have coffeemakers (bring your own coffee even if they do). This is good value if you don't need a phone in your room or other such luxuries. On the other hand, the view is worth a million bucks. Most guests here are American, so the resort quotes its rates in U.S. dollars.

B.P. 8, 98728 Maharepa, Moorea. *C* **56.13.68.** Fax 56.13.27. www.clubbalihai.com. 44 units. US$100–US$115 double; US$185–US$245 bungalow. AE, DC, MC, V. **Amenities:** Restaurant (breakfast and lunch); bar; outdoor pool; activities desk; car-rental desk; coin-op washers and dryers. *In room:* A/C, kitchen (except budget units), fridge, coffeemaker (except budget units), no phone.

The Bali Hai Boys

Californians Jay Carlisle, Don "Muk" McCallum, and the late Hugh Kelley gave up their budding business careers as stockbroker, lawyer, and sporting-goods salesman, respectively, and in 1960 bought an old vanilla plantation on Moorea. Instead of planting, they refurbished a beachfront hotel that stood on their property. Taking a page from James A. Michener's *Tales of the South Pacific*, they renamed it the Bali Hai and opened for business in 1961. With construction of Tahiti-Faaa International Airport across the Sea of the Moon, their timing couldn't have been better. With Jay managing the money, Hugh building the resort, and Muk entertaining their guests, they quickly had a success on their hands. Travel writers soon dubbed them the "Bali Hai Boys."

Supplies and fresh produce weren't easy to come by in those days, so they put the old vanilla plantation to work producing chickens, eggs, and milk. It was the first successful poultry and dairy operation on the island.

Thank Jay, Muk, and Hugh for overwater bungalows—those cabins sitting on pilings over the lagoon, with glass panels in their floors so that we can watch the fish swim below. They built the world's first in 1968 on Raiatea. A novelty at the time, their romantic invention is now a staple at resorts well beyond French Polynesia.

Hotel Kaveka *Value*   Another modest property with a fine view, this all-bungalow hotel sits behind a high rock wall along the road, but its other side opens to Cook's Bay. Noted primarily for its fish burgers, the hotel's overwater **Fisherman's Wharf** enjoys the best view of any Moorea restaurant serving an international menu. The white-sand beach here is compact (a breakwater fronts most of the property), but the snorkeling is very good. The bungalows are made of timber with shingle roofs covering pandanus ceilings. Most have double and single platform beds and smallish, shower-only bathrooms. Two units have two double beds and much better bathrooms. All units have ceiling fans, and some (including beachfront bungalows) have air-conditioners. The least expensive lanai units also lack porches. If your bungalow doesn't have one, you can rent a TV and fridge (as well as a cellphone). The few-frills Kaveka is often the least expensive hotel offered in package trips to French Polynesia.

B.P. 373, 98728 Maharepa, Moorea. © 56.50.50. Fax 56.52.63. www.hotelkaveka.com. 25 units. 11,500CFP–23,500CFP (US$115–US$235) double. AE, MC, V. **Amenities:** Restaurant; bar; watersports equipment/rentals; laundry service. *In room:* A/C (some units), TV, no phone.

La Baie de Nuarei   You can see Tahiti from this small pension, on the north side of Temae Public Beach and near the Sofitel Moorea Beach Resort. Owner Tamara Kindynis, who also operates a Thalassotherapy spa here, has three bungalows in her beachside compound, which is enclosed by a privacy fence. Her "Vaiki" and "Vahia" units have tin-topped thatch roofs and can each sleep up to three persons. The larger "Sakura" bungalow can accommodate four. All have kitchen facilities and tastefully designed bathrooms.

B.P. 605, 98728 Maharepa, Moorea (in Temae). © and fax **56.15.63.** www.labaiedenuarei.pf. 3 units. 12,000CFP–14,000CFP (US$120–US$140). No credit cards. **Amenities:** Spa; free use of bicycles, canoes, and snorkel gear. *In room:* TV, kitchen, no phone.

BETWEEN COOK'S AND OPUNOHU BAYS
EXPENSIVE
Sheraton Moorea Lagoon Resort & Spa ⭐⭐   On the north coast about halfway between Cook's and Opunohu bays, this hotel is not particularly convenient to restaurants and activities, but it does provide shuttles to the Tiki Village Theatre and the Vaiare ferry dock. Two stunning, conical thatch roofs cover the reception area and a French restaurant overlooking a decent beach. Steps lead down to a beachside pool with its own sunken bar. Some guests have complained about the resort's services, but you'll get serious pampering in the Mandara spa. All of the guest bungalows are identical except for their location. A Y-shaped pier—with its own sundowner bar—leads to half of them out over the lagoon. These all have glass floor panels for fish-viewing and decks with steps down into the clear, 4-foot-deep water. The others are situated in a coconut grove by the beach. Every unit is equipped with niceties such as CD players, complimentary snorkeling gear, plush robes, and claw-foot bathtubs, in addition to walk-in showers. The public areas and guest quarters here are the most luxurious on Moorea.

B.P. 1005, 98279 Papetoai, Moorea (between Cook's and Opunohu bays). © **800/325-3535** or 55.11.11 in Moorea. Fax 86.48.40. www.sheratonmoorea.com. 106 units. 34,400CFP–89,000CFP (US$344–US$890) bungalow. AE, DC, MC, V. **Amenities:** 2 restaurants; 3 bars; outdoor pool; 2 tennis courts; health club; spa; watersports equipment/rentals; bike rentals; concierge; activities desk; car-rental desk; business center; 24-hr. room service; massage; babysitting; laundry service. *In room:* A/C, TV, dataport, minibar, coffeemaker, hair dryer, iron, safe, CD player.

MODERATE

Fare Vaihere *(Kids)*   On the eastern shore of Opunohu Bay, this pension has four small bungalows in its tropical gardens and a family-size unit beside the beach and lagoon. Although the buildings all have tin roofs, they are very Polynesian inside, with bamboo walls and bright tropical bedspreads. Each has a front porch. Guests in the family unit have their own kitchen, while everyone else gets a complimentary tropical breakfast and can share cooking facilities in a separate lounge building. You can explore the lagoon with kayaks and snorkeling gear, either from the beach or from a long pier that reaches deep water beyond the fringing reef. Owners Cril and Florence Morize have three youngsters of their own, and your own children should enjoy Fare Vaihere, too.

B.P. 1806, 98729 Papetoai, Moorea (PK 15.5, between Cook's and Opunohu bays). © and fax **56.19.19** or 79.00.97. www.farevaihere.com. 5 units. 16,200CFP–25,000CFP (US$162–US$250). Rates include continental breakfast. MC, V. **Amenities:** Communal kitchen; free use of bicycles, kayaks, and snorkel gear. *In room:* TV (large unit only), kitchen (large unit only), fridge, coffeemaker, no phone.

Pension Motu Iti   Auguste and Dora Ienfa's little pension sits beside the lagoon about 800m (2,625 ft.) west of the Sheraton Moorea Lagoon Resort & Spa. They have no beach, only a bulkhead along the shore, but a pier goes to an overwater cabana for relaxing. Their five bungalows are clean, comfortable, and reasonably spacious, and there's also a small dormitory over the main building. The dining room serves breakfast, lunch, and dinner daily, although the food at **Restaurant Aito** (p. 141) next door is much more interesting.

B.P. 189, 98728 Maharepa, Moorea (between Cook's and Opunohu bays). © **55.05.20.** Fax 55.05.21. www.pension motuiti.com. 5 units, 20 dorm beds (shared bathrooms). 10,500CFP–12,000CFP (US$105–US$120) bungalow, 1,650CFP (US$16.50) dorm bed. AE, MC, V. **Amenities:** Restaurant; bar; free use of kayaks, canoes, and snorkel gear; babysitting; laundry service. *In room:* TV, no phone.

THE NORTHWEST COAST

EXPENSIVE

Inter-Continental Resort & Spa Moorea ★★★ *(Kids)*   Although relatively isolated about 2.5km (1½ miles) east of the Club Med area, Moorea's best all-around resort has plenty to keep its guests busy. The beach and lagoon here aren't Moorea's best, but the resort has the widest range of watersports activities on the island—all of them available both to guests and to nonguests who are willing to pay (see "Fishing, Hiking, Watersports & Other Outdoor Activities," earlier in this chapter). A well-organized children's program also makes this the best family vacation resort in French Polynesia.

The airy central building with a shingle roof houses the hotel's reception, bar, boutiques, car-rental desk, and indoor activities area. It opens to a large pool area surrounded by an ample sun deck. In a tropical setting under a large thatch roof, a dining room opening to the pool offers lunches, light dinners, and snacks. A much larger restaurant provides extensive breakfast buffets and is used for special functions and evening entertainment. The Tahitian weekly dance show on the beach is one of Moorea's most colorful.

Most of the guest bungalows extend partially over the water from manmade islands. They are of European construction, but mat walls and rattan furnishings lend tropical ambience. They're also air-conditioned, unlike the less expensive garden bungalows. A curving two-story building holds 52 spacious hotel rooms. These all have patios or balconies facing the beach, and their combination tub-showers are a rarity on Moorea.

B.P. 1019, 98279 Papetoai, Moorea (between Papetoai and Haapiti). © **800/327-0200** or 55.19.19. Fax 55.19.55. http://moorea.intercontinental.com. 52 units, 102 bungalows. 36,000CFP (US$364) double; 42,000CFP–80,700CFP (US$420–US$807) bungalow. Rates include continental breakfast. AE, DC, MC, V. **Amenities:** Restaurant; bar; outdoor pool; tennis courts; spa; watersports equipment/rentals (free use of snorkel gear, kayaks, and canoes); bike rentals; children's programs; concierge; activities desk; car-rental desk; limited room service; babysitting; laundry service. *In room:* A/C, TV, minibar, coffeemaker, hair dryer.

MODERATE

Fare Vai Moana   The best thing about this little hotel is its charming French restaurant and bar, housed in a beachside building with a natural thatch roof. Otherwise, it's in the center of a busy, crowded neighborhood, which can give it a Grand Central Terminal ambience, especially during mealtimes. On the other hand, more restaurants and a multitude of shops are short walks away. The guest bungalows also have thatch roofs, but most are close together, and some are duplex units, meaning you could have neighbors sharing a common wall. Your best choice is one of three units beside the beach, with unobstructed lagoon views from their porches. These are not screened, but they do have ceiling fans and a mezzanine with extra beds, meaning each can sleep up to five persons. Complimentary continental breakfasts, however, are provided for only two guests in each bungalow.

B.P. 1181, 98729 Papetoai, Moorea (west of old Club Med site). © **56.17.14.** Fax 56.28.78. www.pacific-resorts. com. 13 units. 15,000CFP–22,000CFP (US$150–US$220). Rates include continental breakfast (2 persons per unit). AE, MC. V. **Amenities:** Restaurant; bar; watersports equipment/rentals; activities desk; limited room service. *In room:* Fridge, safe, no phone.

Hotel Hibiscus   Occupying a lagoonside coconut grove in the Haapiti restaurant and shopping district, this hotel has been around for years. Although its 29 bungalows are showing their age a tad, they still have traditional island charms, such as natural thatch roofs that extend over front porches. They also have ceiling fans and kitchenettes, making the Hibiscus attractive for longer-term stays. Next to the pool, a newer building holds 12 less appealing but air-conditioned hotel-style rooms. The beach is minimal here, but a section of the lagoon has been walled off to make a safe swimming hole for children. The beachside **Sunset Restaurant and Pizzeria** serves decent pizzas and pastas, and it's a fine place to sip a cocktail at sunset.

B.P. 1009, 98279 Papetoai, Moorea (in Haapiti, east of old Club Med site). © **56.12.12.** Fax 56.20.69. www.hotel-hibiscus.pf. 41 units. 13,200CFP–25,000CFP (US$132–US$250). AE, MC, V. **Amenities:** Restaurant; bar; outdoor pool; watersports equipment/rentals. *In room:* A/C (hotel rooms only), kitchen.

Hotel Les Tipaniers ⭑⭑ (Value)   One of Moorea's best values, this friendly French-owned establishment sits in a coconut grove beside the sandy beach that wraps around the island's northwestern corner. The widely spaced bungalows stand back in the trees, giving the small complex an open, airy atmosphere. They're also far enough from the road to be quiet. Each "standard superior" bungalow has an L-shaped settee facing a sliding-glass door to a covered porch. Behind the settee, a raised sleeping area supports a queen-size bed, and behind that, a fully tiled bathroom has a sizable shower and vanity space. To the rear of the property, other bungalows are equipped with kitchens and can sleep up to five persons. Also back here is a building that houses four small hotel-style rooms equipped with twin beds (you can push them together), reading lights, and ample tiled bathrooms with showers. Okay for couples, these rooms are the least expensive yet still a comfortable place to stay on Moorea. Unlike the others, however, they do not have phones, fridges, or safes. All units here have ceiling fans but not air-conditioners.

Les Tipaniers Restaurant de la Plage (Restaurant by the Beach; p. 142), with a deck over the white sands, is open during the day, while the hotel's very good **Restaurant Les Tipaniers** (p. 142) serves Italian cuisine at dinner. Guests can make free use of canoes and bicycles, or pay Tip Nautic for kayaking, water-skiing, *motu* trips, and diving with Scubapiti, which is based here.

If you'd like to have a bungalow without the hotel accoutrements, consider **Les Tapaniers Iti,** a five-unit annex near Papetoai village. A shuttle will bring you to the main hotel, where you can make use of its facilities. Rates at the annex are lower than at the main property, and discounts are given for longer stays.

B.P. 1002, 98279 Papetoai, Moorea (in Haapiti, east of old Club Med site). ✆ **56.12.67.** Fax 56.29.25. www.les tipaniers.com. 22 units. 6,900CFP (US$69) double; 13,950CFP (US$140) bungalow without kitchenette; 13,950CFP–15,950CFP (US$140–US$160) double with kitchenette. AE, DC, MC, V. **Amenities:** 2 restaurants; 2 bars; watersports equipment/rentals; free use of canoes and bicycles; babysitting; laundry service. *In room:* Kitchen (6 units), fridge (18 units), safe (18 units).

Residence Linareva   You need not go far for a fine meal here; just stroll out the long pier to **Linareva Floating Restaurant and Bar** (p. 141). Ashore, owner-chef Eric Lussiez has accommodations of varying size beside a very fine beach. All are tropically attired with thatch ceilings, split bamboo walls, and bright fabrics, and all have porches and cooking facilities. They range from the least expensive duplex garden studios, which can sleep two persons, to an air-conditioned beachside bungalow, which can sleep up to six. The restaurant will send breakfast to your unit for an extra fee. This is a gay-friendly establishment.

B.P. 1H, 98729 Haapiti, Moorea (PK 34.5, on the southwest coast). ✆ **55.05.65.** Fax 55.05.67. www.linareva.com. 8 units. 11,500CFP–22,500CFP (US$115–US$225). AE, MC, V. **Amenities:** Restaurant; bar; free use of kayaks, canoes, and snorkel gear; bike rentals. *In room:* A/C (some units), TV, kitchen, coffeemaker, no phone.

INEXPENSIVE

Camping Chez Nelson   All guests share toilets, cold-water showers, and communal kitchen facilities at this campground and hostel in a beachside coconut grove about 183m (600 ft.) west of old Club Med. In addition to camping space on a shadeless lawn, basic accommodations here include small bungalows for couples, four blocks of small dorm rooms (two bunks each), and four other thatch-roofed hostel bungalows down the road (and still on the beach). Each of the latter has a kitchen, modern bathroom, and porch.

B.P. 1309, 98279 Papetoai, Moorea (in Haapiti, west of old Club Med site). ✆ and fax **56.15.18.** www.camping-nelson.pf. 4 bungalows, 15 rooms (shared bathrooms), 20 dorm beds (shared bathrooms). 1,100CFP (US$11) per camper; 1,300CFP–1,600CFP (US$13–US$16) dorm bed; 3,800CFP–5,800CFP (US$38–US$58) double; 4,000CFP–4,700CFP (US$40–US$47) per bungalow. Lower rates for stays of more than 1 night. AE, DC, MC. V. **Amenities:** Communal kitchen. *In room:* Kitchen (bungalows only); no phone.

Mark's Place Paradise   A cabinet maker from Idaho, Mark Walker moved to French Polynesia in 1980 and has put his skills to work on the creatively rustic units at this retreat beside a stream in the Haapiti Valley. No two alike, the accommodations range in size from a honeymoon unit (with TV and DVD player) to one large enough for groups or use as a dormitory. Two studio rooms have TVs, kitchens, and private bathrooms. All other guests—including campers, dorm residents, and those in the

---

Tips **Bring Traveler's Checks, or Card It**

The only banking facility on Moorea's northwest corner is Banque de Polynésie's ATM in Le Petit Village shopping center, opposite the old Club Med site. Since you cannot be assured of withdrawing cash from this machine, and it's a long and expensive trip to the banks at Maharepa, bring traveler's checks if you're staying in this area, or be prepared to put most of your expenditures on a credit card.

---

honeymoon unit—share toilets, showers, and the communal kitchen. Although he isn't on the beach, Mark's attention to his guests makes this an excellent place for budget-conscious travelers and backpackers.

B.P. 41, 98279 Papetoai, Moorea (at PK 23.5 in Haapiti valley). *©* **56.43.02** or 78.93.65. www.marks-place-paradise. com. 5 bungalows (3 with bathroom), 10 dorm beds (shared bathrooms), 25 tent sites. 6,000CFP–7,500CFP (US$60–US$75) bungalow; 1,500CFP–2,500CFP (US$15–US$25) dorm bed; 1,050CFP (US$11) per camper. MC, V. **Amenities:** Communal kitchen; bike and kayak rentals. *In room:* No phone.

Moorea Camping   This establishment in a coconut grove has much more shade and a better beach for swimming than does Camping Chez Nelson. A beachside pavilion covers picnic tables and a communal kitchen. A long plywood house—actually little more than a permanent tent—contains eight rooms with foam mattresses. One bungalow can accommodate up to four persons. The showers dispense cold water.

PK 27.5, Tiahura, Moorea (in Haapiti, west of old Club Med site). *©* **56.14.47.** Fax 56.30.22. einui@hotmail.com. 20 tent sites, 9 dorm beds, 8 rooms (all with shared bathrooms); 5 bungalows (with private bathrooms). 1,100CFP–1,500CFP (US$11–US$15) per camper; 1,200CFP–1,800CFP (US$12–US$18) dorm bed; 2,500CFP–3,800CFP (US$25–US$38) per person in rooms; 4,800CFP–5,800CFP (US$48–US$58) bungalow double. Lower rates for stays of more than 1 night. No credit cards. **Amenities:** Communal kitchen; bike rentals. *In room:* Kitchen (bungalows only), no phone.

7 Where to Dine

The restaurant scene changes quickly on Moorea, so I can only hope the ones I recommend below are still in business when you get here. As on Tahiti, you can save by eating at snack bars for breakfast, lunch, or an early dinner.

THE COOK'S BAY AREA

Nicely spiced pies come from the wood-fired oven at **Allo Pizza,** in Cook's Bay near the gendarmerie (*©* **56.18.22**). There are only two tables, so most folks carry out or call for delivery if they're staying between the Sofitel Moorea Beach Resort and the Sheraton Moorea. Prices range from 900CFP to 1,900CFP (US$9–US$19). Open Tuesday to Saturday from 11am to 2pm and 5 to 9pm, Sunday from 5 to 9pm.

EXPENSIVE

Le Sud *ℱ* SOUTHERN FRENCH   For a pleasant change of French pace, head to this little white house in the Maharepa shopping district for paella, Provençal-style fish dishes, and seafood pastas from *le sud* (the south) of France. The spices definitely reflect Spanish and Italian influences. The *plats du jour* are very good value, especially at lunch. Torches contribute to romantic nighttime dining on the patio.

Maharepa. (? **56.42.95.** Reservations recommended. Main courses 1,900CFP–2,900CFP (US$19–US$29). MC, V. Tues–Sun 11am–2pm and 6:30–9:30pm.

Restaurant Honu Iti (Chez Roger) CLASSICAL FRENCH This bayside restaurant is the domain of owner-chef Roger Iqual, who once won the Concours National de la Poêle d'Or (Golden Pot Contest) in Cannes for a sea-bass concoction. The scenic setting beside Cook's Bay is terrific. Roger devotes much of his time now to painting (his works hang on the walls here), but oversees his and wife Sui-Lane's two sons back in the kitchen. They specialize in fresh seafood—Tuesday and Friday are fresh-tuna days—prepared in the classical French fashion. Be sure to try the lightly smoked slices of mahimahi or haddock served over a piquant potato salad, or the delicate mahimahi mousse. One note of caution: Although I've had very good meals here, some of my friends on Moorea have not.

Pao Pao, north of Municipal Market. (? **56.19.84.** Reservations recommended. Main courses 2,900CFP–3,800CFP (US$29–US$38). AE, MC, V. Sat–Thurs 11:30am–2pm and 6:30–9pm.

MODERATE

Alfredo's FRENCH/ITALIAN Gregarious French restaurateur Christian Boucheron, who worked at hotels in the Washington, D.C., suburbs for 19 years, will make you feel right at home in this old building, a short walk from the Club Bali Hai. In fact, many guests are Americans and other English-speaking visitors who come here as much for fun as food. Local guitarist Ron Falconer usually plays and sings here Thursday and Sunday nights.

Pao Pao, near Club Bali Hai. (? **56.17.71.** Reservations recommended. Pizzas 1,650CFP (US$17); main courses 1,650CFP–3,800CFP (US$17–US$38). MC, V. Daily 11am–2:30pm and 5:30–9:30pm.

Le Mahogany ✸✸ _Value_ CHINESE/FRENCH French chef François Courtien spent 30 years cooking at the former Hotel Bali Hai before joining Tahitian Blondine Agnia at her pleasant little dining spot next to the local gym. It's a favorite with local expatriates who appreciate value and friendly service. Polished mahogany tables, art-adorned walls, and a window opening to a garden provide tropical ambience. A rich avocado-and-shrimp cocktail is a good way to start. Daily specials feature the likes of Moorea-grown shrimp with curry or Provençal sauce, or shrimp and scallops in a puff pastry with a light cream sauce. The Cantonese main courses are better than those at any Chinese restaurant here. Or you can opt for the special tourist menu of a salad, mahimahi grilled or with meunière sauce, and ice cream for desert. Otherwise, end with _tarte tatin,_ a caramelized apple pie served with vanilla ice cream.

Maharepa. (? **56.39.73.** Reservations recommended. Main courses 1,550CFP–2,950CFP (US$16–US$30). Tourist menu 3,100CFP (US$31). MC, V. Thurs–Tues 11am–2:30pm and 6–9:30pm.

INEXPENSIVE

Caraméline PATISSERIE/SNACKS A good choice for a cooked breakfast, this patisserie also offers a selection of pastries, crepes, pizzas, salads, omelets, quiches,

---

Value Call for Transportation

Most Moorea restaurants will either come get you, or pay, half if not all of your taxi fare if you make reservations for dinner. Although they restrict this service to nearby guests, depending on the size of your group, it pays to call ahead and ask.

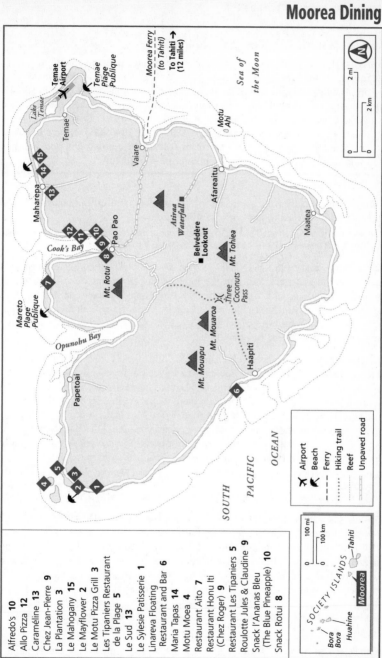

Sea of
the Moon

*Moorea Ferry
(to Tahiti)*
To Tahiti →
(12 miles)

Temae Airport

Temae Plage Publique

Lake Temae

Temae

Motu Ahi

Vaiare

Maharepa

Afareaitu

Atiraa Waterfall

Pao Pao

Cook's Bay

Belvédère Lookout

Mt. Tohiea

Maatea

Mareto Plage Publique

Mt. Rotui

Three Coconuts Pass

Opunohu Bay

Mt. Mouaroa

Haapiti

Papetoai

Mt. Mouapu

SOUTH PACIFIC OCEAN

Airport
Beach
Ferry
Hiking trail
Reef
Unpaved road

Alfredo's **10**
Allo Pizza **12**
Caraméline **13**
Chez Jean-Pierre **9**
La Plantation **3**
Le Mahogany **15**
Le Mayflower **2**
Le Motu Pizza Grill **3**
Les Tipaniers Restaurant
de la Plage **5**
Le Sud **13**
Le Sylesie Patisserie **1**
Linareva Floating
Restaurant and Bar **6**
Maria Tapas **14**
Motu Moea **4**
Restaurant Aito **7**
Restaurant Honu Iti
(Chez Roger) **9**
Restaurant Les Tipaniers **5**
Roulotte Jules & Claudine **9**
Snack l'Ananas Bleu
(The Blue Pineapple) **10**
Snack Rotui **8**

SOCIETY ISLANDS

Bora Bora
Huahine
Moorea
Tahiti

139

Tips **Check Out Moorea's *Roulottes***

As on Tahiti, your best bet for inexpensive nighttime meals are the local *roulottes* (see "Don't Miss *Les Roulottes,*" p. 112). The best of these meal wagons, **Roulotte Jules & Claudine,** at the Municipal Market in Pao Pao (*©* **56.25. 31**), serves a mixed menu of *poisson cru,* chow mein, and char-grilled steaks, chicken, and fish, but the best item is local shrimp in a tasty coconut-curry sauce. Prices range from 800CFP to 1,500CFP (US$8–US$15). No credit cards. Open Monday through Saturday from 6:30 to 8:30pm. You'll find another *roulotte* near Le Petite Village shopping center in Haapiti.

---

burgers, sandwiches, fruit plates, ice cream, sundaes, and other goodies. The patio tables here are a relaxing spot to write a postcard.

Maharepa, next to the post office. *©* 56.15.88. Reservations not accepted. Breakfasts 650CFP–1,550CFP (US$6.50–$16); snacks and light meals 400CFP–1,800CFP (US$4–US$18). MC, V. Daily 7am–5pm.

Chez Jean-Pierre CANTONESE   When my body tells me to eat my vegetables, I get off the tourist track and join the locals at this plain but clean Chinese family restaurant beside Cook's Bay. You can try very good Chinese-style *poisson cru* (it's spicy) or chicken with sweet Moorea pineapple. Everything's fresh and tasty here.

Pao Pao, near Municipal Market. *©* 56.18.51. Main courses 1,350CFP–2,150CFP (US$14–US$22). MC, V. Mon–Tues and Thurs–Sat 11:15am–2:30pm; Thurs–Tues 6:15–9:30pm.

Maria Tapas *(Finds)*   FRENCH/TEX-MEX   You'll hear conversations being held in French, English, and Tahitian—sometimes all three simultaneously—at this lively pub, where the offspring of Moorea's many expatriate residents like to hang out. Happy hours from 6 to 7pm on Thursday and Friday and entertainment on Thursday and Saturday evenings really pack them in. Although Tex-Mex is the official specialty, I stick to burgers, salads, steaks, or French fare. Friendly owners Julie Berten and Herenui Teriitehau stock a wide selection of European beers. You can check your e-mail here every day except Saturday (see "Fast Facts: Moorea," earlier in this chapter).

Cook's Bay, PK 6, in Kilupa Centre. *©* 55.01.70. www.mariatapas.com. Reservations recommended Fri–Sat. Most items 950CFP–2,100CFP (US$10–US$21). MC, V. Restaurant Mon–Thurs 11:30am–2:30pm and 6:30–9:30pm, Fri 11:30am–2:30pm and 6:30pm–1am; Sat 6pm–1am; bar Mon–Thurs 9am–11pm, Fri 9am–1am, Sat 6am–1am.

Snack L'Ananas Bleu (The Blue Pineapple) *(Value)*   BREAKFAST/SNACKS   Matahi Hunter's "snack" occupies what was once the sunken bayside bar at the Club Bali Hai, where a stupendous view of Cook's Bay accompanies the cooked or continental breakfasts and the lunches of big juicy beef, fish, or teriyaki burgers and french fries. Ice cream and fruit drinks provide relief from the midday heat. There's a seafood barbecue on Wednesday night following the hotel's Tahitian dance show.

At Club Bali Hai, Pao Pao. *©* 56.12.06. Reservations not accepted. Breakfast 600CFP–1,500CFP (US$6–$15); burgers and sandwiches 750CFP–1,550CFP (US$7.50–US$16); main courses 1,600CFP–2,000CFP (US$16–US$20). MC, V. Daily 7am–3pm.

Snack Rotui SNACK BAR   This walk-up "snack," run by a Chinese family, is located on the shore of Cook's Bay. For about 500CFP (US$5), you can get a *casse-croûte* sandwich, a soft drink, and a slice of delicious homemade cake. Forget the plate lunches, usually a Chinese dish with rice, which are prepared earlier in the day and served without refrigeration. A few tables under a roof beside the beach catch the breezes off the bay.

Pao Pao, west of the bridge at the head of Cook's Bay. © **56.18.16.** Reservations not accepted. Sandwiches 140CFP–200CFP (US$1.40–US$2). No credit cards. Tues–Sun 7am–6pm.

BETWEEN COOK'S AND OPUNOHU BAYS

Restaurant Aito CORSICAN/FRENCH   Literally extending out over the lagoon, this open-air cafe preserves the old South Seas ambience better than any other on Moorea. Adding to the charm are big *aito* (ironwood) trees growing through the deck and thatch roof (hence the restaurant's name). Owner Jean-Baptiste Cipriani grew up in Marseilles on the cooking of his Corsican ancestors, and he repeats some of those dishes here, including a luscious tomato sauce that requires 10 hours to prepare. You can dip your bread into some *very* spicy Corsican peppers while waiting. This isn't the cleanest place on Moorea, but it's a terrific spot for a lagoonside lunch, as many celebrity visits attest.

PK 13.1, west of Sheraton Moorea between Cook's and Opunohu bays. © **56.45.52.** Reservations recommended. Main courses 1,850CFP–2,600CFP (US$19–US$26). MC, V. Daily 7–9am, 11am–2:30pm, and 6–9pm.

THE NORTHWEST COAST

Restaurants come and go in Le Petit Village shopping center opposite the old Club Med site. Although I wasn't particularly impressed, others have enjoyed the food at the moderately expensive **La Plantation** (© **56.45.10**), opposite the Club Med site; it's one of this area's more romantic restaurants. Soft lighting, music, and dining out on a big porch help set the scene for Polynesian-influenced French fare.

EXPENSIVE

Linareva Floating Restaurant and Bar ♠♠ FRENCH SEAFOOD   You'll pay a price to have dinner here, but Eric Lussiez's restaurant and bar is Moorea's most unusual: It occupies the original *Tamarii Moorea,* the first ferry to ply the waters between Papeete and Moorea. Eric completely rebuilt the old vessel and outfitted the dining room with polished wood, large windows, and plenty of bright brass and other nautical decor. The menu changes with the availability of local seafood, such as shark and emperor fish, expertly prepared with traditional French sauces. Tour groups stop here for lunch, when prices run about half of those at dinner.

Haapiti (7km/4 miles south of old Club Med site). © **55.05.66.** Reservations strongly recommended for dinner. Main courses 1,700CFP–3,850CFP (US$17–US$39). Tourist menu 3,550CFP (US$36). MC, V. Daily 11am–3pm and 5–10pm.

Tips Lunch on a *Motu*

Even if you don't spend a day on a little islet off the northwest coast, you can pop over for a French or Tahitian lunch at **Motu Moea** (© **74.96.96**). Book at your hotel activities desk, since reservations are essential for a boat shuttle leaving at 10am, noon, or 2pm daily. Round-trip boat transfers cost about 1,000CPF (US$10), while main courses average about 2,000CFP (US$20). You'll be on your own out here, so follow the advice of the activities staff and don't swim in the pass between the islets.

MODERATE

Le Mayflower ✿✿✿ (Value) CASUAL FRENCH   This roadside restaurant draws mostly local residents, who rightly proclaim it to be Moorea's best for both food and value. The sauces are lighter than you will experience elsewhere, and there is always a vegetarian selection. I like to start with a salad of warm local shrimp over cool, fresh greens. The house special—lobster ravioli in a cream sauce—is a worthy main choice, as are seafood pasta under pesto or the reliable shrimp in coconut curry. Mahimahi in a lobster sauce highlights a special tourist menu here.

Haapiti, west of old Club Med site. ℂ 56.53.59. Reservations recommended. Main courses 1,650CFP–2,650CFP (US$17–US$27). AE, MC, V. Tues–Sun 11:30am–2pm and 6:30–10:30pm.

Restaurant Les Tipaniers ✿✿ (Value) FRENCH/ITALIAN   This romantic, thatch-roofed restaurant is popular with both visitors and Moorea's permanent residents, who come here for delicious pizzas with a variety of toppings and homemade spaghetti, lasagna, tagliatelle, and gnocchi served with Bolognese, carbonara, or seafood sauce. French dishes include pepper steak and mahimahi in butter or vanilla sauce. Discounted transportation is available for Haapiti-area hotel guests.

At Hotel Les Tipaniers, Haapiti (east of old Club Med site). ℂ 56.12.67. Reservations recommended. Pasta and pizza 1,000CFP–1,550CFP (US$10–US$16); main courses 1,850CFP–2,500CFP (US$19–US$25). AE, DC, MC, V. Daily 6:30–9pm.

INEXPENSIVE

Le Motu Pizza Grill SNACK BAR   You can get a grilled steak with french fries at this open-air restaurant, but it's best for pizzas and burgers. Light fare includes salads, crepes, and soft-serve ice cream, and you can choose from a wide selection of soft drinks, beer, and wine.

Haapiti, opposite old Club Med site. ℂ 56.16.70. Reservations not accepted. Burgers, sandwiches, and salads 500CFP–1,400CFP (US$5–US$14); pizza 1,050CFP–1,300CFP (US$11–US$13). MC, V (2,000CFP/US$20 minimum). Mon–Sat 9:30am–9pm, Sun 9:30am–3pm.

Les Tipaniers Restaurant de la Plage (Restaurant by the Beach) ✿ ITALIAN/SNACK BAR   Under a soaring thatch roof and opening to the lagoon, this is the best place in Haapiti for a lagoonside lunch or sunset cocktail. It offers a good selection of salads (some with fruit) and a big juicy burger. Or you can select one of the pastas that make the hotel's nighttime restaurant popular (see above). Breakfast is also served here.

At Hotel Les Tipaniers, Haapiti (east of old Club Med site). ℂ 56.19.19. Reservations not accepted. Salads, sandwiches, and burgers 550CFP–1,300CFP (US$5.50–US$13); pastas 1,000CFP–1,700CFP (US$10–US$17). AE, DC, MC, V. Daily 6:30–9:30am and noon–2:15pm (bar 6:30am–7pm).

Le Sylesie Patisserie BREAKFAST/SNACKS   This is a good place to start your day with croissants-and-coffee or a full American-style breakfast (served all day). Later you can stop for crepes, burgers, sandwiches, small pizzas, quiches, and pastries. The low-slung building has six tables under cover in front.

Haapiti, west of the Club Med site. ℂ 56.20.45. Reservations not necessary. Breakfast 600CFP–2,200CFP (US$6–US$22); crepes and salads 500CFP–1,500CFP (US$5–US$15). No credit cards. Daily 6am–5pm.

(*Moments* Sunsets with Muk at Club Bali Hai

If I'm on Moorea, you'll find me beside Cook's Bay at the **Club Bali Hai** (© **56.13.68**) swapping yarns with Muk McCallum, one of the original Bali Hai Boys. His bring-your-own happy hours run Thursday through Tuesday between 5:30 and 7pm. This is one of the great vistas in the South Pacific; you'll want to become a modern Paul Gauguin in order to capture the changing colors of the bay, sky, and jagged mountains.

8 Island Nights on Moorea

The one required nighttime activity here is an authentic feast and dance show at **Tiki Theatre Village** in Haapiti (© **55.02.50**). For details, see p. 125.

Moorea's major resorts also have Tahitian feasts and dance shows at least once a week. The most elaborate is the Saturday-evening lagoonside show at the **Inter-Continental Resort & Spa Moorea.** Most charge 7,500CFP to 8,500CFP (US$75–US$85) per person for the dinner and show.

One notable exception is the free show at the **Club Bali Hai** (© **56.13.68**), every Wednesday at 6pm. It's followed by an a la carte seafood barbecue at Snack l'Ananas Bleu (The Blue Pineapple). Depending on what you order, dinner should cost about 2,500CFP (US$25). Reservations are required for the barbecue.

Among the restaurants, **Maria Tapas** (© **55.01.70**) has entertainment on Thursday and Saturday evenings (unless you dine here, expect a cover charge when bands perform), and Scottish-born guitarist Ron Falconer usually plays at **Alfredo's** (© **56. 17.71**) on Thursday and Sunday. See "Where to Dine," earlier in this chapter, for details on both.

6

Huahine

Pronounced Wa-*ee*-nee by the French (who never sound an "h") and *Who*-a-hee-nay by the Tahitians (who always do), Huahine ranks with Easter Island and Raiatea (see chapter 7) as the three most important Polynesian archaeological sites. Here the ancient chiefs built a series of *maraes* on the shores of **Lake Fauna Nui,** which separates the north shore from a long, *motu*-like peninsula, and on Matairea Hill above the lakeside village of **Maeva.** These have been restored, and informational markers explain their history and purposes.

Many honeymooners and other visitors are making Huahine their last vacation stop, drawn by its relaxed ambience, Mooreaesque bays, clear lagoon, and lovely beaches. **Baie Avea (Avea Bay),** on the far southwestern coast of Huahine Iti, is fringed by one of the South Pacific's most glorious beaches. Another is right in the small hamlet of **Fare,** one of the region's best examples of what the South Seas were like in the days of trading schooners and copra planters.

Personally, I think Huahine is the third most beautiful island in French Polynesia (behind Moorea and Bora Bora). Geographically, it is actually two islands—Huahine Nui and Huahine Iti (Big Huahine and Little Huahine, respectively)—enclosed by the same reef and joined by a short bridge, which, in turn, separates two picturesque bays, Maroe and Bourayne. With basaltic thumbs reaching from jagged mountains on either side of the bays, this vista reminds me of Moorea.

France did not annex Huahine until 1897, more than 50 years after it took over Tahiti, and its 5,500 residents are still independent in spirit. When the first Europeans arrived, Huahine was governed as a single chiefdom and not divided into warring tribes as were the other islands, and this spirit of unity is still strong. Pouvanaa a Oopa, the founder of French Polynesia's independence movement, hailed from here. Unrushed by hordes of tourists, the friendly people of Huahine still say *"Ia orana"* to us visitors.

1 Getting Around Huahine

Huahine's airport is on the flat peninsula paralleling the north side of the island, 3km (2 miles) from Fare. Unless you have previously reserved a rental car or are willing to walk into Fare, take your hotel's minibus. At other times, **Moe's Taxi** (© **72.80.60**) or **Enite's Taxi** (© **68.82.37**) will carry you around. Fares are about 600CFP (US$6) from the airport into Fare, about 2,500CFP (US$25) to the southern end of Huahine Iti.

Avis (© **800/230-4898** or 68.73.34; www.avis.com), **Europcar** (© **800/227-7368** or 68.82.59; www.europcar.com), and **Hertz** (© **800/654-3131** or 68.76.85; www.hertz.com) have agents in Fare. Avis charges about 7,500CFP (US$75) a day for a car. Europcar rents scooters for 6,200CFP (US$62) a day, bicycles for 2,000CFP (US$20) a day. On Huahine Iti, **Mara'amu Sailing School,** at Pension Mauarii

Huahine

Aérodrome
de Huahine-Fare

Lac Fauna Nui

SOUTH PACIFIC
OCEAN

Manunu *Marae*

1 Maeva

10

Passe Avamoa

Fare

9

Passe Avapeihi

*Baie
de Cook*

Turi

*HUAHINE
NUI*

Fitii

3

8

7

Faie

2 *Baie
Faie*

Passe Tiare

Passe Farerea

Baie Maroe

Maroe

*Baie
Bourayne*

*HUAHINE
ITI*

Tefarerii

Haapu

Mahuti River

Parea

4
*Baie
Avèa*
*Avea
Beach*
5
6

0   1 mi
0   1 km

N

SOUTH PACIFIC OCEAN

ACCOMMODATIONS ■
Ariiura Camping **5**
Chez Guynette **9**
Huahine Vacances **3**
Pension Fare Maeva **10**
Pension Mauarii **4**
Pension Vaihonu Océan **10**
Relais Mahana **5**
Te Tiare Beach,
  an Outrigger Resort **8**
Villas Bougainville **3**

ATTRACTIONS ●
Anini *Marae* **6**
Eden Parc **7**
Huahine Nui
  Pearls & Pottery **2**
Maeva *maraes* **1**

✈ Airport
↖ Beach
⋯ Reef
📷 Scenic view
▭ Unpaved road

SOCIETY ISLANDS
Bora
Bora
Huahine
Tahiti
Moorea

0   100 mi
0   100 km

> *Fun Fact* **Say Hello to Dorothy**
>
> Be sure to say hello to Dorothy Levy, who runs the snack bar at the Huahine airport. Dorothy's Tahitian father came to Hollywood in the 1930s to work with Clark Gable on the original *Mutiny on the Bounty* movie. He later participated in the first film version of *Hurricane* with Dorothy Lamour, for whom he named this Dorothy.

(© **68.77.10**), rents scooters for 6,500CFP (US$65) a day and bicycles for 1,500CFP (US$15) a day.

Each district has local **buses,** which run into Fare at least once a day, but the schedules are highly irregular. If you take one from Fare to Parea, for example, you might not be able to get back on the same day.

FAST FACTS: Huahine

The following facts apply specifically to Huahine. For more information, see "Fast Facts: Tahiti & French Polynesia," in chapter 2.

Currency Exchange **Banque Socredo** is in Fare, on the road that parallels the main street and bypasses the waterfront. **Banque de Tahiti** is on Fare's waterfront. Both have ATMs.

Drugstores The pharmacist at the drugstore, on the main road between Fare and the airport, speaks English (© **68.80.90**). Open Monday through Friday from 7:30am to noon and 2:30 to 5pm, Saturday from 8am to noon, Sunday and holidays from 8 to 9am.

Emergencies/Police The emergency police phone number is © **17**. The phone number of the **gendarmerie** in Fare is © **68.82.61**.

Healthcare The **government infirmary** is in Fare (© **68.82.48**). Ask you hotel for the name of doctors and dentists in private practice.

Internet Access You can check your e-mail at **AO Api New World** (© **68.70.99**), upstairs over the Manava Huahine Visitors Bureau. Open Monday through Friday from 8:30am to noon and 4 to 7:30pm. Access costs 15CFP (US15¢) a minute.

Post Office The colonial-style post office is in Fare on the bypass road north of the waterfront area. Hours are Monday through Thursday from 7:30am to 3pm, Friday from 7am to 2pm.

Restrooms There are public toilets on the Fare wharf opposite the visitors bureau, but don't expect them to be clean.

Visitor Information On Fare's main street opposite the wharf, **Manava Huahine Visitors Bureau** (© and fax **68.78.81**) is open Monday through Saturday from 8am to noon (more or less). Some local pensions and tour operators have banded together to host **www.iaorana-huahine.com**.

Water Don't drink the tap water on Huahine. Bottled water is available at all grocery stores.

2 Exploring Huahine

VISITING THE *MARAES* ★★★

The village of **Maeva,** beside the pass where Lake Fauna Nui flows toward the sea, was a major cultural and religious center before Europeans arrived in the islands. All of Huahine's chiefly families lived here. More than 200 stone structures have been discovered between the lakeshore and **Matairea Hill,** which looms over Maeva, including some 40 *maraes* (the others were houses, paddocks, and agricultural terraces).

To see the *maraes* on your own, start west of Maeva village at the big reed-sided building known as **Fare Potee.** Flanked by *maraes* and extending out over Lake Fauna Nui, the present building is modeled after a large meeting house that stood here in 1925 but was later destroyed by a hurricane. Take time to read the historical markers outside, which expertly explain the history and use of the *maraes.* Fare Potee has been a museum in the past, and if it has reopened, you'll get to see *adzes* (stone axes), fishhooks, and other artifacts uncovered during restoration work by Dr. Yoshiko H. Sinoto, the chairman of the anthropology department of the Bernice P. Bishop Museum in Honolulu. He has restored this and many other *maraes* throughout Polynesia.

Six *maraes* and other structures, some built as fortifications during the 1844–48 French-Tahitian war, sit on Matairea Hill. The track up the hill can be muddy and slippery during wet weather, and the steep climb is best done in early morning or late afternoon. Better yet, take a tour (see below).

Easier to reach, the large **Manunu Marae** stands on the beach about 1km (½ mile) across the bridge on the east end of Maeva. Follow the left fork in the road after crossing the bridge. The setting is impressive.

From the bridge, you will see several stone **fish traps.** Restored by Dr. Sinoto, they work as well today as they did in the 16th century, trapping fish as the tide ebbs and flows in and out of the narrow passage separating the lake from the sea.

HISTORICAL TOURS

The most informative way to see the historical sites—and much of Huahine, for that matter—is with Paul Atallah of **Island Eco Tours** ★★★ (© **68.79.67;** pauljatallah@ mail.pf). Paul is an American who graduated from the University of Hawaii with a major in anthropology and a minor in Polynesian Island archaeology. He has lived in French Polynesia for more than a decade. His is more than a typical safari expedition, for he gives in-depth commentary about the Maeva *marae* and other historical sites. He charges 5,000CFP (US$50) for morning or afternoon 4-hour trips. They depart

---

Fun Fact Adzes, Fishhooks & Ornaments

When construction began on the now-defunct Hotel Bali Hai Huahine on the north side of Fare in 1973, workers discovered some artifacts while excavating the lily ponds—the only remnants of the hotel left today. Dr. Yoshiko of the Bernice P. Bishop Museum in Honolulu just happened to be on the island and took charge of further excavations. During the next 2 years, the diggers uncovered adzes, fishhooks, and ornaments that had been undisturbed for more than 1,000 years, according to radiocarbon dating of a whale bone found with the items.

daily at 8am and 1pm. He will pick you up at your hotel. Paul can also guide you to the *maraes* on Matairea Hill by special arrangement.

TOURING THE ISLAND

You can rent a vehicle and tour both parts of Huahine in half a day. The main roads around both islands are about 32km (20 miles) long and are paved. Be careful on the steep *traversière*, which traverses the mountains from Maroe Bay to Faie Bay on the east coast. (I would not ride a scooter or bicycle over this road.) Heading clockwise from **Fare,** you skirt the shores of Lake Fauna Nui and come to the *maraes* outside Maeva village (see "Visiting the *Maraes,*" above).

From Maeva, the road heads south until it turns into picturesque Faie Bay. Here you'll pass the landing for **Huahine Nui Pearls & Pottery** ✸ (© **78.30.20;** www. huahinepearlfarm.com), a pearl farm and pottery studio (p. 150). Once you're past Faie village at the head of the bay, the road starts uphill across the *traversière* (see above). At the top, you'll be rewarded with a view down across Mooreaesque **Maroe Bay,** which splits Huahine into two islands.

Turn right at the dead-end by the bay and drive west to the main west-coast road. Turn left and follow it across the bridge over the narrow pass separating Huahine Nui from Huahine Iti. A right turn past the bridge will take you along the winding west-coast road to **Avea Bay,** where Relais Mahana (p. 151) and Pension Mauarii (p. 152) sit beside one of the South Pacific's greatest beaches. Either is an excellent place to stop for refreshment.

Sitting at the end of the peninsula at the south end of Huahine Iti, **Anini Marae** presents a glorious view of the island's southern coast. Nearby is **Parea,** one of Huahine's largest villages. From Parea, you'll skirt the shoreline until you come to the village of **Tefarerii** on the east coast. In between is a pull-off with a marvelous view over the reefs and sea. From here, it's an easy drive to Maroe Bay. The large cruise ships land their passengers at Maroe village on the south side of the bay.

REVISITING THE OLD SOUTH SEAS IN FARE

The main village of **Fare** ✸✸✸ (*Fah*-ray) is hardly more than a row of Chinese stores and a wharf opposite the main pass in the reef on the northwest shore, but it takes us back to the days when trading schooners were the only way to get round the islands. Even today, trucks and buses arrive from all over Huahine with passengers and cargo when the interisland boats put in from Papeete. The rest of the time, Fare lives a lazy, slow pace, as people amble down its tree-lined main street and browse through the stores facing the town wharf. A monument on the waterfront designates it as **Place Hawaiki,** the starting point for October's big outrigger canoe race to Raiatea and Bora Bora.

Tips Fruit Juice & an Exotic Lunch

On your way back to Fare from Huahine Iti, turn off the main road toward Bourayne Bay and drive 2km (1¼ mile) to **Eden Parc** (© **68.86.58;** www.eden parc.org), a lush tropical garden where you can get freshly squeezed fruit juice or enjoy an "exotic" lunch made from produce organically grown on the premises. It's a hot and steamy site, so get out your insect repellent. Open Monday through Saturday from 8am to 2pm.

Moments **Sailboats & Sunsets at Fare**

I thoroughly enjoy strolling along the wharf, poking my head into the shops across the main street, observing the cruising yachts anchored in the harbor, and watching the boats come and go. With Raiatea, Tahaa, and Bora Bora resting on the western horizon, Fare is one of my favorite places to watch the sunset.

Beginning at the **Restaurant Temarara** (p. 154), a pebbly promenade leads north along the waterfront to a sandy swimming beach, which has a daytime snack bar.

3 Lagoon Excursions & Safari Expeditions

LAGOON EXCURSIONS

As on Moorea and Bora Bora, one of the most enjoyable ways to see the island is on a lagoon excursion that includes snorkeling and a picnic on an islet out on the reef. The biggest difference here is that with relatively few tourists around, you and your companions are likely to have the islet all to yourselves.

The all-day excursion with **Huahine Nautique** (© 68.83.15; www.huahine-nautique. com) takes you by outrigger canoe through Maroe Bay and around Huahine Iti. You'll stop for snorkeling and a picnic featuring freshly made *poisson cru,* and you'll observe shark-feeding before returning to Fare. Huahine Nautique's canoes have shade canopies, and the guides speak English as well as French. The excursions cost 8,000CFP (US$80) per person. **Poetaina Cruises (60.60.06)** charges about 7,500CFP (US$75) per person for its all-day trips, but I can't guarantee that you'll have shade on your outrigger. Don't be surprised if you visit Huahine Nui Pearls & Pottery (p. 150).

SAFARI EXPEDITIONS

As on most of the Society Islands, you can make four-wheel-drive expeditions into the mountains here. You will see a bit of the interior of Huahine Nui with Paul Atallah on his **Island Eco Tours** (see "Historical Tours," above), which I would take first. You will repeat seeing the Maeva *maraes,* but either **Huahine Land** (© 68.89.21), which is owned by American expatriate Joel House, or **Huahine Explorer** (© 68.87.33) will also take you to Huahine Iti on its half-day expeditions. Both charge about 5,000CFP (US$50) per person.

4 Watersports & Other Outdoor Activities

FISHING

For lagoon or deep-sea fishing, contact **Huahine Marine Transports** (© 68.84.02; hua.mar.trans@mail.pf), owned by American expatriate Rich Shamel, who has lived on Huahine for many years and who runs the transfer boats for Te Tiare Beach Resort (p. 151). Rich charges US$800 for half a day and US$1,200 for a full day of fishing on his 11m (36-ft.) Hatteras sportfishing boat. He lives and works at the resort's transfer base, just across the bridge on the south side of Fare.

HORSEBACK RIDING

One of the best horseback-riding operations in French Polynesia is **La Petite Ferme (The Little Farm;** © 68.82.98), on the main road north of Fare, just before the airport turnoff. It has Marquesas-bred horses that can be ridden with English or Western saddles along the beach and around Lake Fauna Nui. Prices range from 5,000CFP (US$50) for 2 hours to 9,800CFP (US$98) for an all-day trail ride. The farm also has accommodations, from a dormitory to bungalows.

SAILING

You can go for a half- or full-day cruise with Claude and Martine Bordier of **Sailing Huahine Voile** (© and fax **68.72.49;** www.sailing-huahine.com) on their *Eden Martin,* a 15m (50-ft.) yacht, which they sailed out from France in 1999. A half day of sailing costs about 5,500CFP (US$55) per person; a whole day, 10,000CFP (US$100). Sunset cruises are 4,800CFP (US$48) per person. The boat is also available for 1- or 2-week cruises in the Leeward or Tuamotu islands.

WATERSPORTS

SCUBA DIVING   Huahine's lagoon and fringing reef offer several dive sites with a multitude of sealife, and you don't have to be an experienced diver to see much of it. You'll need a boat to get to it, but even snorkelers will enjoy the **Seafari Aquarium,** inside the barrier reef off Avea Beach on Huahine Iti. Tropical fish congregate around the colorful coral heads that dot the lagoon here, and rays troll the sandy bottom. The aquarium is only 2 to 3m (7–10 ft.) deep. Novice divers can also explore the canyons beyond **Tiare Pass,** off Faie Bay on the eastern side of Huahine-Nui. You will need intermediate skills to explore Huahine's most famous site, **Avapeihi Pass,** the entry through the reef off Cook's Bay and a short boat ride from Fare. Conditions in the pass draw feeding schools of barracuda and other fish, which in turn get the attention of gray reef sharks.

   Pacific Blue Adventure (© **68.87.21;** fax 68.80.71; www.divehuahine.com), Didier Forget's scuba-dive outfitter, has an office on the Fare wharf. Didier charges about 7,500CFP (US$75) for a one-tank dive, during which he might feed the sharks and pet the moray eels.

SNORKELING & SWIMMING   You don't have to leave Fare to find a fine little swimming and snorkeling beach; just follow the seaside promenade north past Restaurant Temarara. **Europcar** (© **68.82.59**) rents snorkeling equipment for 400CFP (US$4).

   Huahine's best, however, is the magnificent crescent of sand at **Avea Beach,** skirting Baie Avea on Huahine Iti. A hilly peninsula blocks the brunt of the southeast trade winds, so the speckled lagoon here is usually as smooth as glass. **Mara'amu Sailing School** (© **68.77.10**), based at Pension Mauarii (p. 152), rents Hobie Cats for 4,000CFP (US$40) for the first hour, 3,000CFP (US$30) for each additional hour, and powerboats for 7,000CFP (US$70) for 4 hours. It also has power- and sailboat tours and will teach you to windsurf, kite surf, or ride a wake board.

5 Shopping

You are not as likely to be pestered to buy black pearls on Huahine as on Tahiti, Moorea, and Bora Bora—another of Huahine's appealing attributes, in my opinion. One stop you should make is **Huahine Nui Pearls & Pottery** ⪕ (© **78.30.20;** www.huahine pearlfarm.com), a pearl farm and pottery studio operated by American expatriate Peter Owen on a *motu* off Baie Faie (see "Touring the Island," above). Peter offers free tours daily from 10am to 4pm, with the boat leaving Faie Bay every 15 minutes. If you aren't going to the Tuamotus, this is a good place to see how black pearls are grown.

Local women sell shell jewelry, bedspreads, and other handicrafts at **Huahine Mata Aiai** (no phone) in a thatch building at the south end of the Fare waterfront. Be sure to look in the small art galleries and other shops along the waterfront.

6 Where to Stay

EXPENSIVE

Te Tiare Beach, an Outrigger Resort 👍👍👍   Rudy Markmiller made a fortune in the overnight courier business in California and then spent more than a decade—and a sizable chunk of his loot—building this luxury resort, one of French Polynesia's finest. Although it's on the main island, guests are ferried here from Fare, which makes this seem like a remote offshore resort (never fear: a shuttle boat makes the 10-minute run to and from Fare every hour from 5:30am to 11pm). You will land at a thatch-roofed, overwater structure housing reception, lounge, bar, and dining room serving excellent international cuisine. A long pier connects this central complex to a west-ward-facing, white-sand beach with gorgeous sunsets over Raiatea and Tahaa out on the horizon. The lagoon is not deep here, but it's still good for swimming and snor-keling over coral heads close to shore. You can use canoes, paddleboats, and kayaks, or cool off in a beachside swimming pool equipped with its own bar. Diving, sailing, fishing, picnicking on a *motu,* horseback riding, and touring the *maraes* costs extra. Jet skis and water-skiing are available, though not in front of the resort.

The 41 spacious bungalows are as luxuriously appointed as any in French Polyne-sia. You won't have a fish-viewing glass panel in the floor, but you can step out to a huge L-shaped deck, half of it under the shade of a thatch roof. The decks also have privacy screens so your neighbors can't see you dining in the altogether, or whatever. Steps lead into the lagoon from the decks of the 11 "deep overwater" bungalows, which have spa tubs as well as showers in their bathrooms (all other units, including five "shallow overwater" models, have large showers). Six bungalows sit beside the beach, but the garden units (the least expensive here) don't have unimpeded views of the lagoon.

B.P. 36, 98731 Fare, Huahine (in Fitii District, 10 min. by boat from Fare). © **888/600-8455** or 60.60.50. Fax 60.60.51. www.tetiarebeach.com. 41 units. 32,000CFP–70,000CFP (US$320–US$700) double. AE, DC, MC, V. **Amenities:** Restau-rant; 2 bars; outdoor pool; watersports equipment/rentals; activities desk; car-rental desk; limited room service; massage; babysitting; laundry service. *In room:* A/C, TV, minibar, coffeemaker, hair dryer, iron (overwater only), safe.

MODERATE

Relais Mahana   This property offers one of the South Pacific's best beach-lagoon combinations, for it sits right on Avea Beach, the white sand stretching along the peninsula on Huahine's south end. A pier from the main building runs out over a giant coral head, around which fish and guests swim. You can just climb down off the pier and swim with the fishes. I cannot tell you much about the accommodations, since a major renovation was upgrading it from *relais* to resort during my recent visit.

Fun Fact **The Swimsuit Models Were Here**

Those extraordinarily beautiful women seen briefly—in both time and cloth-ing—at Te Tiare Beach Resort were recently here to model for the 2006 swim-suit issue of *Sports Illustrated* magazine.

The first stage, to be completed by 2007, aims to enlarge and improve the existing bungalows (heretofore lacking TVs, phones, and other amenities). An infinity pool and other features are to be added later. Be sure to check the website to see if it has reopened.

B.P. 30, 98731 Fare, Huahine (Avea Bay, Huahine Iti). © **60.60.40.** Fax 68.85.08. www.relaismahana.com. 28 units. 21,750CFP–31,000CFP (US$218–US$310) bungalow. AE, DC, MC, V. **Amenities:** Restaurant; bar; watersports equipment/rentals; bike rentals; game room; activities desk; car-rental desk; babysitting; laundry service. *In room:* TV, dataport, minibar, coffeemaker, iron, safe.

INEXPENSIVE

Chez Guynette *(Value)*   Marty and Moe (*Mo*-ay) Temahahe (wife Marty is American; husband Moe is Tahitian) operate this friendly hostel across the main street from the Fare waterfront. A corridor runs down the center of the building to the kitchen and lounge at the rear. The simple but clean rooms and dorms flank the hallway on either side. The rooms have screens, ceiling fans, and their own bathrooms with hot-water showers. The dorms also have ceiling fans; they share two toilets and showers. Marty and Moe offer breakfast and lunch (sandwiches, burgers, salads, and *poisson cru*, plus wine and beer) on their street-side patio. It's the best place in Fare to slake a thirst and get into a good conversation—in English.

B.P. 87, 98731 Fare, Huahine (opposite the town wharf). © **68.83.75.** chezguynette@mail.pf. 7 units, 8 dorm beds (shared bathrooms). 1,750CFP–2,000CFP (US$18–US$20) dorm bed; 5,400CFP–5,700CFP (US$54–US$57) double (higher rates apply to 1-night stays). MC, V. **Amenities:** Restaurant; bar. *In room:* No phone.

Pension Fare Maeva   Located between Fare and the airport, this pension has some features that make it seem more like a cost-conscious resort. It sits beside a white-sand beach, although the lagoon here is so rocky and shallow that you cannot wade in for a swim. You can take a dip in the pool, though, which resides in a beachside lawn in front of the restaurant. The latter is open daily for breakfast and lunch, and occasionally for island feasts and Tahitian music after dark. You can order a cold one at the bar and escape the midday sun under the tin roof of a *fare potee*, or outdoor lounge, beside the pool. The 20 units here are evenly divided between bungalows and hotel-style rooms, all in tropical gardens rather than on the beach. The bungalows are more expensive, but come with kitchens and separate bedrooms. Accommodations are spartanly attired, but tin roofs, tile floors, porches, and simple bathrooms with hot-water showers are common to all units. You'll get a fan, but not window screens. Pension Vaihonu Océan (see below) is a short walk away.

B.P. 675, 98731 Fare, Huahine (2.5km/1½ miles north of Fare). © **68.75.53.** Fax 68.70.68. www.fare-maeva.com. 20 units. 6,000CFP–9,000CFP (US$60–US$90). MC, V. **Amenities:** Restaurant (breakfast and lunch); bar; outdoor pool; bike rentals. *In room:* Kitchen (bungalows only), no phone.

Pension Mauarii *(Value Value)*   Beautifully situated right on Avea Beach, this little budget-minded resort may not offer all the comforts of home, but it oozes charm. Its buildings are constructed of thatch, bamboo, tree trunks, and other natural materials. Although cleverly designed, they seem to be slapped together, which adds to the ambience. Most units are in the tropical gardens, but the rooms open to a long porch right on the beach, as does the one beachside bungalow—my favorite here. All units have ceiling fans, but not all have bathrooms, and their windows aren't screened. The pension offers a host of waterborne activities. The Restaurant Mauarii (p. 154) is the most charming on the island. This is one of the best and most popular small hotels in French Polynesia, so make reservations as soon as possible.

B.P. 473, 98731 Fare, Huahine (Baie Avera, Huahine Iti). ☎ **68.86.49.** Fax 60.60.96. www.mauarii.com. 5 bungalows (2 with shared bathroom), 4 rooms (2 with shared bathroom). 7,500CFP (US$75) double; 10,000CFP–20,000CFP (US$100–US$200) bungalow. AE, MC, V. **Amenities:** Restaurant; bar; watersports equipment/rentals; bike rentals. *In room:* No phone.

Pension Vaihonu Océan   On the shore a few meters south of Pension Fare Maeva (see above), with which it shares a beach beside the shallow, rocky lagoon, this pension offers a wider range of accommodations than any other inexpensive establishment here. Top of the line are two duplex apartments with kitchen and bathroom; the mezzanine level contains two double beds. In the middle are three "beach huts"— actually small, simple bungalows with plywood walls, tin roofs, unscreened windows, and shaded verandas—facing the lagoon across a lawn. Guests in the huts and in the dormitory share toilets, showers, and a sand-floor communal kitchen with campers who pitch their own tents on the lawn. Ariiura Camping (see below) has a better beach and a more picturesque setting, but the location here is much more convenient to Fare, just 2.5km (1½ miles) away.

B.P. 302, 98731 Fare, Huahine (2.5km/1½ miles north of Fare). ☎ **68.87.33.** Fax 68.77.57. www.iaorana-huahine.com/en/vaihonu.html. 2 apartments, 5 beach huts, 7 dorm beds (shared bathrooms), 8 campsites. 7,200CFP–8,200CFP (US$72–US$82) apartment; 4,350CFP–4,850CFP (US$44–US$49) double beach hut; 1,650CFP–2,150CFP (US$17–US$22) per person in dormitory; 1,200CFP–1,700CFP (US$12–US$17) per person camping (higher rates apply to 1-night stays). MC, V. **Amenities:** Communal kitchen; free use of bikes; laundry service. *In room:* Kitchen (apartments only), no phone.

HOUSE RENTALS WITH CARS & BOATS

The two properties below, both on the north shore of Maroe Bay, represent good value since they throw in the use of a car and motorboat in their rates. Neither is a hotel or pension; what you get for your money is a modern house more or less to yourself.

Huahine Vacances *Value*   Bordeaux native Michel Sorin has lived in the islands since the early 1980s, and after a 1998 hurricane ripped up his vanilla plantation, he built three rental houses on the bayside part of his land. Although these modern villas could be at home in most suburbs, the tin roofs and fretwork around the eaves add an old-plantation touch. Two have three bedrooms, while the third has two, making them good choices for groups or families willing to fend for themselves. You'll have a fully equipped kitchen (including a microwave), a large front porch from which to observe the bay, window screens, and your own bathroom with hot-water shower. Michel's Tahitian wife, Jacqueline, will sit the kids while you drive your car into Fare for dinner. The Sorins provide linens, but you do the housework.

B.P. 10, 98731 Fare, Huahine (north shore of Maroe Bay). ☎ and fax **68.73.63.** www.iaorana-huahine.com/en/huahine.html. 3 units. 20,500CFP–27,500CFP (US$205–US$275) depending on number of guests. MC, V. Reduced rates for long stays. **Amenities:** Free use of car, motorboat, canoes, fishing rods; babysitting. *In room:* TV, kitchen, coffeemaker, hair dryer, washing machine, no phone.

Villas Bougainville *Value*   Near Huahine Vacances (see above), the three houses here are a bit larger, as are the surrounding tropical gardens. The two- and three-bedroom villas have wraparound verandas, modern kitchens, and bathrooms with hot-water showers. The bedrooms are somewhat spartan, but all have ceiling fans and some have air-conditioners (for which you must pay extra). Cribs and babysitting are available, but not housekeeping.

B.P. 258, 98731 Fare, Huahine (north shore of Maroe Bay). ☎ **60.60.30** or 79.70.59. Fax 60.60.31. www.villas-bougainville.com. 3 units. 20,500CFP–32,500CFP (US$205–US$325) depending on number of guests and air-conditioning. AE, MC, V. Reduced rates for long stays. **Amenities:** Free use of car, motorboat, canoes, fishing rods; babysitting. *In room:* A/C, TV, kitchen, coffeemaker, hair dryer, washing machine, no phone.

CAMPING

You can pitch a tent or rent a rudimentary thatch-roofed *fare* (cabin) at Cecèle and Upereto Bremond's **Ariiura Camping** (© 68.85.20 or 68.83.78) on the southern end of Avea Beach. The shoreline here has as many coral ledges as sand, but the shady grounds are appealing. Guests share a communal kitchen, tables under a thatch roof, toilets, and cold-water showers (don't expect a showerhead; the water pours directly from a pipe). The cabins have either a double bed or two single beds and range in price from 4,500CFP to 5,000CFP (US$45–US$50), while tent sites are 1,2500CFP (US$13) per person.

7 Where to Dine

You'll meet the locals having breakfast or lunch while watching the passing scene from the patio at **Chez Guynette** in Fare (p. 152). You can also enjoy the fine dining room at **Te Tiare Beach Resort** (p. 151), though you will need to make reservations and pay 500CFP (US$5) for the boat ride there and back.

You'll find Huahine's *roulottes* on the Fare wharf. They're open for both lunch and dinner. See "Don't Miss *Les Roulottes*" (p. 112) for details.

Patisserie Fare *Value* BAKERY This patisserie, under a thatch, lean-to roof extending from a house, is my favorite place for fresh croissants, quiche, or a full American breakfast. Lunch sees the appearance of fresh salads (such as roast chicken with almonds) and country-style French potatoes and bacon. You won't have a sea view here, but the food is both tasty and a good value.

Fare, main road north opposite post office. © 68.77.19. Reservations not accepted. Most items 250CFP–950CFP (US$2.50–US$9.50). No credit cards. Mon–Sat 6am–6pm.

Restaurant La Boussole FRENCH Located in a house on Fare's south side, just beyond the Te Tiare Beach Resort's landing, this restaurant is Huahine's fine-dining outlet, casual though it may be. The menu features fondue Bourguignonne, magret of duck, and steaks and fish in traditional French sauces.

Fare, main road south of downtown. © 68.88.62. Reservations recommended. Main courses 1,650CFP–2,800CFP (US$17–US$28). AE, MC, V. Tues–Sat 11:30am–2:30pm and 6:30–10pm.

Restaurant Mauarii FRENCH/TAHITIAN Assuming the owners haven't taken leave of their senses and moved this restaurant across the road to make room for more bungalows, it will still be sitting almost over the sand, with a great view southward along Avea Beach. It's a charmer, with a thatch-lined ceiling and tables hewn from tree trunks. Lunchtime sandwiches include a "Killer" baguette loaded with grilled fish, fries, and your choice of vanilla or other sauces. For my money, this is a good place to sample Tahitian treats such as chicken with *ruru* (taro leaves) in coconut cream or to sample different dishes on a Polynesian platter. Ask for a menu in English if the friendly staff doesn't figure you out first.

At Pension Mauarii, Avea Beach, Huahine Iti. © 68.86.49. Reservations recommended for dinner. Sandwiches and burgers 600CFP–1,200CFP (US$6–US$12); main courses 1,600CFP–3,200CFP (US$16–US$32). AE, MC. V. Daily noon–2pm and 6–8pm.

Restaurant Temarara ⋆ FRENCH   Facing due west beside the lagoon at the north end of Fare's wharf, this restaurant is everyone's favorite place for a sundown cocktail during half-price happy hour from 5:30 to 6:30pm. The quality doesn't match the great view, but you can get a good beef or fish burger here, as well as steaks and fish with French sauces. The coconut-crumbed mahimahi is a spicy version of breaded fish. If offered, try the parrot fish with lemon butter.

Fare, north end of wharf. ℂ **68.89.31.** Reservations recommended Fri–Sat. Burgers 800CFP–900CFP (US$8–US$9); main courses 1,400CFP–2,200CFP (US$14–US$22). MC, V. Mon–Sat 9am–9pm (bar open all day, to 11pm Fri–Sat).

7

Raiatea & Tahaa

The mountainous clump of land you can see on the horizon from Huahine or Bora Bora may appear to be one island, but it's actually two, Raiatea and Tahaa, that are enclosed by a single barrier reef. Cruising yachts can circumnavigate Tahaa without leaving the lagoon, and Huahine and Bora Bora are relatively easy hauls from here. Accordingly, this is French Polynesia's yacht-chartering center. Except for a few on islets out on the reef and one next to a very shallow lagoon on Raiatea, there are no beaches on either island. Therefore, except for sailing and cruise-ship visits, tourism is not an important part of their economies, which are based on agricultural produce and, in the case of Raiatea, government salaries.

Raiatea, the largest of the Leeward Islands, is by far more important than Tahaa in terms of both the past and the present. In the old days, it was the religious center of all the Society Islands, including Tahiti. Polynesian mythology has it that Oro, the god of war and fertility, was born in **Mount Temehani,** the extinct flat-top volcano that towers over the northern part of Raiatea. **Taputapu-atea,** on its southeast coast, was at one time the most important *marae* in the islands. Legend also has it that the great Polynesian voyagers who discovered and colonized Hawaii and New Zealand left from here. Archaeological discoveries have substantiated the link with Hawaii.

Today, Raiatea (pop. 10,000) is still important as the economic and administrative center of the Leeward Islands. Next to Papeete, the town of **Uturoa** (pop. 4,000) is the largest settlement and one of the most important transportation hubs in French Polynesia, with a modern cruise-ship terminal and welcome center dominating the town wharf. Although most cruise ships prefer anchoring offshore in order to make use of their watersports platforms, Uturoa is the only island port other than Papeete where the larger vessels can spend their nights tied up to a wharf.

Tahaa (pronounced *Tah*-ah-ah) is much smaller than Raiatea in terms of land area, population (about 4,500), and the height of its terrain. It's a lovely island, with a few very small villages sitting deep in bays that cut into its hills. Tahaa has a few family-operated pensions, but other than sailors and guests at the super-luxurious Le Taha'a Private Island & Spa and two other hotels on one of its reef islets, few visitors see it, and most of those who do come on day tours from Raiatea.

If you do make it to Raiatea, Tahaa, or both, you will get a refreshing glimpse of old Polynesia. And as on Huahine, you will meet local residents who are—except on cruise-ship days—unhurried by an over-abundance of tourists.

1 Getting Around Raiatea & Tahaa

The Raiatea airstrip, 3km (2 miles) north of Uturoa, serves both islands. You have to rent a vehicle or take a taxi, since there is no regular public transportation system on either Raiatea or Tahaa.

Raiatea & Tahaa

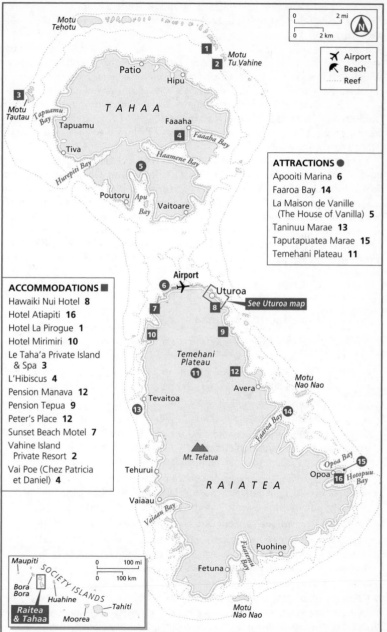

ATTRACTIONS ●
Apooiti Marina **6**
Faaroa Bay **14**
La Maison de Vanille
(The House of Vanilla) **5**
Taninuu Marae **13**
Taputapuatea Marae **15**
Temehani Plateau **11**

ACCOMMODATIONS ■
Hawaiki Nui Hotel **8**
Hotel Atiapiti **16**
Hotel La Pirogue **1**
Hotel Mirimiri **10**
Le Taha'a Private Island
& Spa **3**
L'Hibiscus **4**
Pension Manava **12**
Pension Tepua **9**
Peter's Place **12**
Sunset Beach Motel **7**
Vahine Island
Private Resort **2**
Vai Poe (Chez Patricia
et Daniel) **4**

✈ Airport
🏄 Beach
······ Reef

See Uturoa map

Avis (📞 800/230-4898 or 60.00.95; www.avis.com), **Europcar** (📞 800/227-7368 or 66.34.06; www.europcar.com), and **Hertz** (📞 800/654-3131 or 66.44.88; www.hertz.com) have rental-car offices here. Europcar's prices start at 9,400CFP (US$94) a day, including insurance and unlimited kilometers. It also rents scooters, bicycles, and open-air "Bugster" vehicles. Europcar also has an office at Tapuamu Wharf, on Tahaa's west coast (📞 65.67.00), so you can take the ferry there, rent a car, and drive around the island. You must take a water taxi back to Uturoa.

There is a taxi stand near the cruise-ship terminal in Uturoa, or you can contact **René Guilloux** (📞 66.31.40), **Marona Teanini** (📞 66.34.62), or **Apia Tehope** (📞 66.36.41). From the airport, fares are about 600CFP (US$6) to town and 1,200CFP (US$12) to the Raiatea Pearl Resort.

The passenger ferry *Tamarii Tahaa* (📞 65.67.10) docks in front of the Champion store on Uturoa's waterfront and runs from there to Patio on Tahaa's northern coast. It departs from Uturoa Monday through Friday, usually at 10am and 4pm, and Saturday at 11am. If you're staying in Uturoa, you had best make sure it will return on the same day it leaves. Fares are about 1,000CFP (US$10) one-way. **Dave's Tours** (📞 65.62.42) also runs a shuttle from Uturoa to Tahaa, departing Monday through Saturday at 9am, returning at 4:30pm. Fares are 1,500CFP (US$15) one-way, 2,500CFP (US$25) round-trip. **Water-taxi service** is available at the waterfront (📞 65.66.64); rides cost about 2,000CFP (US$20).

FAST FACTS: Raiatea & Tahaa

The following facts apply specifically to Raiatea and Tahaa. For more information, see "Fast Facts: Tahiti & French Polynesia," in chapter 2.

Bookstores **Librairie d'Uturoa,** on the inland side of the main street in the center of town (📞 66.30.80), carries French books and magazines.

Currency Exchange French Polynesia's three banks have offices with ATMs on Uturoa's main street. There is no bank on Tahaa.

Drugstores **Pharmacie de Raiatea,** in Uturoa (📞 66.34.44), carries French products. Open Monday through Friday from 7:30am to noon and 1:30 to 5:30pm, Saturday from 7:30am to noon, and Sunday from 9:30 to 10:30am.

Emergencies/Police The **emergency police** phone number is 📞 17. The phone number of the **Uturoa gendarmerie** is 📞 66.31.07. The **Tahaa gendarmerie** is at Patio, the administrative center, on the north coast (📞 65.64.07).

Eyeglasses Try **Optique Te Mata Ore,** on Uturoa's main street (📞 66.16.19).

Healthcare In Uturoa, the **hospital,** opposite the post office (📞 66.32.92), serves all the Leeward Islands. Tahaa has an **infirmary** at Patio (📞 65.63.31). Drs. **Sonia Andreu** and **Pascal Diochin** (📞 66.23.01) practice together on Uturoa's main street.

Internet Access **ETS,** in the Gare Maritime on the Uturoa waterfront (📞 60.25.25), has computers with Internet access for 15CFP (US15¢) a minute. It's open Monday through Friday from 7:30am to 5pm, Saturday from 7:30am to noon. You can burn your digital photos to CDs here.

Laundry **Laverie Apetahi,** at Apooti Marina (✆ **66.28.36**), will wash, dry, and fold your laundry for 363CFP (US$3.63) a kilo (2.2 lbs.). Open Monday through Friday from 8am to noon and 1 to 4:30pm.

Post Office The post and telecommunications office is in a modern building north of Uturoa on the main road (as opposed to a new road that runs along the shore of reclaimed land on the north side of town). It's open Monday through Thursday from 7:30am to 3pm, Friday from 7am to 2pm, and Saturday from 8 to 10am.

Restrooms The Gare Maritime on the waterfront has clean restrooms.

Telephones There are *télécarte* phones on the waterfront and at the post and telecommunications office.

Visitor Information **Raiatea Manava** (✆ **60.07.77;** fax 60.07.76; raiateainfo@mail. pf) has a visitor information office in the Gare Maritime on the waterfront. Open Monday through Friday from 8am to 4pm, Saturday from 8am to 3pm (and, when cruise ships are in port, Sun 8am–3pm).

Water Don't drink the tap water on either Raiatea or Tahaa.

2 Exploring Raiatea & Tahaa

Highlights of your time here will include visits to the ancient *maraes,* day trips to and around Tahaa, picnics on small islands on the outer reef, and four-wheel-drive excursions into the mountains.

A paved road runs for 150km (92 miles) around the shoreline of rugged **Raiatea,** the second-largest island in French Polynesia, behind only Tahiti. Its tallest peak, **Mount Tefatoaiti,** at 1,017m (3,337 ft.), occupies the triangular-shaped island's southern end. To the north, the flat top of sacred **Mount Temehani** soars to 792m (2,598 ft.). Much of Mount Temehani is a high plateau, where the five-petal *tiare apetahi* flower grows (see "Delicate Petals," below). Polynesians in ancient times believed that when they died, their souls ascended to the plateau, where they faced a fork in the road. If they were told to go right, they went to paradise. If they went left, it was into the crater and their version of purgatory.

Several rivers carve steep valleys on their way from the Raiatea highlands to six bays indenting the coast. One of them, the **Faaroa River,** is the only navigable waterway in French Polynesia. It empties into mountain-sided **Faaroa Bay,** which provides a protected anchorage for yachts and other small craft. Most charter-boat operators,

---

Fun Fact **Delicate Petals**

Found nowhere else except in Raiatea's mountains, the *tiare apetahi* is a one-sided white flower of the gardenia family. Legend says that its five delicate petals are the fingers of a beautiful Polynesian girl who fell in love with a prince but couldn't marry him because of her low birth. Just before she died, heartbroken, in her lover's arms, she promised to give him her hand to caress each day throughout eternity. At daybreak each morning, accordingly, the *tiare apetahi* opens its five petals.

Fun Fact Omai Scores a Hit in London

Capt. James Cook discovered Raiatea during his first expedition to the islands in 1769. On his second voyage, in 1773, he took home with him a young Raiatean named Mai, or Omai to the English, who was living on Huahine at the time. Like Ahutoru, a Tahitian brought to Paris by the French explorer Antoine de Bougainville 2 years earlier, Omai was seen as living proof of philosopher Jean-Jacques Rousseau's theory of humans as "noble savages." The first Polynesian to visit England, Omai became an instant hit with London society and even met King George III and Queen Charlotte, who apparently were impressed with his grace and good manners. Great artists painted him, and writers spun many words about him (including some pornography). High society soon lost interest, however, and Cook brought Omai home in 1777 on his third and last great voyage of discovery.

---

however, are based at **Apooiti Marina** on the north shore beside the strait separating Raiatea and Tahaa.

With 88 sq. km. (34 sq. miles), **Tahaa** is about a third the size of Raiatea, but it is still French Polynesia's fourth-largest island. Its main villages are **Tapuamu** on the west coast, **Patio** on the north side, and **Haamene** in the center. Tahaa is a rugged island, with its tallest peak, **Mount Ohiri,** reaching to 598m (1,975 ft.). The island's inhabitants live along a narrow coastal plain and at the head of four narrow bays, two of which—**Haamene** and **Harepiti**—almost cut Tahaa into two. Completely surrounded by a deep-water lagoon, and with the sheltered bays providing fine anchorages, Tahaa is a sailor's heaven.

VISITING THE _MARAE_

Raiatea is known as the "Sacred Island" because of its religious importance in pre-European times. On the outskirts of **Opoa** village, 29km (18 miles) south of Uturoa, the **Taputapuatea _Marae_** ✹✹✹ is the second most significant archaeological site in all of Polynesia, behind only Easter Island. Legend says that Te Ava Moa Pass offshore was the departure point for the discovery and settlement of both Hawaii and New Zealand. The large _marae_ on the site was actually built centuries later by the Tamatoa family of chiefs. Vying for supremacy, the Tamatoas mingled religion with politics by creating Oro, the ferocious god of war and fertility supposedly born on Mount Temehani, and by spreading his cult. It took almost 200 years, but Oro eventually became the most important god in the region. Likewise, the Tamatoas became the most powerful chiefs. They were on the verge of conquering all of the Society Islands when the missionaries arrived in 1797. With the Christians' help, Pomare I became king of Tahiti, and the great _marae_ the Tamatoas built for Oro was soon left to ruin, replaced by the lovely Protestant church in nearby Opoa village.

The _marae_ was restored in the 1960s, and more recently Tahiti Museum archaeologists discovered human bones under some of the structures, apparently the remains of sacrifices to Oro. The _marae's_ huge _ahu,_ or raised altar of stones for the gods, is more than 45m (150 ft.) long, 9m (30 ft.) wide, and 3.3m (11 ft.) tall. Flat rocks, used as backrests for the chiefs and priests, still stand in the courtyard in front of the ahu. The entire complex is in a coconut grove on the shore of the lagoon, opposite Te Ava Moa Pass, and legend says that bonfires on the _marae_ guided canoes through the pass at night.

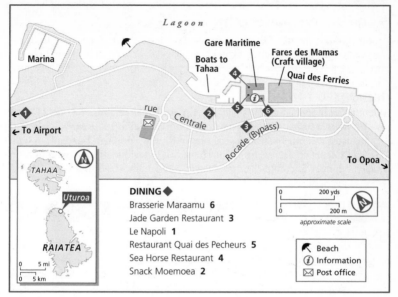

Uturoa

Lagoon

Marina

Gare Maritime

Boats to Tahaa

Fares des Mamas (Craft village)

Quai des Ferries

rue Centrale

← To Airport

Rocade (Bypass)

To Opoa

TAHAA

Uturoa

RAIATEA

0   5 mi
0   5 km

DINING ◆
Brasserie Maraamu   **6**
Jade Garden Restaurant   **3**
Le Napoli   **1**
Restaurant Quai des Pecheurs   **5**
Sea Horse Restaurant   **4**
Snack Moemoea   **2**

0   200 yds
0   200 m
approximate scale

🏖 Beach
ⓘ Information
✉ Post office

Taputapuatea is worth a visit not only for the *marae* itself but also for the scenery here and along the way. The road skirts the southeast coast and follows Faaroa Bay to the mouth of the river, and then back out to the lagoon.

On the west coast, 14.5km (9 miles) from Uturoa, **Taninuu *Marae*** was also dedicated to Oro. Stones bordering the foundation of the ancient chief's home bear petroglyphs of turtles. This is a place of Christian history, too, since the lovely white Eglise Siloama is one of the oldest churches in French Polynesia.

WALKING AROUND UTUROA

There was not even a village at Uturoa before the Rev. John Williams, who proselytized throughout the South Pacific, set up a London Missionary Society headquarters here in the 1820s. The settlement later became the Leeward Islands' administrative center and major trading post. A number of Chinese-owned stores still line Rue Centrale, Uturoa's main street, but the center of activity is the glistening **Gare Maritime,** a cruise-ship terminal built with money from France's economic restructuring fund. You can't miss this big Mediterranean-style building, which houses restaurants, shops, the island's visitor information office, and public restrooms. Needless to say, the waterfront is busiest when a cruise ship arrives, and local women sell handicrafts and souvenirs in small thatch buildings next door known as *fares des mamas* (mamas' houses). A modern produce and fish market is slated to be built nearby.

You can make a walking tour of Uturoa by following the four-lane road northward from the town docks along the shore, past a park built on landfill to the public yacht marina on the northern edge of town. From the traffic circle, follow Rue Centrale back through the business district. Although Rue Centrale was once along the shoreline, landfill has left the street a block inland from the waterfront. Behind it on the mountain side, an expressway speeds vehicles past downtown (there's a traffic circle on each end).

Tips **Avoid Cruise-Ship Days**

Unless you're on one of them, try to avoid visiting Raiatea when cruise ships are in port, since their passengers can monopolize all organized activities here.

ORGANIZED TOURS

American anthropologist Bill Kolans of **Almost Paradise Tours** (✆ **66.23.64**) has lived on Raiatea since sailing his boat down from Hawaii in 1979. He will take you to Taputapuatea and other archaeological sites in his van. Although Bill tends to wander a bit and doesn't appreciate being interrupted, he provides informative commentary about the history and culture of the islands. His 3-hour island tour costs 4,500CFP (US$45) per person.

3 Safari Expeditions & Lagoon Excursions

SAFARI EXPEDITIONS

Either **Raiatea 4×4** (✆ **66.24.16**) or **Jeep Safari Raiatea** (✆ **66.15.73**) will take you via four-wheel-drive jeep into Raiatea's interior, including a ride up to the plateau and into the ancient crater of Mount Temehani; both stop at Taputapuatea Marae before heading back to Uturoa. These expeditions are less thrill ride and more oriented to history and culture than those on Bora Bora. I would opt for Raiatea 4×4, especially if the highly informative Ronnie Moufat is to be your guide. Each outfitter has two trips a day, requires reservations a day in advance, and charges about 4,500CFP (US$45) per person.

The mountains of Tahaa offer much less dramatic scenery than on Raiatea, and the island lacks the historical importance of its big sister. Consequently, safari expeditions here include visits to **La Maison de Vanille** (**The House of Vanilla;** ✆ **57.61.92**), which explains the cultivation and uses of vanilla (Tahaa's major product), and to a black-pearl farm. Most tours follow a four-wheel-drive trail through the mountains from Patio, on the north coast, to Haamene, in the center of the island. These invariably include a refreshment stop high on a ridge with a view over Haamene Bay. I thoroughly enjoyed my expedition guided by the energetic and engaging Roselyne Atiniu of **Dave's Tours** (✆ **65.62.42**). You can also go with **Vai Poe Tours** (✆ **65.60.83**). Either will pick you up at Uturoa.

LAGOON EXCURSIONS

If you can put together your own group (because a minimum of four persons is required), you can take a variety of lagoon excursions and see firsthand the Raiatea-Tahaa lagoon, one of the most beautiful in French Polynesia. All trips include snorkeling, and most include picnics on the *motu* (tiny islets) sitting on the outer reef; unlike the mainland of Raiatea and Tahaa, they have beautiful white-sand beaches. **Motu Toahotu** and **Motu Mahena** are equipped with restrooms and other facilities, for which the locals extract a 500CFP (US$5) per person entrance fee. **Dave's Tours** (✆ **65.62.42**) will take you out from Uturoa.

Marie and Tony Tucker (she's French; he's South African) of **West Coast Charters** (✆ **66.45.39**) offer a complete tour around Tahaa with swimming, guided snorkeling over the magnificent coral gardens next to Le Taha'a Private Island & Spa, a shark-feeding stint, a pearl-farm visit, and lunch for 7,500CFP (US$75) a person. Both Marie and Tony speak fluent English as well as French.

Andrew Brotherson of **Manava Excursions** (© **66.28.26;** fax 66.28.26; maraud@ mail.pf) charges 6,500CFP (US$65) per person for his all-day trips to Tahaa. They include visits to a vanilla plantation and pearl farm, a picnic on a *motu,* and snorkeling over the coral gardens. He also offers a half-day lagoon trip with a *motu* picnic, priced at 1,500CFP (US$15) per person, and a boat trip up the Faaroa River and on to the Taputapuatea Marae, priced at 4,500CFP (US$45) per person.

4 Hiking, Horseback Riding, Sailing & Watersports

HIKING

Just north of downtown Uturoa, the street to the left as you face the gendarmerie leads to a four-wheel-drive track ascending to the television towers atop 291m (970-ft.) **Papioi Hill.** (Be sure to close the gates, which keep the cows out of the station.) From the top, you can see Uturoa, the reef, and the islands Tahaa, Bora Bora, and Huahine.

On the east coast, a trail leads to a waterfall in the valley behind **Kaoha Nui Ranch** (see "Horseback Riding," below), whose guides explain the flora and fauna along the way. The 3-hour guided hikes cost about 3,000CFP (US$30) per person, with at least two persons required.

Serious hikers can take another trail leading to the plateau atop Mount Temehani. The route begins with a four-wheel-drive track about 183m (600 ft.) south of the bridge at the head of Pufau Bay on the northwest coast. It is not marked, so a guide is advisable. Contact the local visitor information office about hiring one (see "Fast Facts: Raiatea & Tahaa," earlier).

HORSEBACK RIDING

You can go horseback riding with **Kaoha Nui Ranch** (© **66.25.46;** www. kaohanui.com), which charges 4,500CFP (US$45) for 2 hours, 6,500CFP (US$64) for half a day. The rides go up the valley and along ridgelines behind the ranch, so you'll be in for some fine scenery. The ranch also offers accommodations for riders, lagoon excursions, and guided botanical walks (see "Hiking," above).

SAILING ★★★

As noted in "Seeing the Islands by Cruise Ship & Yacht" (p. 49), **The Moorings** (© **800/535-7289** or 727/535-1446; www.moorings.com) and **Sunsail Yacht Charters** (© **800/327-2276** or 207/253-5400 in the U.S., or 60.04.85 on Raiatea; fax 66.23.19; www.sunsail.com) are based on Raiatea. Both charter sailboats with or without crew. If a boat is available, it can be chartered on a daily basis. Arrangements for longer charters ordinarily should be made before leaving home.

The Moorings keeps its boats at Apooiti Marina on the north shore, which is more convenient to the popular cruising grounds around Tahaa. Sunsail is based on the north shore of Faaroa Bay.

WATERSPORTS

Raiatea may not have beaches, but the reef and large, clear lagoon are excellent for scuba diving and snorkeling.

SCUBA DIVING   The best wreck dive site in all of French Polynesia is a descent of 15 to 27m (50–90 ft.) above the **S.S.** *Norby,* a three-masted Danish schooner that sunk off Uturoa in 1900. Its main deck has collapsed, so even novice divers can explore its topside. Intermediate divers can swim through the 150-foot-long hull and see a multitude of sealife, including black coral. Although the lagoon can be murky here, the *Norby* makes for good night diving. Nearby, novices can drift dive at Teava-piti Pass, where a coral wall just outside the reef attracts fish; rays; and gray, whitetip, and blacktip sharks. Other sites here, such as the **Little Caves** and the **Mounts of Céran,** both off Tahaa's eastern coast, are known for spectacular underwater scenery.

With bases at the Hawaiki Nui Hotel and at Apooiti Marina, Hubert Clot's **Hémi-sphère Sub Raiatea** (© **66.12.49;** fax 66.28.63; www.multimania.com/diveraiatea) takes divers on one-tank excursions for 6,500CFP (US$65).

SNORKELING You'll have to take a lagoon excursion (see above) to experience the best snorkeling near the offshore islands, especially over the coral gardens off Le Taha'a Private Island & Spa on Tahaa's northwestern coast. Or you can don mask, snorkel, and fins at the Hawaiki Nui Hotel (p. 164), where the overwater bungalows are perched atop a clifflike reef face.

5 Shopping

The Gare Maritime on the waterfront has several black-pearl and other shops. The best is **My Flower** (© **66.19.19**), where owner Flora Hart carries not just floral arrange-ments but also excellent tapa drawings and wood carvings—some from the Marquesas Islands, others done in *hue papaa* wood, a specialty of Raiatea's own carvers.

Other shops line Rue Centrale, the main street. These days, most are built of con-crete and steel, but one wooden building harkens back to the bygone days of clap-board Chinese stores. In it, you'll find the unique **Magasin Vanira** (© **66.30.06**), where owner Jeanne Chane—the *préparatrice de vanille*—prepares many products from vanilla beans: extract, powder, even vanilla soup. The wonderful aroma alone makes it worth a visit.

6 Where to Stay

ON RAIATEA
EXPENSIVE
Hawaiki Nui Hotel ♠ This hotel is of historical importance in its own right, for it was here in 1968 that Moorea's "Bali Hai Boys" built the world's first overwater bun-galows (see "The Bali Hai Boys," p. 132). It was their way of compensating for the lack of a beach here. The hotel has gone through several name changes since its days as the Hotel Bali Hai Raiatea, but those bungalows still stand out on the edge of the reef; from them, you can climb right into the water and get the sensation of flying as you snorkel along the clifflike face.

Also, this is still Raiatea's best hotel. The friendly and helpful staffers speak English, but the ambience is definitely French these days. The land-based bungalows, some of which have two units under their thatch roofs, are either along the seawall or in the gardens beyond. The least expensive units are hotel rooms, which have the same amenities as the bungalows and are air-conditioned. Opening to the pool and lagoon, and serving French fare and libation all day, the hotel's restaurant and bar are favorite local haunts.

B.P. 43, 98735 Uturoa, Raiatea (2km/1¼ miles south of town). © **800/657-3275** or 66.20.23. Fax 66.20.20. www.pearlresorts.com. 32 units. 24,000CFP (US$240) double; 26,000CFP–46,000CFP (US$260–US$460) bungalow. AE, MC, V. **Amenities:** Restaurant; bar; outdoor pool; tennis court; free use of snorkel gear and kayaks; bike rentals; activ-ities desk; car-rental desk; babysitting; laundry service. *In room:* A/C (rooms only), TV, minibar, coffeemaker, hair dryer, safe.

Hotel Mirimiri   Known as Hotel Tenape until taken over in 2005 by veteran hotelier Robert Cazenave, who also owns the fine **Restaurant Quai des Pecheurs** in Uturoa (p. 169), this plantation-style hotel sits in a large lawn across the main road from the lagoon on the west coast. Popular with locals, the restaurant and bar in the middle of the two-story clapboard building open onto the swimming pool out in the front yard. The rooms and one suite extend to each side. The medium-size units are identical, with pine floors, tables, desks, balconies with a view of the lagoon, and bathrooms with open, French-style showers. The suite adds two bedrooms. Robert was planning to repair a pier, which will give access to the lagoon for boating and swimming. The location is a bit remote, but the setting is so peaceful you can hear the birds singing outside your room.

B.P. 1147, 98735 Uturoa, Raiatea (west coast, 8km/5 miles from town). (℃ **60.01.00.** Fax 60.08.01. www.raiatea. com/miri/index.html. 16 units. 18,500CFP (US$185) double; 36,500CFP (US$365) suite. AE, DC, MC. V. **Amenities:** Restaurant; bar; outdoor pool; laundry service. In room: A/C, TV, dataport, safe.

MODERATE
Hotel Atiapiti   Just south of Taputapuatea Marae, this remote but pleasant little hotel sits beside the lagoon facing Te Ava Moa Pass and Huahine. There is no natural beach here, but a row of coconut palms and sand behind a bulkhead makes it seem like a beach resort. Five of the six bungalows directly face this vista. All have stucco sides and wood shingle roofs, which extend over front porches, some strung with hammocks. Each beachfront unit has a separate bedroom with king-size bed, while each garden unit has a double bed and two singles in its main room, plus a small second room with single bed. Owner Marie-Claude Rajaud, who speaks several languages including English, applies her cooking skills to fresh seafood in the French country–style restaurant. It's an excellent stop for lunch while you're visiting the *marae,* but call ahead for reservations if you're not a guest here. This is a relaxing place to stay if you don't mind being a long way from everything except the *marae.*

B.P. 884, 98735 Uturoa, Raiatea (east coast, 30km/18 miles south of Uturoa). (℃ **66.26.65.** Fax 66.16.65. atiapiti@ mail.pf. 7 units. 10,900CFP (US$109) double. MC, V. **Amenities:** Restaurant; bar; free use of snorkel gear; watersports equipment/rentals; bike rentals; car-rental desk; laundry service. In room: TV, kitchen, no phone.

INEXPENSIVE
Pension Manava   Roselyne and Andrew Brotherson rent two rooms in their house and have four bungalows in their lush gardens across the road from the lagoon. The two rooms share a bathroom and the Brothersons' kitchen. The bungalows have corrugated tin roofs, screened louvered windows, double and single beds, and large bathrooms with hot-water showers. Two also have kitchens. Roselyne will cook breakfast and provide free dinner transportation to town on request.

B.P. 559, 98735 Uturoa, Raiatea (6km/3½ miles south of town). (℃ **66.28.26.** www.manavapension.com. 6 units. 4,700CFP (US$47) double (shared bathrooms); 7,000CFP (US$70) bungalow; 8,000CFP (US$80) bungalow with kitchen. No credit cards. In room: Kitchen (2 units), no phone.

Pension Tepua   There's a lot packed into this small parcel of land next to the lagoon south of Uturoa, including a swimming pool and Raiatea's only dormitory, making this pension a good choice for backpackers. Despite being shoehorned into the property, the buildings are tropically attractive, with split bamboo siding and shingle roofs. The choice bungalow sits right beside the lagoon, with a view of Hotel Hawaiki Nui across a small bay. It's the only unit here with a television. Three other bungalows stand away from the lagoon near the pool. Another building houses four hotel-style rooms and the dormitory. The restaurant provides breakfast and lunch to guests and is open to the public at dinner. Dorm residents share toilets and showers, but all other units have private bathrooms with hot-water showers.

B.P. 1298, 98735 Uturoa, Raiatea (2.7km/1½ mile south of Uturoa). ⓒ **66.33.00**. Fax 66.32.00. www.raiatea.com/tepua. 8 units, 12 dormitory beds (shared bathrooms). 6,000CFP (US$60) double; 9,000CFP–12,000CFP (US$90–US$120) bungalow; 1,500CFP (US$15) dormitory bed. MC, V. **Amenities:** Restaurant; bar; outdoor pool; communal kitchen. *In room:* TV (1 unit), no phone.

Sunset Beach Motel ★ (Value   One of the best values in French Polynesia, this is not a motel but rather a collection of cottages, set in a coconut plantation on a peninsula sticking out west of the airport. The cottages sit in a row just off a palm-draped beach, the only one on Raiatea. The lagoon here is very shallow, but the beach enjoys a gorgeous westward view toward Bora Bora, and a long pier stretches to deep water (guests can paddle free kayaks from it). Of European construction rather than Polynesian, the bungalows are spacious, comfortably furnished, and have fully equipped kitchens and large covered verandas facing the sea. Part of the grove is set aside for campers, who have their own building with toilets, showers, and kitchen (bring your own tent). Manager Steve "Moana" Boubée speaks English. There is no restaurant here, but you can order breakfast in your bungalow.

B.P. 397, 98735 Uturoa, Raiatea (in Apooiti, 5km/3 miles northwest of Uturoa). ⓒ **66.33.47**. Fax 66.33.08. www. raiatea.com/sunsetbeach. 22 units. 9,000CFP (US$90) double bungalow; 1,100CFP (US$11) per person camping. MC, V. **Amenities:** Free use of kayaks; bike rentals; laundry service. *In room:* TV, kitchen, no phone.

CAMPING

The best place to pitch a tent is in the coconut grove at Sunset Beach Motel (see above). A less attractive alternative is **Peter's Place,** 6km (3.7 miles) south of Uturoa (ⓒ **66.20.01**). Owner Peter Brotherson has eight very simple and basic rooms in a plywood building, or you can camp in his expansive front yard across the main road from the lagoon. Everyone shares communal toilets, hot-water showers, and a kitchen under its own thatch-line tin roof. Rooms go 1,200CFP (US$12) per person, while campers pay 1,000CFP (US$10) each. Peter does not accept credit cards.

ON TAHAA

Except for Hotel Le Pirogue, Vahine Island Private Resort, and the super-luxurious Le Taha'a Private Island & Spa, all out on islets by themselves, Tahaa's accommodations fall into the anything-but-luxurious pension category. This may change soon, however, since new high-end properties are planned for the *motu* out on the reef.

(Tips **Stuck after Dark**

If you've been to Bora Bora, you'll know that hotel launches regularly ply between the *motu* resorts there, which means guests can easily get over to the main island for activities and dining. Such is not the case at Tahaa. Here, you cannot run over to the mainland from Hotel La Pirogue, La Taha'a Private Island & Spa, or Vahine Island Private Resort and save a few bucks on dinner. They are wonderful places to relax, but once you're out on one of Tahaa's *motu,* you are pretty much stuck out here after dark.

EXPENSIVE

Hotel La Pirogue   Beside a white-sand beach and shallow lagoon on Motu Porou, a small reef islet off Hipu village on Tahaa's northeastern coast, this is the least expensive of the offshore resorts here. All of the buildings have timber sides and natural thatch roofs. Four of the guest bungalows sit beside the beach and have small platforms extending out over the sand, where you can sit and take in the sunsets behind Tahaa and Bora Bora off in the distance. Each unit also has a front porch, a mosquito net over the double bed, a television, and a phone. Separate buildings hold the seafood restaurant and bar. The staff will take you over to Hipu, where you can use bicycles to explore Tahaa.

B.P. 668, 98735 Uturoa, Raiatea (on Motu Porou). ℂ **60.81.45.** Fax 60.81.46. www.hotellapirogue.com. 8 units. 22,000CFP–28,000CFP (US$220–US$280) bungalow. AE, MC. V. **Amenities:** Restaurant; bar; free use of bicycles, canoes, and snorkel gear; limited room service. *In room:* TV, dataport.

Le Taha'a Private Island & Spa ⟡⟡⟡   When I was traveling by yacht back in 1977, we anchored near Motu Tautau, an islet on the reef off Tahaa's northwest coast, and went ashore to get an unsurpassed view of Bora Bora from its outer edge. There was nothing on Tautau then except palm trees, a brackish lake, and several million mosquitoes. Since 2002, the mossies have mostly resided on the sea side of the *motu,* while one of French Polynesia's most luxurious and architecturally creative resorts has occupied the lagoon shoreline. A 40-minute boat ride from the Raiatea airport, or 15 minutes by helicopter from Bora Bora, this Relais & Châteaux hotel sports the territory's most tastefully decorated bungalows. Most stand out over the hip-deep lagoon, where their large decks have privacy fences screening covered sitting areas under thatch roofs. Most face hilly Tahaa, but a few have views of Bora Bora through a shallow reef pass between Tautau and its neighboring *motu.* Ashore beside the brilliant white-sand beach, 12 villa suites are even larger and more private. These have living rooms, bedrooms, and courtyards with plunge pools hidden behind high rock walls. At the center of it all is a stunning two-story central building, where stairs built in a tree lead up to the main bar and casual gourmet restaurant with both indoor and outdoor tables, all with a view. The most romantic tables sit by themselves on extensions from the terrace. Or you can retire inside to the air-conditioned fine-dining restaurant. The resort's infinity pool, a lunchtime restaurant and bar, and full-service spa are on one end of the property, thus removing most daytime activities from the vicinity of the bungalows. There's much to do here, from snorkeling to safari expeditions on Tahaa. This is a marvelous place to chill after the rigors of Bora Bora.

B.P. 67, 98733 Patio, Tahaa (on Motu Tautau). ℂ **800/657-3275** or 69.84.00. Fax 69.84.01. www.letahaa.com. 60 units. 90,000CFP–125,000CFP (US$900–US$1,250) bungalow. AE, DC, MC, V. **Amenities:** 2 restaurants; 2 bars; outdoor pool; tennis court; spa; Jacuzzi; watersports equipment/rentals; concierge; activities desk; limited room service; massage; babysitting; laundry service. *In room:* A/C, TV, dataport, minibar, coffeemaker, hair dryer, safe, CD player.

Vahine Island Private Resort   On Motu Tuuvahine, off Tahaa's northeastern coast, this intimate little hotel offers bungalows both beside a white-sand beach and built out over the sandy-bottom lagoon. Although a tad pricey in my opinion, the overwater units are the pick, since they are larger and more private than the beachside units—and you can climb from your deck right into the shallow water. All are built in traditional Polynesian style, with thatch roofs and native lumber and bamboo inside and out. Each sports a porch with hammock in front and a shower-only bathroom to the rear. Ceiling fans and mosquito nets make up for the lack of air-conditioning and window screens. The dining room serves French fare with island touches. There's a guest lounge with library, TV, and videos. Some travel writers have lumped Vahine Island in with the most luxurious resorts in French Polynesia and Fiji, but I'm not one of them.

B.P. 501, 98735 Uturoa, Raiatea (on Motu Tuuvahine). ℂ **65.67.38.** Fax 65.67.70. www.vahine-island.com. 9 units. 35,000CFP–52,000CFP (US$325–US$520) double. AE, DC, MC, V. **Amenities:** Restaurant; bar; free use of kayaks, canoes, windsurfboards, and snorkel gear; laundry service. *In room:* Minibar, hair dryer.

MODERATE
Pensione Vai Poe (Chez Patricia et Daniel)   Owners Patricia and Daniel Amaru have five tin-roofed bungalows on the lawn of their home on the north shore of Haamene Bay. They also own a pearl farm across the road, where you can learn how the orbs are grown and produced, and they operate Vai Poe safari expeditions (see "Safari Expeditions & Lagoon Excursions," earlier). Two of their bungalows are suitable for couples, while the other three can accommodate small families. Each has a private bathroom with hot-water shower and a fridge stocked with soft drinks. Guests congregate in the veranda-wrapped main house, where Patricia will cook breakfast and other meals on request.

B.P. 104, 98734 Haamene, Tahaa (north shore of Haamene Bay). ℂ and fax **65.60.83.** http://vaipoe.webnui.com. 5 units. 12,000CFP (US$120) double. AE, MC, V. Rates include breakfast. *In room:* TV, kitchen, no phone.

INEXPENSIVE
L'Hibiscus   This lively little pension beside Haamene Bay is the domain of Leo Morou, a bearded Frenchman who "went troppo" years ago, and his wife, Lolita. I stayed here in the early 1990s when they had three simple bungalows sharing communal showers and toilets. Those are still here, but the Morous have added four government-issued bungalows, each with its own bathroom as well as front porch. They also built a 200-seat waterside restaurant and bar, a long pier, and 14 moorings out in the bay, which attract dozens of yachties for a bit of libation and a meal. Parties, music, and Tahitian dance shows have been known to extend well into the night, so you may want to request a bungalow removed from the action.

B.P. 184, 98734 Haamene, Tahaa (north shore of Haamene Bay). ℂ **65.61.06.** Fax 65.65.65. www.tahaa-tahiti.com. 7 units (3 with shared bathroom). 6,000CFP–9,260CFP (US$60–US$93) double. MC, V. **Amenities:** Restaurant; bar; free use of snorkel gear. *In room:* Fridge, no phone.

7 Where to Dine
ON RAIATEA
Les roulottes, Raiatea's inexpensive meal wagons, congregate after dark near the Gare Maritime in the middle of Uturoa's business district. They stay open past midnight on Friday and Saturday. See "Don't Miss *Les Roulottes*" (p. 112) for details.

Brasserie Maraamu *(Value* CHINESE/TAHITIAN   Before it moved into the Gare Maritime, this restaurant occupied a waterfront shack and was widely known for its simple but good Chinese dishes, *poisson cru,* and fried chicken and steaks served with french fries. The chow is still good, as witnessed by the number of local office workers who head here for lunch. Local business types like to hang out over strong cups of morning coffee served in soup bowls, Chinese style.

In Gare Maritime, Uturoa waterfront. ℂ **66.46.64.** Reservations not accepted. Main courses 1,000CFP–1,800CFP (US$10–US$18). MC, V. Mon–Fri 7am–2pm and 6:30–9pm, Sat 10am–2pm.

Jade Garden Restaurant CANTONESE Although not quite on a par with the Sea Horse (see below), this family-run storefront restaurant serves very good Cantonese fare, such as chicken with freshwater chestnuts and pork with cashew nuts. The upstairs dining room is more pleasant than the one on the street level. Both are air-conditioned.

Rue Centrale, Uturoa. ✆ **66.34.40.** Reservations recommended on weekends. Main courses 1,500CFP–2,300CFP (US$15–US$23). AE, MC, V. Wed–Fri 11am–1pm and 6:30–9pm, Sat 6:30–9pm.

Le Napoli ⊛ *Finds* ITALIAN The stack of firewood beside a pond out back (note the Tahitian eels swimming about) gives a clue that the very good pizzas and steaks are cooked in a wood-fired oven in this open-air restaurant, which is dolled up with bamboo trim. The 15 varieties of pizza are all two-person size, so unless you're famished, forget the special tourist menu (which adds *poisson cru* and a dessert).

Main road north of Uturoa, near airport. ✆ **66.10.77.** Reservations recommended. Pizza and pasta 1,250CFP–1,450CFP (US$13–US$15); main courses 1,400CFP–2,000CFP (US$14–US$20). MC, V. Tues and Thurs–Sat 11am–2pm and 6:30–9pm, Wed and Sun 6:30–9pm.

Restaurant Quai des Pecheurs ⊛⊛ *Value* FRENCH Robert Cazenave, one of French Polynesia's top hotel managers, has turned this casual but chic restaurant into Raiatea's best place to dine. A big awning shades tables out on the Gare Maritime's plaza, where you can slake a thirst at the bar or cool off with ice cream at a walk-up counter. Robert's menu features fresh local seafood and New Zealand steaks. The tuna steak in a spicy Creole sauce is a pleasant diversion from familiar French choices. There's music for dancing on Friday nights and a Tahitian dance show on Saturday evenings. Call for free transportation from the Hotel Hawaiki Nui.

In Gare Maritime, Uturoa waterfront. ✆ **66.43.19.** Reservations recommended for dinner. Main courses 1,400CFP–2,950CFP (US$14–US$30). AE, MC, V. Daily noon–2pm and 7–9pm (ice-cream counter and bar 10am–11pm).

Sea Horse Restaurant CHINESE You can dine outside on the plaza or inside this establishment in Uturoa's cruise-ship terminal, where tropical furniture, potted plants, and linen tablecloths set a refined but relaxed ambience for very good Chinese cuisine. Most items on the menu will be familiar, but some such as sea cucumber will not. Check the specials board for the day's fish selections.

In Gare Maritime, Uturoa waterfront. ✆ **66.16.34.** Reservations recommended on weekend evenings. Main courses 1,200CFP–2,100CFP (US$12–US$21). MC, V. Mon–Sat 10am–1:30pm and 6–9:30pm.

Snack Moemoea CHINESE/FRENCH/SNACKS Predating the Gare Maritime by many years, this old corner storefront has tables both outside on the sidewalk and inside on the ground floor or on a mezzanine platform. It's another good place for breakfast, from croissants to omelets. The lunch menu includes *casse-croûte* sandwiches (a sandwich made on a crusty French baguette with any array of fillings), fine hamburgers, grilled fish and steaks, and Raiatea's best *poisson cru*. I love to quench my thirst here with an ice-cold coconut milk.

In Toporo Building, Uturoa waterfront. ✆ **66.39.84.** Reservations not accepted. Breakfast 600CFP–1,500CFP (US$6–US$15); sandwiches 400CFP–700CFP (US$4–US$7); main courses 1,300CFP–1,800CFP (US$13–US$18). No credit cards. Mon–Fri 6am–5pm, Sat 6am–2pm.

ON TAHAA

If you're chartering a yacht, you can have dinner at one of the offshore resorts listed under "Where to Stay: On Tahaa," above. Clients of The Moorings can even dine at the ritzy La Taha'a Private Island & Spa, provided they make reservations in advance.

Chez Louise ☞ TAHITIAN   This local restaurant beside the lagoon in Tiva village, on Tahaa's west coast, is a popular stop for cruise-ship passengers, and it's close enough to Le Taha'a Private Island & Spa that its guests come here for lunch or dinner, too. The *ma'a Tahiti* fare is first rate, as are fresh seafood items such as shrimp and lobster in vanilla sauce. Full meals are served, including wine. Yachties can tie their dinghies up to the pier out front. Reservations are highly recommended so that Louise will have plenty of good local grub on hand.

Tiva village, lagoonside. ℂ **65.68.88** or 72.59.18. Reservations highly recommended. Full meals 3,500CFP–5,600CFP (US$35–US$56). MC, V. Daily 11am–2pm and 6–9pm.

Restaurant Tahaa Maitai FRENCH/TAHITIAN   This French-owned restaurant on the waterfront in Haamene village, at the head of the bay, serves good salads, *poisson cru,* sandwiches, burgers, and French-style main courses. The clientele is mostly local, but yachties drop in here, too.

Haamene village, on the waterfront. ℂ **65.70.85**. Reservations recommended. Sandwiches and burgers 350CFP–1,200CFP (US$3.50–US$12); main courses 1,300CFP–1,600CFP (US$13–US$16). MC, V. Tues–Fri 10am–2:30pm and 6:40–8pm, Sat 6:40–8pm, Sun 10am–2:30pm.

Bora Bora

Because of its fame and extraordinary beauty, little Bora Bora is a playground for the well-to-do, occasionally the famous, and honeymooners blowing a wad. French Polynesia's tourist magnet, it has seen an explosion of hotel construction in recent years, with piers reaching out like tentacles to multitudinous bungalows standing over its gorgeous lagoon. Some of the piers are so long that The Moorings has added them to its sailing charts as hazards to navigation!

Those of us who remember the island in its more natural state often bemoan that development has ruined it. But when I meet someone who is here for the first time, they invariably are as blown away by Bora Bora as I was when I spent a week camping here a few eons ago. If you look beyond the tourists hanging under parasails over the lagoon, you will appreciate why James A. Michener wrote that this is the world's most beautiful island.

Of course, there are more tourists here than on any other French Polynesian island. Thus, some lovers now like to finish their honeymoons on the more peaceful Tahaa or Huahine after the mile-a-minute pace here.

Lying 230km (143 miles) northwest of Tahiti, Bora Bora is a middle-aged island consisting of a high center completely surrounded by a lagoon that's enclosed by coral reef. It has a gorgeous combination of sand-fringed *motus* (small islets) sitting on the outer reef enclosing the multihued lagoon, which cuts deep bays into the high central island. Towering over it all is Bora Bora's trademark, the basaltic tombstone known as **Mount Otemanu** (725m/2,379 ft.). Standing next to it is the more normally rounded **Mount Pahia** (660m/2,165 ft.).

One of the best beaches in French Polynesia stretches for more than 3km (2 miles) around the flat, coconut-studded peninsula known as **Point Matira,** which juts out from the island's southern end.

Bora Bora is so small that the road around it covers only 32km (19 miles) from start to finish. All the 7,000 or so Bora Borans live on a flat coastal strip that quickly gives way to the mountainous interior.

1 Arriving & Departing

Bora Bora's airport is on *Motu* **Mute,** a flat island on the northwestern edge of the barrier reef. U.S. marines built the airstrip during World War II when Bora Bora was a major refueling stop on the America-to-Australia supply line.

You will see the lagoon close up soon after landing because all passengers are ferried across it from the airport. Some resorts send boats to pick up their guests (be sure to tell them your flight number when making your reservations). The major resorts have welcome desks in the terminal to greet you and steer you to the correct boat. It can be a tad confusing out on the dock, where baggage is unloaded. You do not want to end up on the wrong *motu,* so pay attention, and ask someone if you are not sure which boat is yours.

Bora Bora

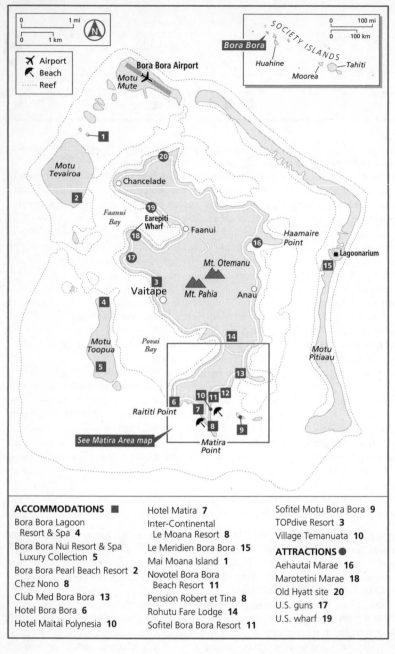

ACCOMMODATIONS ■

Bora Bora Lagoon
  Resort & Spa **4**
Bora Bora Nui Resort & Spa
  Luxury Collection **5**
Bora Bora Pearl Beach Resort **2**
Chez Nono **8**
Club Med Bora Bora **13**
Hotel Bora Bora **6**
Hotel Maitai Polynesia **10**

Hotel Matira **7**
Inter-Continental
  Le Moana Resort **8**
Le Meridien Bora Bora **15**
Mai Moana Island **1**
Novotel Bora Bora
  Beach Resort **11**
Pension Robert et Tina **8**
Rohutu Fare Lodge **14**
Sofitel Bora Bora Resort **11**

Sofitel Motu Bora Bora **9**
TOPdive Resort **3**
Village Temanuata **10**

ATTRACTIONS ●

Aehautai Marae **16**
Marotetini Marae **18**
Old Hyatt site **20**
U.S. guns **17**
U.S. wharf **19**

Impressions

I saw it first from an airplane. On the horizon there was a speck that became a tall, blunt mountain with cliffs dropping sheer into the sea. And about the base of the mountain, narrow fingers of land shot out, forming magnificent bays, while about the whole was thrown a coral ring of absolute perfection. . . . That was Bora Bora from aloft. When you stepped upon it the dream expanded.
                                                    —James A. Michener, *Return to Paradise*, 1951

If your hotel does not send a boat, you will take Air Tahiti's launch to **Vaitape,** the only village and the center of most commerce. Buses will take you from Vaitape to your hotel. Get in the bus displaying the name of your hotel, or ask the driver if you are not sure. Bus fare from Vaitape to the Matira Point hotel district is 500CFP (US$5).

See "Getting to Tahiti & French Polynesia" and "Getting Around Tahiti & French Polynesia," in chapter 2, for more information.

2 Getting Around Bora Bora

There is no regularly scheduled public transportation system on Bora Bora. Buses do ferry passengers from Vaitape to the Matira hotel district on cruise-ship days, though, and anyone can catch a ride for 300CFP (US$3).

Some hotels on the main island shuttle their guests to Vaitape and back once or twice a day, but the frequency can vary depending on how many guests they have. Most resorts out on the islets run shuttle boats to Vaitape. Major exceptions are the Bora Bora Pearl Beach Resort, whose shuttles go to Chancelade on the northwestern corner, and Le Meridien Bora Bora, which sends its *navettes* to remote Anau village on the east coast. Take this into account if you plan to spend time on the main island.

BY RENTAL CAR, SCOOTER & BICYCLE

Europcar (℃ 800/227-7368 or 67.70.15; www.europcar.com) and a local firm, **Fare-Piti Rent a Car** (℃ 76.65.28), have offices at Vaitape harbor. Rates at both start at 8,900CFP (US$89) a day for the smallest cars, including unlimited kilometers and insurance. Both rent open-air "Fun Cars" for about 8,900CFP (US$89) a day. Fare-Piti rents scooters for 7,500CFP (US$75) a day. Both have bicycles for about 1,700CFP (US$17) all day.

The 32km (19 miles) of road around Bora Bora are paved. Most of it is flat, but be very cautious on the unpaved portion, which climbs a steep hill. Always drive or ride slowly and carefully, and be on the lookout for pigs, chickens, pedestrians, and especially dogs.

BY TAXI

No taxis patrol Bora Bora looking for passengers, but several firms have transport licenses, which means they can come get you if someone calls. The hotel desks and restaurants will do that for you, or you can phone **Léon** (℃ 70.69.16), **Otemanu Tours** (℃ 67.70.49), **Jacques Isnard** (℃ 67.72.25), or **Dino's Land & Water Taxi** (℃ 79.29.65). Fares between Vaitape and the Matira Point hotel district are at least 1,500CFP (US$15) from 6am to 6pm and 2,000CFP (US$20) from 6pm to 6am. A ride between Vaitape and Le Meridien Bora Bora's shuttle landing at Anau village costs 5,000CFP (US$50) anytime. (Add up your expected fares; it may be more economical to rent a vehicle.) The taxis aren't metered, so make sure you and the driver agree on a fare before setting out.

If you're staying at a resort on an islet and don't want to wait for the next shuttle boat, you can call **Dino's Land & Water Taxi** (© **79.29.65**) or **Taxi** *Motu* (© **67.60.61**). The ride to the main island costs about 2,500CFP (US$25).

FAST FACTS: Bora Bora

The following facts apply specifically to Bora Bora. For more information, see "Fast Facts: Tahiti & French Polynesia," in chapter 2.

Babysitters The hotels can arrange for English-speaking babysitters, or you can contact **Robin Teraitepo** at Chez Ben's (© **67.74.54**).

Bookstores/Newsstands **La Maison de la Press,** across the main road from the Vaitape small boat harbor (© **60.57.75**), carries the *International Herald Tribune* and *USA Today,* though not today's edition. It also sells film, camera batteries, and prepaid SIM cards for your cellphone.

Camera/Film **Jeanluc Photo Shop,** at the Vaitape harbor (© **72.01.23**), offers professional photo services and overnight processing of color print film.

Currency Exchange **Banque de Tahiti, Banque Socredo,** and **Banque de Polynésie** have branches with ATMs in Vaitape.

Drugstores **Pharmacie de Bora Bora,** north of the small boat harbor in Vaitape (© **67.70.30**), is open Monday through Friday from 8am to noon and 2:30 to 6pm, Saturday from 8am to noon and 5 to 6pm, and Sunday and holidays from 9 to 11 am.

Emergencies/Police The **emergency police** phone number is © **17.** The **gendarmerie** (© **67.70.58**) is opposite the Vaitape harbor.

Healthcare The island's **infirmary** is in Vaitape (© **67.70.77**), as is **Dr. Azad Roussanaly** (© **67.77.95**).

Internet Access Check your e-mail at **L'Appetisserie** in the Centre Commercial Le Pahia just north of the Vaitape harbor (© **67.78.88**), which charges 40CFP (US40¢) per minute of online time. See "Where to Dine," later, for more about this pastry shop.

Post Office The Vaitape post office is open Monday from 8am to 3pm, Tuesday through Friday from 7:30am to 3pm, and Saturday from 8 to 10am.

Restrooms Public restrooms in the small octagonal building on the Vaitape harbor are open sporadically during the day and not at all after dark. It can be a long wait for a shuttle boat back to your resort, so take preventive action as necessary.

Taxes Bora Bora's municipal government adds 100CFP to 150CFP (US$1–US$1.50) per night to your hotel bill.

Visitor Information The **Bora Bora Comité du Tourisme,** B.P. 144, Vaitape, Bora Bora (© and fax **67.76.36;** info-bora-bora@mail.pf), has a visitor center in the large building on the north side of the Vaitape harbor. Open Monday through Friday, and on cruise-ship days, from 8:30am to 4pm.

Water Bora Bora has a huge desalinization plant, so the tap water is safe to drink. Most local residents still drink bottled water, available at all groceries.

3 Exploring Bora Bora: The Circle Island Tour

Most of Bora Bora's residents live on the flat coastal strip that rings the island. The paved round-island road skirts the shoreline and runs in and out of the bays. Because the road is only 32km (19 miles) long, many visitors see it by bicycle (give yourself a full day), scooter, or car.

Some of the sights mentioned below may not be easy to find, however, so consider taking a guided tour around the island. **Otemanu Tours** (© **67.70.49;** otemanu. tours@mail.pf) still uses one of the traditional, open-air *le truck* vehicles, which adds an extra dimension to its trips, but be sure your tour is in *le truck* and not an air-conditioned bus. The cost is about 3,000CFP (US$30) per person; you can book at any hotel activities desk.

If you didn't see enough of Bora Bora on your flight here, you can get a spectacular bird's-eye view of the island with **Polynesia Hélicoptères** (© **67.62.59;** www. polynesia-helicopter.com). It charges about 16,000CFP (US$160) per person for a 15-minute sightseeing flight over Bora Bora and its lagoon. If you've never seen an atoll and aren't going to the Tuamotu Islands, consider a 30-minute flight over Bora Bora and out to Tupai, a ring of flat islets enclosing a lagoon north of Bora Bora; the cost is about 26,000CFP (US$260) per person. A minimum of four passengers is required on all flights. Polynesia Hélicoptères also provides transfers between Bora Bora and Le Taha'a Private Island & Spa, off Tahaa (p. 167).

VAITAPE

If you do the circle island tour on your own, begin at the small boat harbor in **Vaitape,** Bora Bora's only town and its administrative center. The harbor is the center of attention in Vaitape, as Air Tahiti, the cruise ships, and the shuttle boats from the resorts on Motu Toopua (the large islet offshore) land their passengers here. The island's visitor information center and women's handicraft center are in the large building beside the harbor. Viatape's only street is lined with boutiques, black-pearl shops, and other establishments designed to wrench money from your pockets. The post office is to the right as you face the mountains, but most business activity takes place north of the harbor, especially at the modern Centre Commerical La Pahia.

Across the street from the harbor, opposite the gendarmerie, is the grave of famed French socialite, author, and yachtsman **Alain Gerbault,** who single-handedly skippered his boat *Firecrest* around the world between 1923 and 1929, stopping for an extended period in French Polynesia. Gerbault returned to French Polynesia in 1933 and championed the cause of the islanders against the colonial bureaucracy. He also introduced soccer to the locals. Gerbault was interned on Moorea at the outbreak of World War II in Europe because he favored the pro-Nazi Vichy government in Paris, while French Polynesians sided with Gen. Charles de Gaulle and the Free French. He was released on condition he leave the territory. He sailed to Indonesia, where he died

---

Tips A Killer View

The round-island road curves along the shore of **Povai Bay,** where Mount Otemanu and Mount Pahia tower over you. Take your time along this bay; the views here are the best on Bora Bora. When you reach **Bloody Mary's Restaurant & Bar,** go out on the pier for a killer view back across the water at Mount Otemanu.

on Timor in 1941. Six years later, the French navy returned his ashes to Bora Bora, his favorite island.

From the harbor, walk northward through Vaitape, taking in its large Christian church, which stands at the base of soaring Mount Pahia. When you've seen enough of this Polynesian village, turn south and head counterclockwise around the island.

MATIRA BEACH 𝕽𝕽𝕽

After following the shore of semicircular Povai Bay, the road climbs the small headland, where a huge banyan tree marks the entrance to the Hotel Bora Bora on **Raititi Point,** and then follows curving **Matira Beach,** one of French Polynesia's finest. Some of the island's best snorkeling is in the shallow, sand-bottom lagoon off these powdery white sands. People have homes on the other side of the road, but the beach itself is still remarkably undeveloped.

The road follows the beach and then curves sharply to the left at the south end of the island. Watch here for a narrow paved road to the right. This leads to **Matira Point,** the low, sandy, coconut-studded peninsula that extends out from Bora Bora's south end. Down this track about 46m (150 ft.) is a **public beach** on the west side of the peninsula, opposite the Inter-Continental Le Moana Resort. The lagoon is shallow all the way out to the reef at this point, but the bottom is smooth and sandy. When I first came to Bora Bora in 1977, I camped for a week on Matira Point; the Inter-Continental Le Moana Resort is now just one of many structures in what was then a virtually deserted coconut grove completely surrounded by unspoiled beach.

THE EAST COAST

After rounding the point, you'll pass through the island's busy hotel and restaurant district before climbing a steep hill above the Club Med, which sits beside Faaopore Bay. A steep trail begins at a set of steps on the mountain side of the road and goes up to a lookout over the bay. Another trail cuts off to the right on the north side of the hill and goes to the **Aehautai Marae,** one of several old temples on Bora Bora. This particular one has a great view of Mount Otemanu and the blue outlines of Raiatea and Tahaa islands beyond the *motu* on the reef.

You will go through a long stretch of coconut plantations before entering **Anau,** a typical Polynesian village with a large church, a general store, and tin-roofed houses crouched along the road. Anau is the landing point for boats going to and from Le Meridien Bora Bora and the Inter-Continental Resort and Thalasso Spa Bora Bora, whose overwater bungalows you will see out on Motu Pitiaau. The St. Regis Resort Bora and the Four Seasons Bora Bora are slated to joint them out there (see "Where to Stay," below).

The road goes over two hills at Point Haamaire, the main island's easternmost extremity, about 4km (2½ miles) north of Anau village. Between the two hills on the lagoon side of the road stands **Aehautai Marae,** a restored temple. Out on the point is **Taharuu Marae,** which has a great view of the lagoon. The Americans installed more naval guns in the hills above the point during World War II.

THE NORTH & WEST COASTS

On the deserted northeast coast, you will ride through several miles of coconut plantations pockmarked by thousands of holes made by *tupas* (land crabs). After turning at the northernmost point, you pass a group of overwater bungalows and another group of houses that climb the hill. Some of these are expensive condominiums; the

Matira Area

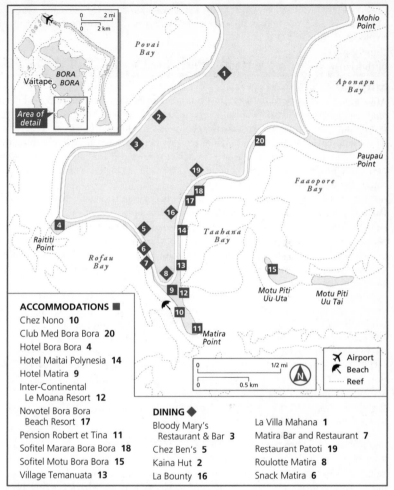

ACCOMMODATIONS ■

Chez Nono **10**
Club Med Bora Bora **20**
Hotel Bora Bora **4**
Hotel Maitai Polynesia **14**
Hotel Matira **9**
Inter-Continental
  Le Moana Resort **12**
Novotel Bora Bora
  Beach Resort **17**
Pension Robert et Tina **11**
Sofitel Marara Bora Bora **18**
Sofitel Motu Bora Bora **15**
Village Temanuata **13**

DINING ◆

Bloody Mary's
  Restaurant & Bar **3**
Chez Ben's **5**
Kaina Hut **2**
La Bounty **16**

La Villa Mahana **1**
Matira Bar and Restaurant **7**
Restaurant Patoti **19**
Roulotte Matira **8**
Snack Matira **6**

✈ Airport
↖ Beach
···· Reef

others are part of a defunct project that was to have been a Hyatt resort. Across the lagoon are Motu Mute and the airport.

Faanui Bay was used during World War II as an Allied naval base. It's not marked, but the U.S. Navy's Seabees built the concrete wharf on the north shore as a seaplane ramp. Just beyond the main shipping wharf at the point on the south side of Faanui Bay is the restored **Marotetini Marae,** which in pre-European days was dedicated to navigators. In his novel *Hawaii,* James Michener had his fictional Polynesians leave this point to discover and settle the Hawaiian Islands. Nearby are tombs in which members of Bora Bora's former royal family are buried. If you look offshore at this point, you'll see the only pass into the lagoon. The remains of two **U.S. guns** that guarded it stand on the hill above, but are best visited on a safari tour (see "Safari Expeditions," below).

As you enter Vaitape, **Magasin Chin Lee** is a major gathering place for local residents. It's a good place to soak up some island culture while trimming your thirst with a cold bottle of Eau Royale.

4 Safari Expeditions & Lagoon Excursions

SAFARI EXPEDITIONS 🐚

The regular tours stick to the shoreline, but safari expeditions venture into the hills in open-air, four-wheel-drive vehicles for panoramic views and visits to the old U.S. Navy gun sites. Compared to safari expeditions on Moorea, Huahine, and Tahaa, which emphasize local culture as well as scenery, here they are more like scenic thrill rides. The journey can be rough, so I do not recommend it for children, the elderly, or anyone prone to carsickness. The mountain roads are mere ruts in places, so you could become stuck if it has been raining.

Your best bet for insight into the island's history and lore is Patrick Tairua of **Patrick's Activities** (© 67.69.94; patrick.bora@mail.pf). Son of the last Polynesian chief of Bora Bora, Patrick (pronounced Pa-*treek* in French) passes along stories gleaned from spending time with the two elders who are responsible for protecting the island's oral history. You'll get out of the jeep and walk through the forest to an ancient *marae* where petroglyphs are carved into the basaltic rock. Patrick also organizes private tours.

Another good choice is **Vavau Adventures** (© 72.01.21; temana689@mail.pf), which has morning and afternoon expeditions around the island and up into the mountains. These tours also emphasize Bora Bora's history, culture, flora, and fauna, and they stop at a fish farm, where you will see tropical species being raised to restock the magnificent lagoon.

The largest operator is the Levard family's **Tupuna Four-Wheel-Drive Expeditions** (© 67.75.06). On this tour, your last stop will be at the Farm, the Levards' black-pearl operation (see "Shopping," below).

Expect to pay about 6,600CFP (US$66) per person for each tour. You can book at any hotel activities desk.

LAGOON EXCURSIONS & SHARK FEEDING 🐚🐚🐚

Bora Bora has one of the world's most beautiful lagoons, and getting out on it, snorkeling and swimming in it, and visiting the islands on its outer edge are absolute musts. Although it's a widespread activity now, this is where **shark feeding** began. That is, your guide feeds reef sharks while you watch from a reasonably safe distance. Some conservationists have criticized shark feeding, but it is guaranteed to leave an indelible imprint on your memory.

Any hotel activities desk can book you on an all-day excursion with one of several operators. My long-time favorite is Nono Levard's **Teremoana Tours** (© 67.71.38), which everyone here calls Nono's Tours. You spend the day going around the lagoon in a speedy outrigger canoe. Depending on the weather, you'll go snorkeling and watch a shark-feeding demonstration in the morning. You'll stop on a *motu* for swimming and a picnic lunch, and then pet stingrays on your way home in the afternoon. Expect to pay about 8,000CFP (US$80) for a full-day outing.

Even if your all-day excursion doesn't feature it, you can still visit the **Bora Bora Lagoonarium** (© 67.71.34), a fenced-in underwater area near Le Meridien Bora

Bora. Here you can swim with (and maybe even ride) manta rays and observe sharks (which are on the other side of the fence here). The Lagoonarium has its own morning tour with shark-feeding and lunch on the *motu,* plus an afternoon excursion with fish-watching. The morning excursion costs 7,800CFP (US$78), the afternoon tour is 6,600CFP (US$66), or you can do both for 11,000CFP (US$110).

You can rent a boat and explore the lagoon yourself, but I strongly suggest this only for those who know what they're doing, and who understand how the color of the water tells its depth. You do not want to ruin your vacation by running onto a shallow reef. If you're still interested in renting a small craft, contact **Taxi Motu,** at the Novotel Bora Bora Beach Resort (✆ **67.60.61**), or **Moana Adventure Tours,** near the Hotel Bora Bora (✆ **67.61.41**).

A much drier way to see the underwater delights is in the semi-submersibles *Spirit of Pacific* (✆ **74.99.99** or 67.55.55; www.spiritofpacific.com) and *Aquascope Bora Bora* (✆ **67.61.92**). These half-submarines operate along the outer edges of the lagoon and along the reef outside the pass. The 50-minute voyages cost about 6,000CFP (US$60) for adults, about half for children 4 to 12. The transfer boats leave the Vaitape small boat harbor several times a day, but call for reservations.

5 Fishing, Hiking, Horseback Riding & Watersports

FISHING

For combined sailing and fishing, American Richard Postma's *Taravana* (✆ **72.39.99** or 67.77.79; taravana@mail.pf) is the world's first sail-powered luxury game-fishing boat. This 50-footer is available for day trips or charters to the other Leeward Islands, including Tupai, a small atoll northwest of Bora Bora. Sailing or fishing costs 90,000CFP (US$900) for a half day, up to 120,000CFP (US$1,200) for a full day; prices include food but not alcoholic beverages. You can go on a nonfishing sunset cruise for about 6,500CFP (US$65) per person. Among Richard's first guests were actors Dennis Quaid and Meg Ryan (when they were still a couple). Former *Baywatch* star Pamela Anderson came along later.

HIKING

On every trip here, I walk along Matira Beach by following the round-island road between the Hotel Bora Bora and Matira Point. It's a flat and enormously beautiful hike. Some maps and older guidebooks show a hiking trail from Faanui village across a pass in the mountains to the east coast, but don't believe them. There is a trail from Vaitape to the top of Mount Pahia, but this is an arduous hike and should be undertaken only with a guide. Otemanu Tours operates **Muont Pahia Excursions** (✆ **67.70.49;** otemanu.tours@mail.pf), which will guide you to the top for about 15,000CFP (US$150) per person. Or contact Stéphane Duwa, the **Trek'in Bora Mountain Guide** (✆ **67.56.40;** duwasteph@yahoo.fr).

HORSEBACK RIDING

You won't be able to ride horses into the spectacular mountains of the main island since **Reva Reva Ranch** (✆ **67.63.63** or 78.26.36; ranchrevareva@hotmail.com) is out on flat Motu Pitiaau on the eastern reef. The 1- and 1½-hour rides along the beach and across the *motu* cost about 6,600CFP to 8,000CFP (US$66–US$80), respectively, including boat transfers from your hotel.

WATERSPORTS

Every hotel has some water toys for its guests to use, and hotel activities desks can arrange fishing, diving, and other watersports. You don't have to stay at the **Novotel Bora Bora Beach Club** (© 60.59.50) to use its equipment and facilities, but you do have to pay a fee. You can go water-skiing, sail on Hobie Cats, paddle canoes, and get a bird's-eye view of the lagoon while hanging below a parasail.

Matira Jet Tours (© 77.63.63) offers lagoon excursions by jet ski as well as inland tours via all-terrain vehicles. Many of the people you'll see riding above the lagoon are with **Bora Bora Parasail** (© 78.27.10). If sailing is more your speed, you can go on a day or sunset sail on the catamaran *Taaroa* (© 24.62.04) for about 4,500CFP (US$45).

KAYAKING   Based at Rohutu Fare Lodge (p. 188), **Bora Bora Kayaks** (© 70.77.99; borarohutu@free.fr) rents one- and two-person sea kayaks ranging from 1,500CFP (US$15) for 1 hour to 6,500CFP (US$65) for a whole day. These quality boats are made in the United States and come equipped with snorkeling and fishing gear.

SCUBA DIVING & SNORKELING 🐟🐟   While snorkeling off the reef face at the Hotel Bora Bora late one afternoon, I was startled to see a large manta ray gliding by virtually overhead, seemingly just a few feet away. It's one of my most indelible Bora Bora moments. You may have one, too, for both divers and snorkelers can swim among the manta rays, eagle rays, sharks, and some 1,000 species of colorful tropical fishes in the lagoon here.

One of the most popular snorkeling sites is over the coral gardens in and near the **Bora Bora Lagoonarium** (see "Lagoon Excursions & Shark Feeding," above). Even novice divers can explore the site known as Anau, in the lagoon between there and Point Haamaire, where manta rays frequently hang out. Divers and snorkelers also share the lagoon off the eastern side of Motu Toopua and the islet next to it, Motu Toopua Iti.

The most easily accessible dive site outside the reef is off Motu Tapu, the islet just south of Teavanui Pass. Two others—the White Valley, off the airport, and Tupitipiti, on the reef's southeastern corner—both require lengthy boat rides and can experience strong currents.

Among the best snorkeling spots are the aptly named "Aquarium," off the southern end of Motu Pitiaau, and around Motu Piti Uuuta, home of the Sofitel Motu. These require boat transportation, but you can walk to the outer reef from the southern tip of Point Matira, thus increasing your chances of seeing more fish than if you snorkel off Matira Beach south of the Hotel Bora Bora. Best of all, in my opinion, are the reef faces, above which sit the Hotel Bora Bora's overwater bungalows.

Every resort has snorkeling gear for its guests as well as a scuba-diving program. They all charge about 7,500CFP (US$75) for 30-minute introductory courses or a one-tank lagoon dive. Open-water and night dives cost about 9,000CFP (US$90).

⟨*Moments* Like Flying Underwater

Shining with every hue on the blue end of the color spectrum, Bora Bora's watery playground is one of my favorite snorkeling spots. Hotel Bora Bora has bungalows sitting right on the edge of a reef that drops precipitously to dark depths. I experience the exhilaration of flying when I drift out over that under-water cliff. If you're lucky, a manta ray will gracefully glide by.

Friendly dive operators Michel and Anne Condesse offer morning, afternoon, and evening dives from their **Bora Diving Center,** adjacent to Hotel Bora Bora (© **67. 71.84;** fax 67.74.83; www.boradive.com). They provide buoyancy compensators, fins, snorkels, wetsuits, regulators, and all other equipment (be prepared for the metric system; depth and pressure gauges display measurements in meters and kilograms). They also teach PADI certification courses. For non-divers, they offer "Aqua Safari" excursions, which entail walking on the bottom while wearing a diving helmet.

The island's largest dive operator is **TOPdive Bora Bora** (© **60.50.50;** fax 60.50.51; www.topdive.com), which has top-of-the line equipment and some of the best dive boats in French Polynesia. Its base is on the northern outskirts of Vaitape.

6 Shopping

Local artisans display straw hats, pareus, and other handicraft items at **Bora Bora I Te Fanau Tahi** in the large hall at the Vaitape harbor (no phone). Open from 8:30am to 4pm Monday through Friday, plus weekends when cruise ships are here.

Boutique Bora Bora   Catering to the cruise-ship crowd, this store has more T-shirts and pareus than most others here, plus it sells wood carvings, books, calendars, curios, and a few black pearls. It's a good place to stock up on Hinano beer glasses. Open daily from 9am to 5:30pm. Vaitape, opposite the small boat harbor. © **67.79.72.**

Boutique Gauguin   In a white house 1.5km (1 mile) north of Hotel Bora Bora, Boutique Gauguin is one of the larger stores here, offering a selection of handicrafts, clothing, black pearls, and curios. This is the best place on Bora Bora to shop for prints of Paul Gauguin's paintings. Some of the pareus here are particularly artistic. Open daily from 8am to 5:30pm. Povai Bay. © **67.76.67.**

The Farm   Since the Farm is owned by the Levard family, you are likely to be deposited here after going on one of their safari excursions. Although the family's main black-pearl farms are on Tahaa, they have about 10,000 oysters growing here, primarily to show you how pearls are grown, harvested, graded, and turned into jewelry. The final products are for sale in the **Bora Pearl Company,** the showroom here. It's worth a visit to see how it's all done. Open daily from 9am to 6pm. Raititi Point, near Hotel Bora Bora. © **70.06.65.**

Matira Pearls ✸✸✸ *Value*   You will have ample opportunities to shop for black pearls on Bora Bora (Vaitape village alone has a dozen outlets), but this is my favorite. It's owned by Steve Fearon, whose family once had a piece of the Hotel Bora Bora, and whose brother, Tom Fearon, has a bungalow resort on Rarotonga in the Cook Islands. Steve's chief assistant is his son, Heirama, who graduated from Pepperdine University in California. Unlike some other stores, their customized settings emphasize the pearl, not the gold. Set and loose pearls start at $100. Open Monday through Saturday from 9am to 5:30pm, Sunday from 10am to 5pm. East side of Matira Point. © **67.79.14.**

7 Where to Stay

Bora Bora has some of the South Pacific's finest—and most expensive—resorts, and it will have a few more of them by the time you get here. Soon to join the fray is the **St. Regis Resort Bora Bora** (www.starwoodspacollection.com) and the **Four Seasons Bora Bora** (www.fourseasons.com), both on the eastern *motus.* Their bungalows, amenities, and room rates should be over the top.

The luxurious **Inter-Continental Resort and Thalasso Spa Bora Bora** (© 800/ 327-0200 or 60.49.00; www.boraboraspa.interconti.com), on Motu Piti Aau off the eastern side of the main island, opened just before press time. Its 80 suite-size bungalows, all built over the lagoon, feature such modern amenities as high-speed Internet access and flat-screen TVs. The resort is the world's first to be entirely air-conditioned using cold seawater pumped from 2,500 feet down in the ocean. The saltwater is reheated for the Thalasso Spa's large swimming pool and unique treatments, some dispensed in overwater rooms with glass floors for fish-viewing. Even the wedding chapel is over the water.

EXPENSIVE

Bora Bora Lagoon Resort & Spa ☆☆
Speedboats shuttle 23 times a day from the Vaitape small boat harbor to this posh resort on the northern end of Motu Toopua, a hilly island facing the rounded peak of Mount Pahia (not Mount Otemanu's tombstone). The main building, under three interlocking thatch roofs, holds a reception area, a bar, and a gourmet restaurant. To the rear, an expansive stone deck surrounds one of French Polynesia's largest swimming pools, where you'll find another bar and daytime restaurant. Long piers with hand-carved railings lead to the 44 overwater bungalows, while the rest of the units sit ashore in tropical gardens. One is a two-bedroom villa well suited to well-heeled families. Three of the beachside bungalows—one of which has a Jacuzzi tub—interconnect to form suites. The units are so close together that, unless you run your air-conditioner, you can overhear your neighbor's favorite TV show (not to mention certain amorous activities). For the most part, the accommodations—while all luxurious—do not live up to the resort's exceptional amenities. The unusual spa here has treatment rooms high up in a banyan tree. *Note:* This resort quotes rates in euros, not CFP.

B.P. 175, 98730 Vaitape, Bora Bora (on Motu Toopua, 1km/½ mile off Vaitape). © 800/860-4905 or 60.40.00. Fax 60.40.01. www.boraboralagoonresort.orient-express.com. 77 units. 395€–1,550€ (US$470–US$1,844) bungalow. AE, DC, MC, V. **Amenities:** 2 restaurants; 2 bars; large outdoor pool; 2 tennis courts; health club; spa; watersports equipment/rentals; game room; concierge; activities desk; limited room service; laundry service. *In room:* A/C, TV, dataport, minibar, coffeemaker, hair dryer, safe.

Bora Bora Nui Resort & Spa Luxury Collection ☆☆☆
This sprawling resort occupies the southern end of hilly Motu Toopua, a 15-minute boat ride off Vaitape. Although this is the island's swankiest property (for the time being, anyway), it faces west toward the sea, thus depriving its public areas and all but a handful of its bungalows of the typical Bora Bora view. They're called "horizon" bungalows here because they look over the sea to the horizon. Only the full-service spa, perched atop the islet's central ridge, looks out at Mount Otemanu. A beachside, two-level infinity swimming pool serves as the focal point of activities. It's backed by two public buildings, one with a large boutique and a casual, sand-floor restaurant offering very reasonably priced lunches and dinners. The other houses a fine-dining outlet, an air-conditioned library, and a fascinating photo collection of U.S. marines building the airstrip on Motu Mute during World War II. Spread out over 6.4 hectares (16 acres) and nearly a kilometer (½ mile) of lagoon (you'll soon learn to call for a golf cart to take you to dinner), the 120 luxurious, suite-size units—84 of them overwater—are some of the largest in French Polynesia (again, for the time being). The overwater bungalows feature separate bedrooms, huge bathrooms with both tubs and walk-in showers, and big decks with privacy screens. Housed in a hillside hotel-style building, the "lagoon-view

suites" are the least expensive units, and they interconnect to accommodate families. Top of the line are the huge royal suites. Unlike Bora Bora's other resorts, room rates here include full breakfast, which the staff will deliver by canoe to your overwater mansion.

B.P. 502, 98730 Vaitape, Bora Bora (on Motu Toopua, 1.5km/1 mile off Vaitape). © 800/782-9488 or 60.32.00. Fax 60.32.01. www.boraboranui.com. 73,800CFP–275,000CFP (US$738–US$2,750) bungalow, 62,000CFP–68,500CFP (US$620–US$685) suite. Rates include full breakfast. AE, DC, MC, V. **Amenities:** 2 restaurants; 2 bars; large outdoor pool; tennis courts; health club; spa; Jacuzzi; sauna; watersports equipment/rentals; bike rentals; children's programs; game room; concierge; activities desk; 24-hr. room service; massage; babysitting; laundry service. *In room:* A/C, TV, dataport, minibar, coffeemaker, hair dryer, iron, safe.

Bora Bora Pearl Beach Resort & Spa 🐠🐠
The most traditionally Polynesian resort on Bora Bora, the Pearl Beach resides on Motu Tevairoa, the largest of the flat islets dotting the outer reef, and it has better views of Mount Otemanu across the lagoon than does the Bora Bora Lagoon Resort to its south (see above). Covered by interconnected conical thatch roofs, the open-air restaurant, main bar, and library stand on a raised earthen platform, which enhances their views over a large swimming pool to the lagoon and mountains. Guests can also enjoy splashing or snorkeling in the natural sand-bottom lagoon (the beach sand is subject to erosion, but dredges replenish it as needed). Gilles Pétré, one of French Polynesia's top dive operators, is in charge of the shop here (and at all other Pearl resorts). Long, curving piers extend out to 50 overwater bungalows that ooze Polynesian charm. The 15 premium units are worth paying extra for, as they're more private than the others and enjoy unimpeded views of Bora Bora. If privacy is more important than the sound of water lapping under your bungalow, consider one of the garden bungalows, which have their own courtyards with sun decks and splash pools. If you bring the kids, opt for a beachside bungalow with a separate bedroom. An annoying drawback here is that the resort's shuttle boats land at Chancelade on Bora Bora's northwestern corner, an expensive taxi ride if you don't catch the infrequent shuttle bus to Vaitape.

B.P. 169, 98730 Vaitape, Bora Bora (on Motu Tevairoa, 1km/½ mile off Farepiti). © 800/657-3275 or 60.52.00. Fax 60.52.22. www.pearlhotels.com. 80 units. 51,000CFP–85,000CFP (US$510–US$850) bungalow. AE, DC, MC, V. **Amenities:** 2 restaurants; 2 bars; outdoor pool; tennis court; health club; spa; watersports equipment/rentals; game room; concierge; activities desk; limited room service; massage; babysitting; laundry service. *In room:* A/C, TV, dataport, minibar, coffeemaker, hair dryer, iron, safe.

Hotel Bora Bora 🐠🐠🐠
This venerable institution opened in 1961, but lost some of its Polynesian character a few years ago when the luxury-laden Amanresorts put more of an Asian imprint on the property. The thatch-roofed central building has always been a key part of the resort's charm, and it still sits atop Point Raititi, a low headland overlooking the start of magnificent Matira Beach. Down below, one of the few real beach bars in the South Pacific rests right on those white sands. The comfortable Tahitian-style bungalows sit among the palm trees on the flat shoreline on either side of the headland. On the north, some of the 15 overwater bungalows are actually perched right on the reef's edge, where coral gives way to a deep blue lagoon (snorkeling off their porches is like flying off a canyon wall). A few others enjoy views of Mount Otemanu's tombstone across Povai Bay. Otherwise, the best units here are on the Matira side of the point; they lack the view but share a much better beach and are more likely to be cooled by the trade winds. Most of the bungalows are relatively small compared to Bora Bora's other resorts, but not the hotel's huge L-shaped units known as "premium beach bungalows." Virtual houses, they all have separate bedrooms, and

---

Tips Be Prepared for Mosquitoes and No-Nos

Keep in mind that mosquitoes and "no-no" sand flies love to feast on guests on Bora Bora's *motus*, so you'll want a good supply of insect repellent if you opt to stay at one of the offshore resorts.

---

the "garden" versions even have their own small swimming pools, surrounded by rock walls for privacy. Furnishings throughout are top of the line, with some Oriental antique pieces here and there. All units have oak-trimmed, claw-foot bathtubs in addition to showers. Avoid units next to the neighboring round-island road, which can send the noise of innumerable scooters into them at the crack of dawn. Also note that you will find no satisfaction here if you need to splash around in a swimming pool or watch TV in your room. *Note:* This hotel quotes rates in U.S. currency, not CFP.

B.P. 1, 98730 Vaitape, Bora Bora (Matira Point, 7km/4½ miles from Vaitape). ℂ 800/421-1490 or 60.44.11. Fax 60.44.22. www.amanresorts.com. 54 units. US$675–US$1,000 bungalow. AE, DC, MC, V. **Amenities:** Restaurant; 2 bars; tennis courts; health club; watersports equipment/rentals; bike rentals; game room; concierge; activities desk; car-rental desk; limited room service; massage; babysitting; laundry service. *In room:* A/C, dataport, minibar, coffeemaker, hair dryer, safe, stereo.

Inter-Continental Le Moana Resort 🏖🏖🏖 Set on the eastern side of the Matira peninsula, this exclusive resort was until recently known as the Inter-Continental Bora Bora Beachcomber Resort (and, like its sibling in Tahiti, may revert back to the Beachcomber name). This is one of the older resorts here, although much improved over the years, especially after a freak ocean wave (no, not a tsunami) did extensive damage and forced it to repair and renovate in 2005. Its bungalows, most of them overwater, are some of the most charmingly designed here. They were the first in which you could remove the tops of the glass coffee tables and actually feed the fish swimming in the turquoise lagoon below. Ashore, 11 beachside bungalows are less enchanting, but like the overwater units, they have Raiatea and Tahaa in their lagoon views. Two suites— one overwater, one ashore—have kitchenettes, making them suitable for families. Also beside the beach, a circular thatch-roofed building houses the reception area, a lounge, and the restaurant and bar, both with outdoor seating. The airy, beachside dining room offers very fine French selections, with an emphasis on seafood.

B.P. 156, 98730 Vaitape, Bora Bora (east side of Matira Point). ℂ 800/327-0200 or 60.49.00. Fax 60.49.99. http://lemoana.intercontinental.com. 64 units. 113,900CFP (US$1,139) bungalow, 101,565CFP–259,300CFP (US$1,016–US$2,593) suite. AE, DC, MC, V. **Amenities:** Restaurant; bar; outdoor saltwater pool; spa; watersports equipment/rentals; bike rentals; concierge; activities desk; car-rental desk; 24-hr. room service; massage; babysitting; laundry service. *In room:* A/C, TV, dataport, kitchen (suites only), minibar, coffeemaker, hair dryer, iron, safe.

Le Meridien Bora Bora 🏖🏖 Located on the northern tip of an atoll-like island stretching 10km (6 miles) along the southeastern side of the outer reef, this well-managed resort is both the busiest and the most unusual on Bora Bora. Most obvious is its Melanesian architecture, like its sister property on Tahiti (see Le Meridien Tahiti, p. 102). The architects also created a seawater-fed, lakelike lagoon, in which you can swim with endangered sea turtles, bred here as part of the resort's award-winning preservation program. Of the 100 identical guest units, 85 are built overwater. Only a few of these have views of Mount Otemanu, whose tombstone is seen from its narrow end out here. Standing over waist-deep water, they are notable for their huge glass floors, which make it seem as if you're walking on air (maids cover the glass with carpets at evening turndown). All units here are smaller than those at Bora Bora's other resorts, however, and you could stumble over too much furniture for the space available. Ten otherwise identical "beach" bungalows actually sit beside the man-made lagoon, but most of them have fine views of Bora Bora. Since the shallow lagoon is safe for swimming, these units are better for families with small children. The broad, brilliantly white main beach here has its own bar. The hotel's launch shuttles guests to Anau village, from where a morning bus goes to Vaitape. Otherwise, it's an expensive taxi ride to town.

B.P. 190, 98730 Vaitape, Bora Bora (on Motu Pitiaau, 1km/½ mile off Anau village). ⓒ 800/225-5843 or 60.51.51. Fax 60.51.10. www.lemeridien.com. 100 units. 72,150CFP–94,350CFP (US$722–US$944) bungalow. AE, DC, MC, V. Amenities: 3 restaurants; 2 bars; outdoor pool; spa; watersports equipment/rentals; game room; concierge; activities desk; 24-hr. room service; babysitting; laundry service. In room: A/C, TV, dataport, minibar, coffeemaker, hair dryer, iron, safe.

Sofitel Bora Bora Resort

Italian movie producer Dino De Laurentis built this resort in 1977 to house star Mia Farrow and the crew working on his box-office bomb *Hurricane.* Formerly known as the Sofitel Marara Bora Bora, it was closed for almost a year in 2005–06 for an extensive rejuvenation and the addition of a full-service spa. A beehive-shaped thatch roof covers the bar and French and Japanese restaurants, all of which open to a walk-in swimming pool sunken into a deck built over Matira Beach and the lagoon. The resort has the island's largest array of watersports activities, which it shares with the Novotel Bora Bora Beach Resort, its Accor Hotels sibling next door (the toys are available to both guests and nonguests). The overwater bungalows have some of Bora Bora's largest decks, but be sure to ask for a unit away from the nearby round-island road. Facing a curving beach of white sand, the land-based bungalows have views of Raiatea and Tahaa on the horizon. Guests here can dine at the Sofitel Motu (see below), but not partake of the activities there.

B.P. 6, 98730 Vaitape, Bora Bora (northeast of Matira Point). ⓒ 800/763-4835 or 41.04.04 in Papeete, or 60.55.00 on Bora Bora. Fax 41.05.05 or 67.74.03. www.sofitel.com. 65 units. 33,000CFP–78,00CFP (US$330–US$780) bungalow. AE, DC, MC, V. Amenities: 2 restaurants; bar; outdoor pool; tennis court; watersports equipment/rentals; bike rentals; concierge; activities desk; car-rental desk; limited room service; babysitting; laundry service. In room: A/C, TV, dataport, minibar, coffeemaker, hair dryer, iron, safe.

Sofitel Motu Bora Bora ⭓⭓

More exclusive and private than its sister property, this intimate, adults-oriented resort sits on a rocky, one-hill *motu* and is a 3-minute boat ride from the Sofitel Bora Bora Resort. Guests here can take the free on-demand shuttle boat and use all of the other hotel's facilities. Sofitel Bora Bora Resort guests, on the other hand, are allowed out here only for lunch and dinner. Unlike any other Bora Bora resort, this one has a gorgeous, picture-postcard view of Mount Otemanu's tombstone face (most but not all units enjoy the view, so ask for one that does). Often-steep stone pathways lead up and downhill to the guest bungalows; for this reason, I don't recommend the Motu to travelers with disabilities or anyone who has trouble walking. Most of the luxurious if not overly spacious units are overwater. Those that are ashore extend on stilts from the side of the hill, rendering great lagoon views. The most expensive unit here is a large villa. Several small beaches are equipped with hammocks and easy chairs, and one has a shower mounted on a tree. Children under 12 can stay at the Sofitel Bora Bora Resort, but not here.

B.P. 516, 98730 Vaitape, Bora Bora (on Piti Uuuta, .5km/¼ mile off Matira Beach). ⓒ 800/763-4835 or 41.04.04 in Papeete, or 60.56.00 on Bora Bora. Fax 41.05.05 or 60.56.66. www.sofitel.com. 31 units. 43,500CFP–120,000CFP

(US$435–US$1,200) bungalow. AE, DC, MC, V. Children under 12 not accepted. **Amenities:** Restaurant; bar; watersports equipment/rentals; activities desk; limited room service; massage; babysitting; laundry service. *In room:* A/C, TV, dataport, minibar, coffeemaker, hair dryer, iron, safe.

TOPdive Resort   Attractive to serious divers who don't need beachside sleeping quarters, this little resort sits beside the lagoon north of Vaitape and is best known for its dive shop and restaurant, both among the island's best (see "Fishing, Hiking, Horseback Riding & Watersports," earlier, and "Where to Dine," below). Closely packed into a small piece of land, the nine bungalows are built of dark wood under pandanus thatch roofs. Each has a front porch, cool marble floors, a king-size bed, and a sofa that can see double duty as a single bed. Three bungalows extend over the lagoon; these are more private and have tubs in their bathrooms as well as showers. Other than their being a bit dark inside, I like these spacious, comfortable units—too bad they aren't on a beach. ***Note:*** This hotel quotes rates in U.S. currency, not CFP.

B.P. 515, 93730 Vaitape, Bora Bora (1km north of Vaitape). ✆ **60.50.50.** Fax 60.50.51. www.topdive.com. 9 units. US$292–US$391 double. MC, V. **Amenities:** Restaurant; bar; outdoor pool; laundry service; coin-op washers and dryers; concierge-level rooms. *In room:* A/C, TV, minibar, coffeemaker, hairdryer, safe.

MODERATE

Club Med Bora Bora *(Value)*   Lush tropical gardens provide the setting for this Club Med, located beside a good beach in a little half-moon-shaped bay north of Matira Point. The focus of attention is a large thatch-roofed beachside pavilion, which houses a reception area, bar, buffet-oriented dining room, and nightclub. Guests pay extra for scuba diving, but all meals (with wine) and a wide range of activities are included in the rates. Considering the prices elsewhere on Bora Bora, this makes Club Med a good value. The accommodations are in a mix of standalone and duplex bungalows and two-story, motel-style buildings. The beachfront bungalows are the preferred choice here, especially for honeymooners and others seeking a degree of privacy. The rooms are comfortably if not extravagantly furnished. If you don't have a roommate, one of the same sex may be assigned.

B.P. 34, 98730 Vaitape, Bora Bora (northeast of Matira Point). ✆ **800/258-2633,** 60.46.04, or 42.96.99 in Papeete. Fax 42.16.83. www.clubmed.com. 150 units. 17,700CFP (US$177) per person double, 21,240CFP–26,000CFP (US$212–US$260) per person bungalow. Rates include all meals (with wine) and most activities. AE, DC, MC, V. **Amenities:** Restaurant; bar; tennis courts; bike rentals; activities desk; car-rental desk; salon; massage; coin-op washers and dryers. *In room:* A/C, TV, fridge, coffeemaker, hair dryer, safe.

Hotel Maitai Polynesia *(Value)*   Like the nearby Novotel, this resort has hotel rooms, but here they climb a hill, giving upper-floor units spectacular lagoon views. Unlike the Novotel, it also has beachside and overwater bungalows, which are among the more reasonably priced in French Polynesia. The bungalows are smaller than those at the more expensive resorts, but they are packed with Polynesian decor, and those overwater have glass floor panels for fish-viewing. The round-island road runs through the property, separating the beach and bungalows from the thatch-roofed main building and hotel rooms. Of its two restaurants, one sits beachside.

B.P. 505, 98730 Vaitape, Bora Bora (northeast of Matira Point). ✆ **60.30.00.** Fax 67.66.03. www.hotelmaitai.com. 74 units. 24,200CFP–35,500CFP (US$242–US$355) double; 39,000CFP–53,300CFP (US$390–US$533) bungalow. Higher rates June–Oct. AE, DC, MC, V. **Amenities:** 2 restaurants; 2 bars; watersports equipment/rentals; bike rentals; activities desk; babysitting; laundry service. *In room:* A/C (hotel rooms only), TV, dataport, minibar, coffeemaker, hair dryer, safe.

Hotel Matira   This is not so much a hotel as a collection of bungalows on and near the beach at the northern end of the Matira peninsula. Imported from Indonesia, the teak units have thatch roofs, porches on one corner, shower-only bathrooms, and pairs of double beds. You'll get a ceiling fan, fridge, and coffeemaker, but forget amenities like TVs, phones, and hair dryers. What you get here is an essentially unscreened cottage, so keep your insect repellent handy. The choicest and most expensive models rest beside Matira Beach, while the others are back in the garden. Ask for a discount if you book directly.

B.P. 31, 98730 Vaitape, Bora Bora (on Matira Beach, south of Hotel Bora Bora). © **67.70.51.** Fax 67.77.02. www.hotel-matira.com. 14 units. 21,000CFP–35,500CFP (US$210–US$355) bungalow. MC, V. **Amenities:** Bike rentals. *In room:* Fridge, coffeemaker, no phone.

Mai Moana Island

More private retreat than hotel, Mai Moana occupies a tiny flat islet on the northwestern side of the reef. It's the home of Stan Wisniewski, a Polish-born, Paris-based documentary and advertising filmmaker, poet, journalist, sailor, and avid ham-radio operator who speaks Polish, French, and English. Stan and wife Malgorzata have three thatch-roof bungalows built on stilts near their white-sand beach. You won't be without luxuries here, since each unit has a TV, phone, minibar, double bed, ceiling fan, bathroom with solar-heated shower, and porch with lagoon view. Nearby are a freshwater swimming pool, library, bar, and sea-view dining room, where Malgorzata serves fresh French- and Tahitian-style seafood. Stan turns the island's generator off at 10pm, but batteries charge the bungalow lights during the night. You can rent the entire island, thus ensuring complete privacy, at a surprisingly affordable price. Even if you don't rent the entire *motu*, Stan permits only six guests here at any one time, and none of them can be under 12 years old.

B.P. 164, 98730 Vaitape, Bora Bora (on Motu Mute Iti). © and fax **67.62.45.** www.mai-moana-island.com. 3 units. 24,000CFP (US$240) double, 45,000CFP (US$450) entire island. MC, V. Children under 12 not accepted. **Amenities:** Restaurant; bar; outdoor pool; boat rental; free use of kayaks; laundry service. *In room:* TV, minibar, hairdryer.

Novotel Bora Bora Beach Resort *Value*

Opened in 2003, this modest but attractive property is one of the better values on the island, especially if you book it as part of a package. It sports a U-shaped, tropical-style public building and an infinity swimming pool beside a palm-draped section of Matira Beach, where the Novotel shares a wide array of watersports with the Sofitel Bora Bora Resort next door. On the other side of the round-island road, the motel-style accommodations occupy two-story buildings dressed up in Tahitian thatch and bamboo; these surround a lush courtyard with lily pond. The medium-size rooms are nicely trimmed with native woods and are comfortably furnished with a queen bed, a built-in settee that can double as a single bed, a desk, a shower-only bathroom, and sliding doors that open to a patio or balcony. You can dine at the Sofitel Motu, but you can't use the other facilities there.

B.P. 943, 98730 Vaitape, Bora Bora (heart of Matira hotel district). © **800/221-4542** or 60.59.50. Fax 60.59.51. www.novotel.com. 80 units. 21,600CFP–28,800CFP (US$216–US$288) double. AE, MC, V. **Amenities:** Restaurant; bar; outdoor pool; watersports equipment/rentals; activities desk; car-rental desk; massage; laundry service. *In room:* A/C, TV, dataport, fridge, coffeemaker, hair dryer, safe.

INEXPENSIVE

Chez Nono

Sitting on the western side of the Point Matira peninsula, this pension is the domain of Noël (Nono) Levard—of *the* Bora Bora Levards, who operate lagoon excursions, safari expeditions, and the Farm black-pearl operation. Since guests here can step from their accommodations right out onto the powdery sands of Matira Beach, this is the most popular beachside pension with French residents of Tahiti (book early). The least expensive units are six simple bedrooms in Nono's house; these all share toilets, hot-water showers, and a kitchen. Two beachside bungalows can accommodate two persons each, while two family-size bungalows are notable for their thatch roofs. All four bungalows have their own bathrooms with hot-water showers, and every unit has an electric fan (much appreciated in the sometimes stuffy house rooms).

B.P. 282, 93730 Vaitape, Bora Bora (Matira Point). ℂ **67.71.38.** Fax 67.74.27. nono.levard@mail.pf. 10 units (6 with shared bathroom). 6,100CFP (US$61) double, 15,000CFP (US$150) bungalow. MC, V. **Amenities:** Communal kitchen; laundry service. *In room:* No phone.

Pension Robert et Tina   This family-run pension consists of three two-story houses right on the southern extremity of Matira Point. One house has six rooms, while the others have three each. You'll share each house's kitchen, toilets, and cold-water showers. If you have a family or group, and don't mind shivering in the shower, Robert and Tina will reduce the rates if you rent an entire house for a week or more. The beach is minimal here, but you can walk across the shallow lagoon to excellent snorkeling near the outer reef. The trade winds can make the point quite breezy and cool during the winter months from June through August.

93730 Vaitape, Bora Bora (Matira Point). ℂ **67.63.55** or 79.22.73. Fax 67.72.92. 15 units (shared bathrooms). 7,700CFP–9,000CFP (US$77–US$90) double. MC, V. **Amenities:** Communal kitchen; laundry service. *In room:* No phone.

Rohutu Fare Lodge ⊛ *Finds*   Almost hidden by botanical gardens on the mountainside overlooking Povai Bay, this little lodge is the creation of Nir Shalev, an Israeli expatriate whom I met shortly after he first arrived on Bora Bora wearing a backpack in 1989. With teak floors and natural thatch roofs, his cleverly designed bungalows are for lovers, definitely not Puritans. In addition to suggestive paintings, statues, and other paraphernalia in the sleeping quarters, faucets in the outdoor bathrooms pour water from certain unmentionable parts of nude statues. (After a night here, you may not be up to the 15-minute bike ride to Matira Beach!) Nir's two lagoon-view bungalows are more charming and have better vistas than his mountain-view unit. They all have ceiling fans, kitchens, decks with lounge furniture, and four-poster beds with mosquito nets. You will not have to leave here to enjoy a view of Mount Otemanu's tombstone face.

B.P. 400, 98730 Vaitape, Bora Bora (hillside in Povai Bay). ℂ **70.77.99.** www.boraboralodge.com. 3 units. 14,900CFP (US$149) bungalow. MC, V. **Amenities:** Kayak rentals; free use of bicycles. *In room:* Kitchen, coffeemaker, safe.

Village Temanuata   On a small part of Matira Beach in the hotel district, this few-frills establishment has 11 thatch-roof bungalows ranging from one-room to family-size units with kitchens and sleeping lofts (over their front porches). All have ceiling fans and private bathrooms with hot water but few other amenities. Choice are the two units directly facing the beach. Four better-equipped models (with TVs and complimentary use of bicycles) are on the other side of the point, between the Hotel Maria and Hotel Bora Bora. The staff will deliver continental breakfast to your bungalow upon prior arrangement. Matira's restaurants and shops are an easy walk away.

B.P. 544, 98730 Vaitape, Bora Bora (heart of Matira hotel district). ℂ **67.75.61.** Fax 67.78.17. www.temanuata.com. 15 units. 13,700CFP–15,900CFP (US$137–US$159) bungalow. MC, V. **Amenities:** Bike rentals. *In room:* TV (4 units), kitchen (6 units), no phone.

8 Where to Dine

EXPENSIVE

A French chef who came here to work at the Hotel Bora Bora took over the restaurant at the **Yacht Club Bora Bora** (ℂ **67.70.69**), on the lagoon about 1.5km (1 mile)

Fun Fact It's a Dog's Life

Despite several neutering campaigns, dogs seem to be everywhere on Bora Bora. You see them all along the roads and even wandering in and out of some restaurants. Their ancestors arrived in the islands with the first Polynesian settlers more than a millennium ago. Along with pigs and fish, they were a prime source of Polynesian protein back then. No longer on anyone's menu, they roam as they see fit.

---

north of Vaitape, after my recent visit. I have since received highly favorable reports about his cooking. Ask your fellow guests if they have had dinner at the Yacht Club.

Bloody Mary's Restaurant & Bar ✿✿✿ SEAFOOD/STEAKS Having a few drinks and a slab of barbecued fish at this charming structure is as much a part of the Bora Bora experience as is taking a lagoon excursion. Ceiling fans, colored spotlights, and stalks of dried bamboo dangle from a large thatch roof over a floor of fine white sand (stash your sandals in a footlocker and dine in your bare feet). The butcher-block tables are made of coconut-palm lumber, while the seats are sections of palm trunks cut into stools. Bloody Mary's is essentially an American-style barbecued fish-and-steak joint—which can be a welcome relief after a diet of lard-laden French sauces. You'll be shown the seafood and beef laid out on a bed of ice. (If it's offered, choose the mouthwatering teriyaki-style wahoo.) The chef will charbroil your selection to order and serve it with a salad, vegetables, and your choice of sauce on the side. The lunch menu consists of burgers, fish-and-chips, and salads, which are not served at dinner.

Open all day, the cozy bar is cut from a beautifully polished litchi tree and is one of my favorite watering holes. You will have an evening of fun, as have the many famous faces posted on a board out by the road. Bloody Mary's American owner, Dexter Hewitt, shares the profits with the staff and sends them all to Las Vegas every December (when the restaurant is closed); given this incentive, the service here is among the best in French Polynesia.

Povai Bay, 1km (½ mile) north of Hotel Bora Bora. © 67.72.86. Reservations strongly recommended. Lunch 950CFP–1,400CFP (US$9.50–US$14); dinner main courses 2,650CFP–3,200CFP (US$27–US$32). AE, MC, V. Mon–Wed and cruise-ship days 11am–3pm, Mon–Sat 6–9pm. Bar Mon–Sat 9:30am–11pm. Closed Dec.

Kaina Hut ✿✿ FRENCH FUSION Restaurateur Gilles Ricaud brings a fascinating combination of French cooking and fresh Polynesian ingredients to this romantic restaurant with a thatch roof and sand floor. This fusion is apparent in the signature dish, gnocchi made from breadfruit instead of potato and served with a light tomato sauce. Otherwise, seafood with Asian influences predominates here. Lunch is served at an open-air snack bar by the lagoon across the main road.

Povai Bay, north of Hotel Bora Bora. © 71.20.73. Reservations recommended. Main courses 2,800CFP–5,500CFP (US$28–US$55). MC, V. Wed–Mon 11am–5pm and 6–10pm.

La Villa Mahana ✿✿✿ INTERNATIONAL You will need one night for fun at Bloody Mary's, another for a romantic dinner at this little restaurant, Bora Bora's finest. Owner Damien Rinaldi Devio, an accomplished young Corsican-born chef, will get you started with a complimentary glass of champagne, perhaps laced with peach liqueur. I started with tuna *tartare exotique*, a luscious version of *poisson cru* with a sharp wasabi-accented sauce. My friends went on to mahimahi perfectly cooked with a subtle version of coconut-curry sauce, while I opted for filet mignon with vanilla-cream gnocchi. Both were outstanding. The four- or five-course fixed-price menus will save you money. The walls of this Mediterranean-style villa are adorned with the works of noted French Polynesian artist Garrick Yrondi, but Damien has only six tables, so consider calling or e-mailing for a reservation well before you get here.

Povai Bay, behind Boutique Gauguin, 1.5km (1 mile) north of Hotel Bora Bora. ⊄ **67.50.63**. damien@villamahana.com. Reservations required. Main courses 3,200CFP–3,600CFP (US$32–US$36); fixed-price dinners 8,500CFP–10,500CFP (US$85–US$105). AE, MC, V. Wed–Mon 6–8pm. Closed Feb.

TOPdive Restaurant ☆☆ NEW FRENCH A soaring thatch roof covers this excellent lagoonside restaurant at TOPdive Resort, north of Vaitape. The kitchen produces wonderful nouvelle cuisine renditions of fresh seafood. For example, you might start with a lobster salad with citrus vinaigrette. Shrimps and scallops in coconut curry sauce is my favorite main. The fixed-price *menu exotique* offers a choice of starters, a main course, and a dessert. You'll need both an appetizer and a main course here because the portions are as small as they are extraordinarily well presented.

At TOPdive Resort, 1km (½ mile) north of Vaitape. ⊄ **60.50.50**. Reservations recommended. Main courses 3,250CFP–6,850CFP (US$33–US$69); tourist menu 6,000CFP (US$60). AE, MC, V. Tues–Sun noon–2pm and 7–9pm. Bar daily 11:30am–9pm.

MODERATE

La Bounty ☆ *Value* FRENCH/ITALIAN This casual restaurant under a thatch roof provides some of the island's best pizza and other reasonably priced Italian (and French) fare. A pie makes an ample meal for one person or can be shared as an appetizer. The spaghetti and tagliatelle are tasty, too, with either smoked salmon, carbonara, Alfredo, Neapolitan, blue cheese, or seafood sauce. Steaks and fish are served under French sauces such as mustard or creamy vanilla. Pizzas are dished up quickly here, but everything else is prepared to order and takes longer. Whatever you choose, it will be excellent quality for the price.

Matira, between Hotel Maitai Polynesia and Bora Bora Beach Resort. ⊄ **67.70.43**. Reservations recommended. Pizza and pasta 1,500CFP–1,650CFP (US$15–US$17); main courses 1,500CFP–2,800CFP (US$15–US$28). MC, V. Tues–Sun 11:30am–2pm and 6:30–9pm.

Matira Bar and Restaurant CANTONESE/FRENCH Literally hanging over the beach, this restaurant is an excellent place to have a lagoon-side breakfast, lunch, a sunset drink, or a good Chinese meal without completely breaking the bank. The menu offers a selection of beef, pork, chicken, duck, and seafood dishes done in the Cantonese fashion, with Hakka overtones (Tahiti's first Chinese immigrants came from the Hakka region of the mainland).

Matira, between Hotel Bora Bora and Hotel Matira. ⊄ **67.70.51**. Breakfast 800CFP–2,100CFP (US$8–US$21); main courses 1,300CFP–2,100CFP (US$13–US$21). MC, V. Daily 7–10am, 11am–2pm, and 6–9pm.

Pirate's Bar & Restaurant FRENCH/PUB FARE Overlooking the lagoon from the Helen's Bay shopping center, north of the small boat harbor, this publike restaurant

---

Tips Call for a Ride

The top restaurants provide free transportation for their dinner guests; always ask when making your reservations.

provides a picturesque setting for a cold one while you're walking around Vaitape. In fact, you'll have a choice of several imported beers, on tap or in the bottle. Lunch features burgers and sandwiches, while French fare leads the nighttime bill of fare. Manta rays expecting a handout from diners on the dock show up in the lagoon here around 7:30pm.

Vaitape, north of small boat harbor, in Centre Helen's Bay. © 60.52.52. Reservations recommended at dinner. Main courses 1,700CFP–2,400CFP (US$17–US$24). Mon–Sat 11am–2:30pm and 6–11pm.

Restaurant Patoti TRADITIONAL FRENCH   On the mountain side of the road, this open-air restaurant draws a mainly local clientele for its traditional French treatment of seafood and meat, sometimes including *exotique* choices such as kangaroo. An ample portion of hearty fish soup will take the chill off the stiff July and August trade winds.

Matira, north of Sofitel Bora Bora Resort. © 67.71.99. Reservations recommended. Main courses 1,800CFP–2,900CFP (US$18–US$29). MC, V. Mon–Sat 11am–2pm and 5–9pm, Sun 5–9pm.

INEXPENSIVE

In addition to Roulotte Matira (see below), other meal wagons roll out near the Vaitape small-boat harbor, some during the day when cruise ships are in port. See "Don't Miss *Les Roulottes*" (p. 112) for details on these inexpensive food wagons. Also in Vaitape, two reasonably priced Chinese restaurants—**Le Panda d'Or** (© 67.72.70) and **Le Cocotier** (© 67.74.18)—can be found north of the small boat harbor.

Bora Bora Burger SNACK BAR   You can get salads, *casse-croûte* sandwiches, hot dogs, burgers, and other daytime snacks at this open-air, order-at-the-counter joint next to the post office in Vaitape. The picnic tables and chairs on the veranda make a good place for refreshment while watching the cruise-ship passengers explore the town.

Vaitape, next to post office. No phone. Reservations not accepted. Most items 250CFP–1,300CFP (US$2.50–US$13). No credit cards. Mon–Sat 8am–5:30pm.

Chez Ben's PIZZA/SNACK BAR   Honeymooners from the nearby Hotel Bora Bora frequently wander to this lean-to across the road from a shady portion of Matira Beach, where Bora Bora–born Ben Teraitepo and his Oklahoman wife, Robin, have been offering American-style cooked breakfasts, lunches, and afternoon pick-me-ups since 1988. The fresh tuna-salad sandwiches, pizzas and pastas, unusually spicy *poisson cru*, tacos, and fajitas are homemade and substantial, although Ben and Robin's company is the main reason to hang out here. They will shoo the dogs and cats away if they're bothering you.

Matira, between Hotel Bora Bora and Matira Point. © 67.74.54. Reservations not accepted. Breakfast 600CFP–1,700CFP (US$6–US$17); sandwiches and salads 250CFP–1,900CFP (US$2.50–US$19); pizzas and meals 850CFP–1,350CFP (US$8.50–US$14). No credit cards. Daily 8am–5pm.

L'Appetisserie ✮ *Value* FRENCH/PASTRIES   I often have breakfast here, for this patisserie bakes excellent croissants, tarts, and quiches to go with the strong French coffee. Also on the menu: sandwiches, pizzas by the slice, and a *plat du jour* at lunch. Order at the counter, at a table inside, or on the shopping-center sidewalk. You can use the computer terminal here to check your e-mail (see "Fast Facts: Bora Bora," earlier in this chapter).

North of the Vaitape small-boat harbor, in Centre Commercial Le Pahia. © 67.78.88. Reservations not accepted. Breakfast 700CFP–2,400CFP (US$7–US$24); pastries and sandwiches 150CFP–1,050CFP (US$1.50–US$11); meals 1,650CFP (US$17). No credit cards. Mon–Sat 6am–6pm.

Roulotte Matira *☆* *(Value* SNACK BAR   This is one of the best *roulottes* in French Polynesia, especially when owner Samuel Ruver cooks tandoori chicken and curries from recipes handed down by his East Indian father. Otherwise, he works at the gas grill to produce steaks and fish, both served with french fries. Anything with legumes will be a so-so Chinese-style stir-fry. You can get a continental breakfast here, too. Grab a white plastic table; there's waiter service.

Matira, at the curve. No phone. Reservations not accepted. Hamburgers 900CFP (US$9); main courses 1,000CFP–1,500CFP (US$10–US$15). No credit cards. Daily 6am–2pm and 6–10pm.

Snack Matira SNACK BAR   Right on Matira Beach and within hailing distance of Chez Ben's, this open-air snack bar is a favorite lunch and afternoon retreat of Bora Bora's French-speaking expatriates. It offers a *roulotte*-style menu of pizzas, salads, omelets, grilled steaks and fish, juicy burgers, and *casse-croûte* sandwiches, plus ice cream and milk shakes. The company is better at Chez Ben's, but not the lagoon view.

Matira, between Hotel Bora Bora and Matira Point. ℭ 67.77.32. Reservations not accepted. Most items 300CFP–1,700CFP (US$3–US$17). No credit cards. Tues–Sun 10am–4pm.

9 Island Nights on Bora Bora

As on Moorea, things are really quiet on Bora Bora after dark (this is, after all, one of the world's most romantic honeymoon hideaways, not a place to practice your dance steps). You might want to listen to a Tahitian band playing at sunset or watch the furious hips in a Tahitian dance show, which all the resorts offer at least once a week. The schedules change, so call ahead.

Even if you're not staying at the **Club Med Bora Bora** (ℭ **60.46.04**), you can have dinner there and watch the nightclub show staged by its staff. The full meal, wine, and show together cost about 6,100CFP (US$61). Call for reservations.

Le Récife Discothèque, about 1km (½ mile) north of Vaitape (ℭ **67.73.87**), is the island's lone nightclub, and it opens only on Fridays and Saturdays at 11pm (that's right, 11pm) and closes at 3am (or later) the following morning. The clientele are mostly Tahitians between 18 and 24 years old, and fights have been known to break out at that late hour. The cover is about 1,000CFP ($10), although women get in free on Friday. Beer costs at least 500CFP ($5).

Maupiti

A favorite pastime throughout the Pacific islands is comparing how one place is like someplace else used to be. For example, locals like to say that Tahiti is like Hawaii used to be, and that Huahine is like Moorea used to be. In the case of Maupiti, French Polynesia's last westward outpost, it is like Bora Bora used to be.

Just 40km (25 miles) west of Bora Bora, this little jewel of an island even resembles its larger neighbor, in that it consists of an outer barrier reef topped by a horseshoe of sand-edged *motus* enclosing a clear lagoon around a high central island. Here, there is more dry land out on the fringing motu than on the main island, which has an area of just 13.5 sq. km (5.2 sq. miles). The road around most of the main island is just 9.6km (5.8 miles) long.

Unlike Bora Bora, Maupiti has not a hint of modern tourism; in fact, its residents have flatly rejected a proposed resort. Most of the few visitors who come here are French residents of Tahiti, who like to spend their weekends relaxing at one of several small pensions, Maupiti's only choice of accommodations. Indeed, Maupiti is definitely a throwback to old Polynesia, when, among other things, very few locals spoke English.

Maupiti reminds me of Bora Bora back when I camped on a nearly deserted

Pointe Matira, now a key part of Bora Bora's booming tourism infrastructure, almost 30 years ago. I am especially reminded of those bygone days at **Plage Tereia** (Tereia Beach), a gorgeous strip of white and pink sand that wraps around a peninsula on the western side of Maupiti. I have no doubt that hotel developers covet this lovely location.

Just as Mount Otemanu's tombstone face is Bora Bora's trademark, Maupiti's distinguishing landmark is **Mount Hotu Parata,** a black-basaltic cliff that dramatically rises 165m (540 ft.) above **Vaiea,** the island's main village. The cliff is pockmarked with caves, which attract a multitude of nesting seabirds.

Despite its small size, Maupiti was an important island in pre-European days. Archaeologists have uncovered both *marae* and petroglyphs on the main island. They have also uncovered human remains and other items out on **Motu Paeao,** a small islet separating two shallow passes on Maupiti's north side. Stone axes, whale teeth, and fish hooks have been dated to about A.D. 850, making it one of the oldest settlements in the Society Islands.

Whether you stay on Maupiti or see it as a day trip from Bora Bora, you are in for an authentic old Polynesian treat.

1 Getting Around Maupiti

Air Tahiti flies to Maupiti from Raiatea about three times a week, with its flights usually geared toward Friday-to-Sunday weekend travelers. The airstrip is on **Motu Tuanai,** the long islet off the northeastern side of the central island. The pensions send

Maupiti

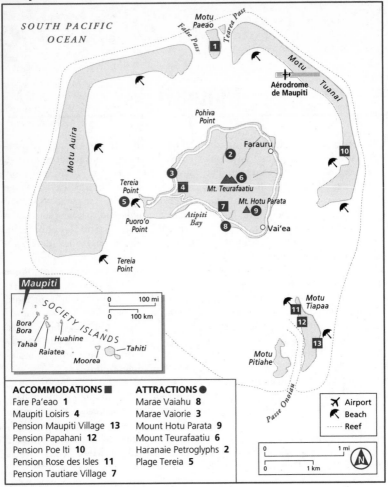

SOUTH PACIFIC OCEAN

Motu Paeao

Tearea Pass

False Pass

1

Motu Tuanai

Aérodrome de Maupiti

Motu Auira

Pohiva Point

Farauru

2

10

3

6

Tereia Point

4

Mt. Teurafaatiu

5

7

Mt. Hotu Parata

9

Puoro'o Point

Atipiti Bay

8

Vai'ea

Tereia Point

Maupiti

0 — 100 mi
0 — 100 km

SOCIETY ISLANDS

Bora Bora

Tahaa

Huahine

Raiatea

Moorea

Tahiti

Motu Tiapaa

11

12

13

Motu Pitiahe

Passe Onoiau

ACCOMMODATIONS ■

Fare Pa'eao **1**
Maupiti Loisirs **4**
Pension Maupiti Village **13**
Pension Papahani **12**
Pension Poe Iti **10**
Pension Rose des Isles **11**
Pension Tautiare Village **7**

ATTRACTIONS ●

Marae Vaiahu **8**
Marae Vaiorie **3**
Mount Hotu Parata **9**
Mount Teurafaatiu **6**
Haranaie Petroglyphs **2**
Plage Tereia **5**

✈ Airport
🏖 Beach
---- Reef

0 — 1 mi
0 — 1 km

N

boats to pick up guests who have reservations (some meet the planes in search of travelers without advance bookings), or you can take the Air Tahiti launch to Vaiea.

The fast ***Maupiti Express*** ferry arrives from Bora Bora three times a week, landing at the island's only wharf, in Vaiea on the southeastern point of the main island. It and all other vessels must negotiate Onoiau Pass, the only navigable entry into the lagoon. The pass is narrow and subject to strong currents and breaking surf. It can be treacherous in rough weather, during which the *Maupiti Express* and other boats cannot get into or out of the lagoon. Keep this in mind when making your plans. See "Getting Around Tahiti & French Polynesia," in chapter 2, for more information.

There is no local transportation system on Maupiti. Since the island is so small, most visitors rent bicycles. Mostly crushed coral, the round-island road is flat and follows the coastline except when it climbs over a steep ridge between Plage Tereia and the south coast. Local residents will be waiting at the wharf when the *Maupiti Express*

Tips Seeing Maupiti as a Day Trip from Bora Bora

You can make a day trip to Maupiti from Bora Bora on the fast ferry *Maupiti Express* (© 67.66.69; maupitiexpress@mail.pf), which departs Bora Bora Tuesday, Thursday, and Saturday at 8:30am, arriving at Maupiti about 10:15am. It leaves Maupiti at 4pm and returns to Bora Bora about 5:30pm. Fares are 2,500CFP (US$25) one-way, 3,500CFP (US$35) round-trip. One caveat: If high waves come up, the *Maupiti Express* may be unable to get out of Maupiti's one pass to return to Bora Bora. In that case, you could be stuck on Maupiti until the sea calms, or until the next Air Tahiti flight departs for Raiatea.

docks to rent bikes for 1,000CFP (US$10) a day. At other times, you can contact the **Total** service station at the wharf (© **67.83.46**), **Puanere Locations** (© **67.81.68;** fax 67.80.85), or **Maupiti Loisirs** (© **67.80.95**). The latter is operated by Ui Terihaunui and Simone Chan of the Maupiti Loisirs pension (p. 199).

FAST FACTS: Maupiti

The following facts apply specifically to Maupiti. For more information, see "Fast Facts: Tahiti & French Polynesia," in chapter 2.

Currency Exchange Maupiti does not have a bank, which explains why the pensions here do not accept credit cards. Bring enough cash or traveler's checks to cover your anticipated expenses.

Emergencies/Police The **emergency police** telephone number is © **17.** Maupiti does not have its own gendarmerie (the nearest is on Bora Bora), so ask your pension staff for assistance in case of emergency.

Healthcare The **government infirmary** (© **67.80.18**) is in the *mairie* (town hall) complex in Vaiea village.

Internet Access The Internet is minimally present on Maupiti. There is no cybercafe on the island, so ask if your pension has, or can arrange, access if you can't live without e-mail or surfing the Web while here.

Post Office The post office is in the *mairie* (town hall) complex in Vaiea village. Hours are Monday through Thursday from 7:30am to 3pm, Friday from 7am to 2pm.

Visitor Information There is no visitor information office on Maupiti, so be sure to pick up an island map before you get here.

Water Don't drink the tap water on Maupiti. Bottled water is available at the grocery stores.

2 Exploring Maupiti

TOURING THE ISLAND

The narrow coastal plain on the east coast is dominated by **Vaiea, Petei,** and **Fararuu,** three villages resting at the base of the Mount Hotu Parata cliff. They run together, so

---

Fun Fact **A Whaler's Tale**

In 1842, a new American whaling ship named the *Charles W. Morgan* put into Maupiti to refresh its crew. One of them was so refreshed by the daughter of a local chief that he stayed behind and founded a large family. The *Charles W. Morgan* kept on working until 1921. The last 19th-century whaling ship still afloat, it's now berthed at Mystic Seaport in Mystic, Conn. (www.mysticseaport.org).

---

you won't know when you've left one and entered another. The great majority of the island's 1,200 or so inhabitants live in these villages, which have the island's only grocery stores and other facilities. You will see very few older homes here, since a hurricane devastated Maupiti in 1997, destroying most of its houses in the process.

The north coast is notable for the **Haranaie Valley,** site of several **petroglyphs,** including one of a turtle. The petroglyphs are not easy to find, so I recommend a guided tour (see below). From the road, you'll have fine views of the three *motu* enclosing the north side of the lagoon. The road rounds the base of Mount Hotu, at the northwestern corner, and then follows the west coast, where you'll pass several ancient *marae,* including **Marae Vaiorie.** This ancient stone structure was built in two parts with a freshwater stream in between.

Go straight when you come to the road junction and follow the sign to the magnificent white and pink sands of **Plage Tereia** ***. Situated in a coconut grove and facing a shallow lagoon, this is one of French Polynesia's best beaches. There are no changing rooms, water fountains, or other facilities to interrupt its pristine character. Only a few trash cans and the occasional drink can remind you that people even come here. At low tide, you can wade across the waist-deep "Baby Sharks Crossing" to **Motu Auira.** (Yes, you may see small sharks in the shallow lagoon.) Motu Auira, the largest of Maupiti's islets, has melon plantations and a wind-generating facility.

From the beach, you will have to backtrack to the road junction, where the *traversière* heads up the ridge between the west and south coasts. Push your bike up the hill for a fine view of the west coast and the lagoon from the top.

The descent will take you down to the populated south coast. On the shore about two-thirds of the way back to Vaiea, you'll come to **Marae Vaiahu,** the most important temple on the island. Maupiti's royalty lived in this area during the olden days, and chiefs from Bora Bora and the other islands often joined them at gatherings at Marae Vaiahu. It's notable for its stone fish box, apparently used in ceremonies to bless the fishing fleet.

ORGANIZED TOURS

In addition to the petroglyphs, some other attractions are not easy to find on your own, so I highly recommend taking a half-day guided tour of the island. Every pension can arrange a tour, or you can do it in advance through **Maupiti Loisirs** (⟨ **67. 80.95**), run by Ui Terihaunui and the English-speaking Simone Chan, who also own Maupiti Loisirs pension (p. 199). Ui and Simone offer two half-day tours. Their regular island tour includes a drive around the central island and a stop for a swim at Plage Tereia (and a wade across to Motu Auira if it's low tide). Their archaeological tour includes stops at the *marae* and a walk to the petroglyphs. The tours cost 1,000CFP (US$10) and 2,000CFP (US$20) per person, respectively. You can also go with Auguste Taurua's **Tefarerii Excursions** (© **67.81.83;** Nicole.richardo@mail.pf). If you cannot understand French, ask for a guide who speaks your language.

3 Hiking, Lagoon Excursions & Snorkeling

HIKING

If you are willing to hire a guide, which you will need, Maupiti has two mountain trails that will test your endurance but reward you with fantastic views. One track leads from Vaiea village to the top of **Mount Hotu Parata,** a hike of about 1 hour. The track is very steep in places, and since the volcanic rock at the top is unstable, you cannot go to the cliff's edge. Another very steep climb ascends **Mount Teurafaatiu** (also known as Mount Nuupure), Maupiti's tallest peak at 380m (1,247 ft.). In places, this trail is more like mountain climbing than hiking.

Ask your pension to arrange a guide or contact Auguste Taurua of **Tefarerii Excursions** (© **67.81.83;** Nicole.richardo@mail.pf). Auguste's prices depend on which track you take and how many people are going.

LAGOON EXCURSIONS

Although Maupiti's lagoon is not as large or deep as Bora Bora's, getting out on it is an essential ingredient of a visit here. (Getting under it is another matter, since at press time, no scuba-diving operator has set up shop on Maupiti.) The excursions pretty much follow the usual script: a boat ride, snorkeling and swimming, a stop to see the ancient ruins on Motu Paeao, and a picnic on a *motu.* Every pension will arrange an all-day lagoon excursion. Or you can contact either of the two leading operators: **Maupiti Loisirs** (© **67.80.95**), based at Maupiti Loisirs pension on the central island (p. 199), or **Maupiti Poe Iti Tours** (© **67.83.14**), at Pension Poe Iti out on Motu Tuanai (p. 198). Both charge about 2,500CFP (US$25) per person without lunch, 3,500CFP (US$35) if a picnic is included.

SNORKELING

There is very good snorkeling in the lagoon around Motu Paeao, between the two shallow entries into the lagoon: **Tearea (Hiro's) Pass** and **False Pass.** The latter is called False Pass because from the sea, it looks likes a navigable pass, while in reality it is only a few feet deep. You'll find more good snorkeling in the south on the lagoonside Motu Tipaa, but be careful of the strong currents into and out of nearby Onoiau Pass.

4 Where to Stay

As mentioned in the introduction to this chapter, Maupiti's residents have rejected proposals to build luxury resorts here. The result: Your choice will be one of the island's small, family-run establishments. A few are on the main island, but the most appealing are out on the skinny islets surrounding the lagoon.

ON THE *MOTU*

Fare Pa'eao   Emile and Jeanine Tavaerii's pension sits by itself on Motu Paeao, the flat islet between the two shallow passes at the northern end of the lagoon. They have six of the government-backed bungalows you see so often in French Polynesia; each has a shingle roof, a front porch, one room with a ceiling fan for sleeping and living, and a bathroom (with cold-water shower) attached to the rear. There is very good snorkeling in this part of the lagoon, and Emile and Jeanine provide free kayaks with which to explore (be careful of the currents in and out of the passes through the reef). Rates here include breakfast and dinner; Janine will also provide lunch at extra cost.

B.P. 33, 98732 Vaiea, Maupiti (on Motu Paeao). ℭ **67.81.01** or 67.81.92. fare.pae.ao@mail.pf. 6 units. 17,500CFP (US$175) double. Rates include breakfast and dinner. No credit cards. **Amenities:** Restaurant; bar; free use of kayaks. *In room:* No phone.

Pension Maupiti Village On the ocean side of Motu Tiapaa, which flanks the channel leading from the main pass into the lagoon, this no-frills pension is one of Maupiti's most basic and least expensive. The buildings consist simply of plywood sides and tin roofs—pretty much what you got before the advent of the more modern government-issued bungalows. Two units are individual bungalows with their own cold-water bathroom. Two rooms in a house and a dormitory all share outside toilets and cold-water showers. A white-sand beach fronts the property, but the lagoon between here and the fringing reef is too shallow for serious swimming. Owner Audine Colomes prepares fresh seafood meals, which guests eat at a long table under a thatch roof.

98732 Vaiea, Maupiti (on Motu Tiapaa). ℭ **60.15.35.** Fax 60.15.36. 5 units (3 with shared bathroom), 6 dorm beds (shared bathrooms). 9,000CFP (US$90) double bungalow; 6,500CFP (US$65) double; 5,500CFP (US$55) dormitory. Rates include all meals. No credit cards. **Amenities:** Restaurant; bar; free use of kayaks. *In room:* No phone.

Pension Papahani Friendly Tahitians Denis and Vilna Tuheiava operate this pension beside a lovely white-sand beach on the lagoon side of Motu Tiapaa. Look to the right as you face the lagoon and you will have a fine view of Mount Hotu Paraoa's cliff above Vaiea village. There are three newer, reasonably spacious "family" bungalows; one of these has a front porch that directly faces the beach. Three older bungalows in the garden are smaller and less comfortable. Except for mosquito nets over their double beds, all are rather sparsely furnished, especially the older units. Each has a private bathroom with cold-water showers. Vilna serves home-cooked French and Tahitian fare in an open-air building by the beach. The lagoon next to the pension is shallow, but you can wade out to deeper snorkeling water. Denis and Vilna speak about as much English as I do French, but they bent over backwards to make my stay with them an enjoyable one. All meals are included in the rates here.

B.P. 1, 98732 Vaiea, Maupiti (on Motu Tiapaa). ℭ **60.15.35.** Fax 60.15.36. 5 units. 9,000CFP–13,000CFP (US$90–US$130) per person. Rates include all meals. No credit cards. **Amenities:** Restaurant; bar. *In room:* No phone.

Pension Poe Iti ✿✿ This excellent pension, set beside a white-sand beach and shallow lagoon on Motu Tuanai, is operated by Gerard and Josephine Sachet, who also own the *Maupiti Express.* Their four units may look like standard government-issue bungalows, but Gerard and Josephine have installed air-conditioners, reading lights beside the double beds, solar-heated showers, and TVs with DVD players (but no over-the-air reception). Although they're located in the gardens rather than beside the beach, these bungalows are the most luxurious I've seen at any pension in French Polynesia, making this my choice on Maupiti. Meals are served family-style in a beachside pavilion, where you will have a fine view of the main island across the lagoon. Breakfast costs 700CFP (US$7); lunch and dinner, 2,500CFP (US$25) each. Morning and afternoon transfers to the main island are complimentary. Gerard speaks excellent English.

B.P. 39, 98732 Vaiea, Maupiti (on Motu Tuanai). ℭ **67.83.14** or 76.58.76. Fax 67.83.14. maupitiexpress@mail.pf. 4 units. 7,000CFP (US$70) double. No credit cards. **Amenities:** Restaurant; bar; free use of kayaks, canoes, and snorkeling gear. *In room:* A/C, TV/DVD player, fridge, no phone.

Pension Rose des Isles Sharing the same beach as Pension Papahani (see above), Rose des Isles has one waterside bungalow built of native materials, making it Maupiti's most authentically Tahitian bungalow. It can accommodate up to five persons and has its own bathroom with cold-water shower. A smaller unit for two persons is back in the garden; its guests share toilets and showers with campers, who can pitch their tents there.

B.P. 55, 98732 Vaiea, Maupiti (on Motu Tiapaa). © **70.50.70.** Fax 67.82.00. 2 units (1 with shared bathroom), 8 tent sites. 8,000CFP–13,000CFP (US$80–US$130) per person room or bungalow (including all meals); 1,000CFP (US$10) per person campsite (no meals). No credit cards. **Amenities:** Restaurant; bar; free use of kayaks. *In room:* No phone.

ON THE MAIN ISLAND

Maupiti Loisirs   This really is a traditional pension, since you'll share the home of Ui Terihaunui and Simone Chan, north of Tereia Beach on the western side of the island. Simone is a former schoolteacher and speaks excellent English, while Ui is a specialist at boat tours around Maupiti. Their guest rooms are a bit cramped, but each has a double bed with mosquito net. The two shared bathrooms—one indoor, one outdoor—have cold-water showers. You can pitch a tent in their yard, or Ui will take you over to a campsite on Motu Auira, where you may have only land crabs and mosquitoes for company. They also rent bicycles for touring the island or making the short ride to the beach. Very good family-style meals are available.

B.P. 66, Vaiea, Maupiti. © and fax **67.80.95.** 2 units (shared bathroom). 5,000CFP (US$50) per person in rooms, 2,000CFP (US$20) per person camping. No credit cards. **Amenities:** Dining room; bike rentals; free use of kayaks. *In room:* No phone.

Pension Tautiare Village   On the southern side of the main island, David and Dawn Domingo's pension consists of one modern house with four bedrooms, each with its own hot-water bathroom, plus one more room in their home, which means you both share their bathroom and see island life first-hand. Guests hang out in the living rooms and on the large verandas.

B.P. 16, 98732 Vaiea, Maupiti. © **67.83.58.** Fax 60.15.91. pension-tautiare@mail.pf. 5 units (1 with shared bathroom). 5,000CFP (US$50) per person. No credit cards. **Amenities:** Restaurant; bar; bike rentals; free use of kayaks and snorkeling gear. *In room:* No phone.

5 Where to Dine

If your choice of pension doesn't include meals in its rates, I strongly advise purchasing at least a *demi pension* meal plan (that is, half board, or breakfast and dinner). This is especially important if you stay out on a *motu,* since you will not be able to go into the village after dark. Expect to pay about 3,000CFP (US$30) for breakfast and dinner, 5,500CFP (US$55) for all three meals. Even on the main island, there is only one nonpension place to dine, to wit:

Snack Tarona FRENCH/TAHITIAN   This snack bar serves as the prime local gathering place for both food and libation. The picnic-style tables and chairs sit on a floor of coral gravel under a thatch-roof pavilion and usually catch the prevailing southeast trade winds, making this a refreshingly breezy location to recover from your bicycle ride around the island. The fare is the typical Polynesian potpourri of *poisson cru,* grilled steaks with french fries, shrimp with coconut-curry sauce, chow mein, and chicken and shrimp sautéed with vegetables. Maupiti's farmers grow vegetables for Bora Bora's hotels, so the tomatoes, cucumbers, and beans here should be straight from the farm.

Farauru (lagoonside in the village). © **67.82.46.** Reservations not accepted. Main courses 700CFP–1,300CFP (US$7–US$13). No credit cards. Mon–Sat 10am–1:30pm and 6–10pm.

10

The Tuamotu Archipelago

When Paul Woodard and I sailed our 41-foot yacht *Felicity* from the U.S. East Coast to Tahiti, our voyage was a relative piece of cake—until we came to the great line of atolls known as the Tuamotu Archipelago. Like a fence stretching for 1,159km (720 miles), the Tuamotu islands block the northeastern approaches to Tahiti. They are so low—never more than 3m (10 ft.) above sea level, not including the height of the coconut palms growing all over them—that hundreds of yachts and ships have been wrecked on these reefs, either unable to see them until it was too late or dragged ashore by tricky currents swarming between the islands and ripping through the passes into their lagoons. Those of us who go down to the sea in yachts well understand why the Tuamotus were once known as the Dangerous Archipelago.

Needless to say, Paul and I had to be on our toes when navigating these waters. While he signaled me from the bow, where he could more easily see coral heads in the water, I steered *Felicity* through narrow Tiputa Pass and into the lagoon at Rangiroa. Once safely inside, the calm water made it seem as if we had sailed into a monstrous lake in the middle of the South Pacific Ocean.

Like all atolls, those of the Tuamotu are necklaces of islets enclosing crystal-clear lagoons. For this reason, they offer a very different kind of experience than do French Polynesia's high, mountainous islands. You will find many black-pearl farms (most of the country's orbs are produced here) and small villages with white-washed churches, but there is much less to be seen aboveground than there is underwater.

Sharks, rays, and more than 400 species of colorful tropical fish inhabit these lagoons, making for French Polynesia's finest snorkeling and scuba diving. Of the 76 atolls, only **Rangiroa, Tikehau, Manihi,** and **Fakarava** have accommodations up to international standard; accordingly, they are the most visited. Only yachties and a few other intrepid travelers go elsewhere.

You will find drier and warmer climes than in the Society Islands, and sand so brilliantly white that it alone requires sunglasses in the midday sun. So grab your hat, your snorkel, and your fins. If you love the water, you are in for a treat up here in the Tuamotu Archipelago.

1 Rangiroa ★★

The largest and most often visited of the Tuamotu atolls, Rangiroa lies 312km (194 miles) northeast of Tahiti. Its ring of low, skinny islets encloses the world's second-largest lagoon. At more than 70km (43 miles) long and 26km (16 miles) wide, it's big enough so that when you stand on one side, you cannot see the other. It's easy to see why it's named Rangiroa, which means "long sky" in the local language. In fact, the lagoon is so large, the entire island of Tahiti could be placed in it, with room to spare.

Northern Tuamotu Archipelago

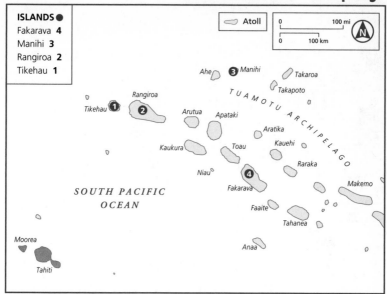

Early mornings and late afternoons, schools of dolphins usually play in **Avatoru Pass** and **Tiputa Pass,** the two navigable passes into Rangiroa's interior lagoon, both on its north side. Currents of up to 6 knots race through the passes as the tides first fill the lagoon and then empty it during their never-ending cycle.

Most visitors come to Rangiroa primarily for French Polynesia's best scuba diving, snorkeling, and fishing. Others venture across the lagoon to Rangiroa's islets, where they can play Robinson Crusoe at a very remote resort.

Rangiroa's airstrip and all but one of its hotels and pensions are on a perfectly flat, 11km-long (7-mile) stretch of sand and palm trees running between Avatoru and Tiputa passes on the northern side of the lagoon. This main island does not have a name, as it actually consists of seven islets separated by narrow and very shallow reef passes. On the western end, **Avatoru** village is the commercial and governmental center for the northern Tuamotu islands. On the eastern end, Tiputa Pass separates the main island from **Tiputa** village. All but a handful of Rangiroa's 2,500 residents live in Avatoru and Tiputa villages.

> ## Impressions
> *At Rangiroa you pick up a hundred natives with pigs, guitars, breadfruit and babies. They sleep on deck, right outside your bunk, and some of them sing all night.*
>
> —James A. Michener, *Return to Paradise*, 1951

GETTING AROUND RANGIROA

Rangiroa's airstrip is on the main island, about equidistant between Avatoru and Tiputa passes. The hotels and pensions send buses or vans to meet their guests. Otherwise, you are on your own, since there is no public transportation on the island.

I usually rent a bicycle, scooter, or car for a day to explore the main island. Its only road crosses six bridges, none of them with guardrails and some of them only one lane

Rangiroa

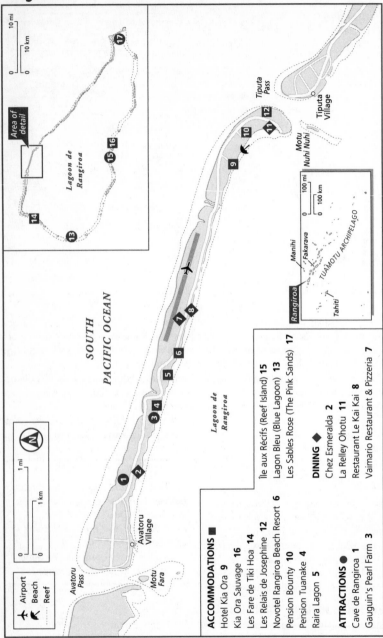

SOUTH PACIFIC OCEAN

Lagoon de Rangiroa

Avatoru Pass

Avatoru Village

Motu Fara

Tiputa Pass

Tiputa Village

Motu Nuhi Nuhi

Lagoon de Rangiroa

Area of detail

Lagoon de Rangiroa

TUAMOTU ARCHIPELAGO

Manihi

Fakarava

Rangiroa

Tahiti

ACCOMMODATIONS ■

Hotel Kia Ora **9**
Kia Ora Sauvage **16**
Les Fare de Tiki Hoa **14**
Les Relais de Josephine **12**
Novotel Rangiroa Beach Resort **6**
Pension Bounty **10**
Pension Tuanake **4**
Raira Lagon **5**

Île aux Récifs (Reef Island) **15**
Lagon Bleu (Blue Lagoon) **13**
Les Sables Rose (The Pink Sands) **17**

DINING ◆

Chez Esmeralda **2**
La Relley Ohotu **11**
Restaurant Le Kai Kai **8**
Vaimario Restaurant & Pizzeria **7**

ATTRACTIONS ●

Cave de Rangiroa **1**
Gauguin's Pearl Farm **3**

Airport
Beach
Reef

Tips **Come up Here First**

Unless you're a serious scuba diver, there isn't a lot to do in the Tuamotu Islands, which makes them great for resting and recovering from your long flight before tackling Tahiti, Moorea, Bora Bora, and the other Society Islands. So come here first for a little R&R, and then hit the more developed mountainous islands.

---

wide. The pavement is uneven, adding to the need for constant caution when driving here.

Rangi Rent a Car is the local agent for **Europcar** (© 800/227-7368 or 96.08.28; www.europcar.com). It has an agency near Avatoru and a desk at the Hotel Kia Ora (p. 206). Scooters and open-air "Fun Cars" (the most you'll need here) cost about 6,500CFP (US$65) for a day (which is longer than you'll need to see the islet). Bicycles rent for 1,500CFP (US$15) for half a day, 1,800CFP (US$18) for a full day. **Arehahio Locations,** in Avatoru (© 98.82.45), rents scooters for 5,200CFP (US$52) a day, bicycles for 1,300CFP (US$13) a day.

You can cross Tiputa Pass to Tiputa village via **Maurice Navette** (© 96.67.09 or 78.13.25), which operates water taxis daily from 6am to 5pm. Call or check with your hotel staff for schedules and fares.

FAST FACTS: Rangiroa

The following facts apply specifically to Rangiroa. For more information, see "Fast Facts: Tahiti & French Polynesia," in chapter 2.

Camera/Film For film, check the drugstore (below) and the boutique at the **Hotel Kia Ora** (p. 206). You won't get overnight processing here.

Currency Exchange Although **Banque Socredo** has an agency with an ATM in Avatoru, I suggest bringing some local currency with you in case the ATM has run out of francs or is otherwise inoperable. The Banque Socredo office is open Tuesday, Wednesday, and Friday from 8am to noon; Monday and Thursday from 1:30 to 4:30pm. **Banque de Tahiti** also has a branch, but not an ATM, in Avatoru. It's open Monday and Friday from 8 to 11am and 1 to 4pm, Tuesday and Thursday from 8 to 11am.

Drugstores **Pharmacie de Rangiroa,** in Avatoru (© 93.12.35), is open Monday through Friday from 7am to 12:30pm and 2:30 to 6:30pm, Saturday from 7am to 12:30pm and 4:30 to 6:30pm, Sunday and holidays from 10 to 11:30am.

Emergencies/Police The **emergency police** phone number is © 17. The phone number of the **gendarmerie** on Rangiroa is © 96.03.61.

Healthcare Dr. Guy Thirouard operates the private **Centre Médical Rai Roa,** in Avatoru (© 96.04.44 or 96.04.33). There are **infirmaries** at Avatoru (© 96.03.75) and across the pass at Tiputa (© 96.03.96).

Internet Access Rangiroa's only cybercafe had closed during my recent visit, so you must rely on your hotel or pension for Internet access.

Post Office The small post office in Avatoru is open Monday through Thursday from 7am to 3pm, Friday from 7am to 2pm.

Telephone Public pay phones are at the post office in Avatoru and at the dock on the Tiputa Pass end of the main island. Residents in the Tuamotus tend to write their phone numbers in groups of three digits—that is, 960 375 instead of 96.03.75.

Water Except at the hotels, the tap water is brackish. Don't drink it.

EXPLORING RANGIROA
THE VILLAGES

Avatoru and Tiputa are typical Tuamotuan villages. I consider **Avatoru** to be the more interesting of the two. Not only is it on the main island (you will need to ride a boat across the pass to Tiputa; see "Getting Around Rangiroa," above), but it is also larger and has a bit more to see. When you get into town, follow the main road straight ahead until it makes a right turn at the picturesque Protestant church beside Avatoru Pass. Along the way, you'll pass the *mairie* (town hall), post office, banks, and three general stores. The whitewashed stone wall along this part of the road is typical of Tuamotuan villages. You can make a loop by following the main street beyond the church; it circles a large public park before returning to the main road.

A BLACK-PEARL FARM

Rangiroa does not produce black pearls in the same quantity as Manihi, but you can visit **Gauguin's Pearl Farm,** west of the airport (© **93.11.30**), and see how it's done. For 5,000CFP (US$50), they will open an oyster for you; you keep any pearl inside. If there isn't one, they keep opening oysters until there is. It's sort of like playing the lottery: You might win big, but then again, you might not. Open Monday through Friday from 8am to noon and 1 to 5pm, Saturday and Sunday from 9am to noon and 3 to 5pm.

A WINERY

You wouldn't expect to be doing any wine tasting in these atolls, but **Cave de Rangiroa,** near Avatoru (© **96.04.70;** www.vindetahiti.pf), is the display room for Vin de Tahiti (Tahiti Wines), French Polynesia's only vineyard and winery. The Carignan, muscat de Hambourg, and Italia varieties were first planted in a coconut grove out on the *motu* west of the main islet in 1999. You can take a half-day tour to the vineyard for 6,000CFP (US$60) per person, or just stay here in the *cave* and taste the results in air-conditioned comfort. Open Monday through Saturday from 9am to 1pm and 3 to 6pm.

LAGOON EXCURSIONS 🎣🎣🎣

Plan to explore this fantastic lagoon. If you're not diving, the best way is on a full-day excursion. The two main attractions are on the eastern and western ends of the lagoon, each at least a 1½-hour boat ride away from the main island each way. That means you will spend at least 3 hours going and coming, so you will need a full day for each of them—and a good set of sea legs if a strong wind kicks up choppy waves on the lagoon. The tours do not operate in bad weather or really rough seas, which are more likely to occur during the austral summer months from December through March. In other words, don't be disappointed if the weather washes out your planned excursion.

Les Sables Rose (The Pink Sands) ⭐⭐⭐, on the eastern end, is a phenomenal beach laden with unusual pink sand. It's one of French Polynesia's most beautiful beaches, and to call it deserted is an understatement. Second on my list is **Lagon Bleu (Blue Lagoon),** a small lagoon carved into the reef on the western edge of the big lagoon. This shallow pool is full of colorful corals and plentiful sea life. Thousands of seabirds nest nearby on aptly named **Île aux Oiseaux (Bird Island).** If you have a third day here and haven't had your fill of boat rides, consider **Île aux Récifs (Reef Island),** on the south side, where erosion has created razor-sharp coral formations (be sure to bring reef shoes on this trip).

You will be able to swim and snorkel at these sites, and the boat staff will prepare a beachside lunch. These trips are not inexpensive: Plan on paying 10,000CFP to 12,000CFP (US$100–US$120) or more per person for a full day's outing, including lunch, soft drinks, and use of snorkeling gear. The hotels and pensions either offer their own or can arrange lagoon excursions.

A shorter alternative if you don't have that much time—or that much spare change—is a **glass-bottom boat ride** over the coral heads inside the passes. You'll see lots of fish and, if you're lucky, a shark or two. Most hotels and pensions can arrange these excursions for about 3,000CFP (US$30) per person.

SCUBA DIVING & SNORKELING ⭐⭐⭐

Rangiroa is one of the world's top diving destinations, with an extraordinary array of sea life. Hurricanes have damaged the coral here, so come to see fish, rays, and especially sharks rather than colorful reefs.

Tiputa Pass is the top dive site in French Polynesia. You can see gray- and black-tipped sharks all year, but the best time is from December to March, when huge hammerhead sharks gather for their mating season. Another good (and less scary) time is between July and October, when manta rays look for mates. Diving in and out of the pass is for intermediate and advanced divers only, since it is both deep and subject to strong currents. Novices can dive inside the reef near Avatoru Pass and around the small islets sitting just inside both passes. Most other dives here are deep and long compared to American standards, so bring a buddy and be prepared to stretch the limits of the dive tables in order to see the magnificent sea life. Divers must be certified in advance and bring their medical certificates.

Snorkelers as well as scuba divers can **"ride the rip"** tide through Tiputa Pass, one of the most exhilarating waterborne experiences in French Polynesia. You are dropped off just outside the reef and literally drift with the incoming current through the pass, which looks like an underwater valley. These so-called drift snorkeling trips cost about 5,000CFP (US$50) and are worth it—if you've got a strong heart.

⟨Moments⟩ Dolphin Watching

All of Rangiroa's hotels and pensions can arrange dolphin-watching cruises, usually for about 3,000CFP (US$30) per person, but you can ride or walk to the public park at the western side of Tiputa Pass and watch them play for free. The best time is late afternoon, when the playful animals frolic in the pass, often leaping high above the waves churned by the strong currents.

While most of its lagoon shoreline consists of pebbly coral, and waves crash directly on the reef over on the ocean side, the main island does have a decent white-sand beach. You'll find it where the island makes a hook on its eastern end—that is, from the Hotel Kia Ora eastward to Tiputa Pass.

Any of the hotels or pensions can arrange scuba dives. The best operators are **Blue Dolphins,** at the Hotel Kia Ora (© **96.03.01;** www.bluedolphinsdiving.com), and **TOPdive Rangiroa** (© **72.39.55;** www.topdive.com). Other outfitters include **The Six Passengers** (© **96.02.60;** www.the6passengers.com), which allows only six divers on its boat at any one time; **Raie Manta Club** (© **96.04.80;** http://raiemantaclub.free.fr); and **Rangiroa Paradive** (© **96.05.55**). One-tank day dives cost about 7,000CFP (US$70). Night dives are more expensive.

WHERE TO STAY
EXPENSIVE
Hotel Kia Ora 𝕲𝕲   This romantic resort in a huge coconut plantation has been Rangiroa's premier lodging for almost 3 decades. Its thatch-roofed buildings look like a lagoonside Polynesian village. White sand is hauled over from the ocean side of the island to create the main island's best beach. It's still is a bit pebbly, but a long pier reaches out into deep water for excellent swimming, snorkeling, and sunset watching, and there's a canoe-shaped swimming pool beside the lagoon. Ten bungalows sit over the reef and share the sunsets. Ashore stand two-story beachside bungalows with bedrooms downstairs and up, plus one-story models with only a downstairs bedroom. These beach units have Jacuzzi tubs set in their partially covered front decks, but they have not one iota of privacy. Much better are three deluxe beach units with their own small pools and bathrooms with outdoor tubs. The much smaller original bungalows have also been spiffed up, but they lack window screens. As at most accommodations on Rangiroa, guests here are overwhelmingly European and Japanese.

B.P. 1, 98775 Tiputa, Rangiroa (3km/2 miles east of airport, near east end of island). © **96.02.22.** Fax 93.11.17. www. hotelkiaora.com. 58 units. 30,000CFP–65,000CFP (US$300–US$650) double. AE, DC, MC, V. **Amenities:** Restaurant; bar; outdoor pool; tennis court; Jacuzzi; watersports equipment/rentals; bike rentals; activities desk; car rentals; massage; babysitting; laundry service. *In room:* A/C, dataport, fridge (stocked on request), coffeemaker, hair dryer, safe.

Kia Ora Sauvage   This outpost offers one of French Polynesia's most remote Robinson Crusoe–like escapes. Guests are transferred daily by a 1-hour speedboat ride from Hotel Kia Ora, which manages this retreat. Once you're out on tiny, triangle-shaped Avearahi *motu,* you will find a thatched main building, where the Tahitian staff cooks up the day's catch, often caught during the guests' lagoon excursions. Accommodations are in five comfortable bungalows built entirely of native materials. They have their own modern bathrooms, but are not screened. Nor do they have electricity. Bring reef shoes, lots of insect repellent, and SPF-60 sun block.

⌒*Fun Fact* **The Exile Islands**

Although the archipelago is now known as the Tuamotu ("many islands"), the chain was once called Puamotu, meaning subservient islands. In the old days, chiefs on Tahiti who did bad things were exiled to the atolls. The indigenous peoples up here refer to the archipelago as Puamotu, its name in those days, and they still speak a distinct Polynesian dialect known in English as Puamotuan.

B.P. 1, 98775 Tiputa, Rangiroa (hotel is 1-hr. boat ride from airport). ℂ 96.02.22. Fax 93.11.17. www.hotelkiaora.com. 5 units. 40,000CFP (US$400) double. Meals and drinks 7,600CFP (US$76) per person per day. Round-trip boat transfers 10,000CFP (US$100) per person. AE, DC, MC, V. **Amenities:** Restaurant; bar. *In room:* No phone.

Novotel Rangiroa Beach Resort

Opened in 2004, this modest but attractive resort sits beside a rocky stretch of lagoon shoreline west of the airport and near Restaurant Le Kai Kai and Vaimario Restaurant & Pizzeria (see "Where to Dine," below). Brilliant white sand has been brought in to form a sunbathing strip along the property. The 38 bungalows and main building (with restaurant and bar) are tightly packed on limited land. The units here come either as individual bungalows or as duplex rooms, which are narrower than the bungalows. Both are tastefully decorated with tropical furniture and fabrics; they also have adequate bathrooms and front porches. Still, you'll have much more room to roam at the Hotel Kia Ora, where you will pay about the same for a garden bungalow.

B.P. 17, 98775 Avatoru, Rangiroa. ℂ 800/221-4542 or 93.13.50. Fax 93.13.51. www.novotel.com. 38 units. 24,600CFP–39,000CFP (US$246–US$390) bungalow. AE, MC, V. **Amenities:** Restaurant; bar; bike rentals; activities desk; car-rental desk; massage; laundry service. *In room:* A/C, TV, dataport, fridge, coffeemaker, hairdryer, safe.

MODERATE

Les Fare de Tiki Hoa

Like Kia Ora Sauvage, this small hotel provides a get-away-from-it-all experience on a *motu* out on Rangiroa's northwestern side, a half-hour by boat from Avatoru. It's a shorter boat ride from here to Lagon Bleu (Blue Lagoon), but much longer to Les Sables Rose (The Pink Sands) on the far side of the lagoon. A nice beach fringes the lagoon side of the islet. Built in 2004, the 10 bungalows have thatch roofs, ceiling fans, and private bathrooms with cold-water showers. Being able to speak a bit of French will be helpful out here.

B.P. 235, 98775 Avatoru, Rangiroa (hotel is 30-min. boat ride from Avatoru). ℂ 58.45.45 or 73.63.10. Fax 58.45.45. 10 units. 12,500CFP (US$120) double. Add 6,500CFP (US$65) per person per day for all meals. MC, V. **Amenities:** Restaurant; bar; free use of kayaks and snorkeling gear. *In room:* No phone.

Les Relais de Josephine ☆ (Value)

You can watch the dolphins frolic in Tiputa Pass from this comfortable inn, the creation of Denise Thirouard, whose husband, Dr. Guy Thirouard, practices medicine in Avatoru (see "Fast Facts: Rangiroa," above). The bungalows flank a Mediterranean-style villa with an expansive veranda overlooking the pass. Guests can relax there or in a lounge equipped with a TV, VCR, and CD player. At night, the veranda turns into Le Dolphin Gourmand restaurant, serving excellent three-course French and Mediterranean meals. Furnished with reproductions of French colonial antiques, the bungalows have thatch roofs over solid white walls. Sliding doors open to the porches, outfitted with high-quality wooden patio furniture. Neither the doors nor the prop-up windows are screened, but the queen-size beds are covered by mosquito nets. The substantial bathrooms have double sinks and walk-in showers. Do anything possible to get one of the three units beside the pass.

B.P. 140, 98775 Avatoru, Rangiroa. ℂ and fax **96.02.00.** http://relaisjosephine.free.fr. 6 units. 14,300CFP (US$143) per person, double occupancy. Rates include breakfast and dinner. AE, DC, MC, V. **Amenities:** Restaurant; bar; bike rentals; laundry service. *In room:* Coffeemaker, safe, no phone.

Pension Bounty

Although it's not directly beside the lagoon, a sandy path leads from this pension to the main island's best beach. Despite not being next to the water, this is the newest and one of the most comfortable pensions on Rangiroa. The attractive, modern bungalows are built of red cedar and local *kohu* hardwood, and each has a kitchen and a ceiling fan to go along with its double bed and private bathroom (with

---

Tips **Expect a Tepid Shower**

I once asked the owner of a Tuamotu pension if the bathrooms in his bungalows had hot-water showers. *"Non,"* he replied. Then they must be cold-water?
"Non," he said again. I must have looked puzzled. *"Regardez,"* he said, telling
me to look at a huge black plastic tank behind the nearest bungalow. As I could
see, gutters divert rainwater from the rooftops into tanks, where it bakes in the
sun until someone turns on a shower. *"Pas chaude, pas froide,"* he said. "Not
cold, not hot." So it is in the atolls, where most fresh water comes not from
wells in the ground but from rainwater, itself a scarce commodity in these semi-
arid islands. Unless you're staying at a deluxe resort with a desalinization plant,
forget lingering in a hot shower.

---

hot-water shower). All of the windows, as well as the sliding doors to each unit's large
deck, are screened. Breakfast and dinner are provided on request.

B.P. 296, 98775 Avatoru, Rangiroa. ✆ and fax **96.08.22**. www.pension-bounty.com. 4 units. 7,000CFP (US$70) per
person. Add 3,000CFP (US$30) per person per day for breakfast and dinner. AE, MC, V. **Amenities:** Restaurant; bar;
free use of bikes. *In room:* Kitchen; no phone.

INEXPENSIVE

Pension Tuanake   This little lagoonside pension sits in a coconut grove on a point
of land fringed by pebbly beaches on two sides. Friendly owner Roger Terorotua has
six bungalows, all with plywood sides, thatch roofs covered with tin, front porches,
mat-lined walls, screened windows, fans, and bathrooms with hot-water showers.
They range in size from small units equipped with two single beds to a family-size
affair with double and single beds both downstairs and in a loft, which can be entered
via its own outdoor stairway. A leader of Haere Mai, French Polynesia's organization
of pensions and small family-run hotels (see "Guesthouses & Family Accommodations," p. 53), Roger speaks enough English to make you feel welcome here. His is a
down-to-earth Tahitian place, so stay somewhere else if you are bothered by chickens
and dogs running free around the property.

B.P. 21, 98775 Avatoru, Rangiroa. ✆ **93.11.80**. Fax 93.11.81. www.tuanake.fr.st. 6 units. 9,500CFP–14,000CFP
(US$95–US$140) double. Add 3,000CFP (US$30) per person per day for breakfast and dinner. MC, V. **Amenities:**
Restaurant; bar; bike rentals. *In room:* No phone.

Raira Lagon   One of the more popular small, family-run hotels here, Raira Lagon
sits beside a rocky beach equipped with chairs under shade trees. Owners Pascale and
Maxime Boetsch, who speak English as well as French, have 10 small thatch-roofed
bungalows equipped with double beds, electric fans, bathrooms with hot-water showers, and front porches. La Margouilat, their brightly decorated lagoonside restaurant,
serves good French fare to both guests and outsiders.

B.P. 87, 98775 Avatoru, Rangiroa. ✆ **99.12.30**. Fax 99.12.31. www.raira-lagon.pf. 10 units. 10,800CFP (US$108) per
person. AE, MC, V. Rates include breakfast and dinner. **Amenities:** Restaurant; bar; bike and scooter rentals; free use
of snorkeling gear. *In room:* No phone.

WHERE TO DINE

Non-guests are welcome at Les Relais de Josephine's (see above) **Le Dolphin Gourmand** restaurant, where the three-course meals cost 3,950CFP (US$40) per person.

Make your reservations before noon. Outsiders are also welcome at the **Hotel Kia Ora** and the **Raira Lagoon** dining rooms.

The local *roulottes* set up shop after dark at the Tiputa Pass wharf, in Avatoru village, and in the center of the main island near Restaurant Le Kai Kai. See "Don't Miss *Les Roulottes*" (p. 112), for details. You'll also find a few inexpensive snack bars in Avatoru.

Chez Esmeralda *(Finds* FRENCH/TAHITIAN   You can stop for breakfast as well as lunch and dinner at this open-air snack bar, beside the main road east of Avatoru. Eye-openers include eggs, omelets, tasty cheese bread, and Tahitian-style fried fish. The rest of the day sees the usual local favorites such as *poisson cru*, grilled steaks and fish, and Chinese dishes. Owner Isidore Tau Maino speaks pretty good English, as well as French and Tahitian.

Main road, east of Avatoru. ℂ 96.04.12. Reservations not necessary. Breakfast 950CFP (US$9.50); main courses 1,100CFP–1,450CFP (US$11–US$15). MC, V. Thurs–Tues 6–9am, 11am–2pm, and 6–9pm.

La Relley Ohotu SNACK BAR   You'll be snacking beside the lagoon at this simple establishment next to the Tiputa Pass dock. It's a local favorite for French- and Tahitian-style breakfasts. The rest of the day brings burgers, sandwiches, *poisson cru*, and grilled steaks and fish served with fries. *Note:* It's open Sunday for breakfast only.

At Ohutu Point (end of the main road at Tiputa Pass). No phone. Reservations not accepted. Burgers and sandwiches 350CFP–800CFP (US$3.50–US$8); main courses 1,000CFP–1,300CFP (US$10–US$13). No credit cards. Mon–Sat 8am–5pm, Sun 5:30–7:30am.

Restaurant Le Kai Kai *⋒* FRENCH   West of the airstrip and near the Novotel Rangiroa Beach Resort, this open-air restaurant with crushed coral floor and mat-lined ceiling is my favorite spot for a casual lunch or dinner. Midday sees a selection of omelets, salads, and *croques* (toasted sandwiches), while dinner turns to French fare with Polynesian ingredients, such as a Tuamotuan-style sautéed pork. Otherwise I stick with the mahimahi, wahoo, or other fresh fish. A special *prix-fixe* dinner menu includes a starter of beef or tuna carpaccio, a main of shrimp in coconut-curry sauce or a filet of beef, and a dessert, such as a Tahitian sundae with coconut and honey. Reserve for a 7pm pickup from your hotel.

Main road, west of airport. ℂ 96.30.39. Reservations recommended. Lunch sandwiches and omelets 400CFP–1,000CFP (US$4–US$10); main courses 1,200CFP–2,000CFP (US$12–US$20); prix-fixe dinner 3,400CFP (US$34). MC, V. Daily 11:30am–2pm and 6:30–9pm.

Vaimario Restaurant & Pizzeria FRENCH/ITALIAN   Single-serving and large pizzas are the highlights at this restaurant in a thatch-roof house just west of the airport. You can dine inside, but the preferred tables are on the coral-floor veranda. The best main courses are grilled fresh fish with vanilla, coconut, or orange and ginger sauces.

Main road, west of airport. ℂ 96.05.69. Reservations recommended. Pizza 950CFP–1,200CFP (US$9.50–US$12); main courses 1,600CFP–2,850CFP (US$16–US$29). MC, V. Wed–Fri and Sun–Mon 11:30am–2pm and 6:30–9pm; Sat 6:30–9pm.

2 Tikehau *⟨★⟩*

Separated from Rangiroa by a deep-water channel, Tikehau is much smaller and less developed than its huge neighbor. Its nearly circular lagoon, 26km (16 miles) across, is no more than 30m (100 ft.) at its deepest. The late Jacques Cousteau found in 1987 that the Tikehau lagoon had more species of fish than any other French Polynesian lagoon. Apparently that's still true, which makes this a great destination for snorkelers and novice divers, as well as providing a substantial income for Tikehau's 400 or so friendly residents, who make more money by trapping and shipping fish to Papeete than from black-pearl farms.

Most local residents live in **Tuherahera,** the only village of any size, on a large *motu* on the southern side of the atoll. It's one of the prettiest Tuamotuan villages; hibiscus, frangipani, bougainvillea, and other colorful flowers seem to grow everywhere. You'll find grocery stores, a post office, and an infirmary in Tuherahera, but **no bank** (bring local currency, especially if your pension does not accept credit cards). The post office sells phone cards, which you can use to make local and international calls at a pay phone outside. As on all the atolls, do not drink the tap water on Tikehau. Bottled water is available at the pensions and from the grocery stores in Tuherahera.

The Tikehau **airport** is on the same island as Tuherahera village; in fact, you can easily walk from the tiny terminal to the village jetty. All of the accommodations will meet you if you have reservations, and all either have, or can arrange, **bicycle rentals** for about 1,000CFP (US$10) a day. There are no rental cars here since there is simply no place to drive them!

Tikehau is an excellent place to stay in one of French Polynesia's many family-run pensions, for half a dozen of them stand beside a long, curving beach of both white and pink sand on the eastern side of Tuherahera. Unlike Rangiroa, where you must ride a boat for more than an hour to see a pink-sand beach, here it's actually in the village. The atoll is also home to the **Tikehau Pearl Beach Resort,** an excellent luxury hotel on a *motu* of its own, a 10-minute boat ride from the village (see "Where to Stay & Dine," below).

LAGOON EXCURSIONS, SNORKELING & SCUBA DIVING

Tikehau has much better beaches than either Rangiroa or Manihi, and you can wade from them into the lagoon off your accommodations for excellent snorkeling. The Tikehau Pearl Beach Resort and the pensions can organize boat trips out on the lagoon to little deserted islets such as **Motu Ohihi,** on the eastern edge of the atoll, where you can swim off a pink-sand beach. Out in the lagoon are **Motu Puarua** and **Motu Oeoe,** the so-called Bird Islands, where noddy birds and snowy white fairy terns nest. These trips often include stops at a black-pearl farm and one of the fish farms, which provide so much of Tikehau's income. In a modern twist on the ancient stone Polynesian fish traps, such as at Maeva on Huahine (p. 147), the locals use bait to lure fish inside the traps and a maze of chicken wire to keep them from escaping. Prices vary from about 6,000CFP (US$60) per person for snorkeling trips to about 11,000CFP (US$110) for a full lagoon excursion, including a picnic on a small islet.

Tikehau's best diving is in and around Tuheiava Pass, the one navigable entry into the lagoon. You will see gray- and black-tip sharks and the occasional manta ray, but the appeal here is the enormous population of colorful fish. **Manihi Blue Nui Dive Center,** based at the Tikehau Pearl Beach Resort (© **996.23.01;** www.bluenui.com), is one of the best in French Polynesia, with top-of-the-line equipment and hard-topped boats with ladders. It charges about 7,500CFP (US$75) per one-tank dive; it also teaches PADI certification courses. Serving the pensions in Tuherahera village, **Raie Manta Club** (© **96.22.53** or 72.89.08; http://raiemantaclub.free.fr) charges about 5,000CFP (US$50) for a one-tank dive, 10,000CFP (US$100) for a two-tanker. It also has snorkeling trips for 2,000CFP (US$20) per person.

Tikehau

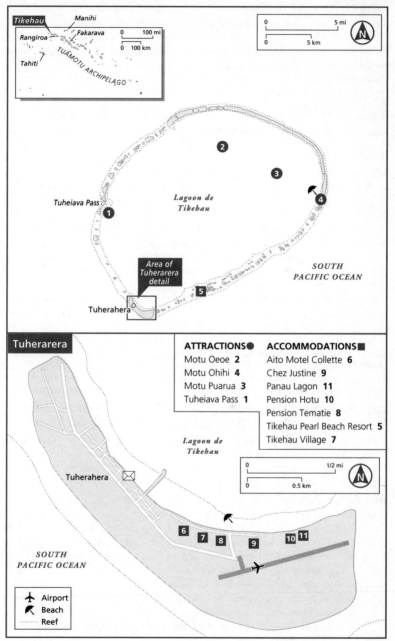

Tikehau

Manihi
Fakarava
Rangiroa
Tahiti
TUAMOTU ARCHIPELAGO

0   100 mi
0   100 km

0   5 mi
0   5 km

Tuheiava Pass ❶

Lagoon de Tikehau

❷

❸

❹ **Motu Ohihi**

Area of Tuherarera detail

Tuherahera

❺

SOUTH PACIFIC OCEAN

Tuherarera

ATTRACTIONS●	ACCOMMODATIONS■
Motu Oeoe **2**	Aito Motel Collette **6**
Motu Ohihi **4**	Chez Justine **9**
Motu Puarua **3**	Panau Lagon **11**
Tuheiava Pass **1**	Pension Hotu **10**
	Pension Tematie **8**
	Tikehau Pearl Beach Resort **5**
	Tikehau Village **7**

Lagoon de Tikehau

Tuherahera ✉

0   1/2 mi
0   0.5 km

SOUTH PACIFIC OCEAN

6 **7** **8** **9** **10** **11**

✈ Airport
➤ Beach
- - - - Reef

WHERE TO STAY & DINE

There are no restaurants or snack bars on Tikehau, and only the **Tikehau Village** pension (see below) welcomes outside guests, so buy a meal plan or pay a room rate that includes at least breakfast and dinner. The pensions listed here have various rates depending on the number of meals provided, so make sure you understand what you're paying for.

EXPENSIVE

Tikehau Pearl Beach Resort ✿✿✿   You may think you have made a horrible mistake as your transfer boat approaches, for rustic Tuamotu-style thatch disguises the luxuries awaiting at this resort, which occupies all of Motu Tiano, a small reef islet that's a 10-minute boat ride from the village and the airport. Other than a concrete patio separating the lagoonside pool from the conical-roofed dining room and bar, everything about it is *très* Polynesian, with beaucoup thatch, mats, and bamboo. The beach here has considerably more white sand than you'll find on Rangiroa and Manihi. Strong currents in a shallow pass rip in and out beneath some of the overwater bungalows, which means you can't go swimming from their decks. Consequently, opt for one of the "premium" suites built over quieter water; these do have ladders leading into the lagoon. Every unit is spacious and well appointed, and the beachside units have large outdoor bathrooms behind high rock walls. The bungalows aren't screened, but the staff closes the windows and turns on the electric mosquito repellents while you're at dinner. Ceiling fans and the trade winds usually provide plenty of ventilation, but opt for a premium overwater or deluxe beach bungalow if air-conditioning is important to you.

B.P. 20, 98778 Tuherahera, Tikehau (on an islet, a 10-min. boat ride from the airport and village). ✆ **800/657-3275** or 50.84.54 for reservations, or 96.23.00. Fax 43.17.86 for reservations, or 96.23.01. www.pearlresorts.com. 37 units. 38,000CFP–75,000CFP (US$380–US$750) double. Meals 10,000CFP (US$100) per person per day. AE, DC, MC, V. **Amenities:** Restaurant; bar; outdoor pool; spa; free use of snorkeling gear, canoes, and kayaks; bike rentals; babysitting; laundry service. *In room:* A/C (in premium overwater and deluxe beach units), TV, minibar, coffeemaker, hair dryer, safe.

INEXPENSIVE

The pensions below are all beside the long white-and-pink-sand beach that begins at Tuherahera village and runs east to the end of the *motu*. They are all cut from the same mold—that is, a few bungalows and a main building, where guests can relax and be fed. The island's airstrip is behind them, but don't worry: At worst only a couple flights arrive and take off each day, and only during daylight hours.

Aito Motel Collette   The closest pension to the village, Aito Motel Collette is named both for its owner and the *aito* (ironwood, or Australian pine) trees which shade her property. The beach here is wide, although the lagoon on this western end is shallow, especially at low tide. The clapboard-sided bungalows have high thatch roofs, now covered by tin painted green, and the front porches are trimmed with treelimb railings, which adds a touch of charm. They come with various bed configurations (two doubles, one double, or a double and a single). Each has its own private bathroom with cold-water shower. Fans and mosquito nets are available. Guests gather in a large living room and on a lagoon-facing veranda, where meals are served.

B.P. 43, 98778 Tuherahera, Tikehau. ✆ **96.22.47.** Fax 96.23.07. 5 units. 9,600CFP (US$96) per person. Rates include all meals. No credit cards. **Amenities:** Restaurant; bar. *In room:* No phone.

Chez Justine   Owner Justine Tetua speaks a bit of English, and she allows campers to pitch tents on the sand, which helps to set her pension apart from the others. Her

---

---

best units are three individual bungalows with private bathrooms by the beach. Two other buildings each have two bedrooms, which share a bathroom. All have front porches and screened windows. All showers dispense cold water. Meals are served in a waterside dining room.

98778 Tuherahera, Tikehau. (C) and fax **96.22.86.** 5 units (2 with shared bathrooms). 8,000CFP–10,500CFP (US$80–US$105) per person in bungalow, 3,000CFP (US$30) per person camping. Bungalow rates include all meals; camping rates include breakfast. No credit cards. **Amenities:** Restaurant; bar. *In room:* No phone.

Panau Lagon   For swimming, the lagoon is better on this eastern end of the beach than nearer the village. Owner Arai Natua, who's also the local cop, has six duplex bungalows—that is, each has two rooms and one cold-water bathroom, making them a decent choice for families or two couples traveling together. All have double beds, ceiling fans, and front porches facing the beach. Meals are served in the main house.

98778 Tuherahera, Tikehau. (C) and fax **96.22.99.** 6 units. 7,000CFP (US$70) per person. Rates include all meals. No credit cards. **Amenities:** Restaurant; bar. *In room:* No phone.

Pension Hotu   Next to Panau Lagoon, this pension is the farthest removed from the village and therefore a bit more private than the others. The lagoon is deeper and better for swimming on this end, too. Friendly owners Isidore and Nini Hoiore keep their three thatch-roof bungalows clean and neat. Two units are minimally furnished, but two have a double bed and a sofa, while the third has two double beds. Each has a front porch and a rear bathroom with cold-water shower. The windows are unscreened, so ask for a mosquito net. Guests share a communal kitchen here, and Nina (who speaks some English) prepares meals in the dining room.

98778 Tuherahera, Tikehau. (C) **96.22.89.** 3 units. 7,500CFP (US$75) per person. Rates include all meals. No credit cards. **Amenities:** Restaurant; bar; communal kitchen. *In room:* No phone.

Pension Tematie   Midway along the beach, and closest to the airport terminal, this pension has the most unusual architecture here. Two of its octagonal-shaped bungalows are built of coral blocks, which owners Nora and Yves-Marie Dubois scavenged from the reef. The bricklike blocks form the walls of the bungalows and of each unit's outdoor bathroom with cold-water shower. The two smaller *fares* have double and single beds. A larger family-size unit has additional beds in its mezzanine. The pull-back windows here are screened, and electric fans are available. Yves-Marie is a French engineer, and he and Nora lived in many countries before settling on Tikehau, her home island. They serve French- and Tahitian-style meals.

98778 Tuherahera, Tikehau. (C) and fax **96.22.65.** 3 units. 7,000CFP–10,000CFP (US$70–US$100) per person. Rates include all meals. No credit cards. **Amenities:** Restaurant; bar; kayak and bike rentals. *In room:* No phone.

Tikehau Village   Often booked solid by Tahiti residents on vacation, this lively little hotel sits just beyond Aito Motel Collette on the widest part of the beach. The lagoon is relatively shallow here, but a pier provides access to deeper water as well as a diving base for Raie Manta Club (see "Lagoon Excursions, Snorkeling & Scuba Diving," above). The bungalows have more Tuamotuan charm than any others here, with natural thatch roofs and walls trimmed with coconut-palm fronds. Each has a front porch, a ceiling fan, and a private bathroom with cold-water shower. Four smaller units are geared for singles and couples, while two larger bungalows attract families. Try to get a beachfront bungalow if you can. Under a big thatch roof to the rear of the property, the moderately priced French and Tahitian restaurant is open to all comers, although reservations are strongly advised.

B.P. 9, 98778 Tueharahera, Tikehau. (©) and fax **96.22.86.** 6 units. 8,500CFP–10,500CFP (US$85–US$105) per person. Rates include all meals. MC, V. **Amenities:** Restaurant; bar; bike rentals. *In room:* No phone.

3 Manihi

Manihi, known for its black-pearl farms, lies 520km (312 miles) northeast of Tahiti. French Polynesia's pearl-farming industry began here in the late 1960s, and although many farms are now closed, the remaining ones seem to sit atop nearly every coral head dotting the lagoon.

Most of the atoll's 800 or so residents live in the only village here, **Paeua,** which sits beside **Tairapa Pass** on Manihi's southern side, the only navigable entry into the lagoon. (Both the village and the pass are also referred to as Turipaoa.) The three pensions here are either very remote or cater primarily to workers at the pearl farms, and as a result, in my opinion, Manihi is a one-horse atoll, that horse being the luxurious **Manihi Pearl Beach Resort** (see below). If you can afford its rates, Manihi offers very good diving and excursions out on its lagoon; otherwise, I would look to another island for my atoll adventure.

From the resort, you can visit Paeua village every day; the hotel launch lands at the jetty inside Tairapa Pass. From there, head inland for 1 block, turn right, and walk to the pass, where there's a grocery store fronted by a huge shade tree. After sipping a soft drink on a bench beside the tree, stroll along the seawall for a sensational view of the outer reef. You'll pass a small, picturesque Catholic church facing the sea.

The **airport** is on the same *motu* as the Manihi Pearl Beach Resort, which sends golf carts to fetch its guests from the terminal (which does not have restrooms). The resort has bicycles for its guests' use, but there are no rental vehicles available here, nor is there public transportation. There is **no bank** on Manihi, so bring local currency if you plan to visit the village. The **post office** (which has pay phones) and the nurse-staffed government **infirmary** (© **96.43.67**) are both in Paeua. Do not drink the tap water; bottled water is available at the resort and from the grocery stores in Paeua.

LAGOON EXCURSIONS, SNORKELING & SCUBA DIVING

At 30km (16 miles) long by 5.6km (4 miles) wide, the clear lagoon is bigger than Tikehau's but not nearly as large—nor as deep—as those in Rangiroa and Fakarava. Like Tikehau, it's better for diving among colorful tropical fish, as opposed to the big

---

Tips Black Pearls

Do not expect to buy the black pearl of your dreams directly from a Manihi farm at a huge discount. Only one farm welcomes guests, and then only on Monday, Wednesday, and Friday. If you must see a Manihi black pearl in the making, plan your visit accordingly.

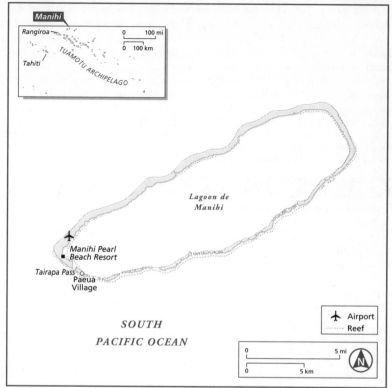

rays and sharks that make diving at Rangiroa so exciting. That's not to say there are no sharks here; to the contrary, the lagoon seems infested with the small reef varieties, and rays feed on plankton near Tairapa Pass, which is wider and deeper than those at Rangiroa. Its strong-enough current makes "riding-the-rip" diving and snorkeling trips a highlight here. All dive sites are in or just outside the pass.

As at Tikehau, Gilles Petrie's **Manihi Blue Nui Dive Center,** based at the Manihi Pearl Beach Resort (see below), provides top-of-the-line PADI diving. It charges about 6,700CFP (US$67) per one-tank dive. The resort also offers fishing (both deep-sea and hand-line in the lagoon), snorkeling trips, picnics on deserted islands, and lagoon excursions.

WHERE TO STAY & DINE

Manihi Pearl Beach Resort ★★ This modern resort and the airstrip share a *motu* on the southwestern end of Manihi's lagoon. As at Rangiroa, the beach here is more pebbly than sandy, but guests can sun themselves on little islets equipped with palm trees and chaise lounges, or on a faux beach beside a lagoonside infinity pool. The thatch-roof pool bar is cozy and conducive to meeting your fellow guests. In addition to diving, activities here include swimming, snorkeling (you can ride the rip tide through the pass), canoeing, visiting pearl farms and the village, lagoon and deep-sea fishing, spending a day on a deserted *motu,* and cruising at sunset. The prevailing trade winds can make for a choppy lagoon under the 19 overwater bungalows. Both the overwater and beachside units have mat-lined walls, natural wood floors, ceiling fans hanging from thatch roofs, king-size beds, writing tables, ample shower-only bathrooms, and covered porches with two recliners. Each beachfront unit also has a hammock strung between two palm trees out front, and the beachfront units' bathrooms are outdoors behind high wooden walls. Although a majority of guests here are European couples, the English-speaking Tahitian staff makes Americans feel at home.

B.P. 1, 99711 Manihi. © 800/657-3275 or 50.84.54 for reservations, or 96.42.73. Fax 43.17.86 for reservations, or 96.42.72. www.pearlresorts.com. 40 units. 28,000CFP–60,000CFP (US$280–US$600) double. Meals 10,000CFP (US$100) per person per day. AE, MC, V. **Amenities:** Restaurant; bar; outdoor pool; watersports equipment/rentals; free use of bikes; game room; activities desk; babysitting; laundry service. *In room:* A/C (in premium overwater bungalows), TV, dataport, minibar, coffeemaker, hair dryer, safe.

4 Fakarava ★★

Southeast of Rangiroa and about 490km (300 miles) northeast of Tahiti, Fakarava's rectangular reef encloses French Polynesia's second-largest lagoon. This 60 by 24km (37×15 mile) aquamarine jewel is filled with such a rich variety of sea life that part of it has been designated a UNESCO nature preserve. Needless to say, there is some very good diving and snorkeling here.

Unlike most Tuamotu atolls, I find Fakarava interesting from an historical standpoint. The airstrip and the main village, **Rotoava,** sit at the atoll's northeastern end, but the first European settlement here was at **Tetamanu,** on the far southern end of the lagoon beside narrow **Tumakohua Pass,** a 1½- to 2-hour boat ride from the airport. Coupled with fine snorkeling and diving in the pass, seeing the crumbling ruins of a prison and an 1834-vintage Catholic church make a visit to the ghostlike Tetamanu one of the more fascinating jaunts in the Tuamotu Archipelago.

The administrative center was moved to Rotoava to take advantage of **Garuae Pass,** the widest in French Polynesia. It's so wide and deep, in fact, that ships as large as the *Queen Elizabeth 2* can safely enter the lagoon and anchor off Rotoava. The cruise ship *Aranui* pulls in here on its way back from the Marquesas Islands (see "Seeing the Islands by Cruise Ship & Yacht," in chapter 2).

From Rotoava, a road—facetiously dubbed "rue Flosse" because former French Polynesian President Gaston Flosse paved part of it prior to a visit by French President Jacques Chirac in 2003—runs for 30km (18 miles) along French Polynesia's longest *motu.* Extraordinarily beautiful beaches border this skinny strip of land, which encloses the northern and eastern side of the lagoon (the western and southern sides consist of reef dotted with a few small islets). As you ride past these deserted beaches in a boat, you'll wonder how long it will be before Fakarava has more than one international-level resort.

Rotoava has a **post office** (with pay phone), **infirmary** (© **98.42.24**), school, whitewashed church, and three general stores, but **no bank.** The island's only resort,

---

Fun Fact R. L. S. Was Here, Too

Before he arrived in Tahiti during his 1888 South Pacific cruise, Robert Louis Stevenson sailed his yacht *Casco* through Garuae Pass. He liked Fakarava so much that he moved ashore and stayed for 2 months in a house near the whitewashed Catholic church, the village's prime landmark.

Legend:
- ✈ Airport
- ···· Reef

Maitai Dream Fakarava **5**
Motu Aito Paradise **7**
Pension Havaiki **3**
Pension Paparara **4**
Pension Tokerau Village **6**
Relais Marama **1**
Vahitu Dream **2**

Map labels: Garuae Pass, Rotoava Village, Rangiroa, Fakarava, Tahiti, TUAMOTU ARCHIPELAGO, SOUTH PACIFIC OCEAN, Tetamanu Village, Tumakohua Pass

the Maitai Dream Fakarava, and most of its pensions accept credit cards, but bring local currency if yours doesn't. Do not drink the tap water on Fakarava; bottled water is available at the resort and the grocery stores in Rotoava.

GETTING AROUND FAKARAVA

The airstrip is on the northern side of the atoll, 4km (3½ miles) from Rotoava. There is no public transportation on the island, so the accommodations meet arriving guests who have reservations. Some pensions rent bicycles to their guests. Anyone can rent a scooter or bike from **Faka Location** (© 78.03.37). Scooters cost 5,000CFP (US$50) for half a day and 8,000CFP (US$80) for 24 hours, while bicycles go for 1,000CFP (US$10) a day. Guests at the Maitai Dream Fakarava resort can charge the rentals to their rooms; everyone else must pay cash.

EXPLORING FAKARAVA
LAGOON EXCURSIONS ✦✦✦

Don't come to Fakarava without spending at least half a day on a lagoon excursion. The pensions will organize these trips. One of the best is **Fakarava Explorer** (© 98. 42.66; fakaravaexplorer@hotmail.com), operated by English-speaking Ato Lissant of Pension Paparara (p. 220). Ato offers dolphin-watching and snorkeling cruises to Garuae Pass, *motu* picnics, and fishing trips.

Moments **History, Snorkeling & a Robinson Crusoe Picnic**

The most enjoyable lagoon excursion I've ever made in French Polynesia was a full-day excursion to the near ghost village of Tetamanu, on Fakarava's far southern end. After a 1½-hour speedboat ride from the resort, guide Coco Randal landed us at Tetamanu for a look at its early-19th-century church and prison ruins and a restored 1862-vintage Catholic church. After petting a huge grouper and drift snorkeling with the current inside Tuamakohua Pass, we went out for a picnic on a tiny islet completely surrounded by brilliantly pink sand. Unlike any other lagoon excursion in the Tuamotu Archipelago, this one adds a bit of history to fine snorkeling and swimming.

I personally prefer those operated out of the **Maitai Dream Fakarava** by Randal "Coco" Neighbors. The son of an American father and Raiatean mother, Coco grew up in the U.S. but has lived here for many years. If you have only half a day, Coco charges 6,000CFP (US$60) per person to drop you off at one of the little *motu* dotting the lagoon for snorkeling. He also has a full-day trip to Topikite, the only rocky islet here and apparently a remnant of Fakarava's past as a high, mountainous island. This adventure costs 9,000CFP (US$90) per head. Best of all are the full-day trips to Tetamanu village (see "History, Snorkeling & a Robinsoe Crusoe Picnic," below). These Tetamanu excursions are usually offered only three times per week; I suggest finding out the schedule from the Maitai Dream Fakarava before planning your trip here.

SCUBA DIVING & SNORKELING ★★★

Garuae Pass is one of the most exciting dive sites in French Polynesia. At nearly a kilometer (⅔ mile) across, it dwarfs all other passes in the Tuamotu and offers just about every kind of fish, shark, and ray you're likely to see in French Polynesia; the coral here is very good, too. As at Rangiroa, hammerhead sharks gather here December through March, manta rays between July and October. July also sees huge schools of marbled groupers. Most dives are of the drift variety; that is, the dive boat takes you beyond the reef and you ride the incoming tide through the 15m-deep (50-ft.) pass back into the lagoon. You had best be an advanced diver to explore Garuae Pass, but those with either advanced or intermediate credentials can dive the much smaller and less challenging Tuamakohua Pass, at the southern end of the lagoon. Novice divers can choose from several sites in the lagoon.

The top dive operation here is Serge and Carine Howald's **Fakarava Diving Center,** at the Matai Dream Fakarava (© **98.43.23** or 77.10.00; www.fakarava-diving-center.com). They charge 6,500CFP (US$65) for a one-tank dive in or near Garuae Pass, or 18,500CFP (US$185) for a full day's outing to Tetamanu, including a picnic lunch and diving in Tuamakohua Pass. The island's other reputable dive center is **Te Ava Nui Plongé,** in Rotoava (© **98.42.50;** www.divingfakarava.com).

A BLACK-PEARL FARM

You can spend a few hours wandering around Rotoava, a typical Tuamotuan village of about 450 residents, and a few more looking at black pearls. **Pension Havaiki** (p. 219) operates a pearl farm on the southern end of the village. **Hinano Pearls,** north of the Maitai Dream Fakarava (© **98.41.51**), also welcomes visitors and will pick up resort guests who call ahead. Neither charges admission to visit. You will have a chance to buy pearls at both, but bear in mind that French Polynesia's wholesalers usually scarf up the cream of the crop before you get a chance to see them. Before shelling out any cash, see "Buying Your Black Pearl" (p. 99). I wouldn't buy set pearls here under any circumstances.

WHERE TO STAY
EXPENSIVE
Maitai Dream Fakarava ★★   A sister of the Hotel Maitai Polynesia on Bora Bora (p. 186), this comfortable, unpretentious resort sits beside the lagoon, a 15-minute ride by *le truck* or boat from the airstrip. A long pier extends from the central building out over the multihued lagoon, but there are no overwater bungalows. Instead, the 28 units sit along or facing the pebbly beach, and all of their front porches have lagoon views. Built of timber with peaked shingle roofs, they are spacious and comfortably furnished with king-size and single beds, desks, and ceiling fans, and their ample bathrooms feature open-air showers and their own outside entrance. The restaurant serves Fakarava's best French fare with Polynesian influences, at both indoor and outdoor tables (be sure to make dinner reservations if you're not staying here). Tahitians put on a dance show once a week. Kayaks, canoes, and snorkeling gear are free, but you'll pay for excellent lagoon excursions and diving (see "Exploring Fakarava," above).

B.P. 19, 98764 Fakarava (14km/8½ miles from airport). ✆ **98.43.00.** Fax 98.43.01. www.hotelmaitai.com. 28 units. 44,000CFP–55,000CFP (US$440–US$550) bungalow. Rates include all meals and airport transfers. AE, MC, V. **Amenities:** Restaurant; bar; free use of kayaks, canoes, and snorkeling gear; bike and scooter rentals; activities desk; laundry service. *In room:* TV, dataport, fridge, coffeemaker, hair dryer, safe.

INEXPENSIVE
At the south end of the lagoon, **Tetamanu Village** (✆ **48.92.40;** www.tetamanu village.pf) enjoys an idyllic location on the lagoon side of Tetamanu village, with its restaurant and some bungalows actually built over the beach. Negative reports have circulated about this pension in recent years, however, so I would tread cautiously before signing on for a 3-night minimum stay at this lovely but very remote islet.

Motu Aito Paradise ★★   If you really want to get away from it all, this pension on beach-fringed Motu Aito, on the far southern end of the atoll, is a less expensive version of Rangiroa's Kia Ora Sauvage (p. 206). It's the creation of Manihi and Tila Salmon, a local couple who lived in New Zealand—where they polished their English—before retiring to their remote corner of paradise. Manihi designed and built the thatch-roof bungalows and most of the furniture out of local materials; hence, they have enormous Polynesian charm if not luxurious amenities. Mat walls and tree limbs are everywhere. Each unit has a double bed and a single bed, both on platforms. You can pull mosquito curtains over the large open windows, although the trade winds should keep the pests at bay out here. Manihi and Tila, who are yoga enthusiasts, usually barbecue freshly caught fish for dinner. They do not have a bar, so bring your own beer, wine, or booze. A 3-night minimum stay is required, understandable since Motu Aito is a 1½-hour boat ride from the airport.

B.P. 12, 98763 Rotoava, Fakarava (on Motu Aito, south end of the lagoon). ✆ **41.29.00** or 74.26.13. Fax 41.29.00. www.fakarava.org. 6 units. 14,800CFP (US$148) double. Rates include all meals and airport transfers. No credit cards. 3-night minimum stay required. **Amenities:** Restaurant; free use of snorkeling gear. *In room:* No phone.

Pension Havaiki ★   Set beside the lagoon on the southern end of the village, this is the most popular pension in Rotoava—and with good reason, since most of its bungalows have front porches right on the beach. Although they have plywood sides and tin roofs, inside they show traditional Polynesian style, with mat walls and ceilings over their double and single beds. The unscreened windows push out, but each bed has a mosquito net. Every unit has a modest private bathroom with cold-water shower. Owner Clotilde "Havaiki" Dariel makes sure all bungalows have fresh flowers, while her husband, Joachim, who speaks fluent English, tends to the family pearl farm at the end of a long pier out over the lagoon. Meals are served family-style in the dining room.

98763 Rotoava, Fakarava (4km/2½ miles from airport). ℂ **98.42.16.** Fax 93.40.16. www.havaiki.com. 5 units. 19,000CFP (US$190) double. Rates include breakfast and dinner. AE, MC, V. **Amenities:** Restaurant; bar; free use of bikes and kayaks. *In room:* No phone.

Pension Paparara   A short walk north of Maitai Dream Fakarava, this is one of the oldest pensions here. Owner Corina Lenior and her English-speaking husband, Ato Lissant, have five A-frame bungalows beside the rocky lagoon shore. Two of these have tiled bathrooms, while the other share toilets and both enclosed and outdoor showers (all showers are cold water, whether attached to a bungalow or not). If you don't mind walking on a crushed-coral floor, the choice unit has a front porch literally hanging over the lagoon; it also has a second double bed up on a mezzanine. Corina serves meals either in their house or at picnic tables under a thatch pavilion. In addition to owning a pearl farm, Ato operates Fakarava Explorer lagoon tours (see "Exploring Fakarava," above).

B.P. 11, 98763 Rotoava, Fakarava (13km/8 miles from airport). ℂ and fax **98.42.66.** fakaravaexplorer@hotmail.com. 5 units (3 with shared bathroom). 15,000CFP–18,000CFP (US$150–US$180) double. Rates include breakfast and dinner. MC, V. **Amenities:** Restaurant; bar; free use of kayaks; scooter and bike rentals. *In room:* No phone.

Pension Tokerau Village ⚓   You can see the pier sticking out from the Maitai Dream Fakarava, which is a short walk north of this pension, one of the more comfortable here. Owner Flora Borders, who speaks English, has four government-backed bungalows separated from a fine beach by her carefully tended garden. Colorfully decorated with Tahitian fabrics, all have shingle roofs, double beds as well as singles, private bathrooms with cold-water showers, and front porches with lagoon views. Their walls are hung with Bordes family photos, including one of Flora with her father when she was 5 years old. Outsiders with reservations are welcome in Flora's open-air restaurant at the rear of the bungalows.

B.P. 53, 98763 Rotoava, Fakarava (13km/8 miles from airport). ℂ and fax **98.41.09.** 4 units. 11,000CFP (US$110) per person. Rates include breakfast and dinner. AE, MC, V. **Amenities:** Restaurant; bar; free use of kayaks and bikes. *In room:* No phone.

Relais Marama   The French term *relais,* which denotes establishments between a pension and a hotel, does not really apply to this establishment, set in a coconut grove on the seaside of Rotoava village. The accommodations consist of six small and basic bungalows with plywood walls and thatch roofs, plus a three-bedroom house. The place is worth mentioning, however, because you can pitch a tent in the coconut grove next to the ocean and share toilets, cold-water showers, and the communal kitchen with other guests. The owners—Frenchman Jacques Sauvage and Tuamotuan Marama Teanuanua—both speak English.

B.P. 16, 98763 Rotoava, Fakarava (4km/2½ miles from airport). ℂ and fax **98.42.51.** teavanui@divingfakarava.com. 9 units (shared bathrooms). 5,400CFP–6,600CFP (US$54–US$66) double; 1,600CFP (US$16) per person camping. No credit cards. **Amenities:** Communal kitchen; bike rentals. *In room:* No phone.

Vahitu Dream   Jacqueline Moeroa's home, on the seaside of Rotoava village, is as much like a bed-and-breakfast as you will find here. Each of her six rooms has a double bed with mosquito net and an electric fan, but you will share two toilets, three cold-water showers, and a TV lounge with your fellow guests. Jacqueline will prepare local-style meals on request.

B.P. 9, 98763 Rotoava, Fakarava (4km/2½ miles from airport). ℭ and fax **98.42.63**. 6 units (shared bathrooms). 3,200CFP (US$32) per person. No credit cards. **Amenities:** Restaurant; bike rentals. *In room:* No phone.

WHERE TO DINE

The **Maitai Dream Fakarava** resort has the best restaurant on the island. All the pensions serve meals to their guests, and **Pension Havaiki** and **Pension Tokerau Village** welcome outsiders who make advance reservations (that is, before 2pm). As everywhere in the Tuamotu Islands, inquire whether the hotel rate you're paying includes meals.

Snack Teanuanua FRENCH/ITALIAN   This open-air lagoonside restaurant, on the south end of the village and a short walk north of Pension Havaiki, is a fine place for lunch while you're touring Rotoava, or for a sunset drink and early dinner anytime. The French owner, who speaks English, offers salads, burgers, *casse-croûte* sandwiches, and grilled steak and fish for lunch. Dinner sees both French and Italian preparation of steaks and fish. Like every restaurant out here in the atolls, she posts a daily fish special.

Rotoava, south end of village. ℭ **98.41.58**. Reservations recommended July–Aug. Burgers and sandwiches 500CFP–700CFP (US$5–US$7); main courses 1,200CFP–1,800CFP (US$12–US$18). MC, V. Daily 11:30am–2pm and 6:30–8:30pm.

11

The Marquesas Islands

Like most sailors navigating down from California or the Panama Canal, I made my first French Polynesian landfall in the Marquesas Islands, at the country's far northeastern edge. These hauntingly beautiful islands were *really* remote those 3 decades ago. Air Tahiti made the 3½-hour flight up here once every 2 weeks, and few cruise-ship passengers ever came close to the Marquesas.

A lot has changed since then. Air Tahiti now flies from Papeete every day to **Nuku Hiva** and **Hiva Oa,** the two main islands, and the cruise ships *Aranui, Tahitian Princess,* and *Paul Gauguin* regularly ply these waters; in fact, the ships are the best way to explore the Marquesas (see "Seeing the Islands by Cruise Ship & Yacht," in chapter 2).

Some things haven't changed, for the Marquesas still seem a world apart from the rest of French Polynesia. They were the first to be settled by Polynesians, who came from Samoa around A.D. 150 and later went on to colonize Hawaii and Easter Island, the northern and eastern outposts of the great Polynesian Triangle. To this day, the Marquesan language is more like Samoan and Hawaiian than Tahitian. Instead of *"Ia orana,"* up here you are as likely to be greeted with *"Kao'a"*—the origin of Hawaiian's *Aloha.*

The Marquesans are proud of their ancient culture with its rich heritage of arts and crafts, especially stone sculpture and wood carving. As in Samoa and Hawaii, their songs are more melodic and their dances are more graceful and not as suggestive as the hip-swinging versions in the Society Islands. Although more Marquesans now live on Tahiti than up here, those who remain are less stressed than their urbanized brethren.

The geography is different here, too. The islands lie between 7½° and 11° south latitude, placing them much closer to the equator than Tahiti. It's warmer here, but the South Equatorial Current brings cool water from South America, thus tempering the climate and impeding the growth of coral reefs. As a result, these rugged volcanic islands drop abruptly into the sea. Many of the bays up here have beaches (most infested with "no-no" sand flies), but with no coral to form lagoons or fringing coastal plains upon which to build round-island roads, getting to them—or anywhere else, for that matter—is a major obstacle in the Marquesas.

In other words, you will be sorely disappointed if you come to the Marquesas expecting a luxurious beach vacation. But if you're an adventurous soul who likes to shop for exquisite handicrafts, go hiking to spectacular waterfalls, ride the descendants of horses brought here from Chile in the 19th century, and see some phenomenally beautiful scenery from a four-wheel-drive vehicle, then you will thoroughly enjoy these remote and fascinating islands.

1 Introducing the Marquesas Islands

Known in French as *Isles Marquises* and in the local language as *Te Henua Enania* (literally, Ground of Men), the Marquesas Islands are a 350km-long (214-mile) chain about 1,400km (850 miles) northeast of Tahiti and some 500km (305 miles) beyond the Tuamotu Archipelago. These distances alone make them seem as if you are visiting another country. In fact, they are farther away from Tahiti than the Cook Islands, the neighboring nation to the west.

The 10 main islands are all high, mountainous, and extremely rugged. Eroding volcanic caldera form high plateaus on some islands, and dramatic ridges fan out like spokes from the craters to form steep valleys on all of them. Black basaltic cliffs, buttresses, and stove-pipe peaks seem to leap from the sea in many places.

Only 6 of the 12 Marquesas Islands are inhabited today, with a total population of about 9,000. There were many times that number when Europeans first arrived, beginning in 1595 with the Spanish explorer Alvaro de Mendaña, who named the group for Marquess Garcia de Mendoza de Canete, wife of Peru's reigning viceroy. When de Mendaña departed, the population had been reduced by 200 Marquesans killed in a skirmish on Tahuata. English Capt. James Cook dropped by in 1774 and estimated 100,000 people lived on the islands. Thanks to disease, a brief Chilean slave trade, and economic opportunities elsewhere, only 2,225 people lived here in 1926. The population has been increasing thanks to a high birth rate and the Marquesas' awakening to the modern world during the 1990s.

In the absence of coastal plains, more ancient Marquesans lived up in the valleys than down by the ocean. Compared to their seaside relatives in the Society Islands and the Tuamotu, they were mountaineers, and their descendants carry an independent mountaineer streak to this day. Given the steep terrain and no shortage of boulders, they built platforms of stone to make both their *marae* (*me'ae* up here) and their houses level. Their me'ae dwarfed most *marae* in the Society Islands and contained even larger *tohua*, or meeting areas. Unlike the puritanical 19th-century Protestant missionaries in the Society Islands, who made the Tahitians destroy their idolatrous stone tikis, the Catholic missionaries had more faith in the heathens up here. As a result, tikis add a delightfully ancient aspect to many Marquesan *me'ae*.

While some *paepae* (stone platforms) are still in use, you will see hundreds of them deserted and overgrown up in the valleys. Coupled with the mango and orange trees the ancients planted near their platform homes, these depopulated valleys make the Marquesas Islands seem mysteriously haunted.

Today, the islands are administratively divided into northern and southern groups. **Nuku Hiva, Ua Pou,** and **Ua Huka** are the inhabited islands of the northern group. About 80km (50 miles) separate them from the inhabited southern islands of **Hiva Oa, Tahuata,** and **Fatu Hiva.**

Fun Fact **In the Middle of Nowhere**

The Marquesas' nearest neighbors to the east are the Galapagos Islands, approximately 3,400 nautical miles away. When you're on a yacht halfway between the two, you are as far away from dry land as you can possibly be on the face of the earth.

The Marquesas Islands

Nuku Hiva is the administrative center of both the archipelago and the northern group, while Hiva Oa is the capital of the southern islands. They are the only islands that are relatively easy to visit—unless you're on a cruise, when they're all easy to see—and the only two with international-level accommodations.

GETTING TO & AROUND THE MARQUESAS

The remoteness of the islands and the scarceness of inter-island transportation deserve special attention when planning your trip, since they can pose problems and unexpected delays.

It's easy to get to Hiva Oa and Nuku Hiva, since **Air Tahiti** flies to both of them from Papeete several times a week. One of these flights, usually on Saturday, stops in Rangiroa before going on to Hiva Oa and Nuku Hiva (in that order), so you can also fly here after visiting the Tuamotu Archipelago.

Air Tahiti's small planes connect Nuku Hiva, Hiva Oa, Ua Huka, and Ua Pou (no other Marquesan island has an airstrip), so don't be surprised if you are ferried on a smaller plane between Nuku Hiva and Hiva Oa to catch your return flight to Tahiti.

Marquises Hélicoptères, based on Nuku Hiva (✆ **92.02.17;** helicon-nuku@pail.pf), a subsidiary of Tahiti-based Polynesia Hélicoptères (www.polynesia-helicopter.com), has connecting flights between Nuku Hiva and Ua Pou for 12,500CFP (US$125) per person; you can charter flights to other islands as well.

> **Tips   Be Prepared to Be Flexible**
>
> Some of Air Tahiti's flights from Papeete to the Marquesas stop first at Hiva Oa before going on to Nuku Hiva. The airstrip on Hiva Oa sits high up on a ridge and can be closed due to fog or rain, especially from March through August. When that happens, the plane skips Hiva Oa and goes directly to Nuku Hiva. Accordingly, pay close attention to the airline's schedule when planning your trip. And always be prepared to be flexible up here.

Otherwise, there is no scheduled transportation system among the Marquesas Islands. You will be on your own in tracking down one of the small boats or trading ships which irregularly connect the islands. This is easily done between Hiva Oa and nearby Tahuata, but not elsewhere. For this reason, I recommend taking a cruise if you want to see more than Nuku Hiva and Hiva Oa in any reasonable amount of time and with as few hassles as possible.

See "Getting Around Tahiti & French Polynesia" and "Seeing the Islands by Cruise Ship & Yacht," in chapter 2, for more information.

VISITOR INFORMATION

Tahiti Tourisme in Papeete distributes information about the Marquesas (see "Visitor Information," in chapter 2). Nuku Hiva and Hiva Oa both have local tourism committees, which have joined together to host a website at **www.marquises.pf**. The committees have visitor information offices on both islands (see the "Fast Facts" sections for Nuku Hiva, below, and Hiva Oa, later in the chapter).

2 Nuku Hiva ★★

Although it appeared on the world's television screens in 2002 as the setting of the fourth *Survivor* series, Nuku Hiva first became famous in the 1840s, when Herman Melville jumped ship and was befriended for several weeks by the otherwise ferocious Taipi tribe in the rugged **Taipivai Valley.** Based on that adventure, Melville's first novel, *Typee,* launched his illustrious writing career.

Then as now, Nuku Hiva is the largest of the Marquesas Islands and the second largest in French Polynesia. It is so rugged that a majority of its 330 sq. km (127 sq. miles) surely goes straight up and down. Two volcanoes formed Nuku Hiva. The large central crater has eroded away on one side, leaving in its bottom the high, cool **Toovi Plateau,** now devoted to farms and pastureland. On the southern coast, half of another crater fell into the sea, creating deep **Taiohae Bay,** the best harbor in the Marquesas and a favorite port for cruising yachts. On the northern side of the crater, **Mount Muake** abruptly rises for 864m (2,834 ft.), forming an awesome backdrop to the town of **Taiohae,** the capital of the archipelago, and its half-moon harbor. Other than arriving by water, the only way into Taiohae is to descend Mount Mauke's cliff-like face.

The central mountains cut off what trade winds blow at this latitude, leaving the western third of Nuku Hiva a desert, known as the **Terre Déserte (Deserted Land).** Rather than being lush and green, the valleys here are dry canyons reminiscent of the American Southwest. With the exception of a few cattle ranches and homes near the airport, this area is quite literally deserted.

Nuku Hiva

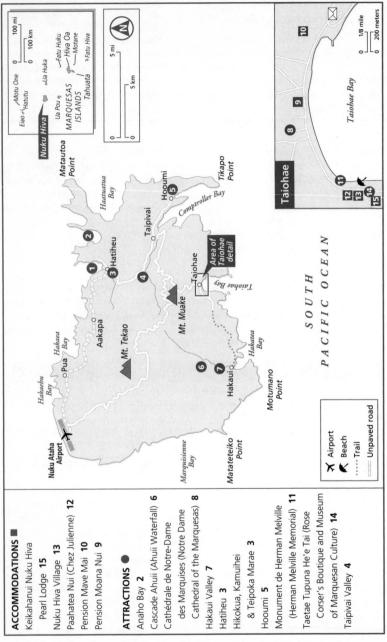

226

ACCOMMODATIONS ■

Keikahanui Nuku Hiva
Pearl Lodge **15**

Nuku Hiva Village **13**

Paahatea Nui (Chez Julienne) **12**

Pension Mave Mai **10**

Pension Moana Nui **9**

ATTRACTIONS ●

Anaho Bay **2**

Cascade Ahuii (Ahuii Waterfall) **6**

Cathédrale de Notre-Dame
des Marquises (Notre Dame
Cathedral of the Marquesas) **8**

Hakaui Valley **7**

Hatiheu **3**

Hikokua, Kamuihei
& Teipoka Marae **3**

Hooumi **5**

Monument de Herman Melville
(Herman Melville Memorial) **11**

Taetae Tupuna He'e Tai (Rose
Corser's Boutique and Museum
of Marquesan Culture) **14**

Taipivai Valley **4**

GETTING AROUND NUKU HIVA

The **airport** is on Nuku Hiva's dry northwestern corner, 48km (29 miles) from Taiohe. The best and by far the quickest way from the airport to Taiohae is a spectacular 10-minute flight over the mountains with **Marquises Hélicoptères** (© 92.02.17; heliconnuku@pail.pf), a subsidiary of Tahiti-based Polynesia Hélicoptères (www.polynesia-helicopter.com), for 75,000CFP (US$75) each way (assuming its one helicopter isn't in the shop for maintenance). Otherwise, your accommodation will send a vehicle to meet you for about 8,000CFP (US$80) per person round-trip. From the airport, it's a tiring ride of at least 2 hours on the winding, mostly dirt road that climbs up and down two steep mountain ridges and across the Toovi Plateau before descending into Taiohae. (You did not misread me; it takes 2 hours to go 48km/29 miles.) Add that to the 3½-hour flight from Papeete, and you can easily eat up a day just getting to Taiohae. There is some great scenery along the way, however, so I look at the ride from the airport to Taiohae as just another four-wheel-drive excursion.

If you're going to get carsick, Nuku Hiva is the place to do it. Although the government is slowly paving them, all of its few roads are narrow, winding, and often treacherous, especially when wet. In places, they are literally blasted into the sides of cliffs. If you miss one of the many 180° hairpin curves, you could plunge more than 1,000 feet to your ultimate demise. For this reason, I recommend exploring by guided tour rather than rental vehicle (see "Exploring Nuku Hiva," below). If you insist on taking your life into your own hands, **Europcar,** in Taiohae (© and fax **92.04.89;** www.europcar.com), rents four-wheel-drive vehicles for about 13,500CFP (US$135) per day. I warned you, though, so don't sue me if you drive off a cliff.

On the other hand, a **bicycle** is a great way to explore the town of Taiohae. Europcar rents them for 1,600CFP (US$16) per day.

There is no regular taxi service on Nuku Hiva as such, but several locals will take you about in their four-wheel-drive vehicles. Your accommodation can make the arrangements, or contact **Nuku Hiva Transports** (© **92.06.08**), **Huku Tours** (© **92. 04.89**), or **Rose Marie Tours** (© **92.05.96**). Fares depend on how far you want to go, so be sure to agree on a price before setting out.

Residents of the outlying villages are as likely to travel by **boat** as they are by vehicle. Several individuals rent crewed boats to take you from place to place, such as from Taiohae around to the Hakaui Valley, or from Hatiheu to Anaho on the north shore. Ask your accommodation to arrange a boat, or contact the local tourism committee for advice (see "Visitor Information" under "Fast Facts: Nuku Hiva," below). The boats moor at the marina on the eastern side of Taiohae Bay.

FAST FACTS: Nuku Hiva

The following facts apply specifically to Nuku Hiva. For more information, see "Fast Facts: Tahiti & French Polynesia," in chapter 2.

Currency Exchange **Banque Socredo** has an office on the waterfront in Taiohae. The ATM is inside the building, so you'll have to come here during banking hours: Monday through Friday from 7:30 to 11:30am and 1:30 to 4pm.

Drugstores **Pharmacie Nuku Hiva,** on the western side of Taiohae (© **91.00.90**), is open Monday through Friday from 8:30am to noon and 3 to 5pm, Saturday from 9 to 11am.

Emergencies/Police The **emergency police** phone number is ⓒ **17**. The phone number of the **gendarmerie** in Taiohae is ⓒ **92.03.61**.

Healthcare Taiohae has a government **hospital** (ⓒ **91.02.00**), and Haitiheu and Taipivai villages both have **infirmaries**. Also in Taiohae, **Dr. Chantel Rigaud-Bermond** and **Dr. Jacques Bermond** (ⓒ **92.08.99**) have a private medical practice, and **Dr. Pierre Puech** (ⓒ **92.00.83**) has a dental office.

Internet Access The island's one hotel and some of its pensions have Internet access for their guests, or you can go to **G-Tech** (no phone), next to Bigot's store in Taiohae. **Nuku Hiva Yacht Services** (ⓒ **91.01.50**; anneragu@hotmail.com) has access for cruising yachts.

Post Office The post and telecommunications office in Taiohae is uphill between the small boat marina and the cruise-ship port. It's open Monday through Thursday from 7:30 to 11:30am and noon to 3:30pm, Friday to 4:30pm.

Telephone There are *télécarte* phones at the Taiohae post and telecommunications office, at the small boat marina, at the ship dock, on the waterfront near the Kovivi restaurant, and in Hatiheu and Taipivai villages. As in the Tuamotu Archipelago, Nuku Hiva residents are more likely to write their phone numbers in two groups rather than three (for example, 920 000 instead of 92.00.00).

Visitor Information The **Comité du Tourisme de Nuku Hiva**, B.P. 32, 98742 Nuku Hiva (ⓒ **92.03.73**; fax 92.03.25; www.marquises.pf), has a visitor information office near the Taiohae *mairie* (town hall). It's usually open Monday through Friday mornings.

Water Don't drink the tap water on Nuku Hiva. The grocery stores sell bottled water.

EXPLORING NUKU HIVA
TAIOHE

It's easy to explore the town of Taiohae either on foot or by bicycle, since its main street follows the curving shoreline of Taiohae Bay for about 3.5km (2 miles). The town hall, wharf, post office, visitor information office, and hospital are on the eastern side of the bay, while most commercial activity is in the middle, or just east of where the airport road comes down off the Mount Muake cliff. The junction is marked by a large seaside cross in honor of the first Catholic mission here.

Follow the next road west inland into the Meau Valley and you'll see the **Cathédrale de Notre-Dame des Marquises (Notre Dame Cathedral of the Marquises),** built in 1977. All of the islands contributed stones and wood carvings to the cathedral. Farther up the valley is a restored *ma'ae,* or Polynesian temple.

On the west side of the bay, you'll pass a large park and then the **Monument de Herman Melville (Herman Melville Memorial),** a terrific wooden sculpture executed in 1991 by noted local artisan Kahee Taupotini. There's a fine view from here back along the bay. This side of the bay is skirted by a black-sand beach, where locals go swimming and launch their racing canoes. For a bit of refreshment and another excellent view, head up the hill to the Keikahanui Nuku Hiva Pearl Lodge, the island's only international-level hotel (p. 233).

Fun Fact **Be Careful around This Tiki**

If you are thinking of infertility treatments, you can save a bundle by visiting Hikokua, the restored *marae* near Hatiheu village. Hikokua has a carved tiki in the shape of a phallus. Any woman who touches it, legend says, will soon become pregnant.

THE NORTHEAST COAST

My most memorable day on Nuku Hiva was spent traveling to the rugged northeastern side of the island in the company of a tour guide. Although it's hardly more than 25km (15 miles) to the end of the road, this excursion required a full day, a good part of it spent just getting from place to place. This is the top trip for anyone to make, since most of Nuku Hiva's key sites are here, especially Melville's **Taipivai Valley** and the highly picturesque northeast shore village of **Hatiheu.** From Hatiheu, you can hike or take a boat to one of the few coral reefs in the Marquesas, at **Anaho** on the island's northeastern corner.

THE TAIPIVAI VALLEY ✹✹   After climbing up Mount Muake out of Taiohae (there's an unbelievably beautiful view of Taiohae Bay from the top), the road follows a mountain ridge, from which you can see one of the beaches used in *Survivor.* It then steeply descends down to **Taipivai** village, at the head of Controller Bay. From there, another coastal road goes southeast to **Hooumi** ✹, a small village on yet another bay. Since access across Hooumi's white-sand beach is easy, cruise-ship passengers land here rather than at Taipivai, beside the shallow Taipivai River.

Backtracking to Taipivai, the road then retraces Herman Melville's footsteps up into the steep **Taipivai Valley.** Your guide will stop about halfway up the valley at the restored *paepae* platforms in a village where Melville is reputed to have stayed. A CITE MELVILLE sign marks the site. You'll see several waterfalls off in the distance as you climb higher into the valley.

HATIHEU ✹✹✹   Once out of the valley, you will soon be looking down at **Hatiheu,** one of my favorite villages in all of French Polynesia. It sits beside a curving black-sand beach. A Mooreaesque ridge topped by basaltic stove pipes dramatically looms over the western end of the beach, creating a quintessentially South Seas scene. Also up on the cliffs, a white statue of the Virgin Mary dates to 1872. Like me, Robert Louis Stevenson was quite fond of Hatiheu and its spectacular setting when he sailed here in 1888. (Great minds do think alike!)

HIKOKUA, KAMUIHEI & TEIPOKA *MARAE* ✹✹✹   Among several restored *marae* in the Marquesas, three of the most impressive are on the Taipivai road above Hatiheu. **Hikokua** is a large open area used for ceremonies, dances, and human sacrifices. Restored for the 1999 Marquesas Festival of the Arts, it has impressive tiki statues. The **Kamuihei** and **Teipoka** sites flank the road higher up in the valley. The expansive Kamuihei part is definitely worth exploring, for it has well preserved tikis, petroglyphs carved into huge boulders, and a pit under an enormous banyan tree, into which human sacrifices were said to have been restrained prior to being dispatched (it's more likely they were used to store food for feasts or to ferment breadfruit *poi,* one of the Polynesians' favorite desserts, which kept well in times of drought). The large size of these *marae* are a testament to how many people once lived in this now deserted valley.

Tips Lunch at Yvonne's

Whether on a tour or on your own, plan to have lunch in Hatiheu at **Restaurant Hinako Nui**, at Yvonne Katupa's **Chez Yvonne** pension across the road from the beach (© **92.02.97;** hinakonui@mail.pf). This thatch-roof charmer specializes in fresh seafood, including delicious shrimp beignets and, from November through January, tropical lobster. Everything comes with fresh local vegetables and bread-fruit fritters, and dessert is often flambéed bananas. Main courses range from 1,550CFP to 2,800CFP (US$16–US$28). If you decide to stay overnight, Yvonne has five simple bungalows to rent in the gardens behind the restaurant for 24,000CFP (US$240) double, including all meals. Bring cash, since Yvonne does not accept credit cards.

ANAHO   Across a ridge east of Hatiheu, the small village of **Anaho** sits beside a white-sand beach in yet another bay visited by Robert Louis Stevenson. This one is unusual, however, because it has one of the few coral formations in the Marquesas, a fringing reef off the beach over which you can snorkel. You can hire a boat at Chez Yvonne (see "Lunch at Yvonne's," above) for the 10-minute ride around to Anaho, or hike over the saddle between the two bays. The path starts at a crossroads about 100m (328 ft.) east of the restaurant. The rather strenuous hike takes about 45 minutes each way, but you'll have a nice view of Anaho Bay from atop 218m-high (720-ft.) Teavaimaoaoa Pass.

HAKAUI VALLEY & AHUII WATERFALL ★★

Over Mount Muake to the west of Taiohae, the **Hakaui Valley** is home to the **Cascade Ahuii,** one of the world's highest waterfalls at 350m (1,159 ft.). The waterfall pours off a high plateau at the head of the valley. This area was a prime set for the *Survivor* television show. Your accommodation can arrange a boat to take you around to Hakaui, from where an ancient stone trail goes upriver to the falls, about a 2-hour walk. Or you can hike or ride horseback from Taiohae to the falls (see "Hiking, Horseback Riding & Scuba Diving," below). However you get here, bring food, water, and insect repellent, and wear shoes suitable for fording the river.

ORGANIZED TOURS

Given the sometimes dangerous condition of the roads and the difficulty of finding things on Nuku Hiva, I recommend seeing the sights on a guided tour. The best are offered by the **Keikahanu Nuku Hiva Pearl Lodge** (p. 233), which offers a full-day tour to the Taipivai Valley and Hatiheu for about 12,800CFP (US$128) per person, including lunch at Chez Yvonne. It also has a half-day version that goes as far as the Taipivai. The lodge's guides speak English.

Another English-speaking guide is French-born, Marquesan-married Jocelyne Mamatui of **Jocelyne Henua Enana Tours** (© and fax **92.00.52;** http://marquisesvoyages. com.pf). She offers several tours, including a full day on the northeastern coast for 16,000CFP (US$160) for one person, 18,000CFP (US$180) for two. Jocelyne is an energetic saleswoman and often shows up at the airport looking for business.

A third option is **Pua Excursions** (© **92.06.87;** www.puaexcursions.pf). Owner Georges "Pua" Taupotini will arrange excursions by land as well as on foot and horseback.

HIKING, HORSEBACK RIDING & SCUBA DIVING

Nuku Hiva has a number of fine beaches, such as those at Hatiheu and Anaho (see "Exploring Nuku Hiva," above), and there's a black-sand beach on the western side of Taiohae. Unfortunately, they are all infested with biting "no-no" sand flies. These nearly invisible pests are particularly aggressive at dusk. If you do go swimming, try to pick a day when the wind is blowing in from offshore, and always lather up with insect repellent.

HIKING   You will have a pretty good hike just walking along the shoreline of Taiohae village. For something a great deal more strenuous, climb the airport road to the top of Mount Muake for its view down over the bay.

In the old days, Marquesans got around by boat or by trails up and over the mountains. Many of these old tracks still exist. One of them begins at the Keikahanu Nuku Hiva Pearl Lodge (p. 233) and goes for 3.5km (2 miles) into **Collette Bay.** The usually deserted beach over there is a fine place for a picnic, but remember to bring—and apply!—your insect repellent.

Rather than taking a boat to Hakaui Valley and Ahuii waterfall (see "Exploring Nuku Hiva," above), you can hike in from Taiohae. It's about a 12km (7½ miles) walk each way, much of it up and down hills and along the river. You can do this on your own, but I recommended a guide. The **Keikahanu Nuku Hiva Pearl Lodge** (p. 233) offers a full day's hiking into and out of the valley for about 10,000CFP ($100) per person, including a picnic lunch at the waterfall. **Marquises Rando** (© 92.07.13 or 21.08.74; frederic.bene@mail.pf) provides professional guides for individuals or groups. Its prices range from 7,500CFP (US$75) per person for a 2½-hour hike to 10,000CFP (US$100) for a 6½-hour trek.

HORSEBACK RIDING   In the 19th century, European whalers and traders brought horses to the Marquesas—plus cattle, pigs, and goats—which soon became wild, and which had a serious impact on native flora and fauna. You are unlikely to encounter a wild pig on Nuku Hiva these days, and most cattle are confined to ranches on the Toovi Plateau, but you will see horses along the roads and goats prowling the rocky mountainsides.

The strong, capable Marquesas horses are prized throughout French Polynesia, and you horse-devotees will have ridden their cousins on Moorea and Huahine. You can ride them here on many of the ancient trails, such as to Hakaui Valley and the Ahuii waterfall.

Up on the plateau just north of Taiohae, Patrice Tamarii of **Le Ranch** (© 92.06.35; danigo@mail.pf) rents horses, leads trail rides, and has 1- to 3-night horseback trips to the north shore, where you camp on beaches. **Alphonse and Sabine Teikiteetini** (© 92.01.52 or 21.24.15; tourisme@marquises.pf) lead half- and full-day rides; contact them for reservations and prices.

SCUBA DIVING   With cliffs plunging into the sea and no fringing coral reefs, the waters off Nuku Hiva present a very different diving experience from that found anywhere else in French Polynesia. The cool South Equatorial Current makes these waters rife with plankton, while limiting visibility to 10m to 20m (33–66 ft.). On the other hand, you may well encounter scalloped hammerhead sharks, melon-headed whales, and other creatures not seen elsewhere in the islands. And even novice divers can enter caves, one of whose sandy floor is populated by stingrays. All of the established sites are off the southern coast, usually within a 30- to 45-minute boat ride from Taiohae.

Rose Corser & Marquesan Art ★★★

Rose Corser and her late husband, Frank, sailed their yacht from California to Nuku Hiva in 1972 to study Marquesan art and culture for a master's degree Rose had in the works. It was a great subject to study, since the islands are justly famous for both their unique culture and their long history of extraordinary art and handicrafts.

More than any other South Pacific islanders, the ancient Marquesans were masters at carving tikis from stone and wooden war clubs and spears from local hardwoods, adorning the latter with the same intricate geometric designs used in their tattoos (which covered most of their bodies) and on the tapa cloth they made from the bark of the paper mulberry tree. Their carving skill was evident even in everyday items such as bowls, axes, pestles, and fishhooks.

The old crafts have been preserved to a remarkable degree, especially carvings made of stone, wood, and bone. The Cathédrale de Notre-Dame des Marquises and the Monument de Herman Melville in Taiohae both are terrific examples (see "Exploring Nuku Hiva," above).

You will come across artisans carving away in their shops in both Taiohae on Nuku Hiva and Atuona on Hiva Oa, and many villages have *centres artisanal* (artisan centers) where the crafts are for sale, especially on cruise-ship days. The best items are often sold in Papeete, however, especially during the *Heiva Nui* festival in July.

Rose and Frank Corser went back to the United States after their 1972 voyage, but they returned for good in 1979. Rose never finished her master's degree, but she founded the marvelous **Taetae Tupuna He'e Tai** ★★★ (© **92.03.82**), also known as Rose Corser's Boutique and Museum of Marquesan Culture, just downhill from the Keikahanu Nuku Hiva Pearl Lodge. Not only is it the best place to buy Marquesan art, but it's also a terrific museum. Here you will see artifacts dating from the Polynesian settlement period of about A.D. 150 to the 1800s. Many of the ancient pieces are on loan from Marquesan families, who have owned them since the dawn of Polynesian time. The carvings, tapa-cloth paintings, grain-seed necklaces, and *kumu hei* (a local lei made of fragrant plants) and other items on sale are all unique pieces of art, not handicrafts. Indeed, Rose's museum is a required stop on your visit to the Marquesas Islands.

At present, Xavier Curvat's **Centre Plongee Marquises,** on the Taihoe waterfront (© and fax **92.00.88;** www.marquises.pf), is the only dive operator in the Marquesas. Bring you own mask, flipper, full wet suit, underwater flashlight, and diving computer. Book well in advance, since Xavier could be leading dive trips to Ua Pou and Ua Huka while you're here. He charges about 6,500CFP (US$68) for a one-tank dive, 12,800CFP (US$128) for two tanks.

WHERE TO STAY & DINE

If you want to stay away from Taiohae, consider **Chez Yvonne,** in Hatiheu village, home of the charming Restaurant Hinako Nui (see "Lunch at Yvonne's," p. 230).

All accommodations here have meal plans. The restaurants at **Keikahanui Nuku Hiva Pearl Lodge, Nuku Hiva Village,** and **Pension Moana Nui** are open to the public, but reservations are advised.

For inexpensive fare, a *roulotte* sets up on the waterfront next to Magasin Kamake (look for the big "Lotto" sign). See "Don't Miss *Les Roulottes*" (p. 112) for more information.

EXPENSIVE

Keikahanui Nuku Hiva Pearl Lodge ✸   Sitting on a hill with a fine view of Taiohe Bay, this is one of the two international-level hotels in the Marquesas Islands, its sister on Hiva Oa being the other. It was originally built as the Keikahanui Lodge by Rose Corser and her late husband, Frank (see "Rose Corser & Marquesan Art," above). Although taken over and upgraded by the Pearl Resort chain in the late 1990s, Rose still owns an interest in the hotel and carefully tends the lush grounds, which are like a botanical garden full of tropical plants. The entire complex blends so well into its natural setting that you hardly notice the shingle roofs when looking this way from Taiohae Bay. Local artisans contributed wood carvings and tapa cloth to the central building and to each of the 20 bungalows, thus giving the entire property a distinctly Marquesan character. The high-ceilinged central building with restaurant, bar, and swimming pool overlooks the bay, as do most of the bungalows (room rates here vary by the quality of each unit's view). Each bungalow has a full picture window in front to take advantage of the bay or garden view, plus a covered porch with wooden lounge chairs. All are equipped with king-size beds and bathrooms with tiled showers. The restaurant, understandably, is the best on the island.

B.P. 53, 98742 Taiohae, Nuku Hiva (western side of Taiohae town). ℂ 800/657-3275 or 92.07.10. Fax 92.07.11. www.pearlresorts.com. 20 units. 18,000CFP–35,000CFP (US$180–US$350) bungalow. AE, DC, MC, V. **Amenities:** Restaurant; bar; outdoor pool; activities desk; limited room service; laundry service. *In room:* A/C, TV, dataport, mini-bar, coffeemaker, hairdryer, safe.

INEXPENSIVE

Nuku Hiva Village   Downhill from the Keikahanui Nuku Hiva Pearl Lodge and across the street from the black-sand beach on the western side of Taiohae, this was once among the better hotels on Nuku Hiva, but it's now down to six functioning bungalows. These simple, oval-shaped units all have small front porches, ceiling fans, double and single beds, and bathrooms with hot-water showers. The thatch-roof restaurant-bar is still popular with locals, who often make merry here on weekend nights.

B.P. 82, 98742 Taiohae, Nuku Hiva. ℂ 92.01.94. Fax 92.05.97. nukuvillage@mail.pf. 6 units. 7,000CFP (US$70) double. No credit cards. **Amenities:** Restaurant, bar. *In room:* No phone.

Paahatea Nui (Chez Julienne)   Also opposite the black-sand beach on the western side of Taiohae, Julienne and Justin Mahiatapu rent three rooms in their house and have six shingle-roof bungalows in their tropical gardens. All of the bungalows and one of the rooms have private bathrooms with hot-water showers, while two in-house rooms share toilets and showers. One family-size bungalow has a kitchen. Guests here are served breakfast, but no other meals.

B.P. 201, 98742 Taiohae, Nuku Hiva. ℂ and fax 92.00.97. paahateanui@mail.pf. 9 units (2 with shared bathroom). 7,000CFP–8,800CFP (US$70–US$88) double. No credit cards. *In room:* Kitchen (1 unit); no phone.

Pension Mave Mai   On a hillside between the boat docks and the center of Taio-hae, Régina and Jean-Claude Tata's pension boasts some of the better-equipped rooms here, with air-conditioning, ceiling fans, balconies or patios, and small private bathrooms with hot-water showers. They occupy a modern, two-story motel-like building, with half the units upstairs, half down. Two units have kitchens. Guests can lounge and have meals on a large patio overlooking the bay.

B.P. 378, 98742 Taiohae, Nuku Hiva. *C* and fax **92.08.10**. pension-mavemai@mail.pf. 6 units. 7,200CFP (US$72) double. AE, MC, V. *In room:* A/C; kitchen (2 units); no phone.

Pension Moana Nui   Across the main drag from the bay in the center of Taiohae, this pension is sometimes called the Hôtel Moana Nui, and with good reason since it doubles as Nuku Hiva's commercial hotel for business types who can't afford the Keikahanui Nuku Hiva Pearl Lodge. The upstairs rooms have televisions (a rarity here), narrow balconies, and private bathrooms with hot-water showers. Four of them are air-conditioned. The owners also rent an air-conditioned bungalow. The pleasant, open-air restaurant serves good French fare, but I was not impressed with the island-style dishes such as shrimp in coconut-curry sauce.

B.P. 33, 98742 Taiohae, Nuku Hiva. *C* **92.03.30**. Fax 92.03.30 or 92.00.02. http://pensionmoananui.ifrance.com. 8 units. 6,900CFP (US$69) double. MC, V. **Amenities:** Restaurant; bar. *In room:* A/C (5 units), TV; no phone.

3 Hiva Oa ★★

Just as Nuku Hiva has had its famous guests in Herman Melville and the sand-fly-bitten cast of television's *Survivor,* so has Hiva Oa, for here lie the remains of French artist Paul Gauguin and Belgian singer-poet Jacques Brel. Gauguin arrived in 1901 to escape what he saw as harassment by French colonial officials on Tahiti. Brel sailed his yacht here in 1975 and just plain fell under the spell of Hiva Oa's beauty and serenity.

The second largest of the Marquesas Islands, Hiva Oa is indeed a place of beauty and serenity. Its rugged scenery was created by a series of volcanoes on an east-west line. One of the craters partially fell into the sea, forming huge **Taaoa Bay** on the south shore and leaving the fishhook-shaped island we see on today's maps. Another crater dominates the center of the island, while a third, on the northeastern coast, also partially collapsed to form **Puamau Bay,** upon whose banks sit one of French Polynesia's most important archaeological sites. In fact, Hiva Oa is pockmarked with the remains of ancient *me'ae,* many of them restored.

Gauguin and Brel both lived in **Atuona,** the island's only town—and my first landfall when I sailed to French Polynesia in 1977. Their graves and an excellent museum dedicated to both of them are highlights of any visit to Hiva Oa. Atuona isn't as physically impressive as Taiohae on Nuku Hiva, but it retains more of a French colonial ambience, with some buildings still standing from Gauguin's day.

GETTING AROUND HIVA OA

The **airport** is at an altitude of 500m (1,650 ft.) up on the Tepuna Plateau, 13km (8 miles) northeast of Atuona. Fog or rain can unexpectedly close the airstrip here, so be prepared to enjoy an extra night or two on Hiva Oa. *Always* plan to fly back to Papeete a few days before your international flight home.

Your accommodation will pick you up if it knows you're coming, or look for **Ida Clark Taxi** (*C* **92.71.33**). Despite her *anglais* name, Ida Clark speaks scant English, but she will take you into Atuona for 1,500CFP (US$15).

Hiva Oa

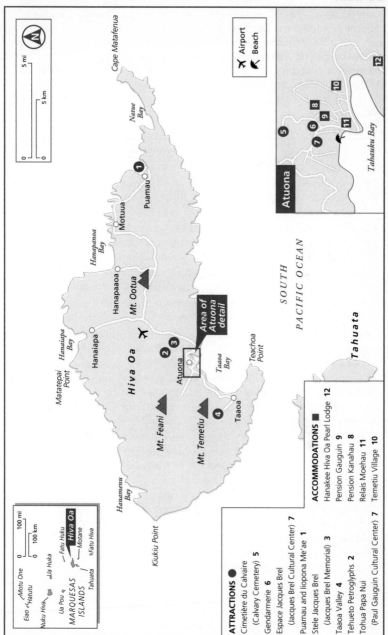

Airport ✈
Beach 🏖

SOUTH PACIFIC OCEAN

Cape Matafenua
Natue Bay
Puamau ● **1**
Motuua
Hanapanoa Bay
Hanaiapa Bay
Hanapaaoa ○ Mt. Ootua ▲
Hanaiapa ○ ✈
Matatepai Point
Hanaiapa Bay
Hiva Oa
2 3
Atuona ○ **Area of Atuona detail**
Taaoa Bay
Teachoa Point
Mt. Feani ▲
Mt. Temetiu ▲ **4**
Taaoa ○
Hanamenu Bay
Kiukiu Point

Tahuata

Atuona detail
5
6 8
7 **6 9** **10**
11
12
Tahauku Bay

Marquesas Islands inset
Eiao ◦ Motu One
◦ Hatutu
Nuku Hiva ▱
Ua Huka ▱
Ua Pou ▱ **Hiva Oa**
MARQUESAS ISLANDS
Fatu Huku ▱
Motane ▱
Tahuata ▱ ◦ Fatu Hiva
0 100 mi
0 100 km

5 mi
5 km
0
0

ATTRACTIONS ●
Cimetière du Calvaire
(Calvary Cemetery) **5**
Gendarmerie **6**
Espace Jacques Brel
(Jacques Brel Cultural Center) **7**
Puamau and Iipona Me'ae **1**
Stele Jacques Brel
(Jacques Brel Memorial) **3**
Taaoa Valley **4**
Tehueto Petroglyphs **2**
Tohua Papa Nui
(Paul Gauguin Cultural Center) **7**

ACCOMMODATIONS ■
Hanakee Hiva Oa Pearl Lodge **12**
Pension Gauguin **9**
Pension Kanahau **8**
Relais Moehau **11**
Temetiu Village **10**

Atuona Rent a Car (℡ and fax **92.67.07** or 72.17.17), **Hiva Oa Location** (℡ **91. 70.60** or 72.83.83), and **David Location** (℡ **92.72.87;** davidkmk@mail.pf) all rent four-wheel-drive vehicles for about 12,000CFP (US$120) a day. The main road is paved from Atuona past the airport going northeast, but be extremely careful when driving here. The north-shore road is so dangerous that I always take an organized tour to see Puamau (see "Exploring Hiva Oa," below).

FAST FACTS: Hiva Oa

The following facts apply specifically to Hiva Oa. For more information, see "Fast Facts: Tahiti & French Polynesia," in chapter 2.

Currency Exchange **Banque Socredo** has an office on the main road in Atuona. The ATM is inside the building, so you'll have to come here during banking hours: Monday through Friday from 7:30 to 11:30am and 1:30 to 4pm.

Drugstores **Pharmacie Atuona** (℡ **91.71.65**) is in the Taiohae *mairie* (town hall) complex in the center of town. It's open Monday through Friday from 7:45am to 12:30pm and 2 to 5:30pm, Saturday from 8 to 11am.

Emergencies/Police The **emergency police** phone number is ℡ **17**. The **gendarmerie** in Atuona (℡ **92.73.61**) is a major landmark in the middle of town.

Healthcare The Atuona government **infirmary** (℡ **92.73.75**) and **dental clinic** (℡ **92.73.58**) are in the Taiohae *mairie* (town hall) complex in the center of town.

Internet Access The island's one hotel and some of its pensions have Internet access for their guests. Otherwise, try **Snack Kaupe,** in the center of Atuona (℡ **92.70.62**).

Laundry If your accommodation won't wash your dirty clothes, contact **Sandra Wullaert** (℡ **27.48.69**) or **Marie-Jo** (℡ **92.73.43** or 26.14.59), both of whom do a booming business during the cruising yacht season from April to September. They will wash, dry, and fold a kilogram (2.2 lbs.) of clothes for about 400CFP (US$4).

Post Office Like most things official in Atuona, the post and telecommunications office is in the *mairie* (town hall) complex. It's open Monday through Thursday from 7:30 to 11:30am and 1:30 to 4:30pm, Friday to 3:30pm. Puamau village also has a post office.

Telephone There are *télécarte* phones at the Atuona and Puamau post and telecommunications offices, as well as at Tahauku harbor in Atuona. As in the Tuamotu Archipelago, Hiva Oa residents are as likely to write their phone numbers in two groups as in three (for example, 910 000 instead of 91.00.00).

Visitor Information The **Comité du Tourisme de Hiva Oa,** B.P. 273, 98741 Atuona, Hiva Oa (℡ and fax **92.78.73;** www.marquises-hivaoa.org.pf), has a visitor information office in a small building near the Gauguin museum. It's open Monday through Friday from 8 to 11:30am and 1 to 3:30pm. **Ernest Teapuaoteani,** who works at the town hall (℡ **92.73.32**), is a font of information about Marquesan culture, and he speaks English as well.

Water Don't drink the tap water on Hiva Oa. The grocery stores sell bottled water. The town of Atuona can run short of water, so don't be surprised if the tap water is suddenly shut off at 8pm.

EXPLORING HIVA OA

A rocky headland divides the town of **Atuona,** on the northern shore of Taaoa Bay, into two parts. Cargo ships and cruising yachts put into **Tahauku Bay,** better known as **Traitors Bay,** a narrow cove on the east of the headland. Other than a black-sand beach and a fresh-water faucet emerging from a cliff, there was little there when I sailed into the harbor back in 1977. Today, a manmade breakwater protects the concrete town dock and small boat marina. From the black-sand beach, the **Faakua Valley** goes off to the northeast.

On the western side of the headland, the original village borders another curving black-sand beach and follows the Vaioa River up into a valley. Unlike Taiohae on Nuku Hiva, where the main road follows the shoreline, here the main street is a block inland, separated from the beach by houses, churches, and parks. Sunset comes early to Atuona, for to the west looms the pointed peak of **Mount Temetiu,** tallest in the Marquesas at 1,190m (3,927 ft.). Atuona's other key landmark is the **gendarmerie,** at the center of town. Two blocks west on the main road is the town's **Tohua Pepeu,** a restored ancient meeting ground where locals stage dance shows and sell handicrafts to visiting cruise-ship passengers.

ATUONA'S TOP ATTRACTIONS

Cimetière du Calvaire (Calvary Cemetery) ★★
Paul Gauguin and Jacques Brel are both buried in this cemetery, on a hill overlooking Atuona. On the way up, you'll pass Brel's home, to the left when the road bends. The large basaltic tombstone bears a plaque with Brel's likeness and that of his mistress and companion, Maddly Bamy (she and Brel's family reportedly are in a constant struggle over the plaque!). I am always amazed at the number of flowers and shell necklaces left on the grave by Brel's fans. Gauguin's tomb is two rows up to the right. You'll recognize it by the sign at his feet and the replica of his *Oviri* statute standing over his head. A frangipani tree constantly deposits its fragrant flowers on the grave. Stop for a few minutes before the cemetery's tall white crucifix and take in the fine view over Atuona and Taaroa Bay.

Atuona, uphill from gendarmerie. Free admission. Daily 8am to sunset. From gendarmerie, follow the signs and climb the inland road uphill.

Espace Jacques Brel (Jacques Brel Cultural Center)
Adjacent to **Tohua Papa Nui** (the Gauguin Cultural Center; see below), this museum recounts the singer's life and displays his airplane *Jojo,* which he used to go back and forth to Tahiti. You will see displays of traditional Marquesan arts and crafts as well. The shop sells CDs and tapes of his albums. The Brel and Gauguin cultural centers share a ticket office.

Atuona, 1 block west of gendarmerie. Admission 500CFP (US$5) adults, 250CFP (US$2.50) children 12–18. Mon–Thurs 8–11am and 2–5pm, Fri 7:30am–2:30pm, Sat 8–11am.

Stele Jacques Brel (Jacques Brel Memorial)
Brel had intended to build a home on a ridge near the airport, spectacularly overlooking Tahauku and Taaroa bays. Construction had not begun when illness cut his life short in 1978 at age 49, but the site is marked by this black rock bearing his portrait and a line from his song *Marquesas.* It's not easy to find, so see it on a tour or ask directions from a local.

Atuona, 5km/3 miles northeast of town on airport road. Free admission. Daily 24 hrs.

Tohua Papa Nui (Paul Gauguin Cultural Center) ★★★
A block west of the gendarmerie is this fine museum, located on the site of Gauguin's last residence. It was opened in 2003 on the 100th anniversary of his death, so discount earlier reports

---

Fun Fact **A Debt Left Unpaid**

Magasin Gauguin, an old clapboard general store beside a huge mango tree near the Gauguin Cultural Center on Atuona's main street, is a relic of the days when Paul Gauguin lived here. It wasn't named Magasin Gauguin in those days, but the painter bought his supplies here, including bottles of liquor, which he kept cool in a well beside his house (he would fetch them with a long bamboo pole). It is said that when Gauguin died on May 8, 1903, he owed the store a considerable debt.

---

about its not being open or not being very good. Start by watching a 2-minute video about Gauguin's life and then take plenty of time to see the reproductions of his paintings by the wife-and-husband team of Viera and Claude-Charles Farina (who could make an illegal fortune as forgers!). Instead of using old copra bags made of jute, as did Gauguin, the Farinas executed these stunningly accurate replicas on real canvas. The exhibition starts with his self-portraits and then follows chronologically. His French Polynesian works, therefore, are near the rear of the building.

Out back is a replica of Gauguin's last residence, which he called his **Maison du Jouir (House of Pleasure)**—an apt name, apparently, since he painted *Barbaric Tales,* one of his best nudes, while living here.

Be sure to shop for Marquesan handicrafts in the boutique, which the center shares with Espace Jacques Brel (see above).

Autuona, 1 block west of gendarmerie. Admission 600CFP (US$6) adults, 300CFP (US$3) children 12–18. Mon–Thurs 8–11am and 2–5pm, Fri 7:30am–2:30pm, Sat 8–11am.

TEHUETO PETROGLYPHS

Reaching northeastward from Traitors Bay, the Faakua Valley is known for its **Tehueto Petroglyphs,** or stone carvings in basaltic rock. Done eons ago, these figures depict human beings with their arms in the air. The site is within hiking distance of Atuona, but I recommend coming with a guide (see "Organized Tours," below).

PUAMAU & THE IIOPONA ME'AE ★★★

Like an excursion to Hatiheu on Nuku Hiva, seeing **Puamau** and its archaeological site is the top trip to make on Hiva Oa. Be prepared for a long day, for it takes 2½ hours to get here from Atuona. The road is paved from town past the airport onto the Tepuna plateau, a cool region with ferns and pines and wild orchids, but it soon turns to gravel and gradually descends to the north shore, where it is literally blasted into cliffs above the serrated coastline. The views are spectacular on this winding road, but it is the most dangerous stretch on Hiva Oa, especially during or just after rain. For this reason, I highly recommend taking an organized tour to Puamau.

On the northeastern side of the island, picturesque Puamau village sits beside a black-sand beach and is surrounded on three sides by the steep walls of an extinct volcanic crater. You may meet some of Paul Gauguin's descendants here, but Puamau's highlight is the restored **Me'ae Iiopona.** One of the most significant ancient temples in French Polynesia, it is famous for the largest stone tiki in all of Polynesia other than the mysterious figures on Easter Island, far off in the eastern South Pacific between here and Chile. In fact, some anthropologists believe the Polynesians who first settled Easter Island came from Puamau. The tallest figure here, a rendition of a Polynesian

Fun Fact **Lunch with Marie-Antoinette**

Most tours stop for lunch in Puamau village at **Pension Chez Marie-Antoinette** (*©* **92.72.27**), which has two simple rooms to rent. On the grounds is Tohua Pehe Kua, the grave of Puamau's last Polynesian queen before the French took over in 1842. She lived until the early 20th century. A popular but unfounded legend says she's buried here with her two bicycles. For sure, Marie-Antoinette's family-style lunches are pure Polynesian: *poisson cru,* goat roasted with onions in coconut milk, boiled mountain bananas, deep-fried breadfruit, and sugary *po'e* (the local version of Hawaiian poi). Lunch is often included in the price of a tour; if not, expect to pay about 2,000CFP (US$20) for a full meal—in cash. You can stay overnight for 6,500CFP (US$65) per person, including all the *po'e* you can eat.

chief named Takai, is much smaller than those on Easter Island, but still stands 2.35m (8 ft.) tall. The most unusual is of a woman lying on her stomach with her hands lifted skywards behind her back, said to be the likeness of a woman giving birth.

Visitors are charged 200CFP (US$2) each to visit Iiopana. It's open daily from 8am to 5pm.

TAAOA VALLEY

About 7km (4¼ miles) by dirt road southwest of Atuona, the **Taaoa Valley** has the greatest concentration of archaeological sites in all of French Polynesia. Some of the more than 1,000 *paepae* (stone platforms) have been restored, but many more still lie in the jungle. Archaeologists believe one of the stone tikis here was used to prepare humans to be sacrificed. Although you can find your way to Taaoa easily enough, the remains occupy most of the valley, so a tour is the best way to see it all.

ORGANIZED TOURS

The best tours with English-speaking guides are organized by the **Hanakee Hiva Oa Pearl Lodge** (*©* **92.75.87**), the island's only international-level hotel (p. 233). It charges 10,500CFP (US$105) per person for an all-day excursion to Puamau, including lunch at Pension Chez Marie-Antoinette. Half-day trips to Taaoa cost 3,500CFP (US$35) per person. One of its guides will take you to the Stele Jacques Brel (Jacques Brel Memorial) or to see the Tehueto Petroglyphs for 2,300CFP (US$23) each. The hotel also has full-day tours to nearby Tahuata island, about an hour's boat ride away across the Bordelais Channel, for 15,000CFP (US$150) per person. You can also contact **Hiva Oa Tours** (*©* **92.70.04;** roga@mail.pf).

FISHING, HIKING, HORSEBACK RIDING & MOUNTAIN BIKING

When you've had enough of Paul Gauguin, Jacques Brel, and ancient archaeological sites, you can hit the great outdoors on Hiva Oa.

FISHING   There's some pretty good hunting for tuna, mahimahi, and other deep-sea game fish in these waters. Your accommodation can arrange a charter boat, or you can contact Gabriel "Gaby" Heitaa, owner of the *Pua O Te Tai* (*©* **91.70.60;** heitaagaby@mail.pf). His is one of the boats that also provides transportation between Hiva Oa and Tahuata.

HIKING   You can hike from Atuona to the Tehueto Petroglyphs and to Taaoa, but I think it's best to go with a guide. The **Hanakee Hiva Oa Pearl Lodge** (✆ **92.75.87**) organizes hiking excursions, or you can contact Bonno Henry of **Hiva Oa Rando-Trek** (✆ **92.74.44** or 27.49.36).

HORSEBACK RIDING   Another way to see the Tehueto Petroglyphs or Jacques Brel's intended home site is on the back of a strong Marquesan horse. Up on the plateau near the airport, **Maui Ranch Tahauku** (✆ **92.47.92**) leads excursions to both sites for about 4,000CFP (US$40) and 5,000CFP (US$50), respectively.

MOUNTAIN BIKING   In addition to horseback rides, the **Hanakee Hiva Oa Pearl Lodge** (✆ **92.75.87**) also organizes mountain-bike excursions to various points in and near Atuona. Contact the hotel for particulars and prices.

SHOPPING

You will see several "Sculpture Traditionnelle" signs around Atuona and Puamau directing you to the workshops of local carvers who are here and at work. The **Comité du Tourisme de Hiva Oa** knows where they are (see "Visitor Information" under "Fast Facts: Hiva Oa," p. 236). The boutique at the **Tohua Papa Nui (Paul Gauguin Cultural Center)** usually has some top-quality pieces and is well worth exploring (p. 237). There's another good handicraft shop across the road from the center.

WHERE TO STAY

All of Hiva Oa's hotels and pensions offer various meal plans. If available, I would opt for a rate that includes breakfast only. You will likely have lunch on an excursion or at a "snack" in town while seeing the sights, so there is little point in paying for that in advance. I also like to dine out while here, so I don't pay for dinner, either.

The most remote place to stay is **Pension Chez Marie-Antoinette,** in Puamau village on the far northeastern shore, at least 2½ hours by road away from Atuona (see "Lunch with Marie-Antoinette," p. 239).

EXPENSIVE

Hanakee Hiva Oa Pearl Lodge ⚐   With a stupendous view out to sea from its perch on a ridge above the eastern side of Tahauku Bay, this is the island's top place to stay—and along with its sister, the Keikahanu Nuku Hiva Pearl Lodge, it's one of the

---

⌒ Fun Fact Play It Again, Gérard

Hotel managers come and go, but you are in for a treat if Gérard Bourgogne is still the boss at the Hanakee Hiva Oa Pearl Lodge when you get here. You see, Gérard only recently came to be a hotelier. In real life—so to speak—he's one of the world's top concert flutists and music teachers. A few years ago, he and wife Nathalie, herself a noted interior decorator, decided they'd had enough of the classical-music scene in Paris. Almost on a whim, they replied to an advertisement looking for someone to manage the Hanakee Hiva Oa. Why not? They stayed at enough hotels during Gérard's concert career that they knew what it takes to make a good one. If Gérard and Nathalie are still here, gorgeous classical music will be softly pervading the hotel's public areas, especially at sunset. In addition to an ear for the note, Gérard also has a nose for the grape, so the hotel's wine cellar should be well stocked with excellent French vintages.

two international-level hotels in the Marquesas. You will be welcomed into the main building by a large and quite immodest Marquesan tiki. It and other carvings throughout the complex will not let you forget where you are. The main building opens to a small infinity-edge pool with a 200° view up the Tahauku Valley all the way around to the Bordelais Channel and (on a clear day) Tahuata island in the distance. Virtually identical to those at Keikahanu Nuku Hiva Pearl Lodge (p. 233), the guest bungalows step downhill below the pool. The most expensive are those with sea views, while the least expensive espy the valley (*Tip:* Bungalow no. 7 looks toward both the sea and the valley). Each unit was decorated by a Marquesan wood carver and has a king-size bed, a porch, and a tiled bathroom with shower. The dining room shares the view and serves very good French fare—it's far and away the best restaurant on Hiva Oa. The hotel offers its guests a wide range of activities (see "Organized Tours" and "Fishing, Hiking, Horseback Riding & Mountain Biking," above).

B.P. 80, 97742 Atuona, Hiva Oa (on airport road 3.5km/2 miles northeast of town). ℭ **800/657-3275** or 92.75.87. Fax 92.75.95. www.pearlresorts.com. 14 units. 28,860CFP–38,850CFP (US$289–US$389) bungalow. AE, DC, MC, V. **Amenities:** Restaurant; bar; outdoor pool; bike rentals; activities desk; limited room service; laundry service. *In room:* A/C, TV, dataport, minibar, coffeemaker, hairdryer, safe.

INEXPENSIVE

Pension Gauguin   The most convenient pension to Atuona's prime attractions, this two-story building sits on a hill behind Snack Make Make (p. 242). It's a bit like an old-fashioned B&B, since the six clean bedrooms share four bathrooms with hot-water showers. The units are equipped with either a double bed or two singles. Guests share a common lounge, dining room, and wide terrace with a view of Taaoa Bay.

B.P. 34, 98741 Atuona, Hiva Oa (in the old village). ℭ and fax **91.73.51.** pens.gauguin@mail.pf. 6 units (shared bathrooms). 3,500CFP (US$35) per person. MC, V. **Amenities:** Restaurant; bar; free use of washers and dryers. *In room:* No phone.

Pension Kanahau 🐾🐾   One of the better pensions in French Polynesia, this fine little inn sits on the ridge between Atuona town and Faakua valley. Marquesan-born owner Tania Dubreuil learned English while dealing with all the yachties who put into Atuona, and she got the idea of building a restaurant where they could come and have dinner overlooking the small boat harbor in Tahauku (Traitors) Bay. Later she installed four standard government-backed bungalows and decorated them in island style, with *tivaivai* quilts on the beds and colorful fabrics on the windows. They also have televisions, ceiling fans, mosquito nets over queen-size beds, sofas that convert to single beds, writing tables, and private bathrooms with hot-water showers. Two of the front porches look across Tahauku Bay to the sea, while the other two face the valley. Most meals are taken under a large shade tree on a patio beside the main house, which has a television lounge. Guests with children can use the kitchen inside. Tania's is a relaxed, friendly establishment that can become quite lively when the yachties are in town from April through September.

B.P. 101, 98741 Atuona, Hiva Oa (Tahuku valley, 2km/1¼ mile east of town). ℭ **91.71.31** or 70.16.26. Fax 91.71.32. http://pensionkanahau.ifrance.com. 4 units. 11,500CFP (US$115) double. No credit cards. **Amenities:** Restaurant; bar; free use of washers and dryers. *In room:* TV, coffeemaker, no phone.

Relais Moehau 🐾   This modern, two-story white building with green-tile roof is the best choice within easy walking distance of Atuona's top attractions. It sits up on a hillside overlooking the black-sand beach of old Atuona. The rooms are all upstairs and open to a veranda that wraps around the building, so you can sit out and admire the view. Although not extravagant, the units are clean and comfortable, each with ceiling fan, a double or two single beds, and private bathroom with hot-water shower. Open to all comers, the downstairs restaurant specializes in wood-fired pizzas as well as French fare. Owners Georges and Gisèle Gramont are originally from the Tuamotu Archipelago. A bit of French will come in handy here.

B.P. 50, 98741 Atuona, Hiva Oa (east side of town). © **92.72.69.** Fax 92.77.62. www.relaismoehau.pf. 8 units. 8,500CFP (US$85) double. MC, V. **Amenities:** Restaurant; bar. *In room:* TV, no phone.

Temetiu Village ✪ Like Pension Kanahau, this is a good establishment on the eastern side of the ridge separating the town from the harbor. Friendly owner Gabriel "Gaby" Heitaa operates the *Pua O Te Tai* fishing boat (see "Fishing, Hiking, Horseback Riding & Mountain Biking," above), while his equally friendly wife, Feli, speaks English. Their seven hillside bungalows all have a view of the bay. Three of them have two bedrooms with three single beds in each. All have televisions and private bathrooms with hot-water showers.

B.P. 52, 98741 Atuona, Hiva Oa (east side of town). © **91.70.60.** Fax 91.70.61. heitaagabyfeli@mail.pf. 7 units. 8,200CFP (US$82) double. AE, MC, V. **Amenities:** Restaurant. *In room:* TV, no phone.

WHERE TO DINE

The **Hanakee Hiva Oa Pearl Lodge** has the best restaurant on the island and a fine view to go with its excellent French and Continental fare. The best pension dining rooms—with the best views—are at **Relais Moehau** (especially if the pizza oven is lit) and **Temetiu Village.** Reservations are essential at both.

Restaurant Hoa Nui MARQUESAN You will have a Marquesan feast at this large restaurant, across the road from the Vaioa River, if you're cruising on the *Aranui,* which must consider it part of your cultural experience. As at Chez Marie-Antoinette in Puamau, the chow is deliciously local, with the likes of goat with onions and coconut milk, fried breadfruit, and sweet banana *po'e.* You can get breakfast and lunch here, but reservations are required by noon for dinner.

Atuona (in Vaioa Valley). © **92.73.63.** Dinner reservations required by noon. Full dinner 2,700CFP (US$27). No credit cards. Daily 7am–10pm.

Snack Kaupe REGIONAL You can get an American-style hot dog at this "snack" next to historic Magasin Gauguin; it's the nearest restaurant to the Gauguin Cultural Center. Otherwise, it serves the usual local collection of burgers, Chinese stir-fries, steak and french fries, and *poisson cru.*

Atuona, center of town behind Magasin Gauguin. © **92.70.62.** Reservations not accepted. Snacks and meals 700CFP–1,100CFP (US$7–US$11). No credit cards. Fri–Wed 6am–8pm.

Snack Make Make REGIONAL East of the gendarmerie, this gaudy green building is another landmark in old Atuona. The menu is typically Tahitian, with burgers, grilled steak or chicken with french fries, poisson cru, chow mein, and shrimp in coconut-curry sauce. You can order to go. The hours can vary here.

Atuona, east of gendarmerie. © **92.74.26.** Reservations not accepted. Snacks and meals 900CFP–1,500CFP (US$9–US$15). No credit cards. Mon–Fri 11am–2pm and 6–9pm, Sat 6–9pm.

Appendix A:
Tahiti & French Polynesia in Depth

Understanding French Polynesia's storied past, the culture and language of its marvelous people, and its fascinating flora and fauna will add an immeasurable richness to your visit here. That's especially true on Tahiti, the first South Pacific island to be examined in detail by Europeans and historically the most significant island in the region. The material in this appendix will give you an in-depth look at the islands. I strongly recommend you read it before beginning your own exploration of these most intriguing specks of land on this vast ocean.

1 French Polynesia Yesterday: History 101

The South Pacific Ocean came to Europe's attention during the latter half of the 18th century with the theory that an unknown southern land—a *terra australis incognita*—lay somewhere in the southern hemisphere. It must be there, the theory went, for otherwise the unbalanced earth would wobble off into space. King George III of Great Britain took interest in the idea and, in 1764, sent Capt. John Byron (the poet's grandfather) to the Pacific in HMS *Dolphin*. Although Byron came home empty-handed, King George immediately dispatched Capt. Samuel Wallis in the *Dolphin*.

Instead of a southern continent, Wallis discovered Tahiti. Surely he and his crew could hardly believe their eyes when they sailed into Matavai Bay in 1767 and more than 500 canoes came out to greet him. Many were loaded with pigs, chickens, coconuts, fruit, and topless young women. The latter, Wallis reported, "played a great many droll and wanton tricks" on his scurvy-ridden crew.

Less than a year later, the Tahitians similarly welcomed French explorer Louis Antoine de Bougainville. Although he stayed at Hitiaa, on Tahiti's east coast, for just 10 days, Bougainville was so enchanted by the Venus-like quality of Tahiti's women that he named their island New Cythère—after the Greek island of Cythera, associated with the goddess Aphrodite (Venus).

Bougainville took back to France a young Tahitian named Ahutoru, who became a sensation in Paris as living proof of Jean-Jacques Rousseau's theory that man was at his best a "noble savage." Indeed, Bougainville and Ahutoru contributed mightily to Tahiti's hedonistic image.

CAPTAIN COOK'S TOURS After Wallis arrived back in England, the Lords

---

Fun Fact **Bougainville and *Bougainvillea***

The French explorer Antoine de Bougainville discovered several islands in Samoa and the Solomon Islands, of which the island of Bougainville—now part of Papua New Guinea—still bears his name. So does the bright tropical shrub known as bougainvillea.

of the Admiralty put a young lieutenant named James Cook in command of a converted collier and sent him to Tahiti. A product of the Age of Enlightenment, Cook was a master navigator, a mathematician, an astronomer, and a practical physician who became the first captain of any ship to prevent scurvy among his crewmen by feeding them fresh fruits and vegetables. His ostensible mission was to observe the transit of Venus—the planet, that is—across the sun, an astronomical event that would not occur again until 1874, but which, if measured from widely separated points on the globe, would enable scientists for the first time to determine longitude on the earth's surface. Cook's second, highly secret mission was to find the elusive southern continent.

Cook set up an observation point on a sandy spit on Tahiti's north shore, a locale he appropriately named Point Venus. His measurements of Venus were somewhat less than useful, but his observations of Tahiti, made during a stay of 6 months, were of immense importance in understanding the "noble savages" who lived there.

Using Tahiti as a base, Cook went on to discover the Society Islands northwest of Tahiti and the Australs to the south, and then fully explored the coasts of New Zealand and eastern Australia. After nearly sinking his ship on the Great Barrier Reef, he left the South Pacific through the strait between Australia and Papua New Guinea, which he named for his ship, the *Endeavor.* He returned to London in 1771.

During two subsequent voyages, Cook visited Tonga and discovered several other islands, among them what are now known as Fiji, the Cook Islands, Niue, New Caledonia, and Norfolk Island. His ships were the first to sail below the Antarctic Circle. On his third voyage in 1778–79, he traveled to the Hawaiian Islands and explored the northwest coast of North America until ice in the Bering Strait turned him back. He returned to the Big Island of Hawaii, where, on February 14, 1779, he was killed during a petty skirmish with the islanders.

With the exception of the Hawaiians who smashed his skull, Captain Cook was revered throughout the Pacific. He treated the islanders fairly and respected their traditions. The Polynesian chiefs looked upon him as one of their own. Cook's Bay on Moorea bears his name. Elsewhere in the South Pacific is a Cooktown, a Cook Strait, any number of Captain Cook's Landing Places, and an entire island nation named for this giant of an explorer.

MUTINY ON THE *BOUNTY* Based on reports by Cook and others about the abundance of breadfruit, a head-size, potato-like fruit that grows on trees

Dateline

- **6th century A.D.** Polynesians arrive (estimated time).
- **1595** Alvaro de Mendaña discovers the Marquesas Islands.
- **1606** Pedro Fernández de Quirós sails through the Tuamotus.
- **1765** Searching for *terra australis incognita,* Capt. John Byron on HMS *Dolphin*

finds some Tuamotu islands but misses Tahiti.
- **1767** Also on HMS *Dolphin,* Capt. Samuel Wallis discovers Tahiti and claims it for King George III.
- **1768** French Capt. Antoine de Bougainville discovers Tahiti.
- **1769** Capt. James Cook arrives to observe the transit of Venus on the first of his three voyages of discovery.

- **1788** HMS *Bounty* under Capt. William Bligh arrives and then takes breadfruit to the Caribbean.
- **1789** Lt. Fletcher Christian leads the mutiny on the *Bounty.*
- **1797** London Missionary Society emissaries arrive, looking for converts.
- **1827** Queen Pomare IV succeeds to the throne.

Fun Fact **Recovering the _Bounty_'s Rudder**

Sunk by the mutineers in 1789, HMS _Bounty_ remained in its watery grave until it was discovered by a _National Geographic_ expedition in the 1950s. The _Bounty_'s rudder is now on display at the Fiji Museum in Suva.

---

throughout the islands, a group of West Indian planters asked King George III if he would be so kind as to transport the trees from Tahiti to Jamaica as a cheap source of food for the slaves. The king dispatched Capt. William Bligh, who had been one of Cook's navigators, in command of HMS _Bounty_ in 1787. One of Bligh's officers was a former shipmate named Fletcher Christian.

Their story is one of history's great sea yarns.

The _Bounty_ was late arriving in Tahiti, so Christian and the crew frolicked on Tahiti for 6 months, waiting for the next breadfruit season. Christian and some of the crew apparently enjoyed the island's women and easygoing lifestyle, for on the way home they staged a mutiny on April 28, 1789, off the Ha'apai islands in Tonga. Christian set Bligh and 18 of his loyal officers and crewmen adrift with a compass, a cask of water, and a few provisions. Bligh and his men miraculously rowed the _Bounty_'s longboat some 4,830km (3,000 miles) to the Dutch East Indies, where they hitched a ride back to England.

Meanwhile, Christian sailed the _Bounty_ back to Tahiti, where he put ashore 25 other crewmembers who were loyal to Bligh. Christian, eight mutineers, their Tahitian wives, and six Tahitian men then disappeared.

The Royal Navy's HMS _Pandora_ eventually rounded up the _Bounty_ crewmen still on Tahiti and returned them to England. Three were hanged, four were acquitted, and three were convicted but pardoned.

In 1808, the captain of an American whaling ship happened upon remote Pitcairn Island, between Tahiti and South America, and was astonished when some mixed-race teenagers rowed out and greeted him not in Tahitian but in perfect English. They were the children of the mutineers, only one of whom was still alive. A handful of the mutineers' descendants live on Pitcairn to this day.

Bligh later collected more breadfruit on Tahiti, but his whole venture went for

---

- **1837** Protestants deny French Catholic priests permission to land. Irate France demands full reparations.
- **1838** Queen reluctantly signs ultimatum of French Adm. du Petit-Thouars.
- **1841** French traders trick Tahitian chiefs into asking for French protection. They later disavow it.
- **1842** Tahiti becomes a French protectorate. Herman Melville jumps ship, spends

time in the _Calaboosa Beretane_ (British jail). He later writes _Omoo_ about his adventures.
- **1844–48** Tahitians wage guerrilla war against the French.
- **1847** Queen Pomare acquiesces to full French protection.
- **1862** Irish adventurer William Stewart starts a cotton plantation at Atimaono.

- **1865** The first 329 Chinese people arrive from Hong Kong to work Stewart's plantation, which fails. Most of the Chinese people stay.
- **1872** Pierre Loti (Julien Viaud) spends several months on Tahiti. His _The Marriage of Loti_ is published 8 years later.
- **1877** Queen Pomare IV dies at age 64.

(continued)

(Fun Fact First Novels

One deserter who jumped ship in the Marquesas Islands and later went to Tahiti, in the early 1820s, was Herman Melville. He returned to New England and wrote two books, *Typee* and *Omoo*, based on his South Pacific exploits. They were the start of his literary career.

---

naught when the slaves on Jamaica insisted on rice.

GUNS & WHISKEY The *Bounty* mutineers hiding on Tahiti loaned themselves and their guns to rival chiefs, who for the first time were able to extend their control beyond their home valleys. With the mutineers' help, a chief named Pomare II came to control half of Tahiti and all of Moorea.

The U.S. ship that found the mutineers' retreat at Pitcairn was one of many whalers roaming the South Pacific in the early 1800s. Their ruffian crews made dens of iniquity of several South Pacific ports, including Papeete and Nuku Hiva in what is now French Polynesia. Many crewmen jumped ship and lived on the islands, some of them even casting their lots—and their guns—with rival chiefs during tribal wars. With their assistance, some chiefs were able to extend their power over entire islands or groups of islands.

Along with the whalers came traders in search of sandalwood, pearls, shells, and the sea cucumbers known as *bêches-de-mer*, which they traded for beads, cloth, whiskey, and guns and then sold at high prices in China. Some established stores that became the catalysts for Western-style towns. The merchants brought more guns and alcohol to people who had never used them before. They also put pressure on local leaders to coin money, which introduced a cash economy where none had existed before. Guns, alcohol, and money had far-reaching effects on the easygoing, communal traditions of the Pacific Islanders.

While the traders were building towns, other arrivals were turning the bush country into coconut and cotton plantations. With the native islanders disinclined to work, Chinese indentured laborers were brought to a cotton plantation in Tahiti in the 1860s. After it failed, some of the Chinese stayed and became farmers and merchants. Their descendants now form the merchant class of French Polynesia.

- **1880** King Pomare V abdicates in return for pensions for him, his family, and mistress. Tahiti becomes a French colony.
- **1888** Robert Louis Stevenson spends 2 months at Tautira, on Tahiti Iti.
- **1891** "Fleeing from civilization," the painter Paul Gauguin arrives.
- **1903** Paul Gauguin dies at Hiva Oa in the Marquesas. All

of eastern Polynesia becomes one French colony.
- **1914** Two German warships shell Papeete, sink the French navy's *Zélée*.
- **1917** W. Somerset Maugham spends several months on Tahiti.
- **1933** Charles Nordhoff and James Norman Hall publish *Mutiny on the Bounty,* an instant best-seller.

- **1935** Clark Gable and Charles Laughton star in the movie *Mutiny on the Bounty.*
- **1942** U.S. Marines build the territory's first airstrip on Bora Bora.
- **1960** Tahiti-Faaa International Airport opens, turning Tahiti into a jet-set destination. Marlon Brando arrives to film a second movie version of *Mutiny on the Bounty.*

Sexy Skin

The United States isn't the only place where it's cool to have a tattoo. With their increasing interest in ancient Polynesian ways, many young Tahitian men and women are getting theirs—but not necessarily with modern electric needles.

The 18th-century explorers from Europe were amazed to find many Polynesians on Tahiti and throughout the South Pacific to be covered from face to ankle with a plethora of geometric and floral designs. In his journal, Capt. James Cook described in detail the excruciatingly painful tattoo procedure, in which natural dyes are hammered into the skin by hand. The repetitive tapping of the mallet gave rise to the Tahitian word *tatau*, which became *tattoo* in English.

Members of the opposite sex rejected anyone with plain skin, which may explain why members of Cook's crew were so willing to endure the torture to get theirs. At any rate, thus began the tradition of the tattooed sailor.

Appalled at the sexual aspects of tattoos, the missionaries stamped out the practice on Tahiti in the early 1800s. Although the art continued in the remote Marquesas and in Samoa, by 1890 there were no tattooed natives left in the Society Islands.

When a British anthropologist undertook a study of tattooing in 1900, the only specimen he could find was on the skin of a Tahitian sailor, who died in England in 1816. Before he was buried, an art-loving physician removed his hide and donated it to the Royal College of Surgeons.

THE FATAL IMPACT   The European discoverers brought many changes to the islands, starting with iron, which the Tahitians had never seen. The Tahitians figured out right away that iron was much harder than stone and shells, and that they could swap pigs, breadfruit, bananas, and the affections of their young women for it. So many iron nails soon disappeared from the *Dolphin* that Wallis restricted his men to the ship out of fear it would fall apart in Matavai Bay. A rudimentary form of

- **1963** France chooses Mururoa as its nuclear testing site.
- **1966** France explodes the first nuclear bomb above ground at Mururoa.
- **1973** Infamous Quinn's Bar closes and is replaced by a shopping center.
- **1977** France grants limited self-rule to French Polynesia.
- **1984** Local autonomy statute enacted by French parliament.
- **1992** France halts nuclear testing, hurting local economy.
- **1995** Conservative French Pres. Jacques Chirac permits six more underground nuclear explosions; anti-nuclear riots take place in Papeete; Japanese boycott Tahiti tourism.
- **1996** France halts nuclear testing, signs Treaty of Rarotonga (declaring South Pacific to be nuclear-free), and tells French Polynesia to start earning its own way.
- **1997** Spurred by economic restructuring funds from Paris, first of several new hotels are built, and Papeete waterfront reconstruction begins.
- **1999** Local officials propose increased autonomy from France.

(continued)

Impressions

It would have been far better for these people never to have known us.

—Capt. James Cook, 1769

monetary economy was introduced to Polynesia for the first time, and the English word *money* entered the Tahitian language as *moni*.

A much more devastating European import were diseases such as measles, influenza, pneumonia, and syphilis, to which the islanders had no resistance. Captain Cook estimated Tahiti's population at some 200,000 in 1769. By 1810, it had dropped to fewer than 8,000.

BRINGING THE WORD OF GOD

The reports of the islands by Cook and Bougainville may have brought word of noble savages living in paradise to some people in Europe; to others, they heralded heathens to be rescued from hell. So while alcohol and diseases were destroying the islanders' bodies, a stream of missionaries arrived on the scene to save their souls.

The "opening" of the South Pacific coincided with a fundamentalist religious revival in England, and it wasn't long before the London Missionary Society (LMS) was on the scene in Tahiti. Its missionaries, who arrived in 1797, were the first Protestant missionaries to leave England for a foreign country. They chose Tahiti because there "the difficulties were least."

Polynesians, already believing in a supreme being at the head of a hierarchy of lesser gods, quickly converted to Christianity in large numbers. As an act of faith, the puritanical missionaries demanded the destruction of all tikis, which they regarded as idols. (As a result, today most Polynesian tikis carved for the tourist souvenir trade resemble those of New Zealand, where the more liberal Anglican missionaries were less demanding.) The missionaries in Polynesia also insisted that the heathen temples (known as *maraes*) be torn down. Many have now been restored, however, and can be visited.

Roman Catholic missionaries made less puritanical progress in Tahiti after the French took over in the early 1840s, but for the most part the South Pacific was the domain of rock-ribbed Protestants. The LMS extended its influence west through the Cook Islands and the Samoas, and the Wesleyans had luck in Tonga and Fiji. Today, thanks to those early missionaries, Sunday is a very quiet day throughout the islands.

- **2001** Long-time pro-autonomy Gaston Flosse is re-elected as president, continuing 20-year control of local government.
- **2004** French Polynesia becomes an overseas collectivity of France with new legislative assembly. Pro-independence leader Oscar Temaru is elected president by a narrow margin, holds office for 4 months until no-confidence vote returns Flosse to power.
- **2005** Special elections on Tahiti and Moorea return Temaru to the presidency. He calls for independence from France over 15- to 20-year period.

THE TRICKED QUEEN   The Protestant missionaries enjoyed a monopoly until the first Roman Catholic priests arrived from France in the 1830s. The Protestants immediately saw a threat, and in 1836 they engineered the interlopers' expulsion by Queen Pomare IV, the illegitimate daughter of Pomare II who had succeeded her father's throne.

When word of this outrage reached Paris, France demanded a guarantee that Frenchmen would thereafter be treated as the "most favored foreigners" on Tahiti. Queen Pomare politely agreed, but as soon as the warship left Papeete, she sent a letter to Queen Victoria, asking for British protection. Britain declined to interfere, which in 1842 opened the door for a Frenchman to trick several Tahitian chiefs into signing a document that in effect made Tahiti a French protectorate.

Queen Pomare retreated to Raiatea, which was not under French control, and continued to resist. On Tahiti, her subjects launched an armed rebellion against the French. This French-Tahitian war continued until 1846, when the last native stronghold was captured and the remnants of their guerrilla bands retreated to Tahiti Iti, the island's eastern peninsula. A monument to the fallen Tahitians now stands beside the round-island road near the airport at Faaa, the village still noted for its strong pro-independence sentiment.

Giving up the struggle, the queen returned to Papeete in 1847 and ruled as a figurehead until her death 30 years later. Her son, Pomare V, remained on the throne for 3 more years until abdicating in return for a sizable French pension for himself, his family, and his mistress. In 1903, all of eastern Polynesia was consolidated into a single colony known as French Oceania. In 1957, its status was changed to the overseas territory of French Polynesia.

A BLISSFUL BACKWATER   French Polynesia remained an idyllic backwater until the early 1960s, except for periodic invasions by artists and writers. French painter Paul Gauguin gave up his family and his career as a Parisian stockbroker and arrived in 1891; he spent his days reproducing Tahiti's colors and people on canvas until he died in 1903 on Hiva Oa, in the Marquesas Islands. W. Somerset Maugham, Jack London, Robert Louis Stevenson, Rupert Brooke, and other writers added to Tahiti's romantic reputation during the early years of the 20th century. In 1932, two young Americans—Charles Nordhoff and James Norman Hall—published *Mutiny on the Bounty,* which quickly became a best-seller. Three years later, MGM released the first movie version, with Clark Gable and Charles Laughton in the roles of Christian and Bligh, respectively.

In 1942, some 6,000 U.S. sailors and marines quickly built the territory's first airstrip on Bora Bora and remained there throughout World War II. A number of

---

Fun Fact **Picking Up a Few Extra Bucks**

Neither Clark Gable nor Charles Laughton came to Tahiti to film the 1935 version of *Mutiny on the Bounty*. While background scenes were shot on Tahiti, they actually performed on Catalina Island, off Southern California. The Mexican actress Maria "Movita" Castenada, who played the chief's young daughter, was later married to Marlon Brando, star of the 1962 version. A young actor named James Cagney, who was vacationing on Catalina at the time, picked up a few extra bucks by playing a sailor for a day.

mixed-race Tahitians claim descent from those American troops.

MOVIES & BOMBS　The backwater years ended in 1960, when Tahiti's new international airport opened at Faaa. Marlon Brando and a movie crew arrived shortly thereafter to film a remake of *Mutiny on the Bounty.* This new burst of fame, coupled with the ability to reach Tahiti overnight, transformed the island into a jet-set destination, and hotel construction began in earnest.

Even more changes came in 1963, when France established the Centre d'Experimentation du Pacifique and began exploding nuclear bombs on Moruroa and Fangataufa atolls, in the Tuamotus, about 1,127km (700 miles) southeast of Tahiti. A huge support base was constructed on the eastern outskirts of Papeete. Thousands of Polynesians flocked to Tahiti to take the new construction and hotel jobs, which enabled them to earn good money and experience life in Papeete's fast lane. Between 1966 and 1992, the French exploded 210 nuclear weapons in the Tuamotu Archipelago, about 1,208km (750 miles) southeast of Tahiti, first in the air and then underground. Their health repercussions are still being debated.

Led by New Zealand, where French secret agents sank the Greenpeace protest ship *Rainbow Warrior* in 1985, many South Pacific island nations vociferously complained about the blasts. That same year, the regional heads of government, including the prime ministers of New Zealand and Australia, adopted the Treaty of Rarotonga, calling for the South Pacific to become a nuclear-free zone. After a lull, French Pres. Jacques Chirac decided in 1995 to resume nuclear testing, a move that set off worldwide protests, a day of rioting in Papeete, and a Japanese tourist boycott of French Polynesia. After six underground explosions,

the French halted further tests, closed its testing facility, and signed the Treaty of Rarotonga.

TO BE—OR NOT TO BE—INDEPENDENT　In 1977, the French parliament created the elected Territorial Assembly with powers over the local budget. A high commissioner sent from Paris, however, retained authority over defense, foreign affairs, immigration, the police, civil service, communications, and secondary education.

Local politics have long centered on the question of whether the islands should have even more autonomy while remaining French, or whether they should become an independent nation. Politicians have been divided roughly into "pro-autonomy" and "pro-independence" camps. On the other hand, neither side wants to give up all that money from Paris!

An additional grant of local control followed in 1984, and in 2004 the islands shifted from an "overseas territory" of France to an "overseas country within the French republic." The local Assembly gained increased powers over land ownership, labor relations, civil aviation, immigration, education, and international affairs (that is, within the South Pacific region). The 2004 law also called for fresh Assembly elections. In a surprise upset, a coalition led by Oscar Temaru, the mayor of independence-leaning Faaa, narrowly ousted long-time pro-autonomy President Gaston Flosse.

Temaru was in office less than 5 months before being toppled by Flosse, who ruled for only 4 months until special elections on Tahiti and Moorea removed him and returned Temaru to the presidency. It was an unsettling period for French Polynesia, but things are stable as we go to press. Although he speaks frequently of independence from France (for which he has been admonished by his French superiors), Temaru has predicted that his goal of complete independence will take as long as 20 years to achieve. In the meantime, he is encouraging economic development at home. The son of a Tahitian father and a Cook Islander mother, he is also improving relations with Tahiti's English-speaking neighbors. And he is insisting that schools from nurseries up teach English as well as French and Tahitian.

2 French Polynesia Today

GOVERNMENT French Polynesia is a "country" within the French system of overseas territories. France sends a high commissioner from Paris and controls foreign affairs, defense, justice, internal security, and currency. French Polynesians have considerable autonomy over their internal affairs through a 49-member Assembly, which selects a president, the country's highest-ranking local official. The Assembly decides all issues that are not reserved to the metropolitan French government.

Local voters also cast ballots in French presidential elections and choose two elected deputies and a senator to the French parliament in Paris (they will pick a second senator beginning in 2007).

The city of Papeete and a few other *communes* have local police forces, but the French *gendarmes* control most law enforcement (they are as likely to be from Martinique as from Moorea).

Local politics breaks down generally into two camps: those who favor remaining French but with increased local autonomy (i.e., pro-autonomy), and those who seek complete independence from France (pro-independence). At press time, the pro-independence party had the upper hand, albeit narrowly. See "French Polynesia Yesterday: History 101," earlier in this chapter.

THE ECONOMY French Polynesia has only two significant industries: tourism and black pearls. More than 200,000 visitors arrive in the islands each year, bringing in more than US$400 million in tourism earnings. Some US$125 million worth of pearls are exported annually, mostly to Japan. Vanilla, copra, coconut-oil cosmetics (you will see the *Monoi* brand everywhere), and an elixir made from the *noni* fruit are minor exports. About 80% of all food consumed here is imported.

French Polynesia would be bankrupt were it not for more than 12€ billion (US$14 billion) poured in by Paris each year. That includes some 150€ million (US$180 million) a year from an economic restructuring fund, set up after France closed its nuclear testing facility in 1996, to foster self-sufficiency by developing the local infrastructure. The fund has paid for public-works projects that have transformed the waterfronts in Papeete and on Raiatea, improved the roads, and built new schools, hospitals, and docks.

In addition, the local government set up highly favorable tax and investment laws, which have spurred hotel construction.

Impressions

Sentimentalists who moan against natives improving their diet with refrigerators and can openers—"Why, they live on Chinese bread, Australian beef and American pork and beans"—could complain with equal logic that dear old ladies in Boston no longer dip tallow candles because they prefer electricity.
—James A. Michener, *Return to Paradise*, 1951

Impressions

You who like handsome men would find no shortage of them here; they are taller than I, and have limbs like Hercules.

—Paul Gauguin, 1891

Bora Bora has most of the new properties, but islands such as Tahaa and Fakarava also received major resorts for the first time. The emphasis has been on the high-end, however, which has done little to reduce the cost to visitors.

All this money translates into both a high standard of living (the *minimum* wage here is about US$1,100 a month plus benefits, compared to about US$850 without benefits in the U.S.) and high prices for everyone. If there is a saving grace for us visitors, it's the lack of tipping and a direct sales tax here, which together can add 25% to your bill elsewhere.

3 The Islanders

Islanders had been living on their tiny outposts for thousands of years before Europeans had the foggiest notion that the Pacific Ocean existed. Even after Vasco Nuñez de Balboa crossed the Isthmus of Panama and discovered this largest of oceans in 1513, and Ferdinand Magellan sailed across it in 1521, more than 250 years went by before Europeans paid much attention to the islands that lay upon it.

The early European explorers were astounded to find the far-flung South Pacific islands inhabited by peoples who shared similar physical characteristics, languages, and cultures. How had these people—who lived a late Stone Age existence and had no written languages—crossed the vast Pacific to these remote islands long before Christopher Columbus had the courage to sail out of sight of land? Where had they come from? Those questions baffled the early European explorers, and they continue to intrigue scientists and scholars today.

THE FIRST SETTLERS The late Thor Heyerdahl drifted in his raft *Kon Tiki* from South America to French Polynesia in 1947, to prove his theory that the Polynesians came from the Americas.

Bolstered by recent DNA studies linking the Polynesians to Taiwan, however, experts now believe that the Pacific Islanders have their roots in eastern Asia. The generally accepted view is that during the Ice Age, a race of early humans known as Australoids migrated from Southeast Asia to Papua New Guinea and Australia, when those two countries were joined as one land mass. Another group, the Papuans, arrived from Southeast Asia between 5,000 and 10,000 years ago. Several thousands of years later, a lighter-skinned race known as Austronesians pushed the Papuans inland and out into the more eastern South Pacific islands.

The most tangible remains of the early Austronesians are remnants of pottery, the first shards of which were found during the 1970s in Lapita, a village in New Caledonia. Probably originating in Papua New Guinea, Lapita pottery spread east as far as Tonga. Lapita pottery was used in the South Pacific islands for a millennium, but by the time European explorers arrived in the 1770s, gourds and coconut shells were the only crockery used by the Polynesians, who cooked their meals underground and ate with their fingers off banana leaves.

THE POLYNESIANS The Polynesians' ancestors stopped in Fiji on their migration from Southeast Asia, but later pushed on into the eastern South Pacific. Archaeologists now believe that they settled in Tonga and Samoa more than 3,000 years ago and then slowly fanned out to colonize the vast Polynesian triangle, which stretches from New Zealand in the south to Hawaii in the north and to Easter Island to the east. In French Polynesia, they landed first in the Marquesas (where the language and culture still have Samoan traces), and then backtracked to Raiatea and the other islands before eventually arriving in Hawaii and New Zealand.

These extraordinary mariners crossed thousands of miles of ocean in large, double-hulled canoes capable of carrying hundreds of people, animals, and plants. They navigated by the stars, the wind, the clouds, the shape of the waves, and the flight pattern of birds—a remarkable achievement for a people who had no written languages.

Their ancestors fought each other with war clubs for thousands of years, and it stands to reason that the biggest, strongest, and quickest survived (many modern Polynesians have become professional football and rugby players). The notion that all Polynesians are fat is incorrect. In the old days, body size did indeed denote wealth and status, but obesity today is more likely attributable to poor diet. On the other hand, village chiefs are still expected to partake of food and drink with anyone who visits to discuss a problem; hence, great weight remains an unofficial marker of social status.

TAHITIAN SOCIETY Polynesians developed highly structured societies. On Tahiti, they were highly stratified into three classes: chiefs and priests, landowners, and commoners. Among the commoners was a subclass of slaves, mostly war prisoners. One's position in society was hereditary, with primogeniture the general rule. In general, women were equal to men, although they could not act as priests.

A peculiar separate class of wandering dancers and singers, known as the *Arioi,* traveled about the Society Islands, performing ritual dances and shows—some of them sexually explicit—and living in a state of total sexual freedom. Family values were the least of their concerns; in fact, members immediately killed any children born into their clan.

The Tahitians had no written language, but their life was governed by an elaborate set of rules that would challenge modern legislators' abilities to reduce them to writing. Everyday life was governed by a system based on *tabu,* a rigid list of things a person could or could not do, depending on his or her status in life. *Tabu* and its variants *(tapu, tambu)* are used throughout the South Pacific to mean "do not enter"; from them derives the English word *taboo.*

Western principles of ownership have made inroads, but by and large almost everything in Polynesia—especially land— is owned communally by families. In effect, the system is pure communism at the family level. If your brother has a crop of taro and you're hungry, then some of that taro belongs to you. The same principle applies to a can of corned beef sitting

Impressions

Now the cunning lay in this, that the Polynesians have rules of hospitality that have all the force of laws; an etiquette of absolute rigidity made it necessary for the people of the village not only to give lodging to the strangers, but to provide them with food and drink for as long as they wished to stay.

—W. Somerset Maugham, 1921

Fun Fact Jotting It Down

No Polynesian language was written until Peter Heywood jotted down a Tahitian vocabulary while awaiting trial for his part in the mutiny on the *Bounty* (he was convicted but pardoned). The early missionaries who later translated the Bible into Tahitian decided which letters of the Roman alphabet to use to approximate the sounds of the Polynesian languages. These tended to vary from place to place. For example, they used the consonants *t* and *v* in Tahitian. In Hawaiian, which is similar, they used *k* and *w*. The actual Polynesian sounds are somewhere in between.

---

on a shelf in a store, which helps explain why most of the grocery shops in French Polynesia are owned by the Chinese. It also explains why you should keep a wary eye on your valuables.

Although some islanders would be considered poor by Western standards, the extended family system insures that few go hungry or sleep without a roof over his or her head. Most of the thatch roofs in Polynesia today are actually bungalows at the resort hotels; nearly everyone else sleeps under tin. It's little wonder, therefore, that the islands are inhabited for the most part by friendly, peaceable, and extraordinarily courteous people.

A HIERARCHY OF GODS The ancient Tahitians worshipped a hierarchy of gods. At its head stood Taaroa, a supreme deity known as Tangaroa in the Cook Islands and Tangaloa in Samoa. *Mana,* or power, came down from the gods to each human, depending on his or her position in society. The highest chiefs had so much mana that they were considered godlike, if not actually descended from the gods.

The Tahitians worshipped their gods on *maraes* (ancient temples or meeting places) built of stones. Every family had a small marae, which served the same functions as a chapel would today, and villages and entire districts—even islands—built large maraes that served not only as places of worship but also as meeting sites. Elaborate religious ceremonies were held on the large central marae. Priests prayed that the gods would come down and reside in carved tikis and other objects during the ceremonies (the objects lost all religious meaning afterward). Sacrifices were offered to the gods, sometimes including humans, mostly war prisoners or troublemakers. Despite the practice of human sacrifice, cannibalism apparently was never practiced in the Society Islands, although it was fairly widespread in the Marquesas.

The souls of the deceased were believed to return to Hawaiki, the homeland from which their Polynesian ancestors had come. In all Polynesian islands, the souls departed for it from the northwest corner of each island. That's in the direction of Asia, from whence their ancestors came.

THE CHINESE The outbreak of the American Civil War in 1861 resulted in a worldwide shortage of cotton. In September 1862, an Irish adventurer named William Stewart founded a cotton plantation at Atimaono, Tahiti's only large tract of flat land. The Tahitians weren't the least bit interested in working for Stewart, so he imported a contingent of Chinese laborers. The first 329 of them arrived from Hong Kong in February 1865. Stewart ran into financial difficulties, which were compounded by the drop in cotton prices after the American

South resumed production after 1868; this led to the collapse of his empire.

Nothing remains of Stewart's plantation at Atimaono (a golf course now occupies most of the land), but many of his Chinese laborers decided to stay. They grew vegetables for the Papeete market, saved their money, and invested in other businesses. Their descendants and those of subsequent immigrants from China now influence the economy far in excess of their numbers. They run nearly all of French Polynesia's grocery and general merchandise stores, which in French are called *magasins chinois,* or Chinese stores.

4 Languages

With the exception of some older Polynesians, everyone speaks **French,** the official language. **Tahitian** is quickly gaining ground as a coequal now that a pro-independence government is in power. **English** is also taught as a third language in most schools (and all of those operated by the Chinese community), and it's a prerequisite for getting a hotel job involving guest relations.

You can converse in English with your hotel's professional and activities staff, but not necessarily with the housemaids.

Some knowledge of French will also be useful on Maupiti and in the Tuamotu and Marquesas islands, where English is not widely spoken. The material in "Appendix B: Useful French Terms & Phrases," will help you get along and make friends while you're at it.

Many young Tahitians are eager to learn English, if for no other reason than to understand the lyrics of American songs, which dominate the radio airwaves in French Polynesia. Accordingly, you can get by with English in shops, hotels,

Sex & the Single Polynesian

The puritanical Christian missionaries who arrived in the South Pacific during the early 19th century convinced the islanders that they should clothe their nearly naked bodies. They had less luck, however, when it came to sex. To the islanders, sex was as much a part of life as any other daily activity, and they uninhibitedly engaged in it with a variety of partners from adolescence until marriage.

Even today, they have a somewhat laissez-faire attitude about premarital sex. Every child, whether born in or out of wedlock, is accepted into one of the extended families that are the bedrock of Polynesian society. Mothers, fathers, grandparents, aunts, uncles, and cousins of every degree are all part of the close-knit Polynesian family. Relationships sometimes are so blurred that every adult woman within a mile is known as a child's "auntie"—even the child's mother.

Male transvestitism, homosexuality, and bisexuality are facts of life in Polynesia, where families with a shortage of female offspring will raise young boys as girls. Some of these youths grow up to be heterosexual; others become homosexual or bisexual and, often appearing publicly in women's attire, actively seek out the company of tourists. In Tahitian, these males are known as *mahus;* in Samoan, *magus;* and in Tongan, *fakaleitis.*

> ### Tips "Oh-oh"—How to Spell Like a Tahitian
>
> When spelling Tahitian words, many cultural activists advocate the use of apostrophes to indicate glottal stops—those slight pauses between some vowels similar to the tiny break between "Oh-oh!" in English. Moorea, for example, is pronounced Moh-*oh*-ray-ah, with a glottal stop between *Moh* and *oh,* and thus is often spelled Mo'orea. Likewise, you may see Papeete spelled Pape'ete. Abundant apostrophes already appear in written Tongan and Samoan, but in this book I have used the traditional spellings, with apostrophes appearing only where they are used in an establishment's name, such as Le Taha'a Private Island & Spa. If you want to spell like a Tahitian, look for a handbook such as D. T. Tyron's *Say It in Tahitian.*

restaurants, and other businesses frequented by tourists. Once you get off the beaten path, however, an ability to speak what I call *francais touristique*—tourist French, as in asking directions to the loo—will be very helpful if not outright essential. I really need my schoolbook French on Maupiti, and it comes in handy in the Marquesas, too.

Not to fear: Tahitians are enormously friendly folk, and most will immediately warm to you when they discover you don't speak French, or that you speak it haltingly or with a pronounced accent.

TAHITIAN PRONUNCIATION A little knowledge of Tahitian will also help you correctly pronounce the tongue-tying place names here.

All Polynesian languages, including Tahitian, consist primarily of vowel sounds, which are pronounced in the Roman fashion—that is, *ah, ay, ee, oh,* and *ou,* not *ay, ee, eye, oh,* and *you,* as in English. Almost all vowels are sounded separately. For example, Tahiti's airport is at Faaa, which is pronounced Fah-*ah*-ah, not Fah. Papeete is Pah-pay-*ay*-tay, not Pa-pee-tee. Paea is Pah-*ay*-ah.

The consonants used in Tahitian are *f, h, m, n, p, r, t,* and *v.* There are some special rules regarding their sounds, but you'll be understood if you say them as you would in English.

USEFUL TAHITIAN WORDS To help you impress the locals with what a really friendly tourist you are, here are a few Tahitian words you can use on them:

English	Tahitian	Pronunciation
hello	**ia orana**	ee-ah oh-*rah*-na (sounds like "your honor")
welcome	**maeva**	mah-*ay*-vah
goodbye	**parahi**	pah-*rah*-hee
good	**maitai**	*my*-tie
very good	**maitai roa**	*my*-tie-*row*-ah
thank you	**maruru**	mah-*roo*-roo
thank you very much	**maruru roa**	mah-*roo*-roo *row*-ah
good health!	**manuia**	mah-*new*-yah
woman	**vahine**	vah-*hee*-nay

English	Tahitian	Pronunciation
man	**tane**	*tah*-nay
sarong	**pareu**	pah-*ray*-oo
small islet	**motu**	*moh*-too
take it easy	**hare maru**	*ha*-ray *mah*-roo
fed up	**fiu**	few

5 The Islands & the Sea: Flora & Fauna

The Polynesian islands were formed by molten lava escaping upward through cracks in the earth's crust as it has crept slowly northwestward over the eons, thus building great seamounts. Tahiti and the Society Islands are called "high islands" because they have mountains soaring into the clouds. In contrast, the atolls of the Tuamotu Archipelago are pancake-flat because they were formed when the islands sank back into the sea, leaving only a thin necklace of coral islets to circumscribe their lagoons and mark their original boundaries. In some cases, geologic forces have once again lifted the atolls, forming "raised" islands whose sides drop precipitously into the sea. Bora Bora is the prime example of a partially sunken island, with the remnants of mountains sticking up in its lagoon.

Most species of plants and animals native to the islands originated in Southeast Asia and worked their way eastward across the Pacific, by natural distribution or in the company of humans. The number of native species diminishes the farther east one goes. Very few local plants or animals came from the Americas, the one notable exception being the sweet potato, which may have been brought back from South America by voyaging Polynesians.

PLANTS   In addition to the west-to-east differences, the flora changes according to each island's topography. The mountainous islands make rain from the moist trade winds and thus possess a greater variety of plants. Their interior highlands are covered with ferns, native bush, or grass. The low atolls, on the other hand, get sparse rainfall and support little other than scrub bush and coconut palms.

Ancient settlers brought coconut palms, breadfruit, taro, paper mulberry, pepper *(kava)*, and bananas to the isolated midocean islands because of their usefulness as food or fiber. Accordingly, they are generally found in the inhabited areas of the islands and not so often in the interior bush.

With a few indigenous exceptions, such as the *tiare* (Tahiti gardenia), tropical flowers also worked their way east in the company of humans. Bougainvillea, hibiscus, allamanda, poinsettia, poinciana (the flame tree), croton, frangipani (plumeria), ixora, canna, and water lilies all give colorful testament to the islanders' love for flowers of every hue in the rainbow. The aroma of the white, yellow, or pink frangipani is so sweet, it's used as perfume on many islands.

ANIMALS & BIRDS   The fruit bat, or "flying fox," and some species of insect-eating bats are the only mammals native to the South Pacific islands. The early settlers introduced dogs, chickens, pigs, rats, and mice. There are few land snakes or other reptiles in the islands. The notable exceptions are geckos and skinks, those little lizards that seem to be everywhere. Don't go berserk when a gecko walks upside-down across the ceiling of your bungalow: They are harmless and actually perform a valuable service by eating mosquitoes and other insects.

The number and variety of species of bird life also diminish as you go eastward. Most land birds live in the bush away from settlements and the accompanying cats, dogs, and rats. For this reason, the birds most likely to be seen are terns, boobies, herons, petrels, noddies, and others that earn their livelihoods from the sea. Of the introduced birds, the Indian myna exists in the greatest numbers. Brought to the South Pacific early in the 20th century to control insects, the myna quickly became a noisy nuisance in its own right. Mynahs are extremely adept at stealing the toast off your breakfast table.

SEA LIFE   The tropical South Pacific Ocean virtually teems with sea life. More than 600 species of coral—10 times the number found in the Caribbean—form the great reefs that make the South Pacific a divers' mecca. Billions of tiny coral polyps build their own skeletons on top of those left by their ancestors, until they reach the level of low tide. Then they grow outward, extending the edge of the reef. The old skeletons are white, and the living polyps present a rainbow of colors; they grow best and are most colorful in the clear, salty water on the outer edge or in channels, where the tides and waves wash fresh seawater along and across the reef. A reef can grow as much as 2 inches a year in ideal conditions. Although pollution, rising seawater temperature, and a proliferation of crown-of-thorns starfish have greatly hampered reef growth—and beauty—in parts of the South Pacific, there are still many areas where the color and variety of corals are unmatched.

Like gigantic aquariums, a plethora of tropical fish and other marine life fill most of the lagoons. Many hotel boutiques and bookstores in the main towns sell pamphlets containing photographs and descriptions of the creatures that will peer into your face mask. Not all sea creatures are harmless, so be sure to read "Be Careful in the Water" (p. 30).

Humpback whales migrate to the islands from June to October, and sea turtles lay their eggs on some beaches from November through February. Sea turtles and whales are on the list of endangered species, and many countries, including the United States, prohibit the importation of their shells, bones, and teeth.

Appendix B:
Useful French Terms & Phrases

It's amazing how a word or two of halting French will often change your hosts' disposition. In my experience, this is especially true of the islanders, who genuinely appreciate your attempts to communicate with them in a language they understand. To be frank, many independence-minded Tahitians are not particularly fond of French people, but they quickly warm to us non-French visitors when they hear us speaking less than perfect *Français*. It's a quick tip-off that we are from someplace other than France.

At the very least, try to learn a few numbers, basic greetings, and—above all—the life-raft phrase, *Parlez-vous anglais?* (Do you speak English?). Many islanders do speak passable English and will use it liberally, if you demonstrate the basic courtesy of greeting them in their language.

Go out, try our glossary, and don't be bashful. *Bonne chance!* (Good luck!)

1 Basic French Vocabulary & Phrases

English	French	Pronunciation
Yes/No	**Oui/Non**	wee/nohn
Okay	**D'accord**	*dah*-core
Please	**S'il vous plaît**	seel voo play
Thank you	**Merci**	*mair*-see
You're welcome	**De rien**	duh ree-*ehn*
Hello (during daylight)	**Bonjour**	bohn-*jhoor*
Good evening	**Bonsoir**	bohn-*swahr*
Goodbye	**Au revoir**	o ruh-*vwahr*
What's your name?	**Comment vous appellez-vous?**	ko-*mahn*-voo-za-pell-ay-*voo*?
My name is	**Je m'appelle**	*jhuh* ma-pell
How are you?	**Comment allez-vous?**	kuh-mahn-tahl-ay-*voo*?
So-so	**Comme ci, comme ça**	kum-*see*, kum-*sah*
I'm sorry/ excuse me	**Pardon**	pahr-*dohn*

GETTING AROUND/STREET SMARTS

Do you speak English?	**Parlez-vous anglais?**	par-lay-voo-ahn-*glay*?

English	French	Pronunciation
I don't speak French	**Je ne parle pas français**	jhuh ne parl pah frahn-*say*
I don't understand	**Je ne comprends pas**	jhuh ne kohm-*prahn* pas
Could you speak more loudly/ more slowly?	**Pouvez-vous parler plus fort/plus lentement?**	Poo-*vay* voo par-lay ploo for/ ploo lan-te-*ment*?
What is it?	**Qu'est-ce que c'est?**	kess-kuh-*say*?
What time is it?	**Qu'elle heure est-il?**	kel uhr eh-*teel*?
What?	**Quoi?**	kwah?
How? or What did you say?	**Comment?**	ko-*mahn*?
When?	**Quand?**	kahn?
Where is?	**Où est?**	oo *eh*?
Who?	**Qui?**	kee?
Why?	**Pourquoi?**	poor-*kwah*?
here/there	**ici/là**	ee-*see*/lah
left/right	**à gauche/à droite**	a goash/a drwaht
straight ahead	**tout droit**	too-*drwah*
Fill the tank (of a car), please	**Le plein, s'il vous plaît**	luh plan, seel-voo-*play*
I want to get off at	**Je voudrais descendre à**	jhe voo-*dray* day-son drah-ah
airport	**l'aéroport**	lair-o-*por*
bank	**la banque**	lah bahnk
bridge	**le pont**	luh pohn
bus station	**la gare routière**	lah *gar* roo-tee-*air*
bus stop	**l'arrêt de bus**	lah-*ray* duh boohss
by means of a car	**en voiture**	ahn vwa-*toor*
cashier	**la caisse**	lah kess
church	**l'église**	lay-*gleez*
driver's license	**le permis de conduire**	luh per-*mee* duh con-*dweer*
elevator	**l'ascenseur**	lah sahn *seuhr*
entrance (to a building or a city)	**une porte**	ewn port
exit (from a building or a freeway)	**une sortie**	ewn sor-*tee*
gasoline	**du pétrol/de l'essence**	duh pay-*troll*/de lay-*sahns*

English	French	Pronunciation
hospital	**l'hôpital**	low-pee-*tahl*
luggage storage	**la consigne**	lah kohn-*seen*-yuh
museum	**le musée**	luh mew-*zay*
no smoking	**défense de fumer**	day-*fahns* de fu-may
one-day pass	**le ticket journalier**	luh tee-*kay* jhoor-nall-ee-*ay*
one-way ticket	**l'aller simple**	lah-*lay* sam-pluh
police	**la police**	lah po-*lees*
round-trip ticket	**l'aller-retour**	lah-*lay* re-*toor*
second floor	**le premier étage**	luh prem-ee-*ehr* ay-*taj*
slow down	**ralentir**	rah-lahn-*teer*
store	**le magasin**	luh ma-ga-*zehn*
street	**la rue**	lah roo
telephone	**le téléphone**	luh tay-lay-*phone*
ticket	**un billet**	uh *bee*-yay
toilets	**les toilettes/les WC**	lay twa-*lets*/les vay-*say*

NECESSITIES

I'd like	**Je voudrais**	jhe voo-*dray*
a room	**une chambre**	ewn *shahm*-bruh
the key	**la clé (la clef)**	la clay
How much does it cost?	**C'est combien?/ Ça coûte combien?**	say comb-bee-*ehn*?/sah coot comb-bee-*ehn*?
That's expensive	**C'est cher/chère**	say share
Do you take credit cards?	**Est-ce que vous acceptez les cartes de credit?**	es-kuh voo zaksep-*tay* lay kart duh creh-*dee*?
I'd like to buy	**Je voudrais acheter**	jhe voo-*dray* ahsh-*tay*
aspirin	**des aspirines/des aspros**	deyz ahs-peer-*een*/deyz ahs-*proh*
condoms	**des préservatifs**	day pray-ser-va-*teef*
a dress	**une robe**	ewn robe
envelopes	**des envelopes**	days ahn-veh-*lope*
a gift	**un cadeau**	uh kah-*doe*
a handbag	**un sac**	uh sahk
a hat	**un chapeau**	uh shah-*poh*
a map of the city	**un plan de ville**	uh plahn de *veel*
a newspaper	**un journal**	uh zhoor-*nahl*
a phone card	**une carte téléphonique**	uh cart tay-lay-fone-*eek*
a postcard	**une carte postale**	ewn cart pos-*tahl*
a road map	**une carte routière**	ewn cart roo-tee-*air*

English	French	Pronunciation
shoes	**des chaussures**	day show-*suhr*
soap	**du savon**	dew sah-*vohn*
a stamp	**un timbre**	uh *tam*-bruh
writing paper	**du papier è lettres**	dew pap-pee-*ay* a *let*-ruh

IN YOUR HOTEL

Are taxes included?	**Est-ce que les taxes sont comprises?**	ess-keh lay taks son com-*preez*?
Is breakfast included?	**Petit déjeuner inclus?**	peh-*tee* day-jheun-*ay* ehn-*klu*?
We're staying for . . . days	**On reste pour . . . jours**	ohn rest poor . . . jhoor
balcony	**un balcon**	uh *bahl*-cohn
bathtub	**une baignoire**	ewn bayn-*nwar*
hot and cold water	**l'eau chaude et froide**	low showed ay fwad
room	**une chambre**	ewn *shawm*-bruh
shower	**une douche**	ewn doosh
sink	**un lavabo**	uh la-va-*bow*
suite	**une suite**	ewn sweet

NUMBERS & ORDINALS

zero	**zéro**	*zare*-oh
one	**un**	oon
two	**deux**	duh
three	**trois**	twah
four	**quatre**	*kaht*-ruh
five	**cinq**	sank
six	**six**	seess
seven	**sept**	set
eight	**huit**	wheat
nine	**neuf**	noof
ten	**dix**	deess
eleven	**onze**	ohnz
twelve	**douze**	dooz
thirteen	**treize**	trehz
fourteen	**quatorze**	kah-*torz*
fifteen	**quinze**	kanz
sixteen	**seize**	sez
seventeen	**dix-sept**	deez-*set*
eighteen	**dix-huit**	deez-*wheat*

English	French	Pronunciation
nineteen	**dix-neuf**	deez-*noof*
twenty	**vingt**	vehn
thirty	**trente**	trahnt
forty	**quarante**	ka-*rahnt*
fifty	**cinquante**	sang-*kahnt*
one hundred	**cent**	sahn
one thousand	**mille**	meel
first	**premier**	*preh*-mee-ay
second	**deuxième**	*duhz*-zee-em
third	**troisième**	*twa*-zee-em
fourth	**quatrième**	*kaht*-ree-em
fifth	**cinquième**	*sank*-ee-em
sixth	**sixième**	*sees*-ee-em
seventh	**septième**	*set*-ee-em
eighth	**huitième**	*wheat*-ee-em
ninth	**neuvième**	*neuv*-ee-em
tenth	**dixième**	*dees*-ee-em

THE CALENDAR

Sunday	**dimanche**	dee-*mahnsh*
Monday	**lundi**	luhn-*dee*
Tuesday	**mardi**	mahr-*dee*
Wednesday	**mercredi**	mair-kruh-*dee*
Thursday	**jeudi**	jheu-*dee*
Friday	**vendredi**	vawn-druh-*dee*
Saturday	**samedi**	sahm-*dee*
yesterday	**hier**	ee-*air*
today	**aujourd'hui**	o-jhord-*dwee*
this morning/ this afternoon	**ce matin/cet après-midi**	suh ma-*tan*/set ah-preh mee-*dee*
tonight	**ce soir**	suh *swahr*
tomorrow	**demain**	de-*man*

2 Food/Menu Terms

English	French	Pronunciation
I would like to eat	**Je voudrais manger**	jhe voo-*dray* mahn-*jhay*
Please give me	**Donnez-moi, s'il vous plaît**	doe-nay-*mwah*, seel-voo-*play*
a bottle of	**une bouteille de**	ewn boo-*tay* duh
a cup of	**une tasse de**	ewn tass duh

English	French	Pronunciation
a glass of	**un verre de**	uh vair duh
a plate of breakfast	**une assiette de le petit-déjeuner**	ewn ass-ee-*et* duh luh puh-*tee* day-zhuh-*nay*
a cocktail	**un apéritif**	uh ah-pay-ree-*teef*
the check/bill	**l'addition/la note**	la-dee-see-*ohn*/la noat
dinner	**le dîner**	luh dee-*nay*
a knife	**un couteau**	uh koo-*toe*
a napkin	**une serviette**	ewn sair-vee-*et*
a spoon	**une cuillère**	ewn kwee-*air*
a fork	**une fourchette**	ewn four-*shet*
Cheers!	**A votre santé!**	ah vo-truh sahn-*tay*!
Waiter!/Waitress!	**Monsieur!/ Mademoiselle!**	muh-*syuh*/mad-mwa-*zel*
appetizer	**une entrée**	ewn ahn-*tray*
fixed-price menu	**un menu**	uh may-*new*
main course	**un plat principal**	uh plah pran-see-*pahl*
tasting menu	**menu dégustation**	may-*new* day-gus-ta-see-*on*
tip included	**service compris**	sehr-*vees* com-*pree*
wine list	**une carte des vins**	ewn cart day *van*

MEATS

beef stew	**du pot au feu**	dew poht o *fhe*
chicken	**du poulet**	*dew poo*-lay
chicken, stewed with mushrooms and wine	**du coq au vin**	dew cock o vhin
frogs' legs	**des cuisses de grenouilles**	day cweess duh gre-*noo*-yuh
ham	**du jambon**	dew jham-*bon*
lamb	**de l'agneau**	duh lahn-*nyo*
rabbit	**du lapin**	dew *lah*-pan
rolls of pounded and baked chicken, veal, or fish (often pike), usually served warm	**des quenelles**	day ke-*nelle*
sirloin	**de l'aloyau**	duh lahl-why-*yo*
steak	**du bifteck**	dew beef-*tek*
veal	**du veau**	dew voh

FISH

English	French	Pronunciation
fish (freshwater)	**du poisson de rivière,** or **du poisson d'eau douce**	dew pwah-*sson* duh ree-vee-*aire,* dew pwah-sson d'o *dooss*
fish (saltwater)	**du poisson de mer**	dew pwah-*sson* duh *mehr*
lobster	**du homard**	dew oh-*mahr*
Mediterranean fish soup or stew made with tomatoes, garlic, saffron, and olive oil	**de la bouillabaisse**	duh lah booh-ya-*besse*
mussels	**des moules**	day moohl
oysters	**des huîtres**	dayz *hwee*-truhs
shrimp	**des crevettes**	day kreh-*vet*
smoked salmon	**du saumon fumé**	dew sow-*mohn* fu-*may*
tuna	**du thon**	dew tohn
trout	**de la truite**	duh lah tru-*eet*

SIDES/APPETIZERS/CONDIMENTS

butter	**du beurre**	dew bhuhr
bread	**du pain**	dew pan
goose liver	**du foie gras**	dew fwah *grah*
mustard	**de la moutarde**	duh lah moo-*tard*-uh
pepper	**du poivre**	dew *pwah*-vruh
potted and minced pork products, prepared as a roughly chopped pâté	**des rillettes**	day ree-*yett*
rice	**du riz**	dew ree
salt	**du sel**	dew *sel*
sugar	**du sucre**	dew *sooh*-kruh

FRUITS/VEGETABLES

cabbage	**du choux**	dew *shoe*
eggplant	**de l'aubergine**	duh loh-ber-*jheen*
french fries	**des pommes frites**	day puhm *freet*
fruit salad	**une salade de fruit/ une macédoine de fruits**	ewn sah-lahd duh *fwee*/ewn mah-*say*-doine duh fwee

English	French	Pronunciation
grapes	**du raisin**	dew ray-*zhan*
green beans	**des haricots verts**	day *ahr*-ee-coh *vaire*
green salad	**une salade verte**	ewn sah-lahd *vairt*
lemon/lime	**du citron/du citron vert**	dew cee-*tron*/dew cee-tron *vaire*
lettuce salad	**une salade de laitue**	ewn sah-lahd duh lay-*tew*
pineapple	**de l'ananas**	duh lah-na-*nas*
potatoes	**des pommes de terre**	day puhm duh *tehr*
potatoes au gratin	**des pommes de terre dauphinois**	day puhm duh *tehr* doh-feen-*wah*
spinach	**des épinards**	dayz ay-pin-*ards*
strawberries	**des fraises**	day *frez*

BEVERAGES

beer	**de la bière**	duh lah bee-*aire*
coffee (black)	**un café noir**	uh ka-fay *nwahr*
coffee (with cream)	**un café crème**	uh ka-fay *krem*
coffee (with milk)	**un café au lait**	uh ka-fay o *lay*
coffee (decaf)	**un café décaféiné** (slang: **un déca**)	un ka-fay day-kah-fay-*nay* (uh *day*-kah)
coffee (espresso)	**un café espresso** (**un express**)	uh ka-fay e-*sprehss*-o (un ek-*sprehss*)
milk	**du lait**	dew *lay*
orange juice	**du jus d'orange**	dew joo d'or-*ahn*-jhe
tea	**du thé**	dew *tay*
tea (herbal)	**une tisane**	ewn tee-*zahn*
water	**de l'eau**	duh *lo*
wine (red)	**du vin rouge**	dew vhin *rooj*
wine (white)	**du vin blanc**	dew vhin *blahn*

DESSERTS

cake	**du gâteau**	dew *gha*-tow
caramelized upside-down apple pie	**une tarte Tatin**	ewn tart tah-*tihn*
cheese	**du fromage**	dew fro-*mahj*
fruit, especially cherries, cooked in batter	**du clafoutis** **une tarte**	dew kla-foo-*tee* tartp ewn tart

English	French	Pronunciation
thick custard dessert with a caramelized topping	**de la crème brûlée**	duh lah *krem* bruh-*lay*
vanilla ice cream	**de la glace à la vanille**	duh lah *glass* a lah vah-*nee*-yuh

Index

See also Accommodations and Restaurant indexes, below.

RESTAURANTS

THE NEW TRAVELOCITY GUARANTEE

EVERYTHING YOU BOOK WILL BE RIGHT, OR WE'LL WORK WITH OUR TRAVEL PARTNERS TO MAKE IT RIGHT, RIGHT AWAY.

*To drive home the point,
we're going to use the word "right" in every single sentence.*

Let's get right to it. Right to the meat! Only Travelocity guarantees everything about your booking will be right, or we'll work with our travel partners to make it right, right away. Right on!

Here's a picture taken smack dab right in the middle of Antigua, where the guarantee also covers you.

The guarantee covers all but one of the items pictured to the right.

For example, what if the ocean view you booked actually looks out at a downright ugly parking lot? You'd be right to call – we're there for you. And no one in their right mind would be pleased to learn the rental car place has closed and left them stranded. Call Travelocity and we'll help get you back on the right track.

Now, you may be thinking, "Yeah, right, I'm so sure." That's OK; you have the right to remain skeptical. That is until we mention help is always right around the corner. Call us right off the bat, knowing that our customer service reps are there for you 24/7. Righting wrongs. Left and right.

Now if you're guessing there are some things we can't control, like the weather, well you're right. But we can help you with most things – to get all the details in righting,* visit **travelocity.com/guarantee.**

*Sorry, spelling things right is one of the few things not covered under the guarantee.

I'd give my right arm for a guarantee like this, although I'm glad I don't have to.